Mine, Mill & Microchip

A CHRONICLE OF
ALABAMA ENTERPRISE

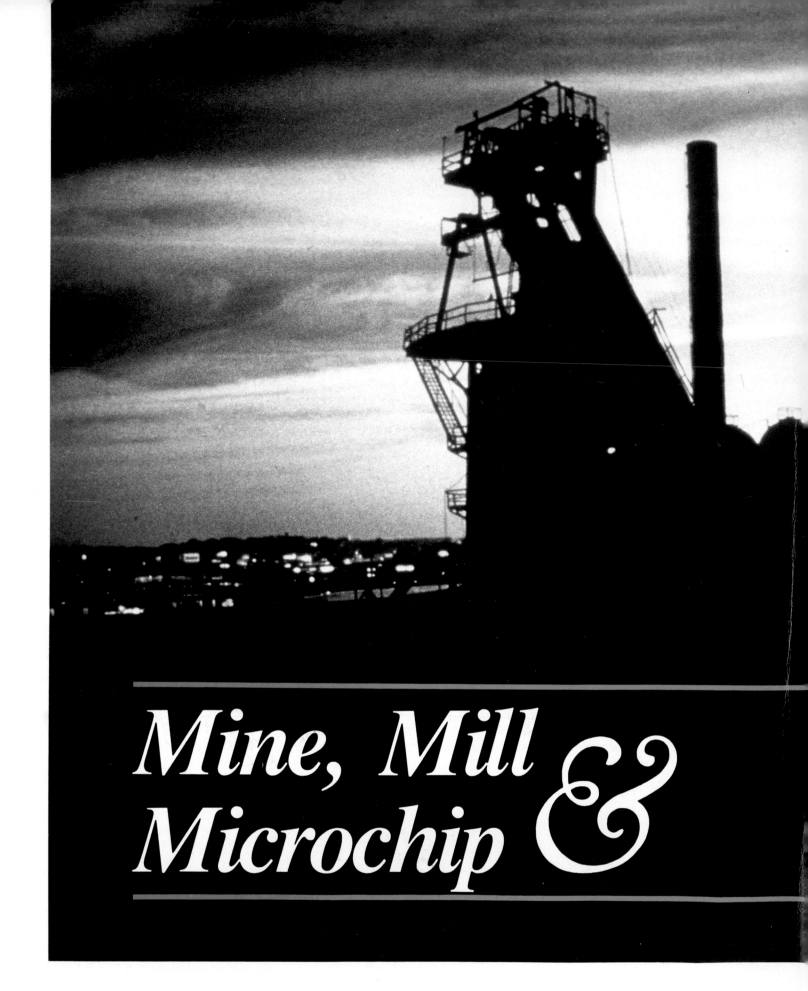

Mine, Mill & Microchip

Produced in Cooperation with the
Business Council of Alabama

Windsor Publications, Inc.
Northridge, California

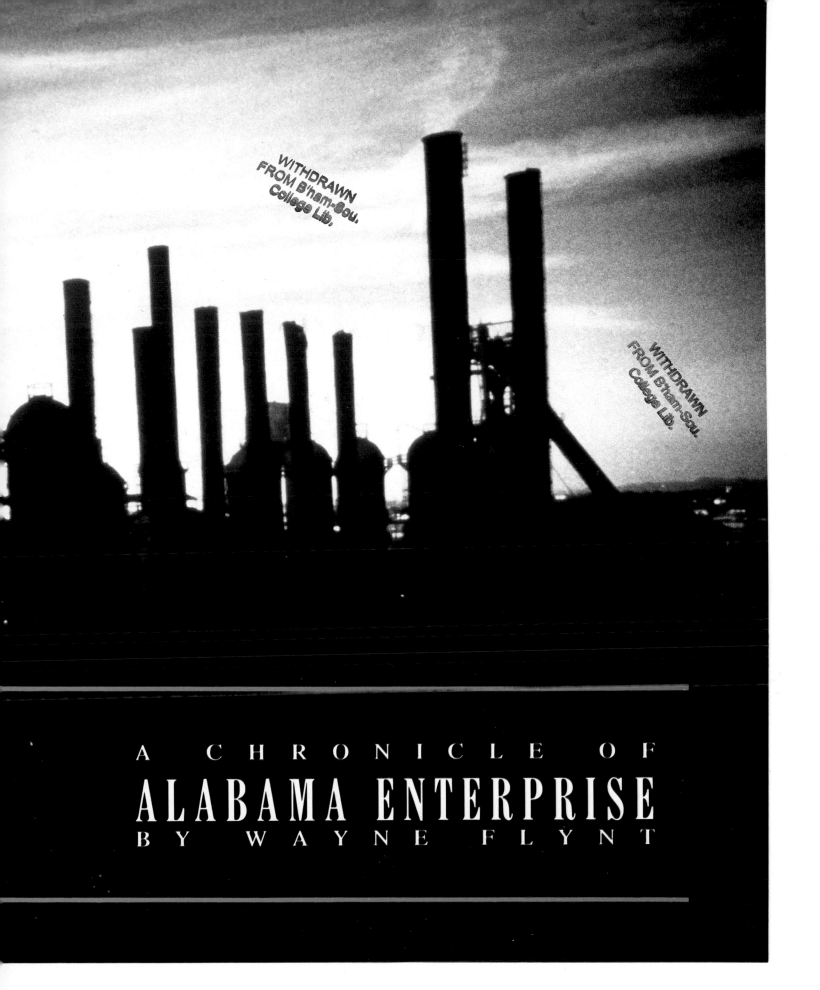

A CHRONICLE OF
ALABAMA ENTERPRISE
BY WAYNE FLYNT

Pictorial Research and Captions by Michael Thomason

"Alabama's Enterprises" by
Peter Cobun, Betty Doyle, Melody Gilchrist, and Marlene Hunt Rikard

Windsor Publications, Inc.—History Book Division
Publisher: Hal Silverman
Editorial Director: Teri Davis Greenberg
Design Director: Alexander D'Anca

Staff for *Mine, Mill & Microchip*
Senior Editor: Pamela Schroeder
Picture Editor: Laura Cordova
Director, Corporate Biographies: Karen Story
Assistant Director, Corporate Biographies: Phyllis Gray
Editors, Corporate Biographies: Brenda Berryhill, Judith L. Hunter
Editorial Assistants: Kathy M. Brown, Susan Kanga, Pat Pittman
Proofreader: Susan J. Muhler
Designer: Thomas Prager
Layout Artist, Corporate Biographies: Barbara Moore
Sales Representatives: John Compton, Melody Gilchrist, William Harrison, Lynn Malone

Library of Congress Cataloging-in-Publication Data

Flynt, J. Wayne, 1940-
      Mine, mill, and microchip.
      "Produced in cooperation with the Business Council of Alabama."
      " 'Alabama's enterprises' by Peter Cobun, Betty Doyle, and Marlene Hunt Rikard:"
p. 265
      Bibliography: 371
      Includes index.
      1. Alabama—Industries—History. 2. Alabama—Manufactures—History. 3. Industry
and state—Alabama—History. I. Thomason, Michael. II. Alabama enterprise. III. Title.
HC107.A4F57   1987   338.09761   87-9192
ISBN 0-89781-215-8

Frontispiece: *An early blast furnace is silhouetted against the setting sun at the Sloss furnace historic site in Birmingham.*

Contents page: *Especially beautiful in the fall, DeSoto State Park in northeast Alabama is a popular destination for travelers. Photo by Chip Cooper*

For

W. Everett Smith

The statue of Vulcan was built by the Birmingham Steel and Iron Company for the 1904 World's Fair in St. Louis. The Roman god of the forge was subsequently on display at Birmingham's fairgrounds until a Depression-era WPA project moved it to Red Mountain, to overlook the city whose economic activity it symbolized. This picture was made in the late thirties, shortly after the WPA project was completed. Courtesy, William Stanley Hoole Special Collections Library, University of Alabama

CONTENTS

Alabama's tall pine forests have played a significant role in the state's economic development. Southern pine provided a larger share of the nation's lumber production than any other species between 1900 and the 1960s, and Alabama was a consistent leader among the Southern states. Courtesy, University of South Alabama

PREFACE

Opp is a town in Covington County, Alabama, near the border with Florida. It sits near the middle of a vast longleaf pine forest which originally stretched along the Gulf Coast from Georgia to Louisiana. In 1900 when the Louisville and Nashville Railroad laid track through the area, local landowner-businessman Alex Hart purchased the site for its potential lumber and turpentine. A town grew up and was incorporated on July 2, 1902, and named for Henry Opp, a railroad attorney for the L & N who lived in Andalusia, a few miles to the west. Through the years it shared a fate common to most Alabama communities, prospering in good times and languishing in bad—tied to the economic cycles in lumbering and railroading, it flourished or declined in obscurity.

Many locals know nothing of Henry Opp. In their folklore they record a different version of how the town got its name: originally called Opportunity, the founders embodied their dreams for a better life in the name of the community. At the time, Covington County was one of the poorest in Alabama, its soil inadequate for cotton and its sole natural resource its tall trees. Upon those trees, and the railroad that carried them to Mobile and Pensacola, the founders pegged all their hopes. But as the years passed, the timber disappeared, the hard times multiplied and the original name seemed unduly complicated and inaccurate. Opportunity was shortened to Opp, and a legend was born.

Residents of south Alabama's Wiregrass region are not the only ones who came to the heart of Dixie seeking opportunity. People came by the thousands and tens of thousands, some bringing millions to invest, others carrying no more than what they wore or carried in their carpetbags. Some built factories, others worked in them; but they shared a dream common to most Americans, a dream of upward mobility, increased prosperity, and a better life. Some realized the dream; many did not.

This history briefly tells the story of the people who built Alabama's industries, both successfully and unsuccessfully. I tell the story as frankly and honestly as sources permit, and not without respect and even admiration. Their motives were seldom as pure as they alleged, and seldom as crass as their opponents charged (the reader can judge such matters for himself); but they deserve a better fate than they have received, which is to be largely ignored. I offer this volume as a corrective to that oversight and in hopes of enlarging our understanding of the whole human family that forged our common heritage.

This undertaking has left me indebted to many people. Dean Edward Hobbs and Vice President Taylor Littleton provided the research leave which made the book possible. Auburn University President James Martin persuaded me to remain a faculty member at Auburn, thereby releasing me from the burden of administration and returning me to the oasis of scholarship. Flora Moss typed draft after draft without demonstrable evidence of resentment.

Numerous persons provided information and photographs: Martha "Marty" Garrett, a research specialist with the Huntsville Chamber of Commerce; Linda Bayer, a staff member in the Huntsville Planning Department; university archivists Elizabeth Wells at Samford University and Allen Jones at Auburn University; Auburn University librarian Bill Highfill, and Special Collections librarian Gene Geiger; April Martin, Director of Marketing for the Alabama Shakespeare Festival; and faculty colleagues Dean Gjerstad and Warren Flick of the Auburn School of Forestry. Michael Thomason deserves special thanks for tracking down and producing the photographs and writing the captions. Marlene Rikard and other able historians prepared the histories of individual companies. Most of all I owe a debt of gratitude to W. Everett Smith, who directs Technical Operations and Mineral Resources for the Geological Survey of Alabama. He first introduced me to this largely unknown agency, which has played such a key role in Alabama's industrial history. Stretching across the decades, it has served the state diligently and professionally. Although no state agency entirely transcends politics, the Geological Survey comes as close as any. Under a variety of able state geologists, the agency has studied and publicized Alabama's resources, and has sought within the limits of its budget and charge to foster manufacturing growth without violating environmental integrity. Had all state development efforts been as well coordinated, as devoted to the welfare of the state, and as professionally competent, Alabama would be a good deal closer to its goal of a decent life for all.

W. Everett Smith read the entire manuscript and saved me from a multitude of embarrassing inaccuracies, both technological and historical. A fine example of a historian without a degree in the discipline, I wish to dedicate this book to him. Its remaining mistakes must be attributed to me.

—Wayne Flynt,
Auburn, Alabama

In 1805 John Hunt settled near the site of modern Huntsville, attracted by the abundant fresh water from the Big Spring. By 1850, the town had grown to become a center for banking and textile manufacturing in the Tennessee Valley. In the foreground of this picture, painted in 1850 by William Frye, spring waters drive a gristmill and feed one of the state's earliest canals, which was used to transport cotton to nearby gins and mills. Courtesy, Huntsville/Madison County Public Library

Chapter 1

THE VISION
OF INDUSTRIAL ALABAMA

This circa 1900 photograph depicts a spoon tipple at #3 slope at the Woodward Iron Company. The devise was used for loading and unloading iron ore from the mines to railroad cars. Courtesy, Birmingham Public Library

The American dream of progress was never uniform. Success for many individualists meant subsistence agriculture on a family farm. For some the dream was more complicated; they became skilled craftsmen transforming simple materials into intricate, useful designs and products. Others thrived in the world of machines, content to operate instruments that standardized products and reduced their prices for a mass market. Still others eschewed sinew and muscle work for more cerebral undertakings; their contributions were made in board rooms and professions. Circumstances trapped many in unhappy jobs, yet some chose their courses freely. Whatever the motivation, the genius of America has been embodied in the diversity of aspirations and occupations of its people. In fact, in the long run those states or regions dominated by a single vision of success have tended to be the least prosperous and the most vulnerable to economic cycles. To some degree the vagaries of weather have determined that vision. To an even greater extent the patterns of geology and geography have defined the economic possibilities of America's states and regions.

Alabama was no exception to any of these generalizations. The antebellum dream shared by most of its people matched its weather and soil but largely ignored its geology. Because short-term market conditions favored them, the state's cotton farmers thrived for a time; some, though not so many as the romantic lore of the South would have us believe, built splendid mansions and imported English furnishings. The uncle of an aspiring migrant, Phillips Fitzpatrick, captured the dream precisely, if ungrammatically, in an 1849 letter of advice to his young nephew:

Now as you are a young man and on your first legs and wishes to become rich and have a plenty of money and every other thing around you that heart could wish, this would be my plan to obtain it fairly, honestly and above board, is to get you a piece of good land and a healthy situation with plenty of good timber and water, with a good range or a range that will hardly ever give out, where a boat will come and carry off everything that you might have to ship off; and stick down upon it with some good woman for your wife (for without a good wife it is hard to get along), and raise everything, and only wait for the woom of time to bring everything to bar.

Many Alabamians agreed. The best life was life closest to the land. Imbued with Thomas Jefferson's agrarian vision of America, they believed that factories and cities imperiled true democracy, seduced the nation's youth into degeneracy, fostered special privilege, and exacerbated class conflicts.

Dissenters offered a different opinion, but their task was never easy. Even in good times the lack of economic diversity made Alabama dependent upon other states and regions for products essential to its well-being; and in bad times the state's slavish devotion to cotton threatened catastrophe. The dissenters, some native born but most from beyond Alabama's borders, pleaded for state help to develop its abundant mineral resources, broaden its markets through modern transportation, and transform its base with stable banking. However, the preachments were largely drowned out by the strident roar of Jacksonian rhetoric, which glorified the common man and ridiculed bankers and entrepreneurs as effete dandies and seekers after special status. The result was a time quite different from the tranquil and united antebellum world depicted in so many stories of Alabama before the Civil War.

Nature provided the key arguments for the debate over Alabama's future. The northern half of the state resembled Wales, whence came many of the state's early iron makers. Deep valleys and high mountain ridges made transportation difficult. Infertile rocky land, except in river bottoms, afforded hardy people a poor living on small patches of corn, potatoes, and wheat. Riches in these parts lay beneath the soil, not on top of it. Five physiographic regions of north Alabama covering 10,000 square miles and twenty-eight counties contained important minerals: the Highland Rim, which included deposits of limestone, iron ore, asphalt, bauxite, phosphate rock, clay, natural gas, sand, gravel, and building stone; the Cumberland Plateau, which included the Warrior and Plateau coalfields and associated deposits of fireclay, building stone [flat

Riverboats were the principal vehicle by which cotton was brought to Mobile for almost 100 years until early in this century. This picture *was made circa 1900 on one of the rivers above the city. Courtesy, Alabama Department of Archives and History*

slabs of sandstone], and natural gas; the Appalachian valley and ridge, which contained brown iron ore, hematite (red iron ore), limestone, dolomite, lead, zinc, bauxite, barite, talc, manganese, sand, gravel, building stone, natural gas, coal (in the Cahaba and Coosa coalfields), silica, and clay; the Piedmont Upland, which contained the greatest diversity of minerals and which would later support the mining of gold, iron ore, marble, graphite, mica, copper, dolomite, clay, sand, and gravel; and a part of the east gulf coastal plain, which contained sand, gravel, clay, ocher, natural gas, and oil.

Awareness of the state's diverse mineral resources came slowly. Minerals that were recognized early and which formed the foundation of the state's antebellum mineral industry were brown iron ore, coal, hematite, limestone, dolomite, gold, copper, lead, and zinc. Although antebellum south Alabama produced some burned lime, building stone, phosphate, rock and clay, industrialists utilized the mineral resources of this region only in later years.

Few American states could equal Alabama's abundance of good-quality water resources. These resources would be vitally important to a beginning industrial economy, for early industry relied upon waterpower and cheap transportation via the river system. Moreover, many of the early industrial operations required great amounts of clean water for manufacturing processes. Rivers drained most regions of the state and permitted riverboat transportation as far north as the fall line. The mighty Tennessee River, coursing from east to west near the northern boundary of the state, provided the rich bottomlands of the Tennessee River Valley. Along the eastern border, the Coosa, Tallapoosa, and Chattahoochee rivers rose in Georgia but poured their waters into their sister state to the west, or along the boundary. The Cahaba and Warrior rivers drained the north central mineral belt before joining other streams for their journey to the port at Mobile Bay. The Cahaba joined the Alabama River near Selma, then transported the cotton crop grown on the rich ebony soil of the Black Belt, a rich district of dark, fertile soil stretching across central Alabama from Georgia to the Mississippi border.

The Warrior merged with the Tombigbee near Demopolis, whence it paralleled the Mississippi boundary south. Where the Tombigbee and Alabama rivers joined just north of Mobile, they created a gigantic system of swamps and deltas before emptying into Mobile. Though some parts of the state contained a larger share of nature's bounty than others, none could complain, and each prospered in its own way and time.

That so many early pioneers ignored the state's industrial resources is not surprising. Many Americans were first-generation immigrants from land-starved Europe. Few had owned land there, so ownership of a small plot was a symbol of America's opportunity. Alabama soil, especially in river valleys and the Black Belt, produced abundant crops and could be acquired for low prices or by merely squatting and waiting for the government to allow them to assume ownership. With such bounties of timber and foodstuffs on top of the soil, it seldom occurred to anyone that even greater potential waited just below. Nor did the primitive state of technology promise much; although coal mining and iron making were already important to the economies of Wales and northern England, the occasional outcropping of Alabama iron ore was seen as more of a curiosity or a source of dye than an attractive alternative to the riches being made in the state's cotton fields. Planters plowed every cent of profit back into the purchase of slaves and land, leaving little capital for risky manufacturing ventures. They knew about cotton but, generally, lacked the managerial skills and technical knowledge needed for manufacturing. Most plain folk preferred farming; in fact, they associated hard industrial labor with slavery as something to be avoided. The agrarian, Jacksonian values—which glorified unlearned men and disdained the accumulation of wealth and power—pervaded the entire society.

These attitudes found political expression in a state that was surprisingly liberal: by providing universal manhood suffrage, the state constitution guaranteed that Alabama's economic destiny would be controlled by popular sentiment.

Class divisions appeared early in Alabama's history. Democrats convinced most citizens that they championed the interests of farmers and plain folk against the "commercial element" and the wealthy. Alabama Whigs, claiming the state's urban middle class, merchants, manufacturers, and large planters as a constituency, were on the defensive. They favored state funding of transportation systems, economic diversification, and public assistance for education and mental health. Legislators representing poorer folk imposed a tax system which fell heaviest on the wealthy and blocked state funding of internal improvements, such as canals, state-chartered railroads, and banks. A future president of the state senate articulated the sentiment of many Alabamians in 1839:

Incorporated companies create no wealth; they fatten upon the labor and industry of the poor man who lives by the sweat of his brow. Let these combinations then of wealth against labor, of the rich against the poor be regarded as engines of popular oppression.

The most practical expression of such sentiments, and the one most detrimental to the growth of Alabama industry, was opposition to banks. In 1816 LeRoy Pope and eight friends established the first bank in the Alabama Territory, the Planters and Merchants Bank of Huntsville. The bank gained such power that many yeoman farmers came to view it as a threat to their liberties. In their view, the exclusive function of a bank was to provide money for the purchase of land. In that sense, banks were commercial extensions of an agricultural society. As a result of hostility to Pope's early domination of state finances, the legislature created a state bank in 1823. Basically, Alabamians had concluded that banks should serve the public interest; and the state bank, through its branches in Tuscaloosa and elsewhere, did precisely that— using its limited capital primarily to provide agricultural credit. Legislators agreed to charter several private banks at St. Stephens and Mobile, but only because these banks' officials were not hostile to the state bank. LeRoy Pope paid for his opposition to the state bank by the revocation of his bank charter in 1825.

Unfortunately, the state bank never operated effectively. Money drained from its weakest branches to its strongest, and from the strongest branches of the state bank to the strongest private bank, the Bank of Mobile.

Public confidence in the state bank declined markedly during the Panic of 1837, a calamity caused partly by political manipulation of banks, corruption, and poor banking practices which fueled speculation in land. Legislative attempts to regulate the state bank did little to improve conditions but did involve legislators and government officials in a network of cotton speculation and corruption.

Alabama's banking experience was typical of four other southern states—Arkansas, Florida, Mississippi, and Tennessee—which had small business communities and undeveloped commercial resources. As in those states, Alabama's leaders relied upon the government to direct economic growth through a state bank rather than rely on market conditions. Southern states with more developed commercial structures—Virginia, the Carolinas, Georgia, and Louisiana—encouraged competition in their banking systems and relied far less on state banks to generate economic activity.

Given such prejudices and conditions, it was not surprising that most Alabamian industries were somehow related to agriculture. Throughout the antebellum period the state's largest industry, both in value and industrial employment, was gristmilling; its second most extensive was saw milling. Gristmills simply transformed agricultural crops into foodstuffs for local markets.

Timber, however, afforded more commercial opportunities. By 1860 Alabama ranked fourth among southern states in the value of its sawed and planed lumber, and Mobile had become the major export center draining southern Alabama, Mississippi, and West Florida; but even lumber was basically a rural industry centered in Mobile Bay and along the major rivers emptying into it. Plantation slaves freed from agricultural labor during the winter cut most of the timber. The industry was primarily a way of supplementing the income of plantations and more efficiently utilizing the slave labor force.

The waterpowered sawmills of the early nineteenth century produced only a thousand board feet of lumber a day, but the increasing use of steam-powered mills allowed rapid expansion of

the industry. Between September 1, 1831, and the same date a year later, Alabama exported more than 1.5 million board feet of lumber. That figure more than doubled to 3.5 million during the same period of 1846-1847. It nearly tripled to 12.5 million during 1853-1854. The total value of lumber, staves, shingles, and masts shipped in 1854-1855 exceeded $200,000. Most products were shipped to the West Indies, especially Cuba, which took 80 percent of the 1860 exports. But France, Spain, and England also became lucrative markets.

Transportation rivaled banking in importance to the state's manufacturing economy. In antebellum times geography largely determined routes: river systems ran approximately north to south across the state; but dangerous rapids along the streams that crossed the central Alabama fall line effectively limited upstream navigation by commercial shallow-draft boats. During high water, most streams were used for downstream transport of goods by crude flatboats. Canals and railroads were also limited by geographic factors. The mountains and stream valleys of north Alabama proved to be formidable barriers to railroad construction. Hence, efficient transportation was limited to the Tennessee Valley in the extreme northern part of the state, and to north-south rivers and east-west stagecoach and railroad lines in the southern part.

In 1821 a stagecoach line opened between Montgomery, Alabama, and Milledgeville, Georgia. By the mid-1820s eight stages per week carried passengers between the two towns. A stage line from Montgomery to Tuscaloosa opened in 1830. It allowed eager travelers to depart at 4:00 a.m. on Monday and arrive by noon Friday, if they were lucky. The arduous 104-hour journey covered 150 miles, an average of one-and-a-half miles per hour at a rate of twelve-and-a-half cents per mile. Passengers were often required to walk up steep grades. It is most probable also, that when it came to eating and sleeping arrangements it was "each to his own." Passengers carried their fifteen-pound

Alabama's strongest bank was the privately owned Bank of Mobile. Mobile was the state's wealthiest city, and the competing state banks' political ties so weakened it that it nearly failed in the Panic of 1827. Unfortunately the financial strength of the bank was little protection against fire, and it burned to the ground in Mobile's great fire of 1839. The bank is on the left in this engraving of that fire. Courtesy, Historic Mobile Preservation Society

baggage allowance at their own risk.

North-south travel relied initially on the excellent river system. Flat-bottomed boats, propelled by strong currents from spring rains, carried products downriver to Mobile. North of the rapids this was risky business. Coal floated down the Coosa River on flatboats had to cross the deadly "devil's staircase," a wide series of shoals above Wetumpka. The intrepid men who transported the coal were renowned not only for their skills in maneuvering their primitive vessels, but they also entered Ala-

bama folklore for their feats on land, one group allegedly walking ninety miles from Montgomery back to Calhoun County in only two days. From central Alabama to Mobile, the perils of river travel were less but the time spent on sluggish rivers longer.

To the east, along the boundary between Alabama and Georgia, the Chattahoochee River afforded commercial opportunities. It drained parts of Georgia, Florida, and Alabama through the port of Apalachicola, which by the Civil War had be-

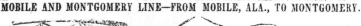

MOBILE AND MONTGOMERY LINE—FROM MOBILE, ALA., TO MONTGOMERY.

The subscriber respectfully begs leave to adopt this method of informing the public that he has now in successful operation a lendid Line of DAILY STAGES, between MOBILE and MONTGOMERY, which affords every facility of ease and comfort passengers travelling in that direction. He pledges himself to use every possible exertion to render those favoring him with eir custom, all the comfort and safety, which is to be derived on any other stage line in the South. WARD TAYLOR, Proprietor.
OFFICES—Opposite Mansion House, MOBILE; Planter's Hotel, MONTGOMERY.

Above: *In 1821 Alabama's first stagecoach line opened between Montgomery and Milledgeville, Georgia. Other routes followed, linking the state's major towns, but the roads were often little more than tracks, and a stage trip was long and difficult despite the image presented in ads such as this in a Mobile City Directory. Courtesy, Local History Division, Mobile Public Library*

Right: *Alabama's extensive river system made possible transportation of commodities such as cotton, coal, and timber. In this illustration from Ballou's Pictorial slaves load cotton onto a riverboat on the Alabama River. Scenes such as this were common throughout the antebellum period. Courtesy, University of South Alabama*

come the third busiest on the Gulf of Mexico. Steamboats traveled upriver as far as Columbus, Georgia, to pick up cargoes of lumber, cotton, and tobacco. The river made Eufaula a bustling manufacturing town with a shipyard which built the steamboats *Mary A. Moore* and *Eufaula* in 1845.

The Alabama River was the chief component of the longest water system in the state, 776 miles from northern Georgia to Mobile. Eleven miles below Wetumpka the Coosa joined the Tallapoosa to form the Alabama. The Tombigbee merged 312 water miles further south to form the Mobile River some 44 miles north of Mobile. In its natural state, low-water depths on the river system varied from three to fifteen feet, which made it navigable for light-draft boats throughout most of the year. The Alabama traversed the Black Belt, which contained some of America's most fertile soil, and early planters bought large tracts along its banks so they could easily ship their cotton downstream. By statehood in 1819, huge flatboats carrying up to 100 bales of cotton were floating downriver. If

the physical dangers were less than on the northern reaches, the time consumed was much greater. Henry Goldthwaite, a prominent citizen of the capital, took three months in 1819 to float downstream from Montgomery, then pole his boat back upstream. The round trip never required less than two months.

Steamboats solved the problem of long delays. The first was built at St. Stephens Steamboat Company in 1818, but the boat, appropriately christened the *Alabama,* lacked the power to move back upstream against the current. By the fall of 1821 the *Harriet* made it all the way upriver to Montgomery, reducing the journey to a matter of days. The steamboat age had dawned.

Overland transportation declined as water traffic increased. River towns such as Claiborne, Cahawba, Selma, and Montgomery thrived on steamboat trade. Planters built more than 300 docks along the Black Belt section of the Alabama River, and each landing was a social occasion, the boats' whistles attracting crowds of curious spectators. Towns and plantations supplemented their incomes with a bustling trade in pine logs used to

fuel the boilers.

At first the steam vessels were primitive and carried few passengers, but in time they reached a length of 250 feet and contained three decks, each varying in creature comforts. Some featured elegant cabins, bars, gaming tables, a dance floor, even a calliope. The lower deck held up to 3,000 bales of cotton and the upper decks could accommodate 150 passengers.

However, such travel entailed risks. Sunken logs and snags could puncture a hull and send boats swiftly to the bottom. Fires and exploding boilers often turned ships into raging infernos. The *Orline St. John* burned in March 1850, killing forty of the sixty aboard. Sandbars and low water could transform a normal three-day trip into an arduous three-week ordeal.

Situated strategically at the terminus of this vast drainage system was Alabama's port of Mobile. The city's golden age was later clouded in obscurity by the railroad era, but during the 1830s the city led the nation in population growth. By 1860 Mobile contained three-fifths of Alabama's urban population. So cosmopolitan had the city become that a fourth of its inhabitants were immigrants, mainly from Ireland and Germany. Most immigrants worked in railroad construction or manufacturing. Boasting the state's most respected private bank, the city also contained sawmills and textile factories. By 1850 women comprised 8 percent of its industrial work force. Ten years later Mobile had become the second largest port on the Gulf Coast and one of the busiest in America, shipping large quantities of cotton and lumber around the world.

One man attracted by Mobile's 1830s boom was Philip Phillips, a young Jewish lawyer from Charleston, South Carolina. When he arrived in 1835 he brought what he believed to be a hefty inheritance of $5,000, but so hard was space to acquire that he had to spend $1,500 of that for his first year's rental of a law office. Phillips plunged into Democratic party politics, serving as president of the 1838 state convention and two terms in the house of representatives. In the legislature he became the chief advocate of state funding for internal improvements, predicting that someday minerals would eclipse cotton as Alabama's most valuable product. In 1844 he introduced a bill calling for a thorough geological survey of the state. When fellow legislators did nothing, he renewed the campaign for industrialization as president of the 1849 railroad convention. During the decade of the 1840s he became the chief spokesman for a scheme to connect north and south Alabama by railroad and river systems.

Such a proposal was not original. As early as 1819 Governor William Wyatt Bibb had anticipated the Tennessee-Tombigbee Canal by recommending a waterway across northwestern Alabama to connect the Tennessee and Mobile rivers, thus bypassing New Orleans. In 1836 the legislature chartered the Selma and Tennessee Railroad in a futile attempt to unify the two sections of the state, but the economic panic of the following year made short work of that plan. Due primarily to Philip Phillips' indefatigable lobbying, the legislature tried again in 1850, chartering the Alabama and Tennessee Rivers Railroad and the Tennessee and Coosa Rivers Railroad. The lines were designed to run northeast from Selma, connecting that town to Montevallo and Gadsden, thence by the Tennessee and Coosa rivers to Gunter's Landing on the Tennessee River. They would cross diagonally through the mineral belt. Few of these elaborate plans materialized, and by 1852 the state possessed only 165 miles of track, forty-four on the Memphis and Charleston Railroad, eighty-eight on the Montgomery and West Point line, and thirty-three belonging to the Mobile and Ohio Railroad. Other railroads existed only as charters on pieces of paper.

The Decatur and Tuscumbia Railroad, begun in 1829, met the most embarrassing fate. Although favorably located to haul both cotton from the rich Tennessee Valley lands around the Tennessee River shoals at Florence/Sheffield, and iron from the state's first furnace at Cedar Creek in Franklin County, the railroad extended only forty-six miles by 1834. The locomotive soon malfunctioned, and curious residents beheld the sorry spectacle of mules pulling railroad cars along the track.

In 1840, only six years after the legislature chartered the second state railroad, the Montgomery Western, citizens voted overwhelmingly for macadamized roads instead of railroads. This process of road construction piled successive layers of small broken stone on a dry earth roadbed. Citi-

zens accepted proponents' arguments that such roads were less vulnerable to accidents than railroads, but they were also slower and less efficient. The voters' decision provoked the editor of De Bows *Commercial Review of the South* to scold the state: "God may have given you coal and iron sufficient to work the spindles and navies of the world, but they will sleep in your everlasting hills until the trumpet of Gabriel shall sound unless you can do something better than build turnpikes."

Perhaps because the textile industry was tied more directly to the state's agriculture it experienced fewer problems than railroads. Charles Cabaniss established the first cotton mill between 1815 and 1817 about twelve miles northeast of

In 1837 Daniel Scott built a three-story textile mill on the Cahaba River near Tuscaloosa. Although it lost money at first, by 1858 the mill employed 100 people, paid healthy dividends to its shareholders, and good wages to its white employees. The Tuscaloosa Manufacturing Company, shown here in a postwar photograph, was one of the state's larger manufacturing enterprises in 1860. Courtesy, William Stanley Hoole Special Collections Library, University of Alabama

Huntsville on the Flint River. His son managed the business for fifty years from an office in Huntsville. Two more yarn mills followed shortly, all using the waters of the Flint River to drive waterpowered looms. A series of mergers before 1832 resulted in a 100-acre tract containing a gin, gristmill, distillery, and textile mill which performed carding, weaving, and dyeing. The Bell Factory, so-called because a large bell summoned employees to work, used slave labor to tend its 100 looms and 3,000 spindles. Located a few miles from Huntsville, it consumed fifty bales of cotton a month and was successful enough that when it burned in 1841 its owners rebuilt it immediately.

Perhaps the success of the Bell Factory inspired the Tuscaloosa Manufacturing Company to build a three-story mill on the Cahaba River between Centerville and Tuscaloosa in 1837. The company, like so many early Alabama ventures, began with insufficient capital. The mill, called Scottsville in honor of Daniel Scott, one of its founders, lost money the first four years, but Scott turned his first profit in 1841 and used it to purchase a family of slaves for $2,200. This investment demonstrated one of industry's major problems in the state. The value of the slave family rapidly increased to $10,000, appreciating faster than the products they produced on Scott's looms. He was one of the few businessmen to employ a racially mixed work force efficiently and profitably. Perhaps he owed his success to unusually high wages paid to his white employees, thus minimizing their racial hostility. Scottsville paid a dividend of at least 10 percent each year after 1841. By 1858 Scott's capital stock amounted to $117,000 and his work force had grown from twenty to 100. His facility in Bibb County contained the original brick factory, gristmill, sawmill, store, blacksmith, wheelwright, hotel, flour mill, church, and cottages.

The key figure not only in textiles, but in all antebellum Alabama manufacturing, was Daniel Pratt. A native of Temple, New Hampshire, Pratt was a deeply religious man dominated both by a Puritan work ethic and an altruistic desire to help his fellow man. Practicing the trade of carpentry, Pratt moved first to Georgia, then in 1833 to Alabama. He began building cotton gins, then constructed an iron factory, a door and sash factory,

Daniel Pratt, the state's leading antebellum industrialist, was a New Hampshire native. He came to Alabama via Georgia in 1833, and is best known for his cotton gin manufacturing company at Prattville in Autauga County. Courtesy, Alabama Department of Archives and History

and a textile mill. He located in a rural part of Autauga County because he feared the demoralizing and radical tendencies of urban populations. Within twenty years he had transformed Prattville into the most diversified manufacturing town in Alabama. When he opened his mill in 1846 he employed 160 people, preferring family units though he did allow children and a few single girls. The poor white labor force he recruited learned slowly and made many mistakes, but Pratt persisted. Ever the paternalist, he furnished cottages for low rents, a day-care center for mothers, and a school for children of workers. He prohibited the sale of liquor within two miles of his village and required all children to attend Sunday School. His average 1850 wage of nine dollars per month for women and sixteen for men attracted ample numbers of indigent whites. By 1850 Autauga County contained 5,962 spindles, twice as many as any other county, and Pratt operated 2,682 of them at his Prattville Manufacturing Company. His osnaburg, a cheap, coarse cloth used mainly to clothe slaves, even won markets abroad. Unfortunately, his missionary efforts among poor whites did not fare so well. In the next decade he switched to a racially mixed labor force because so many white operatives succumbed to lethargy, insobriety, unreliability, and poor health.

Pratt, not content with his own success, tried to persuade fellow citizens to adopt a similar vision for his adopted state. In his "Letter to the People of Alabama" written in 1847 he argued that $50,000 invested in a plantation might wear out the land, causing the planter to sell and move, but the same amount invested in manufacturing created "permanent wealth." Even if a business failed, he reasoned, someone would buy the equipment and carry on. Although he conceded that agriculture might be basic to the economy, he believed farming and industry could thrive together.

He urged planters to invest some of their profits in factories and legislators to grant liberal charters to bankers and manufacturers. Two years after his 1847 open letter he wrote: "Show me the states that are most prosperous and I will show you the states that have the largest banking privileges. Banks may be an evil, but at present they are necessary evils; and no manufacturing state can prosper without them." He felt no sympathy for narrow-minded state legislators who opposed banks at every opportunity. "Why is it," he asked, "that we cannot for once lay politics aside and both parties look strictly . . . to the interest of the state?" He was in course a Whig, a Know-Nothing, and finally, in 1860, a follower of John Bell's Constitutional Union Party. At the time of his membership, each was most congenial to southern manufacturing interests.

Whether because of his persuasive rhetoric or his rapidly increasing bank account, many enter-

prising Alabama capitalists took Pratt's words to heart. Chief Justice Henry W. Collier endorsed the cotton mill crusade in 1846. They were essential, he warned, if poor whites were not to remain "an incubus on the bosom" of society. Scoffing at rumors of crowded, unhealthful conditions and long hours in the mills, Collier assured fellow citizens there was nothing in a cotton factory "prejudicial to health . . . , nothing in tending a loom to harden a lady's hand . . . , nothing to cause the rouge upon the cheek to fade, although the skin may become bleached by remaining so much in the shade."

More importantly, some planters and merchants began to invest dollars, usually citing the same moral justification of helping poor whites advanced by Pratt. In 1849 Henry Collier, then serving a term as governor, warned planters that during hard times lower-class whites might blame their troubles on slavery. He urged planters to pa-

tronize those mills that provided employment to poor whites. In Mobile civic leaders established the Dog River Factory to employ the city's growing number of unskilled immigrants. A new mill in Autaugaville employed mainly young white women. In 1845 the planter-owner opened the Tallassee Factory with a half-slave, half-white work force. Some five years later he gave up on slave labor and used only poor whites. The Fish Pond Factory on Elkahatchie Creek in Tallapoosa County provided the only manufacturing employment for the county's whites. Wages were low, averaging less than six dollars a month; but annual profits were high, never amounting to less than 25 percent of the original investment. The mill on Socapatoy Creek in Coosa County paid higher wages and also imposed the moral values of its owner on workers—it prohibited liquor sales, compelled children to attend Sunday School, church, and school. A Florence entrepreneur believed his cotton mill provided a better life for poor whites and improved citizens for Alabama. Like Pratt, he established schools and churches for them: " . . . in this way we hope to benefit them, while we benefit ourselves."

Many of these mills failed both in their civic and entrepreneurial goals. Poor management and under-capitalization caused many to collapse, while market fluctuations and the planters' unwillingness to patronize local industries brought down others. Periodic national depressions also contributed to the problem.

And in the mill villages poor whites did not necessarily prosper economically or morally. One laborer in Daniel Pratt's mill wrote retrospectively of his fifteen years' labor: "I have about paid my expenses and no more . . . " The standard work day of fourteen hours had been the hardest of his life and had wrecked his health. Poor whites bitterly denounced planter-managers for using slaves in the mills, thus depriving them of even the meager wages offered. Politicians took up the cry, and mill owners increasingly feared an aroused white working class. Owners turned to slave labor as an alternative. The mill villages provided no sense of kinship between indigent whites who aspired to become planters and their white "betters." Few of them moved upward into the middle class and many resented the restrictions placed on their personal conduct.

All these factors conspired to hobble the industry. Despite successes by men such as Pratt, Alabama contained only twelve functioning mills in 1850, employing a total of 715.

The story of great promise shackled by limited

Daniel Pratt had very specific ideas about relations between employer and employees. He paid his workers well, and forbade the sale of alcohol in the village he built for them adjacent to his cotton mill and gin factory. He constructed churches and schools for his employees in addition to the cottages he supplied to them for nominal rent. Unfortunately his somewhat utopian mill village had little appeal to the rural white frontiersmen who then lived in Alabama, and Pratt was forced to use slaves to keep his mill and factory profitable. Courtesy, Alabama Department of Archives and History

vision, managerial skill, capital, and by public misunderstanding applies just as well to Alabama's mineral resources. Although most people associate the mineral age with the emergence of Birmingham industry a half century later, antebellum developers first explored the potential that lay beneath the surface.

Prospectors discovered gold in Alabama in about 1830. The gold district stretched like a triangle across east-central Alabama with its apex at the Georgia border in rough country between the Tallapoosa and Little Tallapoosa rivers. From there the northern leg ran through Cleburne, Clay, Coosa, and Chilton counties, ending near Verbena. The southern leg crossed Randolph and Tallapoosa counties. In all, the area embraced some 3,500 square miles.

The early strike brought prospectors pouring into the hill counties, wading their creeks with sloshing gold pans or wielding picks and shovels on their hillsides. The area contained both placer gold deposits in streams and gold in hard-rock quartz veins. Miners panned the placer deposits by hand or with rocker boxes and washers. The primitive washing and sluicing operations relied primarily on wooden troughs containing cross riffles made of small wooden strips. Miners mounted the entire assembly on rockers. As water and alluvium poured in, they rocked the trough, and the heavier gold settled to the bottom where it was trapped by the riffles. Some operations used sluice troughs where huge amounts of alluvium could be washed with large hoses.

By 1840 intrepid pioneers had mined fortunes in gold. Single nuggets sold for as much as $1,200. Land prices in the gold district soared; in fact, it is probable that speculators made far more money selling land to prospectors than miners made mining gold. Towns like those which later dotted the California goldfields sprang up almost overnight. Arbacoochee grew from a small mining camp in the 1830s to a bustling community of 5,000 by 1845. It boasted twenty general stores, five bars, two hotels, a racetrack, fire department, 100 houses, a school, two churches, and innumerable tents and shacks.

To the southeast of Arbacoochee, the Goldville district in northern Tallapoosa County ran south six miles along Hillabee Creek. At its height the town of Goldville contained 3,000 people and served the gold mines at Hog Mountain, Birdsong, and Dutch Bend.

Southeast of Goldville the Devil's Backbone gold district ran for three miles along a rugged line of ridges in Tallapoosa County. Although it contained fairly low-grade ore, it supported, in time, a number of mines such as Silver Hill, Blue Hill, and Gregory Hill. The gold "leads" in this area were typical of many of the Alabama districts, consisting of numerous quartz veins and quartzite bodies.

The United States Mint recorded only $367,000 worth of Alabama gold sent to the mint between 1830 and 1860, but this figure almost certainly represented only a fraction of the precious metal actually mined. Prospectors exchanged gold for provisions, and much of it never reached a mint. They were a notoriously secretive lot who neither advertised their claims nor, contrary to Hollywood's version, boasted of their finds. Perhaps the most notable contribution of the Alabama and Georgia gold rushes was the training of a generation of miners in technology which they would later apply to the great California fields.

If gold mining was a temporary though spectacular phenomenon, coal mining was a long-term proposition. It became Alabama's primary mining industry for a simple reason: coal deposits lay in the subsurface of more than twenty north Alabama counties stretching from the northeastern corner of Georgia-Tennessee to the western boundary with Mississippi. The coal is classed as bituminous and ranks among the best bituminous coals in the United States.

Geological forces folded and bent the coal beds and weathering of the strata frequently exposed the beds on the land surface. So the earliest coal explorations, like those of gold and iron ore, consisted of visual contact with coal bed outcrops or evidence such as alluvial coal fragments along a stream or hillside.

Early settlers began to mine coal almost as soon as Alabama became a state in 1819. The first coal mined, in what later would become the Birmingham district, came from the area of the confluence of Turkey Creek and the Warrior River. Other

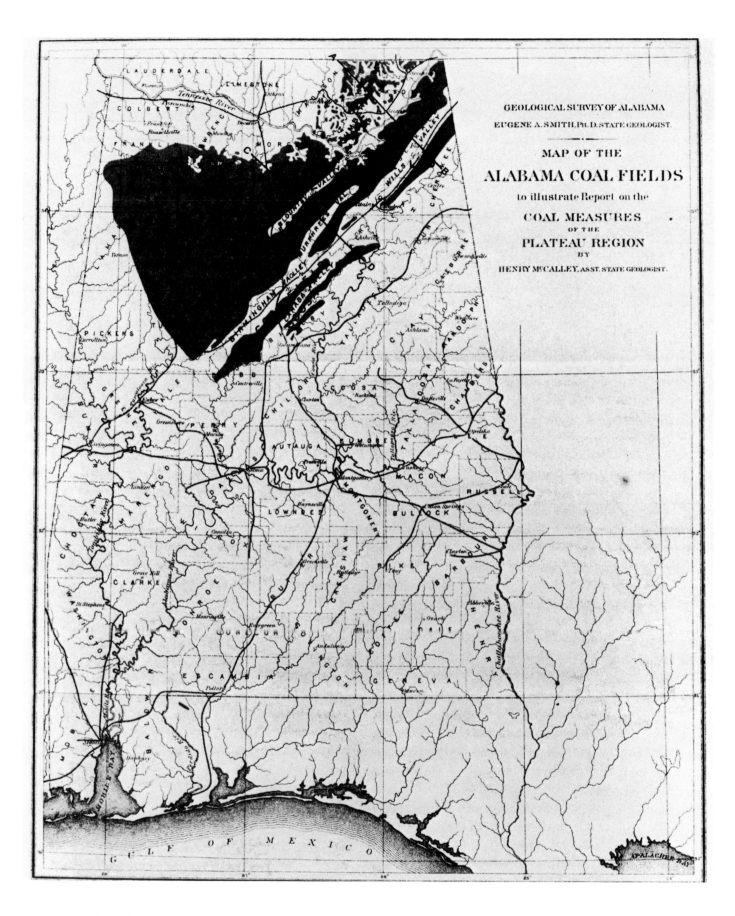

Coal deposits are found across twenty counties in northern Alabama. The bituminous or soft coal is easily burned, and since some of the mineral lies at or near the surface of the ground, coal mining began early in Alabama's history. However, the exact location and extent of the state's coal deposits were not known until the eve of the Civil War, and many coalfields were not accessible before the days of the railroads. Lacking transportation, working capital, and maps such as this, Alabama's antebellum coal mining industry showed little development. *Courtesy, University of South Alabama Library*

mines opened soon in nearby Walker County. Miners along the Locust Fork of the Warrior River in Blount County sent coal downriver to Mobile on flatboats as early as 1827 or 1828. Soon the banks of the Warrior were dotted with coal operations. One operator built two flatboats out of poplars and anchored them beside a coal outcropping in the river. He loosened the coal with crowbars driven into the ledge, then broke off chunks into the river. Teams of divers retrieved them from the water, sometimes hauling aboard large blocks weighing 1,000 pounds by a primitive crane and chain rigged on deck. Along the banks miners worked coal mines in drifts and headings, following a seam into the hillside at a declining slope. Horses or mules pulled coal-laden carts up the inclines to the surface, then hauled them to the river for loading aboard flatboats.

Next came the long voyage to Mobile. David Hanby, who entered the state with Andrew Jackson during the Indian wars, purchased land along Turkey Creek near Hagood's crossroads. His sons built corn, flour, and sawmills in addition to the family's mining operations. Hanby soon became the foremost coal shipper; but nearly every year he lost a flatboat trying to navigate the treacherous rapids. One year he lost five flatboats from his fleet of twelve.

Nor did safe passage to Mobile ensure success. When his first two boatloads of coal arrived in the port city, no one would buy the black chunks. He had to give it away and dispatch a Negro boy with every bucketful to instruct people in how to light and burn it. The lessons apparently took because by 1844 Hanby sent eight to ten boatloads downriver and in later years as many as seventy-five. His business produced an income of $6,000 a year, earning four to seven dollars a ton in Mobile. The local gas company became his best customer.

Antebellum coal production never reached gigantic proportions. As late as 1860 the state census listed only fifty-four coal miners, but they produced for an eager market and were the best-paid industrial workers in the state, earning an average annual wage of $344. Production increased steadily from 946 tons in 1840 to 1,500 tons in 1845 to 2,500 in 1850.

Coal became inseparably linked to iron ore.

Narrow red-ore seams paralleled the coal beds running northeast to southwest from the Tennessee-Georgia borders as far as Tuscaloosa County. These hematite ores extended, with some significant breaks, from central Alabama to northern Maine and into New Brunswick, Canada. The Red Mountain Formation crops out on the flanks of Red Mountain across DeKalb, Etowah, St. Clair and Jefferson counties. The formation reached a maximum thickness of 700 feet, though the famous Jefferson County sequence along Red Mountain ranged from 400 to 650 feet in thickness and was exposed in outcrop over approximately twenty-five square miles. Several red-ore seams of variable thickness occurred at different intervals in the Red Mountain Formation. In only a few places, such as in the Birmingham and Attalla areas, was the red ore of sufficient thickness and quality to be mined and transported economically. Mining was at first restricted to the slopes of Red Mountain, where the southeastward dipping beds could be mined from pits or inclined drifts. Later, ore mines extended great distances into the subsurface where the ore seams were almost horizontal.

Where a red-ore seam was exposed to the surface, or where it occurred in the shallow subsurface, atmospheric agencies had leached the ore from some of its lime and much of its phosphorus content. The term often applied to this weathered ore was soft ore. Hard ore included a higher lime and phosphorous content and a lower lime content. The best grades of soft (weathered) ore contained more than 50 percent iron and the best grades of lime ore carried about 37 percent iron.

The physical appearance of hematitic ore varied considerably according to seams. Sometimes it was fine-grained; some seams consisted of hematite particles as large as one-eighth inch in diameter. Because the ore occurred in seams, mining was a predictable process, though variation in iron content and lime caused early miners and iron makers much grief.

Goethite or so-called brown iron ore existed in many regions of north Alabama and were the first ores used by the early iron makers. Although the brown ore constituted the best material for iron making, its production costs proved in time to be prohibitive. Unlike the hematite which occurred in

Alabama's first blast furnaces looked like truncated pyramids in which iron ore and flux were placed in the top with charcoal below. The heat from the charcoal fire melted the ore which ran out of the furnace in molten form. When cool it was known as "pig" iron. Courtesy, Birmingham Public Library

beds of generally consistent thickness, the brown ore occurred in pockets of clay and sand residuum. The pockets varied widely in size both laterally and vertically and followed no predictable pattern. Early miners joked that no one knew about a brown ore "bank" beyond the length of his pick.

The two general types of brown ore recognized by the miners, lump and gravel, presented common problems. Chert fragments (high in silica impurities) adhered to the ore, and clay filled the voids in the ore fragments. The lumps varied from the size of a fist to several tons; but most brown iron came in sizes which miners described as "between a pigeon egg and a goose egg." Early mining techniques involved literally cutting away a huge bank of limestone residuum in sections with picks, shovels, and mule-drawn scoops. Upon finding a lump, miners dug away the surrounding clay and sand, broke up the mass with hammers or dynamite, and loaded it on wagons. Mules and scoops, dynamite, sledge hammers, and strong muscles provided the necessary technology. Wagons then hauled the ore to nearby washers, thence to furnaces or to water

or rail loading facilities. A thorough washing, which removed the embedded sand and clay, resulted in a purer grade of ore. Only a small amount of flux (limestone) was used in the early brown iron ore smelting process. The red ore required variable amounts of limestone or dolomite flux, depending on the amount of lime already in the ore. In the smelting process impurities in the ore combined with the flux and produced slag. Producers came to prefer dolomite because it withstood higher temperatures than limestone and reduced sulphur in the iron, creating a high quality pig iron. Fire clay underlying the coal beds was used for making heat-resistant brick for furnaces.

As the decades passed, geologists, chemists and other specialists developed sophisticated technology and quality control for the iron making processes, but during the antebellum years the industry was primitive.

Alabama's first blast furnace began operating about 1815 near Russelville in Franklin County using the local brown iron ore. Entrepreneurs built several furnaces in North Alabama in the early 1840s, one on Cane Creek in Calhoun County, another in Roupe Valley where Tuscaloosa, Jefferson, Bibb, and Shelby counties met. A cotton planter named Ninion Tannehill purchased this furnace when it went idle and put it back into operation in 1836. Moses Stroup from a Pennsylvania iron making family bought and remodeled it in the 1850s. A furnace began operating in Shelby County about the same time and at least three more went into blast between 1840 and 1860.

Many smaller forges and large blacksmith shops produced iron, though none really fit the definition of furnace. Such operations might be as primitive as the one described by Frederick L. Olmstead on a journey through north Alabama. He observed white women, half naked for comfort under the blazing June sun, shoveling away a hillside. A man with pick worked nearby helping them uncover iron ore. Women and children shoveled the ore onto kilns of charcoal where it was fired, then taken to a forge. The women worked as hard as the men, and children of eight or ten carried lumps of ore.

The seven or so blast furnaces established between the War of 1812 and the Civil War relied on a similar process. Operators built them on a stream near an iron ore deposit and timber. Water turned a wheel which powered a blowing apparatus, either a large leather bellows or wooden tubes. Water-

Antebellum Alabama's nascent iron industry relied on charcoal to fuel its furnaces. The apparently limitless forests of the state provided the logs which were stacked, covered with dirt, and set on fire. After smoldering for a week or so, the wood, now reduced to charcoal, provided a sulfur-free fuel for iron making. Scenes such as this were common near the furnaces since it took nearly 100 bushels of charcoal to produce a single ton of iron. Charcoal continued to be used in Alabama iron making until the 1890s. Courtesy, Alabama Department of Archives and History

into operation. The Cane Creek furnace operated in about the same manner, producing 600 bushels of charcoal each twenty-four hours.

The furnaces usually consisted of stone blocks laid somewhat in the design of a truncated pyramid. The stone furnaces were lined with refractory bricks handmade from fire clay. Furnace operators placed charcoal, raw ore, and flux into the top of the thirty- to forty-foot-high furnace, which they built against a hillside and connected with a wooden bridge to the hill. When smelting began the ore was oxidized to metallic iron which was periodically run into sand molds known as "pigs." Depending on the grade of ore and the skill of the operator, such a furnace could produce between two and five tons of pig iron a day. Because of droughts and floods which prevented the use of waterpowered apparatus, most furnaces operated only twenty to thirty weeks a year, though one on an exceptional stream might produce nine months a year.

Charcoal fueled the early furnaces. Huge stands of cedar, pine, or hardwoods were felled, dried for a time, then cut into sections and stacked in huge piles. Workers then covered the piles with dirt and pine straw to exclude air and set them afire. The wood smoldered for a week or so, creating an excellent fuel which did not add sulphur to the iron in the ore-smelting process. Producing a ton of iron from brown ore required approximately 100 bushels of charcoal and resulted in a better quality pig iron than later coke furnaces.

Reducing timber to charcoal required both tremendous acreage and great expanse. Timber had to be felled by hand, then cut into sections and stacked. As forests closest to the furnace came

powered hammers fell of their own weight on the iron yielded by furnaces to produce bar iron. Their thunderous noise was audible for miles.

The state geologist described a furnace on Talladega Creek which employed fourteen people: one or two hammermen, two firemen working at the forge, one who stamped and roasted the ore, four wood choppers, three teamsters, and two colliers. The facility cost only 2,500 to 3,000 dollars to put

down, workers had to move further and further afield, adding transportation costs to the labor.

Because none of Alabama's coal could be used directly in iron furnaces it had to be reduced to coke. It was placed in beehive-shaped ovens for several days and heated without air like the piles of timber. Then workmen watered it down and produced a substance almost entirely carbon, like charcoal but with higher heating value. The disadvantage was greater sulphur content; the advantage over charcoal was a significant reduction in labor costs.

Slaves performed most of the hard labor. Since the busiest furnace season was often the slack time for agriculture, operators could usually rent them from nearby plantations. Slaves mined the ore, felled trees, produced charcoal, quarried limestone, transported it to the furnace, and loaded it. White supervisors directed the operation.

After transforming the ore into pig iron, domestic ware, or bar iron, owners shipped the products by wagon, boat, or train to nearby forges, blacksmiths, or stores. At the blacksmith operations the bar iron was heated again and worked into domestic items such as horseshoes, nails, or machinery. Furnace operators also bartered a good deal of iron locally with farmers for crops to feed the slave labor force.

Horace Ware was by far the most notable figure in the early years of iron making. Born in Massachusetts to an iron making family, Ware moved to Bibb County, Alabama, in the early 1830s where his father constructed a forge. Horace moved to Shelby County and established the state's third furnace about 1840 or 1841. Using brown ore and charcoal, he produced a fine grade of iron which he sold to Daniel Pratt for the construction of cotton gins and other machinery. In time he extended his markets to Montgomery and Mobile, added a forge, foundry, and rolling mill, purchased additional skilled slaves, and built a company town for 300 operatives. His Shelby Iron Company became one of the largest facilities in the South and a precious resource for the Confederate army later.

But Ware was neither a farsighted financier nor a skilled technical iron maker. He constantly suf-

fered from inadequate capital and did not get along well with other businessmen. His early experience with charcoal and brown ore and the excellent iron it produced caused him to ignore the later opportunity to help develop the red-ore-and-coke industry in the Birmingham district. In the antebellum years, however, his contributions to iron making matched Daniel Pratt's to textiles. Ware's

wife recalled years later: "He was pioneering all his life. I remember, even in driving anywhere he always took the roughest places in the road because he used to say nobody else would take them, and they must be smoothed down."

That epitaph could well serve an entire generation of entrepreneurs who began Alabama's industry and manufacturing.

The burning of the capitol on December 14, 1849, is depicted in this daguerrotype made at the time of the fire. The blaze broke out shortly after Montgomery had been made the state capital, after Tuscaloosa. Though only the walls of the capitol were left standing, it was completely rebuilt by 1851. Jefferson Davis was later inaugurated here as president of the Confederacy. Courtesy, John Engelhardt Scott, Jr.

Chapter 2
YEARS OF
TRIUMPH AND APOCALYPSE

Histories of Alabama traditionally divide the state's economic development at 1865. Before that date they suggest that cotton plantations and slavery predominated, after 1865 that industry boomed and cotton declined. These generalizations are not entirely accurate. During the years 1850 to 1865, Alabamians who envisioned an industrial state made significant progress toward their goal. Following the war, cotton production actually expanded. At the same time many planters converted into enthusiastic advocates of manufacturing. The decade and a half between 1850 and 1865 was as much a watershed for Alabama's manufacturing and commerce as the Civil War was for its politics. During those years citizens engaged in a furious debate over the state's future course and the wisdom of a more diversified economy. Several factors contributed to the change.

Concern over the fate of tens of thousands of poor whites motivated some industrial crusaders. Although many entrepreneurs cast this argument in paternalistic and humanitarian terms—factory jobs could provide a decent income and a better life—others worried about the potentially radical masses of poor whites collecting in Alabama's expanding towns. One planter spokesman boasted that the South prospered because poor whites remained "wholly rural; hence, the South will ever remain secure against any species of agrarianism, since such mob violence always originates in towns and cities, wherein are herded together an unthinking rabble . . . "

Despite attempts by Daniel Pratt and others to locate their mills in rural districts, towns were filling up with sullen whites. Artisans, mechanics, teamsters, mill workers, boatmen, among others earned

a precarious existence and often appeared on urban relief rolls. A November 1851 issue of the *Alabama Beacon* blamed urban destitution for driving such people begging from house to house. They were "roving, worthless creatures" who slept where they could and caused urban fires and other outrages.

Providing manufacturing jobs became more than a humanitarian urge; some planters perceived it as an act of self-preservation. Poor whites had to be absorbed into the economic structure somehow and the plantation system provided no possibility of doing that. In 1848 Montgomery's *Tri-Weekly Flag and Advertiser* asserted that the state contained 50,000 poor and idle whites who were available for employment. The following year Governor Henry Collier urged planters to patronize factories that employed poor whites, thereby producing consumers of local mechanical services and food products. Although many planters denounced industrialization because they believed it would produce a southern proletariat class, concern about poor whites was a major factor in the growth of the textile industry during the decade.

Southern nationalism played an even larger role in the manufacturing crusade. Many of the state's pro-slavery newspaper editors urged Alabama to diversify its economy in order to make the region independent of the North. An Alabama correspondent for De Bow's *Review* wrote in 1853 that "No state . . . possesses to a greater degree materials for a proud independence, than does Alabama . . . Too much time is given to growing cotton . . . How long, with all the advantages which God has given her, shall Alabama remain in the background, with her countless millions of wealth buried beneath her soil?" A Lauderdale County booster believed his county would become the "Lowell of the South." A Mobilian extolling one of the city's cotton factories in 1850 called it "one of the pillars of Southern independence . . . We must diversify our labor, build up factories and forges, if we desire real independence." A new quarry inspired a Talladega editor to write that same year: "One such enterprise as this will do more towards establishing the independence of the South than all the indignation meetings that can be drummed up . . . " The opening of a cotton mill in Autaugaville afforded an

example of how the South was "gradually freeing herself from northern bondage." In an 1859 epistle to Alabama citizens, Daniel Pratt argued that southern nationalists should make fewer fiery speeches and instead should "use our own iron, our own coal, our own lime, our own marble, etc." This nationalistic advocacy of industrialism in order to rid the South of reliance on the North became one factor leading to antebellum southern separation. Paradoxically, after the Civil War proponents of industrialism based their appeals on its capacity to heal the breach between sections and restore harmony to the Union.

Scientific exploration provided a third stimulant to manufacturing. As late as the 1840s citizens knew little about the state's resources. But in 1847 Michael Tuomey decided to make his home in Ala-

bama. A native of Cork, Ireland, Tuomey came to America as a young man in the 1820s. After farming briefly in Pennsylvania and teaching school in Virginia, he began his lifetime career of scientific investigation. South Carolina appointed him state geologist in 1844 and three years later he accepted an appointment to the faculty of the University of Alabama. Although the state appointed Tuomey its first state geologist in 1848, it appropriated no money for the position until 1854. This funding allowed Tuomey to resign his teaching position and work full time as state geologist.

For ten years between 1847 and 1857 Tuomey mapped Alabama. Tuscaloosa newspapers first publicized his findings. Then the state published his reports in 1850 and a second more detailed account posthumously in 1858. The reports were

models of that era's geological knowledge and provided the first guide to the state's mineral resources. Dissemination of his findings created a minor sensation. One Talladega County planter reported that "our country is all 'agog' with the mineral fever. Our people from the hills bring in pockets and saddle-bags full of rocks . . . " In some counties coal mining and iron making followed almost immediately the publication of his reports.

Politicians could not ignore such pressure, and they held the levers of power. With cotton prices booming and planters investing every available cent in slaves and new land, little capital remained for machinery and factories. It cost nearly $30,000 to lay one mile of rail and the only source of such funding was governmental. Either federal or state governments had to subsidize such internal im-

Above: Cotton was antebellum Alabama's most profitable product. Large plantations shipped bales on steam-powered riverboats to Mobile, the state's only seaport. Often the cotton went down long covered chutes, from high bluffs to the riverboats below, where slaves stacked the bales on the lower deck. This illustration shows this dangerous work as the cotton hurtled down from the bluff above. Courtesy, Mobile Public Library

Opposite: This lithograph by A.R. Waud depicts a riverboat on the Alabama River at Montgomery in the 1850s. Riverboats were then the principal means of transport for the state's largest cash crop, cotton, which was exported from Mobile. The capitol can be seen in the background. Courtesy, Will Hill Tankersley

provements. Democrats, who had long controlled the mechanisms of power both in Washington and Montgomery, opposed internal improvements at taxpayers' expense.

This dilemma made the challenge facing industrial boosters formidable, but they put their minds to the task with a will, believing that both the future of Alabama and their personal fortunes de-pended upon state subsidies. Henry W. Collier brought a pro-banking, pro-business attitude into the governor's office in 1849, but that same year the internal improvements faction lost badly in the legislature. Philip Phillips, elected to a second leg-islative term by his pro-business Mobile constitu-ents, led the proponents of state aid. As chairman of the House Committee on Internal Improve-

Above: *In 1854 the state legislature appropri-ated $10,000 to conduct a geological survey undertaken by Michael Tuomey, the first state geologist. Completed in 1855, but not pub-lished for more than two years, the survey cre-ated a sensation, and mineral fever swept the state. Tuomey's untimely death in 1857, before publication of his report, was a severe blow to hopes for rapid economic diversification in Al-abama. Courtesy, University of South Alabama Library*

Right: *Cotton was Mobile's most important export and the basis for the city's antebellum growth and prosperity. Although timber was a valuable commodity nothing could challenge the ascendancy of King Cotton before 1860. Steamers loaded with passengers and hun-dreds of cotton bales made their way down to Alabama's port, while on the return trips they took all the imported and manufactured goods the city's merchants sold to the Black Belt plantations. Courtesy, Mobile Public Library*

ments, he chided colleagues for their niggardly support of business. Alabamians, he warned, seemed determined "to grow old and poor together." In the summer of 1851 he organized a public meeting in Mobile which endorsed state aid for railroads.

But the Senate counterpart of Phillips' committee more accurately mirrored public sentiment. It reported that although Alabama's mineral resources attracted much public attention, "the whole public mind and many private interests" were still "in their transition state in respect to this new class of industrial enterprises." The internal improvement forces lost again in 1851.

During the next two years sentiment began to swing. In 1854 the legislature chartered the Mobile

Above: One of the great success stories of antebellum railroad building, the Mobile and Ohio ran for 200 miles northwest from the port city into Mississippi when this ad appeared in the Mobile Register. Financially supported by Mobile's business community and investors on both sides of the Mason-Dixon line, construction of the M & O was to expand the hinterland served by Alabama's port city. Unfortunately the outbreak of war delayed the realization of this goal for many years. Courtesy, Historic Mobile Preservation Society

Above, right: In the mid-1850s, facing a legislature determined to appropriate state money to subsidize railway construction, Governor John A. Winston vetoed dozens of such bills. While the legislature overrode some of his vetoes, Winston courted popular feelings of disdain for corporations, and the legislature backed down for a time. In 1859, led by pro-railroad legislators, new subsidies were passed but the coming of the war overwhelmed the state's infant railroad system. Winston effectively managed to block much-needed railroad construction for nearly a decade. Courtesy, Alabama Department of Archives and History

Chamber of Commerce, the first such organization in the state. Pro-railroad Democrats won many legislative seats from north Alabama where Tuomey's geological reports dazzled citizens with visions of untold fortunes to be made from the region's minerals. Phillips manipulated his advocacy of state assistance into a congressional seat when he was elected to represent the Mobile district in 1853, despite the fact that he was a pro-Union, anti-secessionist Democrat.

The legislature in 1853 finally approved a package of pro-business legislation. It chartered many new corporations and approved loans to the Mobile and Ohio and the Tennessee and Coosa railroads. These actions guaranteed that the question of state subsidies would become the central issue in the 1853 elections. Although north Alabama elected pro-railroad Democrats, the state as a whole elected John A. Winston governor, and he bitterly opposed state subsidies. Winston vetoed thirty-six bills in one session alone, though legislators overroad twenty-seven of his vetoes; sixteen of the overrides granted privileges to corporations.

But Winston was not easily discouraged. He took his case to the people and stimulated their intrinsic disdain for privilege. Public reaction forced repeal of previous aid bills in the 1857 session. But the pro-railroad faction rallied again and in 1859 enacted the most extensive system of state aid to railroads in Alabama history.

These almost biennial legislative reversals demonstrate both how acrimonious and equally balanced the pro- and anti-manufacturing forces were within the state. During the midst of Winston's resurgence in 1856, De Bow's *Review* editorialized: "Under the regime of the cotton planters Alabama is weak in her internal improvements, weak not only in the little already accomplished, but weak in the disinclination of capitalists to invest their means in a way to advantage the people and promote state welfare." The editor noted that in 1850 Alabama had investments of one million dollars in twelve cotton mills and fourteen forges and furnaces; meanwhile Georgia had two million dollars and Tennessee three million invested in the same industries. He attributed Alabama's backwardness to "lack of public spirit, no foresight, an utter indifference to the future, . . . an unsettled state of feeling as though Alabama were a temporary, not a permanent home . . . "

The story was not quite so bleak as De Bow's editor seemed to think. Optimistic signs appeared with increasing regularity. Even Philip Phillips' long crusade to build railroads bore fruit.

During the decade of the 1850s the Alabama legislature chartered seventy-three railroad companies. Most never laid track because of Governor Winston's opposition to state aid, but Tuomey's reports made it clear that the prerequisite to exploitation of the state's mineral resources was a transportation system. As late as 1852 Alabama possessed only 165 miles of track. In one decade following 1850 the state's entrepreneurs laid 610 miles of track costing more than fifteen million dollars. By 1860 the state contained nearly 800 miles of rail, much of it in the mineral belt. Unfortunately much of the track was small, detached, and supported by underfinanced individual capitalists or subscribers.

Charles T. Pollard possessed the clearest vision of the future. Keying his lines to commercial centers, he saw them not as supplements to steamboat traffic but as an alternate transportation system. First connecting his hometown of Montgomery to Columbus and Atlanta to the east, he then turned south with lines toward Pensacola and Mobile. Later he envisioned a western link from Selma to Meridian and a northern line through the mineral belt. Although by 1861 he had completed only the eastern and southern lines, his South and North Alabama Railroad had already reached as far as the mineral-rich hills of Shelby County. State government played the coquet in Pollard's courtship, regularly pledging aid in the legislature, then denying it in the governor's office. This charade provoked a more favorably inclined governor, A.B. Moore, to tell the legislature in 1859:

It is hard for a man who has lived in Alabama seven years to account for the deep and widespread suspicion and want of confidence in railroad . . . investments. There seems to be a holy horror . . . of all railroad corporations. We cannot understand why it is, that whilst the states all around us . . . are using every exertion to build railroads, the people of Alabama seem to regard them with suspicion and distrust.

In a dramatic about-face, the legislature both adopted his report in 1860 and loaned the South and North Alabama Railroad $663,135, allowing the railway to cross the Cahaba coalfield from Calera to Brocks Gap on Shades Mountain, overlooking the Birmingham coal and iron ore fields.

The legislature's waffling on banking was even more dramatic than on railroad subsidies. In 1850 the state possessed only two banks, the Bank of Mobile and the new Southern Bank began that October. Together they owned $2 million in specie, had $3.5 million in circulating notes, deposits worth $1.5 million, and loans valued at $4.5 million. By 1860 Alabama's eight banks held $2.75 million in specie, had doubled circulating notes, had tripled loans and deposits.

Once again the legislature played a key role in this reversal. The pro-banking wing of the Democratic party gained strength during the decade. In 1850 the legislature allowed a slightly regulated free market banking system. A tremendous demand for credit and money multiplied the number of banks operating in the state and even these could not satisfy the demand which resulted from the demise of the state-owned bank. Huntsville lawyer H. Lawson Clay summarized the situation in 1855: "money, money, money is the cry here from morning till night and if I were disposed to shave notes or lend at usurious rates of interest, I could almost double my means in twelve months." The regulations imposed by the legislature were not merely forms of harassment but intelligent attempts to guarantee sound practices and win public confidence. It mandated thorough state examinations and attempted to eliminate paper currency issued by banks outside the state.

Even this multiplication of banks underestimates the extent of financial activity, as Lawson Clay's letter demonstrates. Individual farmers, planters, lawyers, and merchants extended loans and performed other financial operations. When such stores and businesses are added to the banks, perhaps the total number of lending institutions reached seventy by 1860. Their financial ventures helped fund Alabama's manufacturing, stabilize the state's economy, and control inflation.

The state's furnaces, forges, and foundries also expanded rapidly during the 1850s. By the end of the decade some twenty facilities produced iron products worth $800,000 annually. The industry continued undercapitalized and oriented toward agriculture, however. The owner of one large foundry wrote: "If we had more capital, we could employ fifty more workmen in our general business, chiefly in grist and saw mills for the planters." Coal production, which stood at 2,500 tons in 1850, increased to 6,000 tons by 1855, and to 10,200 tons in 1860.

The textile industry followed the same pattern. Its 1,312 operatives, double the 1850 figure, made it Alabama's second largest industry by 1860. The value of their workmanship more than doubled, from $380,000 in 1850 to $1 million ten years later. Wages of textile mill workers remained low, averaging only $151 annually, the lowest of twelve industrial occupations listed in the 1860 census. Daniel Pratt's factory alone consumed 1,200 bales of cotton in 1857 and shipped its coarse fabric to

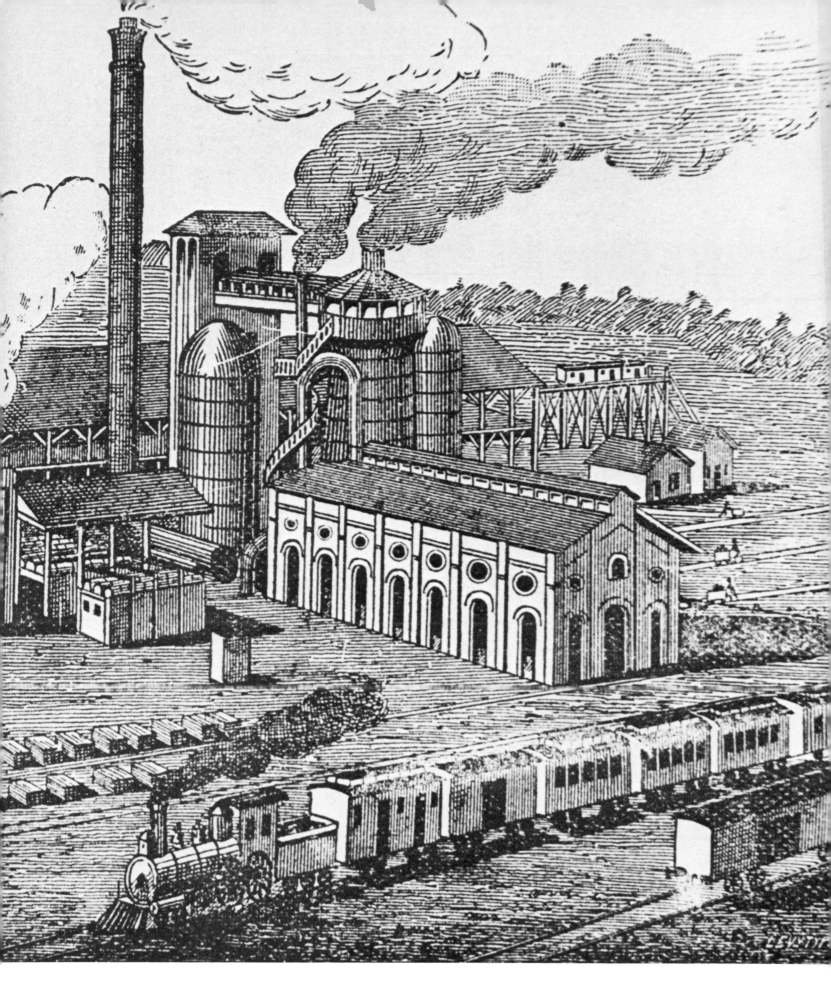

In 1883 Henry F. DeBardeleben and William T. Underwood developed the Mary Pratt Furnace Company, named for DeBardeleben's daughter. They purchased thirty acres off First Avenue near Avondale from the Elyton Land Company and the new furnace went into blast in 1883. Courtesy, James F. Sulzby, Jr.

Prussia, South America, and French Africa as well as to cotton states.

In a closely related industry, Alabama actually led the nation. Sixteen factories produced cotton gins worth half a million dollars. Pratt's factory dominated the industry as the largest single producer in the nation and as fabricator of one-fourth of Alabama's total.

Adding together the income from all of Pratt's enterprises reveals him to have been one of the nation's most successful businessmen. Between 1857 and 1860 he averaged an annual gross income of $632,652, impressive by modern standards and phenomenal in antebellum times.

Even industries which did not share in the general prosperity of the decade found new outlets. The lumber industry experienced a slight decline. High freight rates due to competition for available shipping reduced the timber market during the late 1850s, but even with that decline, 339 Alabama sawmills produced more than $2 million worth of lumber in 1860 and paid $430,000 in wages. Out of

Below: Henry Hilliard was the anti-secessionist editor of the Alabama Journal, *a leading Whig newspaper, and chief opponent of William L. Yancey, a brilliant orator in the cause of secession. Courtesy, Alabama Department of Archives and History*

Below, right: Sawmills were the state's leading industrial employer on the eve of the Civil War, and with gristmills accounted for one-third of all the state's industrial establishments and a quarter of its industrial work force. The timber industry was especially important in southwest Alabama and would become even more so after the war. Sawmills such as this one near Mobile depended upon water transport for logs, and railroads and the port of Mobile to transport the finished lumber to a variety of foreign and domestic markets. Courtesy, University of South Alabama

a total state manufacturing force of 6,792, sawmills employed 1,647 to lead all industries. Lumber companies also began exploiting the turpentine resources of the pine belt. Southwestern Alabama forests produced $650,000 worth of turpentine in 1860.

Taken together, these developments promised to deflect Alabama's economy in a new direction. By the eve of the Civil War, 10.5 percent of Alabama's white males worked in manufacturing or industrial jobs. Towns grew rapidly as did the number of businesses. Alabama's 1860 industrial product was valued at $10.5 million, twice the value of ten years earlier. Railroad track, either planned or already laid, crisscrossed the state.

On the debit side, most manufacturing in 1860 consisted of light industry; 40 percent came from just two sources, sawmills and gristmills. These accounted for 572 of the state's 1,459 manufacturing establishments and employed 25 percent of Alabama's industrial work force. Even in cities, the impact of factories was limited. In Mobile, Ala-

bama's largest city with a population of 29,258, only 764 persons worked in factories. Though progress seemed incredible compared to the state's condition ten years earlier, it was less impressive when matched with other states. Illinois had been paired with Alabama when both entered the Union in 1819, but by 1860 its annual industrial production exceeded Alabama's by five times. Even the industrial production of Indiana, primarily a farm state, bettered Alabama's by four times. Compared to more industrial northeastern states such as New York, Massachusetts, or Pennsylvania, Alabama almost disappeared from the scale.

Nonetheless, the progress was real enough, and Alabama seemed poised for a great leap forward in the 1860s. That such a spurt hardly left a blip on the historical landscape is due mainly to the Civil War.

Like most armed conflicts between peoples, the Civil War was an economic stimulant. It multiplied the economic developments of the 1850s. This pattern became well-known in the North, where the

1850s had also produced notable manufacturing growth. The war accelerated industrialization so rapidly that tremendous economic momentum was created for the following half century. This period of growth made America the dominant industrial nation in the world. Less well-known is the fact that Alabama contained resources which equalled or exceeded some of the northern states and that

Brigadier General Josiah Gorgas headed the Confederacy's Ordnance Department. A native of Pennsylvania, he had been stationed in Mobile before the war where he met and married his wife, Amelia Gayle. When the South seceded he took up its cause and directed a great deal of wartime investment to Alabama. After years of scarce capital, industrial development in Alabama boomed during the early part of the war. Courtesy, Alabama Department of Archives and History

it also stood poised to join the industrial revolution. The first stages of war affected Alabama's economy much the same way as it affected its industrial neighbors to the north.

When Confederate artillerymen fired the first shots at the federal garrison defending Fort Sumter they could not appreciate the difficulty of their position. The cannon they fired was precious beyond comprehension because only the Tredegar Iron Works in Richmond, Virginia, could cast heavy artillery for southern armies. The Tredegar facility was to Confederate technology what Virginia was to southern politics, a strategic keystone that had to be defended at all costs. From the outset Confederate planners realized the folly of relying exclusively for so important a resource upon a factory only 100 miles from Washington, D.C.; but where should an alternative be constructed?

The primary figure in making this decision was not unknown to Alabama. Brigadier General Josiah Gorgas headed the Confederate Ordnance Department and probably did more to spur Alabama's mining and manufacturing than any antebellum figure. Like so many other early developers, he was not a native son. A native Pennsylvanian, he had attended the Military Academy at West Point, then served a distinguished career as an ordnance officer in the United States Army. In 1853 fate served the future Confederacy when he received a billet near Mobile. There he met and married Amelia Gayle, daughter of a distinguished Mobile judge and politician. When Alabama seceded, his new family ties bound him to the South. That the Confederacy survived as long as it did is a testimony to his administrative genius.

His tasks were enormous. Rural areas produced tough, hardened soldiers but not the rifles, artillery, wagons, trains, rail, ships, and matériel to equip them. The South, scornful of factories and the urban world they spawned, launched a war which it was woefully unprepared to fight. Creating an industrial structure was the order of the day. This Gorgas did by heavy reliance upon his adopted state.

Between 1862 and 1865 Alabamians erected thirteen new blast furnaces in the state, all funded wholly or in part by the Confederate government. The furnaces received in wartime what they had

During the Civil War John T. Milner, pictured here, and Frank Gilmar used Confederate government funding to establish the Red Mountain Iron and Coal Company. Its blast furnace at Oxmoor produced much of the iron used by the military arsenal at Selma. By 1865 the Oxmoor facility was producing up to ten tons of iron a day. Courtesy, Alabama Department of Archives and History

never gotten in peace: abundant capital. The Confederacy provided as much as $100,000 for each. Building the new furnaces was simpler than operating them. Shortages of skilled labor, food, and draft animals crippled production. Furnace owners and government officials quibbled endlessly about procedures and prices. The Confederacy fixed iron prices it was willing to pay, but spiraling inflation quickly destroyed the scales. Finally in 1863 the government brought all iron manufactur-

ing under military jurisdiction. In order to supply adequate labor, Confederate armies detailed soldiers with iron making experience to duty at the furnaces.

As a result of governmental stimulus, activity quickened across the mineral belt. Entrepreneurs in Lamar County erected the Murdock Iron Works in 1862 using slave labor and skilled machinists assigned by Confederate officials. Thomas H. Owen, a planter and merchant in Jefferson County, began a forge near Tannehill employing an expert iron maker from Tennessee to operate it. Tannehill Furnace converted to military production, making cannonballs, gun barrels, and ordnance. Confederate funding allowed Frank Gilmer and John T. Milner to start Red Mountain Iron and Coal Company. Their furnace at Oxmoor produced ten tons of iron per day by 1865, most of it hauled by train to Selma for use by the ordnance works located there. The Mt. Pinson Iron Works on Turkey Creek in northern Jefferson County trained slaves as blacksmiths. W.S. McElwain, a native of Massachusetts, began the Cahaba Iron Works at Irondale in 1864. Foundrymen began other furnaces in Talladega, Calhoun, Jackson, and Cherokee counties. Supervised by many foreign-born iron makers from Wales and England, the crude furnaces strained to supply Confederate armies. By early 1865 the state contained sixteen blast furnaces, nearly twice as many as in 1860, and six rolling mills. Nine counties produced iron for the Confederacy. The largest furnace, at Brierfield, reached a capacity of twenty-five tons of iron a day.

Subsidiary industries thrived as well. Coal production, which had reached 10,000 tons in 1861, climbed to 15,000 tons by 1863. Although lack of capital hindered the industry, technological advances partly compensated. The first systematic underground mining began in the Cahaba coalfields in Shelby County during 1856. Construction of the South and North Railroad carried the line into the Cahaba field just before the war and proved a critical lifeline in the narrow artery that pumped blood into the Confederacy. Coal production in Tuscaloosa, Jefferson, Walker, St. Clair, Bibb, and Shelby counties presaged the abundant riches their rolling hills would surrender in years to come.

Manufacturing establishments multiplied in the towns. Tallassee and Demopolis businessmen began small arms factories. The new Alabama Arms Manufacturing Company in Montgomery produced Enfield rifles. Patriotic entrepreneurs in Clarke County built a navy yard on the banks of the Tombigbee River for constructing small ships, but the most elaborate facilities belonged to the river town of Selma.

Long a busy antebellum commercial entrepôt supplying the Black Belt, Selma was entirely unprepared for the fate that awaited it in the early 1860s. The Confederate government awarded its first contract for iron in 1861 and by late 1862 had developed a large ordnance facility at Selma, including an arsenal and naval foundry. As the boom gained momentum, twenty-four buildings were improvised from cotton warehouses or built from scratch. Businesses sprang up like weeds during spring rains: Central City Iron Works, Central City Foundry, Dallas Iron Works, Alabama Factory, Phelan and McBride Iron Works, Campbell's Foundry, Selma Shovel Factory, and Selma Iron Works. At its peak the Confederate war effort employed 10,000 industrial workers at Selma, more than the entire state contained in 1860. The Confederate government alone employed 6,000 people in factories which covered fifty acres along the banks of the Alabama River. The factories produced a variety of products including rifles, swords, shot, shell, muskets, pistols and caps, heavy ordnance, and ironclad ships. Selma factories produced perhaps half the cannons and two-thirds the ammunition used by Confederate armies during the last two years of the war. By 1863 the city had become the second largest manufac-

After the Union fleet cleared the guns of Ft. Morgan, the only effective resistance left was provided by the CSS Tennessee. A formidable warship built in Mobile with engines, guns, and armor plate manufactured in Selma, it engaged the entire Union fleet single-handedly for several hours until, having lost its smokestack and steering gear, it finally surrendered. In this engraving it is engaging Farragut's flagship, the Hartford. Courtesy, William Stanley Hoole Special Collections Library, University of Alabama

Alabama's oldest textile mill, the Bell factory, was established on the Flint River twelve miles northeast of Huntsville. The mill was chartered in 1932, burned and rebuilt in 1841,

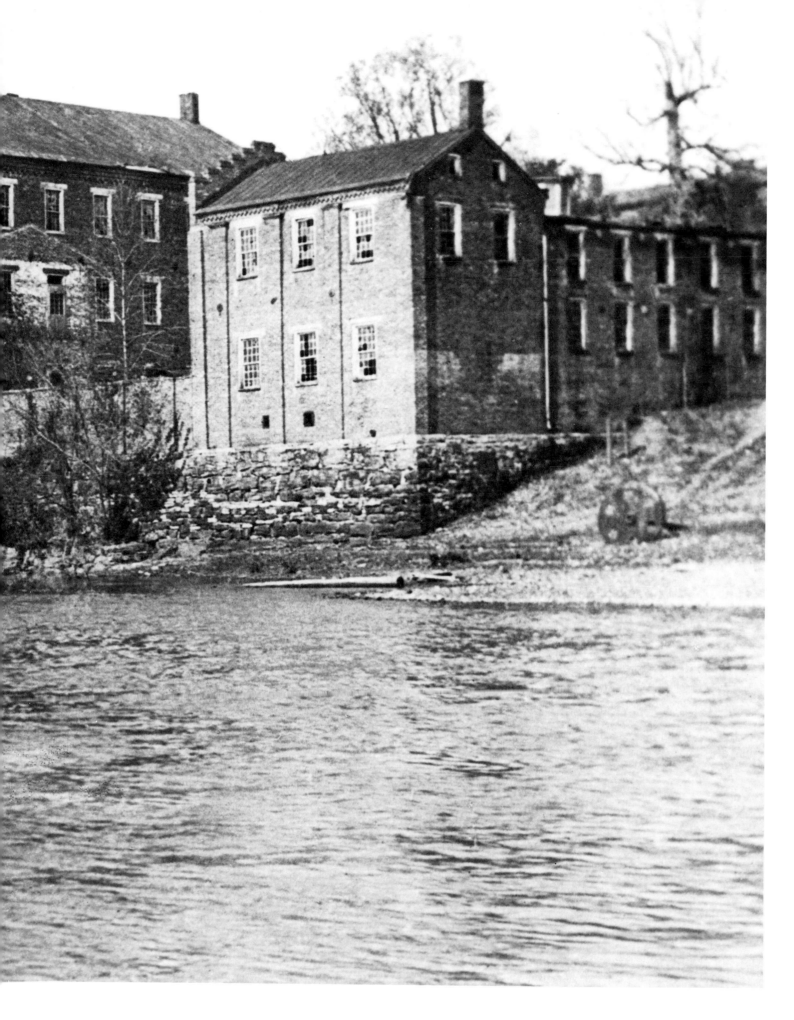

and closed in 1885. It got its nickname from the massive bell used to summon its workers.

Although most of Alabama was spared the physical destruction that occurred in northern Virginia, Selma was a notable exception. As a center of the Confederacy's munitions production, it was razed by Wilson's raiders. Even the cotton warehouses along the bluffs of the Alabama River were not spared, leaving an image of destruction as vivid as any in the old Confederacy. This view of Selma was sketched early in 1866. Courtesy, William Stanley Hoole Special Collections Library, University of Alabama

turing center in the Confederacy, exceeded only by Richmond.

Expert iron makers and engineers descended on the town in large numbers, perhaps the best known being George Peacock. A native of Yorkshire, England, who had learned his iron trade there, Peacock became superintendent of the naval foundry. A technological wizard, he discovered the first Alabama coal useful for making coke and instituted a number of innovations. Shelby Iron Works and Brierfield Furnace furnished excellent iron for making heavy naval artillery. Wood cut from nearby forests provided the skeleton and planking for the *Morgan, Selma, Gaines,* and *Ten-*

nessee, the naval fleet defending the strategic harbor of Mobile. Iron from Shelby and Brierfield furnished the *Tennessee's* iron skin and its guns. Admiral David Farragut discovered the skill of Peacock's 3,000 craftsmen during the Battle of Mobile Bay, when his large armada forced passage between Forts Morgan and Gaines and overwhelmed the small fleet inside the harbor. But his shells bounced harmlessly off the *Tennessee,* which inflicted heavy losses on the Union fleet before her surrender.

The Civil War presided both as midwife and undertaker for Alabama industry. Economic buds set with so much promise in the springtime of the Confederacy wilted and died as the war wound toward its conclusion. Banks which had made such progress during the previous decade collapsed under the dual blows of inflation and Confederate confiscation. The Bell Factory near Huntsville and most other textile mills in the Tennessee Valley fell victim to federal occupation. Coal production peaked in 1864 at 15,000 tons, then declined to 12,000 the next year.

The iron industry suffered even greater destruc- *(continued on page 65)*

This is a typical scene of logging operations in the pine forests above Mobile. The high-wheeled logging cart dragged logs to the railroads or rivers for shipment to Mobile. Timber was as big an export item as cotton by 1900. Courtesy, Alabama Department of Archives and History

Top, left to right: LeRoy Pope was one of the fathers of Huntsville and the founder of the state's first bank, The Planters and Merchants. He was a leader of the Georgia Party, the state's first political organization. Courtesy, Alabama Department of Archives and History

Henry Collier, Alabama governor from 1849 to 1847, was from Limestone County. He was an early promoter of economic development and railroad construction in the state. Courtesy, Alabama Department of Archives and History

Charles Pollard was the most active railroad builder in antebellum Alabama. He built a railroad from near Mobile to Montgomery, having a vision of long-range transport based on rail, not river, networks. The Civil War interrupted his plans. Courtesy, Alabama Department of Archives and History

Henry DeBardeleben was the premier industrialist in late nineteenth-century Alabama. He was a "savagely energetic, restless, impatient capitalist," in the words of Ethel Armes, noted Birmingham historian. Courtesy, Birmingham Public Library Archives

Right: Mobile's City Hall and Market built in 1857 has been in continuous service ever since and is one of the nation's oldest seats of municipal government. Courtesy, Museum of the City of Mobile

Above: *Mobile's fishing fleet docked at the wharves circa 1900. Mobile was one of America's oldest ports and a source of some of the nation's finest fish and shellfish by the time this picture was made around the turn of the century. Courtesy, University of South Alabama*

Opposite, top: *This is a view of Birmingham's main business district, Twentieth Street, looking north circa 1900. Coal and iron built Birmingham, and Twentieth Street was an expression of the city's wealth and power in early twentieth-century Alabama. Courtesy, Birmingham Public Library*

This page, middle: *This is a view of the TCI mill village at Ensley, with the giant steel mill in the background, circa 1915. Courtesy, Birmingham Public Library*

This page, bottom: *The Statue of Vulcan, Roman god of the forge, was constructed for the 1904 St. Louis World's Fair. After that it was on display at the fairgrounds in Birmingham until it was placed on Red Mountain in the 1930s. Courtesy, Birmingham Public Library*

The Ensley Steel Mill, owned by TCI, is pictured here circa 1910. The Ensley mill was one of the largest in the Birmingham area. Courtesy, Birmingham Public Library

This is the hospital built in Fairfield for its employees by Tennessee Coal, Iron, and Railroad. The hospital was a result of the policies of George Gordon Crawford and Dr. Lloyd Noland, who tried to improve the living and working conditions of all TCI employees. Courtesy, Birmingham Public Library

The Dwight Cotton Mill in Gadsden is seen here circa 1930. It was one of the larger mills in the state at that time. Courtesy, Birmingham Public Library

Mill owners often encouraged employee activities such as picnics, pageants, and, in this case, the Mignon Band at the Avondale mill, Sylacauga. Courtesy, Birmingham Public Library

This cotton mill in Mobile was typical of mills found all across the state early in this century. At one time cotton mills were the largest industrial employer in the state. Courtesy, University of South Alabama

This night view depicts Twentieth Street, the main street in Birmingham at the turn of the century. Courtesy, Birmingham Public Library

tion. General John T. Croxton's raid late in the war destroyed the Tannehill and Oxford furnaces. General James H. Wilson led 14,000 cavalry troops through Alabama in the spring of 1865, razing facilities throughout the mineral belt. Only the small furnaces in Hale and Lamar counties escaped destruction. Worse for the future, just six of the state's sixteen Civil War furnaces would go into blast again and only two would survive into the twentieth century (Shelby and Oxmoor). Some of the casualties were personal. David Hanby, father of the Warrior River coal trade but then an old man, was shot down in a federal volley while talking with Confederate troops near Hagood's Crossroads.

Alabama could absorb the loss of one man better than it could the destruction of Selma. Wilson's troops overwhelmed the tiny force defending the town, then put it to the torch. The five large buildings belonging to the naval foundry, the Selma Iron

The largest blast furnace in operation in Alabama during the Civil War was built at Brierfield in Bibb County. It produced twenty-five tons of iron a day for the Selma ordnance works, which in turn manufactured weapons for the Confederacy. Near the end of the war Union forces destroyed the facility at Brierfield along with most others in the state. Courtesy, Birmingham Public Library

Works, the Powder Mill and Magazine, five privately owned iron works, the Selma arsenal with twenty-four buildings, gun carriages, 60,000 rounds of artillery and one million rounds of small arms ammunition, all went up in smoke and flame. Selma had experienced her industrial moment of grandeur. She would retrieve her role as marketing center, but the industrial center which Wilson reduced to rubble would not rise Phoenix-like from the ashes.

Throughout southern Alabama logs were floated down creeks and rivers to sawmills, or directly to the port of Mobile for export. By 1900 timber was Mobile's largest export commodity. In this picture which was made at the port of Mobile early in this century more than a million board feet of poplar logs were being loaded for export. Courtesy, University of South Alabama

Chapter 3
RECONSTRUCTION
A MIXED ECONOMIC LEGACY

Whether or not Reconstruction was a critical watershed in Alabama's history is much debated. Many planters and industrialists lost both their financial resources and their will. Others shrewdly transferred their bank accounts to gold, sent the bars to Liverpool or London, and emerged from the war with fortunes intact. Within two years they had reestablished a labor force, switching from black slavery to biracial farm tenancy. Planters lost political power for less than ten years, reestablishing conservative Democratic control by 1875.

Under the spell of Henry Grady and other "New South" evangelists, many planters converted to a secular gospel of economic diversification, urbanization, and industrialization. They renounced past sins of agrarianism, secession, and slavery while enthusiastically proclaiming the efficacy of manufacturing, railroads, and the federal union. Most remarkable of all, they not only welcomed their erstwhile enemies to invest in the South, they actively recruited them. Some fiscally conservative planters, who had often supported the Whig party before the war, even earned the approbation of their neighbors by turning "scalawag" and joining the Republican party.

The collective efforts of outside investors and native industrial boosters changed Alabama's economy perhaps more rapidly than any other southern state. Alabamians began to utilize natural resources which had lain dormant. Factories sprang up as if by magic, and whole towns appeared in what seemed no more than a fortnight. Within a span of twenty years between 1880 and 1900 Alabama enthusiasts predicted a New South, chronicled its growth, and proclaimed its triumph.

The evidence does not quite match the boast. Compared to the economic conditions of 1860, the New South crusade did transform the state, particularly its northern third. But using a different measurement, growth within the eastern and midwestern industrial states which furnished Alabama's economic competition, the progress was sporadic and uneven. Relative to the rest of the nation, the South stood at no higher levels in 1900 than it had in 1860, and in some categories it had lost ground. Like Alice in Wonderland, southern industrialists had to run faster and faster just to stand still.

Alabama industry after the Civil War was similar to that of underdeveloped, Third-World economies in the twentieth century. It relied on abundant raw materials, outside capital and management, and cheap labor. It produced roughly finished products which were refined in other regions which reaped the highest profits. The economy was essentially colonial, with many of the businesses

Above: Birmingham was certainly the state's "Magic City" in the 1880s as its population and economy grew by leaps and bounds. Real estate speculation was fueled by the enormous profits successful speculators reaped buying and selling Elyton Land Company parcels. This 1887 Harper's Weekly illustration captures the sense of excitement in Birmingham during the 1880s. Courtesy, Alabama Department of Archives and History

Opposite: During the 1880s, having made a substantial fortune from his plantation in Barbour County, Braxton Bragg Comer moved on to Anniston as a merchant. In 1897 he went to Birmingham, where he bought the City National Bank and founded the Avondale Mills to manufacture cotton cloth. Comer's success brought him into conflict with Milton Smith and the L & N Railroad, whose rate structure he criticized, and catapulted him into the governor's office shortly after the turn of the century. Courtesy, Alabama Department of Archives and History

owned by northerners or Europeans. Profits flowed outside the region. Entrepreneurs who contributed money, time, and expertise to the civic betterment of Pittsburgh, New York, Baltimore, and even London, contributed little to solving similar problems in Birmingham, Anniston, or Gadsden. Ironically, sometimes the efforts of these outside entrepreneurs on behalf of the region exceeded those of native-born industrialists whose proclamations about saving poor whites by affording decent jobs masked a crass materialism more concerned with making a buck than saving a soul. Yet the twin goals of profit and philanthropy were often interdependent and compatible; when they were, Alabama's industrialists operated within the restraints of accepted legal and ethical practices. But when necessity demanded they could exploit their own people as callously as any Yankee capi-

talist, a fact well-documented by the excesses of peonage, the convict lease system, and child labor, to cite only three examples.

The postwar era opened amid chaos and confusion. Historian/journalist Ethel Armes speculated that as many as two-thirds of the shareholders of Alabama's mining and furnace companies who survived the Civil War were ruined financially. Most of the furnaces had used unskilled slave labor, a source temporarily eliminated by emancipation. Federal raids late in the war had toppled furnaces and destroyed facilities and equipment.

Most of these problems were short-term; but more serious structural economic troubles awaited resolution. Unreliable transportation crippled recovery. Lack of capital resulted in underfunding of most new manufacturing ventures, which were even then heavily dependent on northern and Eu-

ropean funding. Experienced managers and technical experts were harder to locate than money. Most of the South's wartime entrepreneurs in iron had been lawyers or merchants interested in industrial development, but possessed little if any experience or technical knowledge in operating furnaces or marketing iron products. As long as the Confederate government guaranteed them a market they could compete, but cast adrift in a competitive world they were hopelessly outmatched by experienced northern iron makers.

During the Civil War, seventeen Alabama blast furnaces had supplied iron to the Confederacy. Six furnaces never went into blast again after the war because they were too small to be profitable or too remote for economical transportation. Alabama ranked fourteenth nationwide in pig iron production in 1860, but fell to sixteenth place in 1870.

Above: Fire ravaged all of Alabama's cities during the nineteenth century, and adequate fire protection was hard to come by. In this rare tintype, a photographer has captured the men and machines of the Huntsville Fire Department. The fire station was located on Clinton Street between Washington and Jefferson. In addition to Engine House No. 1, the building housed the city scales where a fair weight of cotton and other bulk goods was assured. Courtesy, Huntsville/Madison County Public Library

Opposite: The forlorn landscape in this picture reflects the destruction Union General John H. Wilson's troops had wrought in the spring of 1865 and the hard times the South faced immediately after the war. In 1866 the Alabama and Tennessee Railroad stretched from Selma to Blue Mountain, the future site of Anniston, when this photograph was made in Selma. Courtesy, Samford University Library

Some furnaces reopened that might as well not have. Josiah Gorgas, Confederate cabinet officer who was largely responsible for Alabama's wartime industrial growth, decided to gamble on the future profitability of Brierfield Iron Works. Without any funds of his own, he persuaded friends to invest nearly $100,000 in the purchase and repair of the furnace in 1866; but the nearest rail line was miles away, and its spur line to the furnace operated on an irregular and unreliable schedule. When his iron reached the main line the railroad charged exorbitant freight rates. Freedmen made unreliable laborers, disappearing at the most critical times. Despite his initial success at raising money, subsequent attempts to obtain credit failed; nor did Gorgas prove as skillful in managing his own resources as he had in managing those of the Confederacy. Perhaps the hard times and economic

depression that gripped the South in the late 1860s doomed his efforts anyway. At any rate, by 1869 the company had failed, and Gorgas was forced to take a position as headmaster of the Junior Department at the University of the South in Sewanee, Tennessee.

Railroads fared no better during Reconstruction. Most Alabama railroads were small independent lines. Only by the broadest definition of the term could it be said that Alabama had a railroad system in 1865. After the war legislative fraud and incompetence replaced the antebellum legislature's refusal to provide state funding. So even though the Reconstruction government gave millions to individual companies, it received little return on its investment. By the time conservative whites regained control in 1875, the state and its railroads were insolvent. Many towns and counties

which had subscribed to railroad stocks in a desperate attempt to procure lines shared a similar fate.

Reconstruction politics and racial tension compounded the problems of railroads. By 1861 its founders had completed the Alabama and Tennessee Railroad from Selma as far as Blue Mountain, location of the future town of Anniston, but they abandoned the project during the Civil War. During Reconstruction, New York investors gained control of the line, which they renamed the Selma, Rome, and Dalton. They employed Captain E. G. Barney, a native of Ohio, to manage construction. He moved the headquarters from Selma to Patona in Calhoun County, and began recruiting black labor at Talladega College, a new institution just opened to educate former slaves. He hired an employee of the college, Methodist minister William

Opposite: In 1866 Josiah Gorgas obtained the astronomical sum of $100,000 in war-ravaged Alabama to repair and reopen Brierfield furnace. Plagued by erratic and expensive rail service, an undisciplined work force, and the hard times of Reconstruction, Gorgas went bankrupt in 1869. Courtesy, Birmingham Public Library

Below: The roundhouse at the Memphis and Charleston Depot in Huntsville is pictured here in about 1863. An adjacent engine house, a car shop, and a machine shop were constructed to handle repairs and to rebuild the rolling stock. Courtesy, Huntsville-Madison County Public Library

The state's second largest cotton mill, the Tallassee Manufacturing Company, established in the 1840s, had grown to contain 18,000 spindles and 360 looms in the late nineteenth century.

Located at the Tallassee Falls on the Tallapoosa River and operated by water power, the mill produced sheetings, shirting, osnaburgs, and ducks. It was located next to the main line of the

Western Railroad of Alabama, the state's principal east-west line, which facilitated shipping. Courtesy, Alabama Department of Archives and History

Luke, as the railroad's bookkeeper. Barney encouraged Luke to start Bible study and a school for blacks. Using northern and Negro labor, the railroad rapidly expanded into Alabama's largest line.

Then trouble began. In late June 1870, night-riding terrorists threatened to burn the railroad's buildings. They cut trees across the track, toppled rocks onto night trains, and fired shots at locomotives and depots. Barney petitioned the governor to station federal troops in Jacksonville, the county seat, to protect railroad property and personnel from Ku Klux Klan terrorism. The company was powerless, he wrote, to protect itself from "disguised ruffians." Pondering why Alabamians would attack a railroad which offered them economic opportunities, Barney concluded that the "better classes" respected the line; but the "ignorant short-sighted and those blind to the interests of the country" caused the trouble. When local klansmen lynched William Luke in 1870, the culprits included a Baptist preacher and small farmers, people outraged perhaps by the railroad's threat to their agrarian way of life as well as by its iconoclastic racial policies.

The economic distress of the times, abusively high freight rates and political corruption, combined to create such public hostility. The new legislature in its 1878-1879 session had to pass laws imposing stiff penalties for throwing rocks or shooting at trains, destroying track, bridges, or trestles, or for salting tracks in order to attract cattle and wreck trains.

Despite the problems, the Reconstruction years did not pass without development, some of it important to the future. Shelby Iron Company underwent reorganization, but was the only furnace to function throughout the period from Reconstruction to the 1890s. Giles Edwards, a native of Wales who had learned the iron trade in Pennsylvania and Tennessee, raised northern capital to improve his furnace. Thanks to good railroad transportation and management, Shelby Iron became one of the three leading U.S. iron manufacturers for railroad car wheels. By 1880 the company sold to customers in Kansas City, Toronto, and many other cities.

Even more dramatic events occurred in Jefferson County. W.S. McElwain, owner of Cahaba Iron

Top: A train leaves the Woodward ore mines. The Woodward brothers came to Birmingham in the boom years of the 1880s, and the Woodward Iron Company's first furnace went into blast in 1883 on a farm where the town of Woodward was located. Courtesy, William S. Hoole Special Collections, University of Alabama

Above: Pictured are the Oxmoor furnaces in Oxmoor, Alabama. Eventually, these furnaces became part of the Tennessee Coal, Iron and Railroad holdings. Courtesy, James F. Sulzby, Jr.

Opposite: In 1880, despite the developments which were occurring in the Birmingham area and throughout the mineral district, the most common industrial establishment was a grist-mill such as this one near Auburn which was operated by water power. Saw mills were in second place, reflecting the rural nature of the state a century ago. Courtesy, Auburn University Archives

Works, left for the North in 1865 to procure financing. He returned from Ohio with pledges of support and used this funding to employ 500 men to reopen his wrecked works at Irondale. By early 1866 his new furnace produced ten tons of pig iron a day.

Daniel Pratt and his son-in-law Henry F. DeBardeleben came to Birmingham in the spring of 1872. They gained control of Red Mountain Iron and Coal Company, with Pratt and Henry D. Clayton of Eufaula supplying the capital. They reopened Oxmoor Furnace and converted it from charcoal to coke, an experiment that produced a marketable grade of pig iron at less expense, and propelled Birmingham into dominance of the state's industry.

Progress on state railroads was also uneven. The most notable and revealing battle involved the South and North Railroad. The postwar president

of the line, Montgomery cotton factor John Whiting, wanted the railroad to turn northeast from Red Mountain and connect to Chattanooga, thus bypassing the heart of the mineral district. Chief engineer Frank Gilmer continued to press for the original route north to Nashville. With the key support of John T. Milner, Gilmer carried the day, but lack of capital forced the line to detour, climb hills, and snake through turns in order to avoid costly grading, tunneling, and trestle-making.

Milner, typical of Alabama industrialists eager to forget sectional animosities and determined to press on with economic development, allied with John C. Stanton. Stanton, a Boston "carpetbag" legislator who had gained control of the Alabama and Chattanooga Railroad, agreed to assist Milner and others in purchasing a large tract of land where the railroads crossed in order to establish a new in-

dustrial city, but Stanton saw no reason to retain his partners and tried to force them into bankruptcy. Milner forged a new alliance which included planters such as Bolling Hall and formed the Elyton Land Company. The company purchased land surrounding the tiny community of Elyton in 1871 and named the new town Birmingham in hopes that their project would develop an industrial economy to match its English namesake.

Thus, the Reconstruction economic legacy was mixed. So-called "Radical Republican" leaders envisioned a modernized Alabama. Without a planter wing to resist manufacturing, and influenced by many northern carpetbaggers who favored industry, Republican legislators provided state aid to private corporations, a practice which led to numerous abuses. The legislature also created two new offices to publicize and promote the state's industrial opportunities: the commissioners of industrial resources and of immigration. Radical legislators generally favored corporate development. They drafted a constitution in 1867 which limited corporate stockholder liability and allowed formation of new corporations without the burdensome procedure of individual charter by the state legislature. The return to power of Democratic conservatives in 1875 brought a renewed agrarianism complete with attacks on corporations and glorification of planter values. Paradoxically, Radical Republicans proved more friendly to industrialization than did conservative Democrats, who often reflected the views of planters; but by no means

While this 1852 broadside implies that the railroad linked Savannah and Huntsville, a passenger would have had to travel at least from Huntsville to Stevenson by stage, for the Memphis and Charleston tracks between the two cities were not completed until 1856.

CENTRAL RAILROAD,

FROM SAVANNAH TO MACON, GA.,
190½ Miles.

Passenger Trains leave Savannah daily, at......8 00 A. M.
"   "   "   Macon daily at ....8 00 A. M.
"   "   arrive daily at Savannah at....6 15 P. M.
"   "   "   " at Macon, at......6 45 P. M.

This Road in connection with the Macon and Western Road from Macon to Atlanta, and the Western and Atlantic Road from Atlanta to Dalton, now forms a continuous line of 391½ miles in length from Savannah to Dalton, Murray county, Ga., and with the Memphis Branch Rail Road, and stages, connect with the following places:

Tickets from Savannah to	Jacksonville, Ala.,	$20.00
" " "	Huntsville, } Ala.,	22.00
	Decatur, }	
" " "	Tuscumbia, Ala.,	22.50
" " "	Columbus, Miss.,}	28.00
" " "	Holly Springs, }	
" " "	Nashville, Tenn.,}	25.00
" " "	Murfreesboro' }	
" " "	Memphis, Tenn.,	30.00

An extra Passenger Train leaves Savannah on Saturdays, after the arrival of the steamships from New York, for Macon, and connects with the Macon and Western Rail Road ; and on Tuesdays, after the arrival of the Macon and Western cars, an extra Passenger Train leaves Macon to connect with the steamships for New York.

Stages for Tallahasse and intermediate places connect with the road at Macon on Mondays, Wednesdays, and Fridays, and with Milledgeville at Gordon daily.

Passengers for Montgomery, Mobile, and New Orleans, take stage for Opelika from Barnesville through Columbus, a distance of 97 miles, or from Griffin through West Point, a distance of 93 miles.

Goods consigned to Thos. S. Wayne, Forwarding Agent, Savannah, will be forwarded free of commission.

Wm. M. WADLEY, Sup't.

Savannah, Ga., 1852.

did all planters agree on the best course for the state, a fact well-demonstrated by the boom times of the 1880s.

Whatever progress toward recovery the South made during Reconstruction ended in the Panic of 1873. Failures of banking houses and companies on both sides of the Atlantic plunged the nation into a long depression. As the depression of 1873-1877 loosened its grip, economic activity quickened. The panic resulted in a shakedown of existing Alabama firms with many of the weaker ones disappearing. Usually a stronger company backed by northern or European capital bought smaller and weaker firms.

As a result of consolidations between 1879 and 1881, four major railroad systems emerged: the Queen and Crescent (funded by German and English capital); the East Tennessee, Virginia, and Georgia (New York capital); the Central of Georgia; and the Louisville and Nashville (which purchased the South and North). The Richmond Terminal system swallowed three of these (all except the Louisville and Nashville) during the 1880s. When the Richmond corporation fell on hard times in the 1890s, J.P. Morgan and Samuel Spencer purchased it and combined it into the Southern Railway (1894).

Although such monopolies led to abuses and struck many Alabamians as vaguely un-American, consolidation did solve some problems. The new lines were better managed and funded. Attracted by the tremendous freight possibilities of Alabama's coal, coke, iron, stone, lumber, and cotton, railroads vied with each other for control. Total rail mileage increased steadily: 1,843 miles in 1880; 3,422 miles in 1890; 4,197 in 1900; 5,226 in 1910.

Despite competition from strong adversaries, the Louisville and Nashville dominated the state. Milton H. Smith, the L.&N.'s dynamic president, understood as well as any single person Alabama's vast economic potential. He and vice-president Albert Fink helped Birmingham's early developers defeat an effort to divert railroad traffic away from the mineral district, but the price Smith demanded was control of the South and North Railroad to Nashville, which gave him a link from Louisville straight through to Pensacola. Because of the South and North's economies of construction, he had to virtually rebuild the line upon acquiring control. This acquisition gave him an enormous stake in Birmingham's development which he aided in every way possible. He favored the district with low freight rates on iron and coal, sold L.&N. mineral lands to developers, and even loaned them money to begin operations. Then he built branch lines into remote regions to provide efficient transportation. Ethel Armes, with little exaggeration, called Smith "the strongest force in the industrial history of Alabama."

In many ways Milton Smith embodied both the best and worst values of the late nineteenth-century entrepreneur. Fearless and imaginative, he possessed an intuitive sense of economic destiny. He could survey a virginal mountainous landscape and envision belching smokestacks and streams of boxcars groaning beneath loads of coal, but he exacted a steep price for his investments. He fiercely opposed state regulation. "In our efforts to protect the property of the company," he wrote, "we must do what we can to conciliate and placate and prevent . . . injurious, destructive, or confiscatory legislation." He tried to prevent establishment of a state railroad commission in 1881, and failing that, he successfully lobbied to restrict its role to purely advisory. He showered railroad commissioners with free passes on the line they were supposed to regulate and in time extended his largess to legislators, journalists, and governors. Because the railroad conducted legal business in every community through which it passed, he placed a prominent local attorney on the L.&N. payroll. Many of them entered politics where they usually protected the railroad's interests.

Thomas G. Jones was one such friend of Smith and the L.&N. Jones defeated a populist candidate for governor and served two terms in the 1890s. A former L.&N. attorney, Jones received many favors such as a luxurious free railroad car for trips. When he contemplated resigning in 1893, Smith dissuaded him, arguing that remaining in office was both in the best interests of the state and "the Louisville and Nashville R'd [railroad] Co. as well as other companies operating in the state . . ." Jones also reflected Smith's attitude on legislative regulation; instead of restrictions, he urged measures "which can be extended by any legislation to

Thomas Goode Jones, who had been an attorney for the L & N Railroad, served two terms as Alabama's governor in the 1890s. While in office he did all he could to help Milton Smith's L & N avoid meaningful railroad regulation. Jones was a typical politician of the New South, favoring rapid industrialization, laissez faire policies, and very low tax rates. Courtesy, Alabama Department of Archives and History

these great developers." So influential was Smith that Alabama retained one of the least regulated railroad systems of any southern state, and so despised was he by many merchants and farmers who had to use his railroad that L.&N. became the abbreviation for the "Long and Nasty."

The same laissez-faire spirit encouraged other industrialists. Daniel Pratt and Henry F. DeBardeleben were cut from the same cloth as Smith. They purchased 30,000 acres of coal lands and in 1878 organized the Pratt Coal Company. DeBardeleben, J.W. Sloss, and other partners laid

track, and in 1879 began shipping high-grade coking coal into Birmingham. Oxmoor Furnace had produced the first pig iron from coke in 1876, and the Pratt company's steady supply of coal brought Birmingham to life. Annual coal production in Alabama increased from 224,000 tons in 1878 to 324,000 two years later. By 1882 the figure had reached 896,000 tons and the following year it nearly doubled again to 1,568,000 tons. Before the depression of 1893 cut production, the state's coal mines produced 5,529,000 tons. By 1900 produc-

In 1881 Colonel James Withers Sloss organized the Sloss Furnace Company with the encouragement of Henry F. DeBardeleben. As president of the Nashville and Decatur Railroad and later as a partner in Pratt Coal and Coke Company, Sloss had been involved with the development of Birmingham since its inception. In 1881 he built the city's second blast furnace on First Avenue. The Sloss furnace, with many modernizations, continued in operation for nearly nine decades and is now a municipally-owned museum. Courtesy, Birmingham Public Library

Below: *In 1872 Daniel Pratt and his son-in-law, Henry DeBardeleben, gained control of the Red Mountain Iron and Coal Company and reopened the Ironton (Oxmoor) furnace using coal coke, not charcoal. Since there were abundant supplies of coal in the area, the success of the Oxmoor experiment enabled Birmingham to dominate Alabama's iron industry. This photograph shows the principal blast furnace where the iron was produced at Ironton. Courtesy, Alabama Department of Archives and History*

tion had recovered to 8,394,000 tons.

DeBardeleben dominated the 1880s coal and iron industry as thoroughly as Smith did Alabama's railroads; and like Smith, he was the product of a swashbuckling age of enterprise. A practical man, he debunked education and history: "The rocks and the forest are the only books I care about reading... The future is what a man looks to. Who cares a hang about the past—things that are over and done?" Operating on the principle that "life is one big game of poker," he waged war on his rivals. "I was the eagle," he boasted, "and I wanted to eat all the crawfish I could—swallow up all the little fellows, and I did it!" As he surveyed his domain of 15,000 acres of mineral lands in the late 1880s, the largest empire in the South at the time, he expressed his desire for mastery over nature as well as rivals: "Break a young mustang into a fox-trotting gait—that's what we did to the Birmingham District." Or as he phrased his ambition more lyrically:

> There's nothing like taking a wild piece of land, all rocks and woods, ground not fit to feed a goat on, and turning it into a settlement of men and women, making pay rolls, bringing

Above: On November 23, 1880, Henry DeBardeleben's "Little Alice" furnace went into blast, the first actually built in the city of Birmingham. Within three years it was joined by "Big Alice" and Sloss furnaces. This 1987 Harper's illustration shows the interior of one of these early furnaces as it is being tapped to produce the pig iron for which Birmingham became famous. Courtesy, Alabama Department of Archives and History

> the railroads in, and starting things going. There's nothing like boring a hillside through and turning over a mountain. That's what money does, and that's what money's for. I like to use money as I use a horse,—to ride!

In time larger eagles than DeBardeleben would swoop down on Birmingham and swallow him as he had swallowed others. One imagines that he had a grudging respect for J.P. Morgan, the most voracious eagle of them all, but in his heyday DeBardeleben could wheel and deal with the best of his opponents.

Together with his father-in-law Daniel Pratt, he established one enterprise after another. In 1880 they put the Birmingham Rolling Mill into operation. The same year DeBardeleben and T. T. Hillman began the "Little Alice" Furnace, the first in the city proper. Alice Furnace produced fifty-three tons of iron per day, a record for Alabama. Although the furnace was a success from the start, successive modifications increased its capacity to 300 tons of pig iron a day by 1912. DeBardeleben utilized English capital to form DeBardeleben Coal and Iron Company in 1886. Realizing the tremendous potential of western Jefferson County he also founded the industrial city of Bessemer. Like most of the early coal and iron men he incorporated real estate companies and banks.

Although DeBardeleben dominated development, others competed for choice properties. Sloss Iron and Steel opened a facility in the 1880s which would become the most long-lived of the early furnaces. In 1886 the Tennessee Coal, Iron, and Railroad Company bought Pratt Coal and Iron. Relying on the innovative ideas of mining engineer Erskine Ramsay, T.C.I. quickly cornered a major share of the southern iron market, but the ever-present problem of raising capital plagued the new enterprise. In 1888 a group of New York City financiers gained control of T.C.I.; then southern investors repurchased the corporation in 1891, though many directors and much of the capital continued to come from New York. In the 1890s better funding allowed T.C.I. to purchase DeBardeleben Coal and Iron and the Cahaba Coal Mining Company. With these transactions the corporation acquired the historic Oxmoor furnaces, the Bessemer furnaces, the Red Mountain iron ore deposits, the coalfields near Helena, and other important properties. Subsequent acquisitions just after the national depression of 1893-1897 merged some sixteen companies into T.C.I. The corporation retained many of its officials. Henry DeBardeleben became first vice-president and the resourceful engineer, Erskine Ramsay, served as chief engineer.

By the mid-1880s Birmingham was a full-fledged boomtown. Population surged from 3,000 at the beginning of the decade to 26,000 at its end. Six new furnaces opened, giving the town a total of ten. Iron production, which placed Alabama eighth among all states in 1880, increased twelvefold during the decade. By 1887 the Birmingham

Opposite: Cotton was commonly sold around the Public Square in turn-of-the-century Huntsville. This view, taken from the northwest corner looking east, shows the second Madison County Courthouse at right. Courtesy, Huntsville-Madison County Public Library

Below: The Sloss furnace shown in the background of this picture was Birmingham's second oldest. As this early photograph suggests, the "Magic City's" growth depended upon its close proximity to natural mineral resources and adequate rail transportation. Colonel Sloss built his blast furnace next to the main yards of the L & N Railroad to take full advantage of this combination. Courtesy, Samford University Library

district contained thirty-three coal and iron companies. Following a substantial crisis during the 1890s depression, the industry recovered rapidly in 1898 led by T.C.I.'s vigorous expansion. Northern firms began to pay close attention to the region as the quality of iron improved and as Birmingham's cost advantages began to cut into Pittsburgh's markets. In 1899 the Republic Iron and Steel Company of Pittsburgh bought the Pioneer Company in order to establish a foothold in Alabama. Eight years later U.S. Steel fashioned one of the most significant takeovers in southern history when it eliminated a formidable rival by purchasing T.C.I.

Although activity was centered in the new city of Birmingham, satellite towns shared the riches. The prosperity of the coal and iron boom spread through Walker and Etowah counties into the Tennessee Valley. Of fifty-five Alabama blast furnaces in 1893, thirty-three had been built since 1885, and twenty-five were located in boomtowns other than Birmingham. The Tennessee River community of Florence acquired two furnaces in the 1880s. Decatur, which lay in ruins at the end of the war, obtained a blast furnace in 1887. This facility in turn spawned a number of iron manufacturing plants, including L.&N.'s Consolidated Car Construction and Repair Shop, the largest factory of its kind south of the Ohio River when it opened in 1887.

Perhaps no single community epitomized the New South spirit better than the northeast Alabama town of Anniston. It was the creation of two men, Samuel Noble and Daniel Tyler. Noble, an English-born ironmaster who learned his trade in Pennsylvania, moved to Rome, Georgia, and

opened an iron works before the Civil War. Tyler, a Connecticut Yankee with ample capital, entered the region because of the interest of his son, who became vice-president of a South Carolina railroad during Reconstruction. In 1869 the Tyler and Noble families bought iron ore lands in Calhoun County, and in 1872 created Woodstock Iron Company. They laid out a model community complete with schools and churches. For eleven years the community remained purely a company town. Its founders personally recruited business and professional men, prohibited alcohol, imported skilled foreign labor, and handpicked workers for the Woodstock Company. Railroad expansion drove the price of iron to $52 a ton and earned the company a profit of $87,000 its first year of operation. Despite the 1870s depression, which closed 71 percent of the nation's charcoal furnaces, Woodstock

*The Spring City Mills **(opposite)**, the Yarbrough Grocery **(top)**, and the Huntsville Grocery Company **(above)** were all thriving enterprises in turn-of-the-century Huntsville. Courtesy, Huntsville-Madison County Public Library*

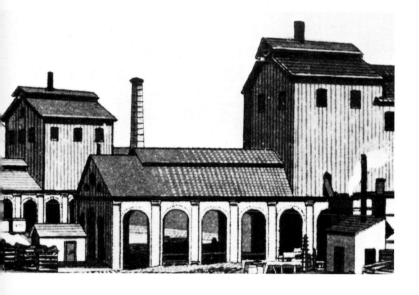

survived by its quality products, the only charcoal furnace in the state to remain in blast throughout the depression. By 1880 Woodstock was the second largest producer of charcoal pig iron in the world.

The company funded the city, installing Alabama's first effective system of electric lights and paying above-average wages. Even these salaries did not provide a high level of living, so the town's founders built Anniston Cotton Manufacturing Company in 1880 to offer employment to the wives and children of foundrymen. They constructed a three-story brick building which was the largest mill in Alabama at the time. Most of the 250 operatives who tended 11,000 spindles and 320 looms were female. The company imported an experienced mill superintendent from Providence, Rhode Island, and produced coarse cloth, 30 per-

Top: In 1872 Samuel Noble and Daniel Tyler created the Woodstock Iron Company and laid out a model community for its employees. Thus Anniston came into being as a paternalistic company town with schools, churches, and no alcohol. Woodstock made most of its iron using charcoal long after most other Alabama furnaces had converted to coal coke, but the quality of its product was high and in great demand. When these engravings were made, Woodstock was the world's second largest producer of charcoal pig iron. Its charcoal-fired furnace produced 50,000 tons of pig iron annually. *Courtesy, Alabama Department of Archives and History*

Middle: Anniston, like Birmingham, benefited from the close proximity of iron ore and rail transport. The Woodstock Iron Company owned mines such as this which produced red hematite ore, accessible by surface mining operations. Lacking an adequate supply of coal, the Woodstock Company used charcoal until the 1890s to produce an unusually pure grade of iron. *Courtesy, Alabama Department of Archives and History*

Bottom: The Anniston Manufacturing Company, the largest cotton mill in Alabama when it was built in 1880, hired the wives and children of the men who worked for the Woodstock Iron Company. It employed some 1,250 workers. Women and children traditionally comprised the bulk of the work force in textile mills throughout the South. *Courtesy, Alabama Department of Archives and History*

cent of which was exported to China. The textile mill's annual profits of 7 percent were about average for the industry.

When the Georgia Pacific Railroad crossed the Selma, Rome, and Dalton line in 1883 it made Anniston an important rail junction, but one observer noted it also "made it impossible to observe the same degree of exclusion of the lower grades." So the Nobles and Tylers conceded the inevitable and offered real estate for public sale. Henry Grady, the founder of the New South movement, came from Atlanta for the dedication ceremonies and praised the community as a model of the new commercial spirit. Population rose spectacularly from 941 in 1880, to 6,000 in 1884, to 9,695 in 1900. The Nobles moved their iron car wheel works from

The wages paid to the women and children who worked in Alabama's cotton mills were low, but when combined with those of the head of the household (if he was working) the resulting "family wage" was adequate to sustain life. This mill was owned by Mobile investors but located just over the Mississippi border on the M & O Railroad line. Courtesy, University of South Alabama

Rome, making the Anniston Car Wheel Works the largest such concern in the South, serving twenty-nine different railroad customers. Fortunately for Anniston, the city's founders quickly diversified into producing textiles, cast-iron pipe, iron stoves, and nails. As the nation's railroads converted to

In the 1890s the Tennessee Coal, Iron and Railroad Company, led by Erskine Ramsay, became one of the largest producers of iron in the South. In the process it acquired competing companies such as DeBardeleben Coal and the Cahaba Coal Mining Company whose Blocton, Alabama, coke ovens are shown in this circa 1890 photograph. Courtesy, Birmingham Public Library

president of Alabama Rolling Mill at age twenty-three. Before coming to Birmingham he had been chief chemist for Youngstown Steel Company and at Spang Steel and Iron in Pittsburgh. On February 27, 1888, Henderson Steel produced Birmingham's first steel. The event created a media sensation, but the company did not prosper. Though succeeding in the technology of steel production, its management failed in entrepreneurship. They could not obtain capital for expansion or markets. Finally Henderson's high operating costs made it a commercial failure.

New technology and industries provided Alabama a spectacular episode quite different from other southern states, but quantitatively its manufacturing remained mired in more traditional ruts. According to the 1880 census the leading industries in value of finished products among Alabama's 2,070 manufacturing establishments were flour, meal, and cereal milling, followed by sawmills in second place, iron and steel in third, and textile mills in fourth. The first three industries accounted for 8.25 million of total capitalization of 9.5 million dollars.

The textile industry made steady progress from Piedmont through north Alabama. Predicated on the "family wage," mills opened in thriving industrial towns on the assumption that a male head of family could barely survive on his salary. Hence cotton mills afforded jobs for his wife and children. Antebellum mills had often been located in rural areas, but they fell upon hard times after the war. For instance, the Bell Factory near Huntsville was reorganized in 1868 as Bell Factory Manufacturing Company with more than 600 employees. It closed in 1885 because the railroad had provided such an

advantage to new mills in Huntsville ten miles away that it could no longer compete.

Daniel Pratt's multifaceted empire in Prattville continued to thrive. Absorbing hundreds of poor white operatives, the mills produced coarse fabrics for finishing elsewhere. After Pratt's death his son managed Daniel Pratt Gin Company, which by 1899 was the largest producer of cotton gins in the world. In that same year Daniel Pratt, Jr., sold out to Continental Gin Company, a merger of several large concerns fashioned by Birmingham businessmen.

Each town seemed to covet a cotton mill as a source of income for penniless poor whites crowding in from the countryside. Huntsville attracted its first cotton mill in 1881 by exempting the factory from taxes for ten years. Anniston's founders established the Anniston Cotton Manufacturing

The larger lumber companies rented housing to their employees, which was graded according to race and pay scale. These views of company housing in Fulton, Alabama, taken about 1900, illustrate clearly this range and diversity. The skilled white workers' homes are on the top in this picture, and the housing available for the blacks is on the bottom. Courtesy, University of South Alabama

Opposite: *W.H. Hassinger founded the Henderson Steel Company to produce steel using a new process developed by James Henderson. The company managed to produce Birmingham's first steel in 1888, but not profitably. Although the Henderson Steel Company would not be able to capitalize on its innovation, other Birmingham firms, notably Tennessee Coal, Iron and Railroad Company, would a decade later successfully use the open hearth process to make steel. Courtesy, Birmingham Public Library*

William H. Echols, who led the way toward Huntsville's "New South" position, served as a civil engineer for the Memphis and Charleston Railroad, then ran the Bell Factory Cotton Mills from 1874 to 1884. As president of the First National Bank of Huntsville, he continued as a leader in the community until his death in 1909. Courtesy, Huntsville Public Library

Company as an additional source of family income for iron workers.

A mixture of philanthropic and personal motives also inspired Alabama's most distinguished textile man, Braxton B. Comer. He seemed an unlikely candidate to become a manufacturing tycoon. Born on a plantation in Barbour County, he made his early fortune in the mercantile business. Using the profits of his store, farm, and gristmill, he accumulated 30,000 acres of land. Unlike many planters who resisted industrialization from their islands of prosperity in the Black Belt, the commercial possibilities of north Alabama captivated Comer. When Anniston opened its doors to the public, he moved there in 1885 where he became a wholesale merchant, miller, and cotton factor. Crippled by high railroad freight rates, he relocated his milling business to Birmingham, then bought the City National Bank, and in 1897 he established Avondale Mills with initial capital of $350,000 and employed 400 operatives. According

to family history, Comer began the mill at the request of the Chamber of Commerce in order to employ the city's poor whites. From his base at Birmingham, he purchased or began other mills in Eufaula and Sylacauga. Steadily expanded by his son Donald, Avondale Mills employed 8,500 by the 1940s.

The timber business also thrived in the new industrial climate. When the Civil War ended, the vast longleaf yellow pine forests of south Alabama remained largely untouched. The region belonged to the Southwestern Pine Hills stretching from the Savannah River in Georgia through West Florida and south Alabama to Mississippi's Pearl River. The longleaf pine had a long taproot which allowed it to flourish in the infertile sands of the pine barrens. By destroying pine straw and undergrowth, occasional fires seemed to help more than they hurt. This allowed seeds to germinate in clean, bare soil. The pines grew forty to sixty feet with scant foliage, except for a crown at the top.

Straight, permeated with resin which made them extremely durable, and containing a solid heart and little waste in branches, longleaf pines were a lumberman's dream.

Before 1880 Alabamians cut more trees to clear land for farming than for commercial timber, but the industrial surge of the 1880s caught everything in its sweep. Railroads needed 3,000 cross ties per mile of track and had to replace 200 ties per mile annually before modern wood preservatives appeared. As a result farmers began to supplement their incomes during the winter months by cutting cross ties.

The lumber business grew in the same bursts of energy as coal, iron, and steel. When the Civil War ended, Alabama contained more than 32 million acres of public land; by 1876 only 4,600,000 remained. The government sold most of the rest in 1876 for $1.25 per acre. Since an acre of longleaf pine yielded between 6,000 and 12,000 board feet of lumber, timberland was one of America's greatest bargains.

Many shrewd lumbermen got the land for nothing by merely filing homestead claims for forty acres. They hired prostitutes, tramps, and ne'er-do-wells, anyone capable of signing a name. They had no intention of improving the land as the Homestead Bill required, but planned merely to clear-cut the timber. Others, less imaginative, simply poached timber off public lands without so much trouble or formality.

By the late 1880s large lumber companies, often funded by European or northern capital, entered the market and began to impose some order. Lumbering was an extractive industry, an example of economic colonialism which combined the most wasteful practices of laissez-faire capitalism.

The companies employed a racially mixed labor force which lived in mobile lumber camps as wild as any western frontier town. At first they lived in tents and shacks, though when logging trains entered the scene, they moved into boxcars which contained twenty double-decker bunks and were called "shaking Jacobs." The train usually provided a kitchen car and two dining cars, one for blacks and another for whites.

Skill with an ax was the primary requirement until the 1890s when the crosscut saw revolutionized the industry. A skilled axman could hew a log square with such skill that one had to search carefully to see the ax marks, but use of the crosscut saw tripled production.

Because of the expense of laying even narrow gauge track and operating trains and other mechanical devices, the large logging companies began "clear cutting" forest regions. Unlike smaller operations which only went after the larger trees worth the muscle power required to cut and remove them from the forest, "clear cutting" harvested every available tree in an area. It was a system profitable to the companies and devastating to the land. Courtesy, University of South Alabama

Above: *Before 1880 most trees were cut so farmers could clear land for planting. Stumps were pulled both to facilitate cultivation and as a source of lighter wood. These men are using a mule powered puller and twin blade axe to remove pine stumps. The photograph was made in 1895 at the height of the lumber boom in southern Alabama. Courtesy, University of South Alabama*

Opposite: *Logging was the most important economic activity in rural south Alabama during the late nineteenth century. However, moving the logs from forest to mill was a difficult task. Wherever possible, logs floated on the numerous creeks or rivers, but any overland transport depended on high-wheeled logging carts such as this, pulled by oxen. Courtesy, Alabama Department of Archives and History*

The most difficult work was hauling logs. At first loggers cut along rivers and creeks so they could float logs downstream to Pensacola or Mobile. Then oxen pulled them to the nearest water, or huge two-wheeled carts handled them, with one end of the log attached to the cart and the other end dragging behind.

Lumbermen collected the logs in streams until huge rafts could be floated in rivers engorged by rains. In November 1895, 117 rafts, each averaging 120 logs, waited for fall rains to raise the waters of Murder Creek some three miles from Brewton.

Although water transportation remained important throughout the nineteenth century, railroads became increasingly competitive. Lumbermen began to experiment with a variety of techniques. The typical cost of $20,000 to $35,000 a mile precluded full-fledged roads which could operate only

until the lumber was exhausted, but W.T. Smith Lumber Company of Chapman constructed a railroad of wooden spikes fastened to cross ties by pegs or iron. The train was called a "gravity tram" because when workmen removed chocks from the wheels, the cars rolled downhill until they stopped at the planing mill. Oxen or mules then towed the empty cars back uphill to the sawmill. Companies tried other ingenius devices. One placed peeled logs side by side pegged to the ground. Then animals or steam engines moved cars over the pole road. This device reduced the price of hauling a log up to five miles by oxen (sixty-five cents) by more than two-thirds (sixteen-twenty cents).

The most important experiment began in 1883 when Emory F. Skinner heard about a narrowgauge logging railroad in Michigan. He visited it and believed it would solve the South's log hauling problems. He ordered six miles of track and a locomotive, and his project was a success from the start. After 1890 most large companies copied his idea. W.T. Smith Lumber Company built a network of 100 miles of three-foot-wide gauge. Kaul Lumber Company of Tuscaloosa laid seventy-five miles of track. The companies used secondhand rail and wood-burning locomotives to reduce costs.

The introduction of logging railroads dramatically changed the industry. They gave a distinct advantage to large, well-financed corporations that could afford costs of more than $1,000 a mile for track. One secondhand locomotive could do the work of ten to thirty oxen teams depending on the distances involved. The annual operating costs of thirty teams and their drivers was $27,000; a train and crew, plus maintenance cost of the track, averaged about $7,000. But the roads dictated cutting

scended from prewar planter families. Although self-made men such as T.R. Miller appeared on the list, they were exceptions. Among the 186, 25.8 percent of their fathers had been businessmen, another 24.2 percent professionals. Many of them were well-educated (37.1 percent had attended college), had served in the Confederate army (45.2 percent), were active politically, usually in the Democratic party (43 percent), and were church members (79.1 percent, led by Episcopalians, Methodists, and Baptists).

Their success was not accidental. New South advocates became skilled publicists. Between 1885 and 1893 Alabama boosters promoted twenty-four towns with publicity campaigns that were often as

shameless as they were exaggerated. The Fort Payne area contained thin coal and ore veins too sparse to support a major iron works; but the town's promotional literature referred to "inexhaustible" quantities of ore and coal. Pamphlets christened Fort Payne at the foot of remote Lookout Mountain, "The New England City of the South." Gadsden became "The Hub of the Mineral Belt," Tuscaloosa "Alabama's Natural Pittsburgh," Sheffield "The Iron Manufacturing Center of the South," Birmingham "The Magic City," Anniston "The Model City." An Augusta, Georgia, visitor to Anniston returned home thoroughly disgusted. In Anniston, he complained, "every bunch of sassafras is a mighty forest, every frog pond a

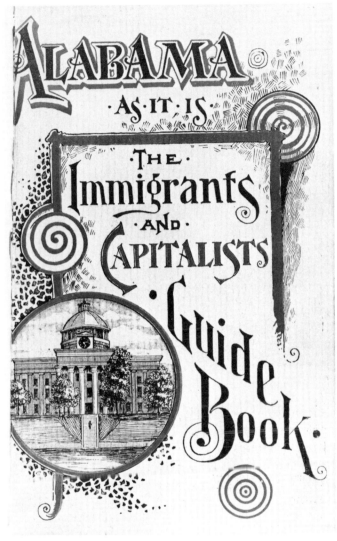

sylvan lake, every waterfall a second Tallulah, every ridge of rocks a coal mine, . . . and every man a liar."

Promoters raised capital, built a hotel and perhaps a blast furnace, produced elaborate pamphlets and brochures complete with geological and engineering reports, then chartered trains to transport prospective investors and speculators. During land auctions they sometimes offered fictitious bids to drive up prices.

The state joined this promotional effort, employing a talented Baptist preacher-writer, B.F. Riley, to author a volume entitled *Alabama As It is; or The Immigrant's and Capitalist's Guide Book to Alabama.* Published in 1888, the first edi-

Above: In 1888 B.F. Riley wrote Alabama As It Is *or* The Immigrant's and Capitalists' Guide Book to Alabama. *Riley's work was part of a Victorian publicity campaign to attract capital and newcomers to the state. Courtesy, Alabama Department of Archives and History*

Opposite: Birmingham's dramatic growth in the 1880s was as much a product of the boom in railroad construction as of its mineral wealth. The most important railroad for the city was Milton Smith's L & N. The L & N built an appropriately ornate Union Station to serve Birmingham's passengers, but it was the branch lines to remote coal fields and blast furnaces around the city, and the long distance routes that carried products to regional markets, that made the difference for the "Magic City." Courtesy, Birmingham Public Library

tion of 5,000 copies sold out almost immediately. Officials ordered 25,000 additional copies for eager prospective investors. The handsome volume contained information on everything from average rainfall and temperature to descriptions of geography, towns, manufacturing in each community, schools, and railroads. So successful was this effort that officials began publishing an annual "Handbook of Alabama" which included the same type of information.

Such unseemly eagerness to attract manufacturing at any price left some Alabamians cynical and hostile. Some of this criticism occurred within the business community itself where one set of interests clashed with another. B.B. Comer is a perfect example. During his brief sojourn in Anniston as a wholesale grocer, discriminatory freight rates had denied him access to nearby Georgia markets. The Georgia Railroad Commission fixed rates in that state well below prevailing Alabama levels, meaning that Georgia wholesalers could ship goods further distances at cheaper prices. When Comer entered the milling and banking business in Birmingham he remembered his earlier problems.

With the assistance of Rufus Rhodes, publisher of the Birmingham *News,* and other businessmen, he organized mass meetings to protest excessive freight rates. This injustice inspired Rhodes, Comer, and eighty-five other businessmen to organize the Commercial Club of Birmingham in May 1893. The club's primary task was to negotiate more favorable railroad charges for Birmingham. Failing this, Comer began attacking state officials, such as Governor Thomas G. Jones, who had been railroad attorneys. Such persons, Comer complained, used their influence to promote the interests of their clients rather than those of Alabama's ordinary citizens.

B.F. Roden, a grocery wholesaler, detailed charges against the railroads in a speech before the Commercial Club. According to his figures wholesalers in Nashville and Memphis could ship goods to Cullman and Jasper, each within sixty miles of Birmingham, cheaper than Birmingham wholesalers could. Although the railroads disputed his statistics, the Birmingham movement for regulation of railroad rates gave significant impetus to the progressive reform crusade in Alabama. By the

Rufus N. Rhodes, publisher of the Birmingham News, *joined with B.B. Comer and other businessmen to protest freight rates which discriminated against products made in Birmingham. In 1893 they formed the Commercial Club, and from that forum and in the editorials of the* News *Rhodes fought for railway regulation and other Progressive reforms. Courtesy, Alabama Department of Archives and History*

turn of the century, railroad regulation had become a major political issue arraying textile companies and merchants against railroads. Comer's election as governor on a regulatory platform in 1906 reduced the influence of railroads on Alabama politics.

Not all criticism of business came from within the fraternity, however. In fact, B.B. Comer's textile mills were the largest employers of child labor in the state. By 1900, 25 percent of Alabama's textile workers were under the age of sixteen, and their illiteracy rate was three times as high as that of nonworking children. The source of this abuse was complex. Many industrialists paid the heads of families so poorly that the "family wage" became an economic necessity. Bell Factory paid its textile workers an average wage of thirty-five cents for a twelve-hour day in 1875, but many poor families, fresh into town from tenant farms, believed that rudimentary education sufficed and that children should earn a wage as soon as they were able. Alabama farmers found hard work for their children to do as soon as they were old enough to wield a hoe or plow a furrow. Why should industrial work

be any different?

Thus Alabama's new industrial labor force took on new configurations. In textile mills most laborers were women and children. The iron and steel industry employed a biracial male workforce. At first entrepreneurs recruited foreign-born workers; Birmingham contained 5,000 immigrants in 1890. Then they relied on blacks and poor whites; Birmingham's black population increased from 20 percent in 1870 to 40 percent twenty years later. Three groups comprised the state's mining force in 1889. Native-born whites made up 34.9 percent. Nearly 19 percent came from abroad, mostly from England, Scotland, and Ireland. Blacks constituted the largest segment, 46.2 percent.

Economic expansion combined with low wages and dangerous conditions to disrupt Alabama's labor force. Owners looked to the state for aid and received it in the form of the convict lease system. The system solved a multitude of problems. Even when labor could be obtained, workers from rural backgrounds often proved unreliable and highly mobile. Conservative Democratic officials opposed taxes and resented having to provide even minimal

state services such as jails and prisons. Hence officials jumped at the opportunity to avoid penal costs by leasing convicts to private companies and actually making a profit on the deal. The Stollenworck Lumber Mill in Butler County began using convicts in the early 1890s. Soon the practice spread to include the L.L. Moore Mill at River Falls and the Flowers and Flowers Lumber Company of Bolling. Some of the worst abuses of prisoners occurred in lumber and turpentine camps.

When T.C.I. took over Pratt Coal and Coke Company in 1886, some 600 convicts mined coal for the corporation. Two years later T.C.I. obtained a ten-year lease for all state convicts. The state renewed this lease for 1898 to 1903 and again for 1903 to 1908. By 1894 the Tennessee Company worked 1,138 convicts at an annual cost of about $108 per head. The Sloss Company worked 589 convicts at its Coalburg mines.

The presence of convict labor caused resentment among free miners who believed convict labor depressed wages. This and fluctuations in coal demand during the 1890s led in 1894 to one of the state's largest strikes. Early organizing efforts of the United Mine Workers succeeded in reaching 8,000 miners who waged bloody war with management during that depression year.

Not all antagonism to New South industrialists

came from businessmen and workers. In fact, people from rural backgrounds leveled the most scathing criticism. Throughout most of the nation's history Americans had glorified farming as the ideal occupation and farmers as model citizens. Farmers felt neither besieged nor that their interests differed fundamentally from those of business and industry. But all that changed in the late nineteenth century. Mechanization and the settling of the Great Plains toughened competition. Cyclical depressions and natural disasters wrought havoc. Farmers lost world markets to overseas producers, and they blamed much of their trouble on American industry. Railroads monopolized lines and

The Tennessee Coal, Iron and Railroad Company was the state's largest employer of convict labor. This, coupled with falling demand for coal and the organizing gains made by the United Mine Workers among TCI employees led to a protracted strike in 1894. The company hired armed men such as the Erskine Ramsay Guards shown here protecting TCI's Slope #5, brought in scab laborers and evicted strikers from company housing. After several bloody clashes the UMW was broken and the strike collapsed, but its bitter legacy of industrial animosity endured. Courtesy, Birmingham Public Library

overcharged farmers for storage and transportation. Trusts gouged them for everything from bagging for cotton bales to shoes. By the last decade of the century farmers had concluded that the interests of farmers and industrialists-businessmen were antithetical.

Farmers and their allies among small-town editors, merchants, ministers, and physicians expressed their reservations about industrialization and urbanization in many ways. The Athens *Alabama Farmer* in December 1888 editorialized that "It was the intention of the omnipotent, as well as omniscient God, that man was to have been an ag-

riculturist." A minister in Livingston believed that "A filthy city always has been, and always will be, a wicked place." An editor in Anniston warned notoriously wicked Birmingham residents to "remember the fate of Sodom and Gomorrah."

Gradually the fabric of Alabama society split like a piece of wood whose veneer has come unglued. Local business and political elites in many towns and cities banged the drum for new mills and furnaces. In the hinterland all around angry farmers railed against "trusts," "monopolies," "Wall Street," and the "money power." They rejected the materialism associated with New South values, the

The steamboat Alabama *is viewed loading cotton on the Alabama River, circa 1890. Courtesy, John Engelhardt Scott, Jr.*

desperate grasping for money which seemed to animate so many entrepreneurs. They condemned local and state politicians as minions of the exploiters. To them industrialism threatened the small farm, an independent way of life, a whole system of rural values, and warm human relationships symbolized by home, family, and local community. One farmer, opposing local boosters determined to build a railroad, argued in 1888 that "railroads and free Negroes are of but very little benefit to poor people."

Agrarianism found its political expression in the Farmers' Alliance and Populist party. The Alli-

ance began as an educational movement to raise farm income and worked within the dominant Democratic party, but reforms came slowly if at all, and the more radical wing of the Alliance finally formed a third party in the 1890s. Although technically called Jeffersonian Democrats, the party was in fact the local manifestation of the Populist movement. Its gubernatorial candidate, a planter and former agricultural commissioner named Reuben F. Kolb, criticized some industrial abuses such as convict leasing and discriminatory railroad rates. He flayed his gubernatorial opponent, Thomas G. Jones, as a pawn of the L.&N. Railroad. But in his two narrow losses in 1892 and 1894 he tried to avoid polarizing the state along purely industry/anti-industry lines. Recognizing that new businesses did create opportunities, he called for regulation but not for exclusion: "I am friendly to corporations ... Individuals cannot develop our mineral resources, cannot easily build furnaces and factories. Corporations are, therefore, necessary to the workingmen and to the general well being of the community."

Kolb embodied the ambivalence of many Alabamians toward manufacturing. Desperately seeking the economic opportunities it promised, they nonetheless feared its excesses and the erosion of rural values. If only they could have the benefits and avoid the pitfalls, but no such choice awaited them. Industrialization was all of a piece, and Alabama gained its payrolls, comforts, and technological miracles along with its pollution, ugly slums, and political manipulation.

In 1897 the Tennessee Coal, Iron and Railroad Company turned its attention to overcoming the problems associated with making steel from Birmingham's red hematite-coke fired iron. TCI built ten new open hearth furnaces at Ensley which went into production in 1899, giving the company a definite edge in production costs by comparison with Northern rivals. Unfortunately, mismanagement and labor troubles prevented the company from exploiting what should have been a decided economic advantage. By 1907 TCI teetered on the brink of bankruptcy. Courtesy, University of Alabama in Birmingham

Chapter 4

INDUSTRY
COMES OF AGE

If the Victorian era epitomized rugged individualism, consolidation, and laissez-faire, the early twentieth century introduced different themes. Reacting to social dislocation, sharp divisions of income, and conditions bordering on economic anarchy, many industrialists took a long, sober look at industrial America. They did not like what they saw. As Birmingham's experience demonstrated, they reacted in a variety of ways. Some industrialists sought to prevent industrial unionism by introducing welfare capitalism. Others devised plans to involve employees in decision making and even ownership. Many joined the Progressive political movement, which tried to rationalize and organize the chaotic economic and social changes of the previous thirty years.

Birmingham was the setting for most of these changes. As Alabama's largest city, it dominated the state's industrial life by 1900. Consolidations late in the 1890s had produced a triumvirate of iron and steel companies. T.C.I., created by mergers and purchases in 1886, led the pack. Sloss-Sheffield Coal and Iron, formed by a combination of twelve smaller companies in 1899, followed in second place. Republic Iron and Steel, which entered the district in 1899 by purchasing Pioneer Mining and Manufacturing, challenged the two front-runners. All followed familiar patterns. They relied heavily on outside capital and expertise, dispersed facilities across the mineral district, and purchased large tracts of land in order to guarantee adequate supplies of iron ore, coal, and limestone.

Each also experienced internal problems. Obtaining reliable labor posed the greatest challenge. For years the South had attracted industry by advertising its huge reservoir of docile, hardworking, desperately poor farmers; but the economic upswing which followed the 1893-1897 depression threatened to denude the landscape of every tenant farm family willing to move. Labor recruiters vied with each other as they toured country regions, pockets bulging with greenbacks. At just the right moment they would dramatically display rolls of bills to mesmerize farmers and send them scurrying home to load wives and children aboard wagons for the trip to Birmingham.

Rural people did not adjust easily to urban industrial jobs. Day-long shifts six days a week with occasional Sunday work on dirty, dangerous, unfamiliar jobs wrecked families and lives. Without leisure time for hunting, fishing, visiting relatives, drinking, or playing, workers simply "laid out" a few days when the urge struck them. Saloons and bordellos flourished in sections of Birmingham known locally as Scratch Ankle, Beer Mash, and Buzzard's Roost. Violence was so common that the city earned the sobriquet "Bad Birmingham, Murder Capital of the World."

Above: This bustling street scene shows Court Square, as seen from North Court Street, in turn-of-the-century Montgomery. Courtesy, John Engelhardt Scott, Jr.

Opposite: By the 1920s the streets of Birmingham were crowded with cars. Though streets in downtown Birmingham were wide enough to accommodate the new vehicles, the cars created congestion on roads designed for horse and buggy. Courtesy, James F. Sulzby, Jr.

The company store was a common feature in mining camps, lumber- and textile mill villages. Often employees were paid in scrip that was redeemable only at the company-owned store, where goods were overpriced. This was especially true in the more isolated lumber mill villages in southern Alabama and mining camps. Courtesy, Birmingham Public Library

Poor health compounded other problems. In 1912 T.C.I. employees reported 8,000 cases of malaria. In most mining camps the only garbage collectors were pigs, buzzards, and chickens. Outdoor toilets, often suspended over a creek or drainage ditch, were actually an improvement over no sanitary facilities at all. As a result hookworm debilitated the population.

Companies tried a variety of strategies to obtain adequate labor. Several leased state or county convicts. Others hired many more workers than they needed. T.C.I., the largest local company, employed 18,567 men in 1913 in order to obtain 13,622 daily workers. Early in the century T.C.I.'s employment turnover rate reached the phenomenal total of 400 percent per year. The corporation also dispatched labor recruiters to Europe, with the result that some 5,000 Italian workers moved into the steel mills and coal mines, along with a smaller number of eastern European immigrants; but this expedient solved the problem only partially. By 1913 white native-born Americans comprised 37.2 percent of T.C.I.'s labor force and worked an average of 20.5 days per month. Immigrants constituted 7.6 percent of the workers and averaged 20.4 days. Blacks made up 55.2 percent and worked an

FIRST CAR LOAD OF STEEL MADE IN BIRMINGHAM ALA.
JULY 22, 1897.

average 16.8 days. The working month for the entire labor force averaged only 18.3 days.

Many managers tried to whip into line a labor force which they held in contempt. A T.C.I. official referred to his workers as "shiftless, thriftless, sloppy and dirty." Colonel John C. Maben, president of Sloss-Sheffield, responded to an inquiry about the wretched conditions in his company town by noting that he did not believe in "coddling workmen." One mine owner hired only workers who could not read, regretting that there were no longer enough illiterate blacks to go around. "They're spoiling them now-adays by educating them," he said.

Such attitudes, reflecting the frontier conditions of Henry DeBardeleben's Birmingham, held sway for decades and created an adversarial relationship between management and labor. Workers responded in predictable ways. The United Mine Workers of America organized north Alabama in the 1880s and 1890s. Birmingham workers began publishing the *Labor Advocate* in 1890 and hosted an American Federation of Labor convention in 1891. They launched bloody strikes in 1893, 1904, and 1908. Extensive violence by both sides accompanied the strikes, requiring the governors to send

This 1897 photograph records the first carload of steel to be made in Birmingham, Alabama's industrial center.

117

units of the state militia to restore order. During the 1908 strike Birmingham-area industrialists formed the Alabama Coal Operators Association committed to the open shop and preventing unionism. Obviously there had to be a better way to conduct business than hiring armed company guards, importing strikebreakers from other regions, or fighting pitched battles in the hollows and hills of north Alabama.

George Gordon Crawford best articulated that better way. A native Georgian and graduate of Georgia Tech, Crawford had supplemented his engineering education by study in Germany. He had moved rapidly up the executive ranks of several companies, most notably the giant U.S. Steel Corporation. Financial genius J.P. Morgan formed U.S. Steel in 1901 but did not participate in the actual management of the firm. Judge Elbert Gary became chairman of the company's finance committee, where he wrested control from the operating steel men who ran various subsidiaries. Gary favored a cooperative relationship with workers, calling for fair wages, safety measures, pensions, and other benefits. Although his paternalistic proposals operated from the top down and were designed partly to prevent unionization, many

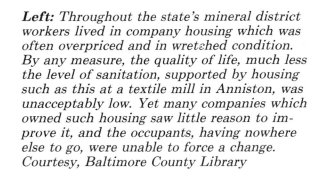

subsidiary presidents believed he was coddling workers and inviting trouble. One of them summarized his philosophy in a sentence that would have won applause from many chief executives in north Alabama: "I have always had one rule—if a workman sticks up his head, hit it." Gary, searching for a new kind of leadership, liked the cooperative approach of the bright young technical steel man, George Crawford; but Crawford might never have brought his innovative ideas to Birmingham except for a series of unfortunate events which befell T.C.I.

The chief technological problem afflicting

Above: U.S. Steel Company sent George Gordon Crawford to Birmingham in 1908 to manage the Tennessee Coal, Iron and Railroad Company which it had acquired during the Panic of 1907. Crawford, a native Georgian with a degree in engineering from Georgia Tech, undertook a series of sweeping reforms which modernized company operations and improved employee relations. In an unprecedented example of welfare capitalism Crawford dramatically improved workers' health care, educational, recreational, and housing opportunities. Courtesy, Alabama Department of Archives and History

Birmingham's iron industry was extractive metallurgy. In 1900 two-thirds of the nation's iron production was converted into steel. Birmingham concentrated on iron making and neglected developing its steel making capability. This policy resulted from the fact that much of the red hematite ore when processed with coke yielded a product high in phosphorous, sulphur, and silica, all undesirable. The Bessemer process could not convert such iron into high-quality steel. Competing ore from the Great Lakes area contained lower quantities of phosphorous and could be made into good quality steel by Bessemer technology. In 1897 T.C.I. finally committed the necessary resources to construct ten new open-hearth furnaces at En-

sley for the production of steel. When these went into operation on Thanksgiving Day, 1899, the company gained on its northern competition. Because Great Lakes ore required transportation to Pittsburgh for smelting and manufacturing, Birmingham won a substantial cost advantage.

Yet once again Alabama squandered the advantage nature afforded by failing to attract adequate corporate leadership. In 1901 T.C.I. selected Don H. Bacon to lead the company. A native of Pennsylvania who had worked in the iron business for thirty-two years in Michigan and Minnesota, he seemed a good choice. He agreed to come when U.S. Steel absorbed his company in 1901, as part of the merger which created the gigantic corporation. When he

arrived in Birmingham he discovered an empty treasury and a backward operation. Flabbergasted by labor problems and employment turnover, he set about to modernize T.C.I. by increasing the loyalty and efficiency of employees. Bacon was not, however, a technical steel man nor an expert in manufacturing. Though he improved the mining end of the company, he made mistakes in constructing new steel plants. He resigned when new ownership purchased T.C.I. in 1906. A new interim management team was no sooner in place than the economic panic of 1907 struck. The company could not pay its debts and threatened to carry several important New York banking firms into bankruptcy with it. T.C.I. dispatched a team to New

York and Washington where feverish negotiations persuaded J.P. Morgan to purchase the company. After clearing the deal with Theodore Roosevelt in order to avoid a trustbusting suit by the Justice Department, Morgan purchased T.C.I. in November 1907 for $35 million.

Opinions regarding the takeover varied. Many national observers believed that Morgan had jumped at the opportunity to eliminate a major competitor to U.S. Steel which had been underselling Pittsburgh and capturing its markets. Morgan strenuously denied each allegation and depicted his purchase as a public service to end the 1907 panic. Whatever his motive, Alabama lost its major locally based industry. Birmingham leaders,

Alabama's river systems augmented by the locks and dams on the Black Warrior River made inexpensive long-distance transport of iron and coal possible. This picture shows the Central Iron and Coal Company's facility at Holt near Tuscaloosa which had access to both rail and water transport. The river barges in the foreground are loaded with coal bound for Mobile, while the blast furnace's pig iron can be shipped throughout the region by rail. Courtesy, University of South Alabama Library

far from expressing concern over northern control, rejoiced that at last T.C.I. would obtain adequate funding and stability.

Judge Gary now had to decide who to dispatch to Birmingham to manage the new facility. His eye fell on the cooperative young Georgian who shared his management philosophy. The thirty-nine-year-old Crawford arrived in the city in 1908 with a mind full of ideas for a company full of problems. Some of the problems were technical: unmechanized ore mines, outdated coke ovens, poor transportation, inferior quality steel, and inadequate industrial water supply. Others involved service: poor customer relations and limited markets in a rural region. Labor problems provided the largest challenge: poor morale, unhealthy and unsafe conditions in mill villages and factories, and inadequate housing and schools. Crawford addressed these issues believing that it was "good business as well as good ethics to treat employees as human beings." Although the company welfare program he inaugurated did inhibit unionism, his motivation seemed broader than that. Improving labor conditions and stablilizing the work force served both the interests of labor and management. The 1908 strike no doubt hastened his determination to improve labor conditions, but he had already drafted many reforms before the strike began.

Crawford introduced his welfare program in stages. First he commissioned a number of surveys on conditions in T.C.I.'s factories and industrial villages. Next he established divisions of the company to implement reforms. Then he hired social workers and medical experts to head and staff the new divisions. He was the first Birmingham-area industrialist to hire social experts to design company programs for workers. As president of T.C.I., Crawford endorsed Judge Gary's programs more fully than any other U.S. Steel subsidiary executive, and implemented it most completely in Birmingham.

The keystone of the program was the new de-

Above: *Loom workers at the Dallas Mills in Huntsville are pictured in about 1900. In 1882-1883, the men were paid an average daily wage of 68 cents for working more than ten hours per day. Courtesy, Huntsville-Madison County Public Library*

Opposite: *The Ensley steel facility was as modern as any in the world, but it was handicapped by labor difficulties and poor management. This mill produced steel rails, I beams, and billets, and had an annual capacity of 150,000 to 300,000 tons. After U.S. Steel took over TCI this factory was completely replaced, more than quadrupling its production capacity. Courtesy, Alabama Department of Archives and History*

Dr. Lloyd Noland was responsible for developing a department of health for Tennessee Coal, Iron and Railroad Company. He built an operation that employed thirty-five physicians and a dozen dentists, operated a large hospital, and established a sweeping medical insurance program. Noland's medical insurance program was so popular that almost all of TCI's employees signed up and paid seventy-five cents a month for health care. Courtesy, Birmingham Public Library

partment of health. Crawford sailed to the Panama Canal Zone in 1913 and hired Lloyd Noland to organize T.C.I.'s medical services. Noland proved the ideal choice because of his experience with tropical diseases, sanitation, and industrial accidents. The physician created one of the largest departments of industrial medicine in the United States. He tried to visit each one of the twenty coal and iron camps frequently to personally supervise sanitation and health work. He requested that the company buy him a 1912 Cadillac Roadster, and he put 37,000 miles on the speedometer in only two years of driving dangerous mountain roads. He employed thirty-five physicians and a dozen dentists, built a 345-bed hospital, and instituted a pre-paid medical insurance program supplemented by company funds. His reforms bore immediate results. Malaria cases fell from 8,000 in 1912 to 370 in 1913, then 264 in 1914, and only 30 in 1917. T.C.I. employees could use company dispensaries, doctors, or hospitals by agreeing to a payroll deduction of seventy-five cents a month until the 1930s, when it increased to $1.25. Virtually all employees opted to participate. Crawford's program of welfare capitalism was the most extensive in the South, a fact reflected in the price tag of these benefits. In 1916 employee fees amounted to $130,000, with T.C.I. providing $83,500. Gradually, by 1938, the company share declined to $43,500.

Although health care constituted the core of Crawford's welfare program, he also hired teachers, social workers, and other experts to staff schools, design mining villages, and institute recreation programs. By 1913, 34 percent of T.C.I.'s 45,000 laborers and family members lived in com-

Above: Steam-powered sawmills ringed Mobile in the late nineteenth century as the large lumber companies clear cut the virgin forests of southern Alabama. Unguarded saw blades, uncovered drive belts, and an absence of protective clothing made the work hazardous; accidents were common. Courtesy, William E. Wilson Collection/Historic Mobile

Below: The Merrimack Mill in Huntsville was Alabama's largest when it opened in 1900. Adjacent to it was the mill village, a company school, churches, and company store for employees. The playground shown in this picture was available for children of employees, some of whom worked in the mill themselves. The mill also offered a night school for illiterate employees over the age of sixteen. But despite the benefits, wages in all of Alabama's industrial establishments were low, working hours were long, and conditions often dangerous. While the industrial component of Alabama's economy was growing throughout the first thirty years of this century, little progress can be seen in the standard of living enjoyed by most employees. Courtesy, H.E. Monroe Collection, Huntsville, Alabama

pany housing (65 percent of black workers and their families did so). As a result the company's employees enjoyed better health care, schools, housing, and recreation facilities than their neighbors. In 1909 Crawford began subsidizing schools in T.C.I. villages that made them among the best in the state. He built community bathhouses and a model industrial town at Corey (later called Fairfield).

Such efforts resulted in dramatic improvements for the company. In 1912, the year before Lloyd Noland arrived, T.C.I.'s labor turnover rate was 400 percent. By 1919 it was down to 145.3 percent, by 1923 to 57.4 percent, and in 1929 to 13.3 percent. The average number of days worked per month also increased. Although general economic conditions contributed to the solution, Crawford's programs were primarily responsible. A muckraking review of the Birmingham area by *Survey Magazine* in 1912 contained a generally favorable review of T.C.I.

Welfare capitalism had a brief lifetime in ica. The economic collapse of 1929 large stroyed the resources with which companies had funded such programs; and the New Deal substituted a system of collective bargaining for company benevolence. Most T.C.I. programs were reduced or eliminated by the 1930s. Yet even in the post-World War II period the staff and services of T.C.I.'s department of health constituted one of the largest pre-paid medical plans in America. Even labor historians concede that welfare capitalism was a step in the right direction of humanizing industrial relations for workers. Many employees, desperately poor before they left worn-out land for

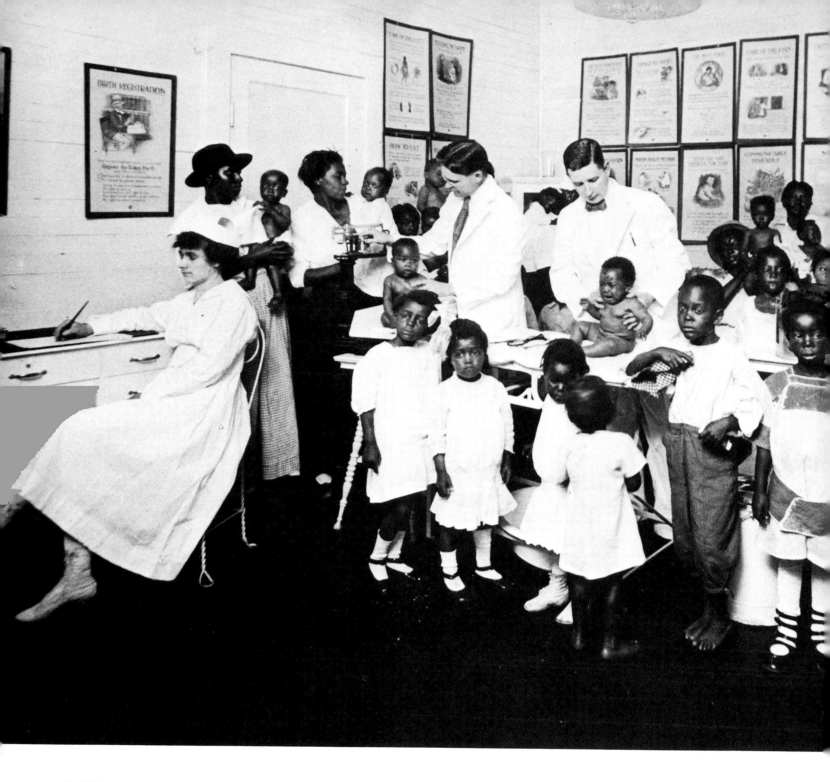

T.C.I.'s mines and factories, remember the services and salaries as providing the best years of their lives.

John J. Eagan tried a more radical and solitary approach to labor relations. Born in Griffin, Georgia, Eagan inherited money and began a distinguished business career in Atlanta. A devoted churchman, he served for thirty years as superintendent of the Sunday school at Central Presbyterian Church, as an elder, and as a member of the denomination's Home Mission Board. He read widely in the new sociological literature, and though he rejected Socialism, he supported many aspects of the Social Gospel. He endorsed prison reform and prohibition, opposed child labor and

the exploitation of workers. Eagan sympathized with labor in several 1913 strikes, speaking at their rallies and winning the praise of Atlanta's *Journal of Labor.* In 1919 he was elected first president of the Council of Interracial Cooperation which he helped establish, but his most famous expression of social Christianity occurred in Birmingham.

In 1905 Eagan helped organize the American Cast Iron Pipe Company, or ACIPCO as it was called in Birmingham. He served as president of the company from 1905 until 1915 when he became chairman of the board. Although he had always tried to operate his business according to the ethical principles of the golden rule, in 1921 he decided to allow ACIPCO's workers to share in the opera-

tion and profits. His "Eagan Plan of Business Administration" was simple but radical: the company must pay every employee a reasonable living wage; it must provide constant employment despite prevailing economic conditions; and the golden rule must govern employer-employee relations. When Eagan died, his will transferred all the company's common stock jointly to the boards of management and operators. The board of directors retained final authority over both management and labor. Workers annually elected their own representatives to the board of operators, and shared dividends. The company provided medical and hospital services, pensions, group insurance, funeral expenses, emergency loans, a co-op store, res-

Above: *TCI's paternalistic policies included providing facilities for the children of its workers. This 1917 photograph, made in the TCI village next to the Muscoda Ore Mine, shows children getting a hot meal in decent surroundings with adequate supervision. Lloyd Noland's reforms had begun to bear fruit. Courtesy, William Stanley Hoole Special Collections Library, University of Alabama*

Opposite: *Under the leadership of Dr. Lloyd Noland, the Tennessee Coal, Iron and Railroad Company embarked on an extensive health care program for its employees and their dependents. Within a few years of Dr. Noland's arrival in 1913, clinics such as this one for black employees and their families were in operation throughout the TCI system. Courtesy, Birmingham Public Library*

taurant, gardens, a savings bank, housing, athletic teams, and other recreational facilities. Each new employee received a copy of *John Eagan: His Business Practices and Philosophy* which contained a brief biography and a lengthy exposition of the founder's ethical principles.

B.B. Comer tried yet another approach to creating a new industrial order. For years he had waged war with Milton H. Smith and the L.&N. Railroad. At the root of their struggle were two different philosophies of business. Smith, a classic nineteenth-century individualist and advocate of laissez-faire, opposed all regulatory authority and believed that no railroad rate was unreasonable. He opposed state taxes and free public schools. Because Alabama's conservative legislative attitude toward property rights coincided with his own philosophy and partly resulted from the L.&N.'s spirited lobbying, he invested heavily in the state. Comer on the other hand believed L.&N. rates to be excessive and argued that lower charges would generate

The Crews family, pictured here in 1913, worked at Merrimack Mills in Huntsville. As one writer summarized the life of the mill worker: "It was theoretically possible that a man's mother might attend a pre-natal clinic established by the mill, that the baby be born in a mill-owned hospital and delivered by a mill-paid doctor, that he be educated in a mill-supported school, married in a mill-subsidized church to a girl he had met in the mill, live all his life in a house belonging to the mill, and when he died be buried in a coffin supplied at cost, by the mill in a mill-owned cemetery." Courtesy, Huntsville-Madison County Public Library

heavier traffic, especially in farm products, and thus higher profits. Their disagreement involved many elements: an agrarian versus industrial society; retailers and wholesalers versus unregulated railroads; absentee owners opposed to local businessmen; and vested interests which stood in opposition to popular majorities; the precarious balance

between excessive regulation which could cripple economic development and unregulated capital ism which might unreasonably exploit the state and its people. The animosity between Comer and Smith became intensely personal. On one occasion Smith called Comer "an impossible man. A disordered mind ... his insane desire for political preferment and notoriety [caused him to act] like a lunatic ..."

Comer ignored such insults and shrewdly conducted his campaign in stages. In 1901 he put together an incongruous coalition which included the Birmingham Trades Council (A.F. of L.), the United Mine Workers Union, the Wholesale Grocers' Association, the Shippers' and Buyers' Association, the Freight Bureau, and commercial clubs (chambers of commerce) in Mobile, Huntsville, Florence, Sheffield, Anniston, Selma, and elsewhere. They lobbied Alabama's 1901 constitutional convention to include an elected railroad commission in the new state constitution. On the opposite side were the L.&N. together with most railroads and the iron and steel industry, which received excellent rates because it provided through traffic. Though failing in 1901, Comer's coalition succeded in pushing such a bill through the 1903 legislature. Alabama citizens elected Comer president of the new commission in a bitter 1904 campaign; but his associate commissioners blocked rate revision. Comer then switched the arena to the 1906 gubernatorial contest where the race focused so completely on railroad regulation that one pundit described his campaign as a "lyre with one string."

The 1906 gubernatorial race reflected the multiple dimensions of Alabama's Progressive movement. On one side different segments of business condemned each other. Defenders of the railroads countered Comer's appeal to workingmen and farmers by reminding them that he used more child labor than any single employer in the state. Organized labor refused to support him because of his alleged abuse of laborers and employment of children. But Comer not only won the governor's office, he also carried into office a legislature committed to lower railroad rates. He pushed through a package of twenty laws designed to reduce rates and railroad influence in Alabama politics. Although the roads won most cases appealed to federal courts, Comer forced concessions by threatening to cancel their licenses to operate in the state. Backed by tremendous public support, Comer found that railroads made excellent whipping boys. One legislator phrased the fight as one between freedom and "industrial peonage to railroads." Actually the stakes were not nearly so dramatic, and the reforms wrought by Comer's administration probably improved the lives of industrial workers less than the welfare programs instituted by George Crawford.

Although the search for a new industrial order continued for a long time, manufacturing hardly languished during the interval. With T.C.I. stabilized, the most immediate problem for Birmingham's thirteen furnaces was less one of production than of marketing. U.S. Steel predetermined markets to a large extent by imposing the "Pittsburgh Plus" system of pricing T.C.I. steel. Under this system local steel sold for the cost of production plus a profit and the cost of shipping the steel from Birmingham to Pittsburgh, even if the steel was sold locally. This effectively negated T.C.I.'s cost advantage and largely confined its steel to a regional market, thus eliminating competition with the parent company. But Crawford was one of the best technical steel men in America and

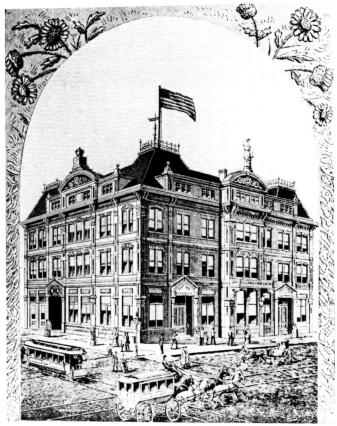

his skillful management of T.C.I. solidified its dominance of the industry in the South and Southwest.

Other entrepreneurs succeeded on a more modest scale. T.T. Hillman, Erskine Ramsay, and others organized Pratt Consolidated Coal Company in 1904 by merging six companies. Operating in the Warrior coalfield, their fifty-four mines made Pratt the largest coal company in the Birmingham district. In 1910 Alabama produced sixteen million tons of coal, more than half of it in Jefferson County. By 1914 the state ranked seventh in U.S. coal production.

By-products of iron and steel making, together with new technologies, increasingly altered Birmingham manufacturing. Solon Jacobs and Henry L. Badham organized Birmingham Slag Company to utilize waste from iron and steel making. When Henry Ford marketed his Model T in 1909, Jacobs and Badham realized that primitive southern dirt roads would not serve the vehicle

Above: The Mobile Chamber of Commerce, the state's oldest, joined with its sister organizations to support B.B. Comer's efforts to get a railroad commission to regulate the L & N and other railroads. In 1903 it succeeded, but it would be years before the commission accomplished much. Mobile felt that it was especially in peonage to the railroads since they owned most of the city's port facilities and showed no interest in expanding them, fearing the competition of efficient water transport. Courtesy, University of South Alabama

Opposite: In 1913 Alabama Power Company launched a twenty-year construction project, eventually building a chain of six hydroelectric dams on the Coosa and Tallapoosa Rivers which produced 600,000 KW of electrical power. The Lay Dam on the Coosa was the first in this chain coming on line in 1914 with a capacity of 81,000 KW. Courtesy, Alabama Department of Archives and History

The DeBardeleben Coal Company's Birmingham store sold provisions to company employees. The pot-bellied stove was a gathering place in winter. Courtesy, Jackie Dobbs, Old Birmingham Photographs

well. Believing that slag provided the ideal aggregate for highway construction, they installed a plant in 1910 at Ensley's T.C.I. slag pit. Their small operation included three steam shovels, a railroad car dump, crushing and conveying equipment, and a railroad car reloading facility. So successful was their operation that in 1916 Charles L. Ireland, an Ohio banker, and his three sons purchased controlling interest in the company. One of the sons, Glenn Ireland, had operated stone quarries in Kentucky and West Virginia. He realized the tremendous potential of slag as an aggregate and road-building material and operated Birmingham Slag so successfully that it functioned with only one loss in its history, that in 1932. The Irelands expanded their holdings by organizing the Montgomery Gravel Company in 1923 and the Atlanta Aggregate Company the following year. From such modest beginnings Vulcan Materials later emerged as the largest aggregate company in the world.

Other newcomers fared as well as the Irelands. J.R. McWane came to Birmingham in 1904 at the urging of the city's Commercial Club. As president of Birmingham Steel and Iron Company, he presided over the casting of the giant statue of Vulcan,

the Roman god of fire and forge. Later he moved to ACIPCO where he served as president from 1915 until Eagan determined to will the company to his employees in 1921. Then he organized McWane Cast Iron Pipe Company. An innovator in technology, McWane was granted seventy-five patents for improved foundry processes and pipe products.

Symbols of the new affluence sprang up throughout the city. In 1906 local developers erected the sixteen-story Brown-Marx building, the state's largest skyscraper. It provided offices for T.C.I., Pratt Consolidated Coal Company, and many other local corporations. Across town the gigantic statue of Vulcan brooded over the city's factories from its perch on Red Mountain. Cast by local foundries of Red Mountain ore, the giant symbolized Birmingham's industrial potential at the 1904 Louisiana Purchase Exposition in St. Louis where it was first displayed.

Charles Ireland and his sons bought out Birmingham Slag in 1916. Skillful management
and the purchases of Montgomery Gravel and
Atlanta Aggregate built a successful company
which eventually became Vulcan Materials.
Courtesy, Auburn University

Above: Employees of the Birmingham Coca-
Cola Bottling Company pose for the camera in
1903. Courtesy, Jackie Dobbs, Old Birmingham Photographs

Below: Coal became more and more important
as fuel with the demise of charcoal-fired blast
furnaces and the transition to the production
of steel. In this photograph, coal is being loaded
into a railroad car at slope #2 of the Pratt
Mines Division of the Tennessee Coal, Iron
and Railroad Company around 1900. Jefferson
County was the center of the state's coal mining, and by 1914 Alabama had become the nation's seventh largest coal producer. After a
1904 merger, the Pratt Consolidated Coal
Company dominated coal production in the
Birmingham district. Courtesy, Birmingham
Public Library

Marketing Alabama's industrial resources became as complicated as selling Birmingham's iron
and steel. Here again the strategy represented a
quantum leap from the naive brochures of the
1880s. Alabama's Geological Survey continued to
play a major role through its maps and site studies.
In addition the Survey published authoritative
books on industrial resources and practices such
as William B. Phillip's *Iron Making In Alabama,*
published in 1912.

The most enduring marketing resource actually
came from the pen of journalist Ethel Armes. She
began to write for a Birmingham newspaper in
1905. Shortly thereafter Robert Jemison, Jr., president of the Commercial Club, commissioned her
to write an industrial history of Alabama. Her business sponsors provided access to a multitude of
first generation industrialists who were still alive
and active. She pursued these contacts with dili-
gence and enthusiasm and used many sources later
lost to historians. The result, *The Story of Coal and
Iron in Alabama,* is considered the classic account.
Published in 1910, the lengthy treatise glorifies the
rugged spirit and daring of Alabama's industrial
pioneers. She ignored the seamier side of the story
reflected in child labor, peonage, and the convict

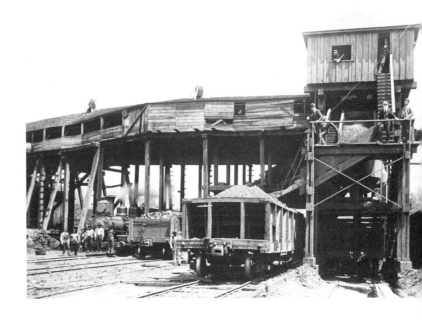

lease system. Her content reflected both the work's sponsor and her own inclinations.

Her journalistic career revealed another Birmingham, one she described two years later in a special issue of *Survey Magazine* devoted to examining several of America's most dynamic cities. Her essay criticized the lack of civic responsibility among many of the city's industrial founders: "Few dollars of theirs have gone to boost along any public welfare moves. 'Before God,' said one of these, 'I will be damned before I will put my hand in my pocket for anything!'" As a consequence, she wrote, social, educational, artistic, or philanthropic activities "have not as yet become strong-winged." In fact the entire city was merely a by-product of its industrial plants, "utterly jagged and uneven, raw in spots, 'picayunish,' and provincial—'get-rich-quick.'" Although privately she recognized exceptions to her generalizations, especially T.C.I.'s George Crawford, she became progressively more frustrated at the reactionary attitudes in the city. Finally she advocated unionism as the best way for workers to improve their status and even spoke at the 1913 convention of the United Mine Workers.

Nor was Armes the only writer struck by Birmingham's contradictions. Carl Carmer, a New Yorker teaching English at the University of Alabama in the early 1920s, could hardly believe his eyes when he drove out of the desolate hills and encountered a copy of the Roman temple of Vesta on the summit of Shades Mountain. To Carmer, the classic building made of cheap materials with a garage in its base symbolized Birmingham. A city of the nouveau riche, her wealthy residents spent large sums on second-rate art. People who earned their fortunes by daring and unconventional methods purchased only trite and conventional landscapes. Even religion succumbed to advertising. A huge banner hung across the city's busiest street announcing that Birmingham enrolled more Sunday school students per thousand than any other city in America. At the same time the banner proclaimed the city's devotion to religion, Ku Klux Klansmen unmercifully flogged three local citizens, and more than half the city's ministers during the 1920s belonged to the klan. To Carmer, Birmingham was an industrial monster in the midst

of a slow-moving pastoral landscape. A new city in an old land, it characterized Alabama's heterogeneity and grotesqueness.

The evaluations by Armes and Carmer were both incisive and one-sided. Armes' lament over lack of philanthropists ignored men such as Erskine Ramsay, whose contributions of time and money were seldom exceeded in any southern city. And Carmer's depiction of klan-style terrorism and a reactionary business community ignored the

tendencies of many local businessmen and their spouses. Pattie Ruffner Jacobs would have surprised Carmer had they met. Encouraged by her husband, Birmingham Slag's founder Solon Jacobs, she crusaded for women's rights with a skill few could match. Protected by her husband's influence and drawing talent from among the well-educated wives and daughters of his associates, Mrs. Jacobs lobbied the 1915 Alabama legislature so successfully that it seriously considered extend-

This Huntsville school operated from 6 a.m. to noon, after which the students went to work in the mill. The photographer, Lewis Hine, was dubious of the school's educational value. He believed it was in existence solely to comply with a state law requiring eight weeks of schooling each year. Courtesy, University of Maryland Baltimore County Library

ing the vote to women. When the federal government accomplished this task in 1919, she became the first Democratic National Committee Woman from Alabama, secretary of the National League of Women Voters, and later head of the New Deal's Woman's Consumer Division of the National Recovery Administration. Poet John Beecher, son of a T.C.I. official, became a political radical and one of the city's fiercest critics. Even Carmer commented on the irony of a city whose industrialists ran Alabama government but which also contained the state's only viable Socialist organization.

Elsewhere in the state manufacturing followed various patterns. Anniston shifted increasingly to cast-iron pipe. By 1920 the city's ten plants produced 250,000 tons of sewer pipe and fittings per year which it shipped to almost every country in the world. As the world's largest producer, the Anniston industry provided an annual payroll of two-and-a-half million dollars. Diversification continued to broaden the town's economy. A chemical plant built after World War I introduced an important new source of income.

Blacks also played a larger role in the manufacturing economy. Booker T. Washington and George Washington Carver at Tuskegee Institute had feared the corrupting influence of factories and cities on black life, but economic reality continued to drive Negro sharecroppers off the land. George Crawford solicited Tuskegee graduates and furnished good jobs for them at T.C.I. In towns such as Anniston, blacks tried to enter the world of entrepreneurship. A group of blacks tried to organize the Afro-Alabama Cotton Mill Company in the 1890s, but could not raise the necessary capital. Dr. Charles E. Thomas, the first black practicing physician in Alabama, opened a drugstore in Anniston which was the largest owned and operated by blacks in the nation. A local black Baptist minister established *The Baptist Leader* and invested in local businesses. Together Anniston's black leaders organized a Negro Business Men's League

In 1910 Solon Jacobs organized the Birmingham Slag Company to use steelmaking's waste products to manufacture paving material for dirt roads, realizing that the dawning automotive age would require hard-surfaced roads. Beginning in a small way at TCI's Ensley slag pit, his company was immediately successful. Courtesy, Auburn University

in the early 1900s paralleling the white chamber of commerce organized a few years earlier.

Some thirty miles north of Anniston, the town of Gadsden made notable industrial progress. Its economy became a profitable mixture of textiles, steel, and rubber. Dwight Manufacturing Company employed 2,000 operatives and followed a familiar pattern of northern financing and management. Gulf States Steel employed 3,000 and anchored the industry. Alabama Steel and Wire Company built five open-hearth furnaces in the city during 1903-1904, and despite several name changes, provided an important component of the local economy. Goodyear Tire and Rubber Company located in Gadsden in 1929, attracted by the large number of poor white farmers in the mountains surrounding the city. Goodyear hired 1,500.

An element in Gadsden's success was creation of the Alabama School of Trades. First conceived by State Representative Watt T. Brown of Ragland in 1911, the idea won legislative approval but

no funding. In 1923 the legislature finally funded the school, but decided to locate it in Gadsden rather than Ragland. One of the school's functions was to provide skilled workers for local industry, and Gadsden's rapid progress had eclipsed its smaller competitor. The school opened in September 1925, the South's first state supported and operated trade school. It accepted males over the age of sixteen regardless of previous education and provided for many boarding students from beyond Etowah County. During the 1931-1932 academic year, the school enrolled 27 students from Gadsden and 103 from across the state. The total cost of $225 included room, board, and tuition.

The original curriculum included printing, electricity, cabinetmaking, and bricklaying, but soon added sheet metal work, welding, drafting, and automobile mechanics, the latter at the insistence of Governor Bibb Graves. The governor was driving to Demopolis when a tire blew out on his car, which swerved and landed in a swamp. After a wait of several hours, a farmer and his mule pulled the damaged car out of the swamp. On his next journey Graves motored to Gadsden where he told L.R. Fuller, the Trade School's director, "What this state needs is automobile mechanics, and the only way to get them is to train men for the job."

Mobile continued to rely on her proximity to open water and river transportation. A constitutional amendment ratified in 1922 authorized a $10 million bond issue for construction of state docks. Completed in 1923, the docks expanded in subsequent years into a vast system that efficiently moved the products of Alabama's factories and forests into the open seas. Large quantities of cotton, lumber, iron, steel, naval stores, textiles, coal, coke, tobacco, machinery, masonite, and canned goods passed through Mobile on their way to world markets.

Montgomery not only became the home of a bustling textile business, it also led the state in developing hydroelectric power. The miracle of electricity had first appeared in Anniston in 1882 when Woodward Iron lighted its furnace operations and city streets. Four years later Montgomery had installed the nation's first practical electric streetcar system called the "Lightning Route" because the train could race along at the breathtaking speed of six miles an hour. In 1902 the city began operating its own electrical power plant at a dam some twenty-five miles away on the Tallapoosa River. Many small companies tried to match this successful project and obtained rights to build dams on the state's numerous rivers. Such competition threatened endless litigation concerning navigation and flood rights. A company might build a dam downriver which flooded the site of a company further upstream. As always, attracting investors for numerous companies proved difficult.

Another familiar theme of Alabama industrialization was the mixture of local and outside management. James Mitchell, one of the founders and the first president of the Alabama Power Company, was a Canadian who had moved to Massachusetts. Later he helped develop the electrical systems of Brazil and London. He came to Montgomery to help William P. Lay organize the Alabama Power Company in 1906 with only $5,000 capital. In 1912 Lay and Mitchell persuaded a

Booker T. Washington's Tuskegee Institute was founded on the proposition that blacks would forever be second-class citizens until they had the practical skills to get decent jobs.

While segregation thwarted much of Tuskegee's success, some employers, such as George Crawford, did respond by offering graduates of the Institute good jobs with the Tennessee *Coal, Iron and Railroad Company. Courtesy, Tuskegee Institute*

young Montgomery attorney, Thomas W. Martin, to become the firm's general counsel. Martin's father had brought the family to the capital from Scottsboro when young Thomas was only eight years old. The elder Martin had entered politics, serving as Alabama's attorney general from 1889 until 1894, and young Martin entered law practice with his father in 1901.

Thomas Martin's association with the new company paralleled a period of vigorous expansion. He helped negotiate agreements with textile magnate Benjamin Russell of Alexander City who was building a dam to provide electrical power for his mills. Martin also negotiated the purchase of Montgomery's dam on the Tallapoosa. The new corporation attracted English capital and sold bonds to finance a twenty-year expansion program. It began serving customers in 1913 and completed a turbine dam at Gadsden on the Coosa River the following year. Its dams on the Coosa—Lay, Mitchell, and Jordan—and Martin Dam on the Tallapoosa achieved their goals in less than twenty years. By the 1930s Alabama Power Company controlled a chain of six dams in east Alabama, and in 1917 the company opened the Gorgas plant in Walker County using coal as a fuel. Martin became president of the company in 1920 and chairman of the board in 1949.

More traditional industries not only survived into the new century but thrived in the heady atmosphere of economic expansion. As one of the four leading southern textile mill states (together with the Carolinas and Georgia), Alabama continued to attract New England cotton mills because of its proximity to raw materials, an excellent transportation and water supply, and a large pool of poor, unorganized white workers. Between 1880 and 1910 the state acquired forty-five new mills, although its share of the nation's facilities actually declined from 10 to 8 percent. New mills dotted the landscape providing clusters of new jobs in the Fairfax-Lanett-Opelika area of east central Alabama and throughout the northern counties.

Benjamin Russell's career typified the industry's growth. Born in 1876 on a farm near Alexander City, he earned a law degree at the University of Virginia and practiced briefly in Birmingham. After his father died, he sold the family mercantile business and used the proceeds to start a bank in 1900. Shortly afterward he left the banking business to his brother and purchased a Georgia knitting mill. He moved the six knitting and ten sewing machines into a 50-by-100-foot wooden building in Alexander City. Although he lost money the first year, he added a spinning operation in 1908. In 1911 he acquired a dam site on the Tallapoosa River five miles east of town. Because Alabama Power Company claimed prior flood rights to the site, Russell began tedious negotiations. Finally he agreed to sell his unfinished dam in return for a power line into Alexander City and reduced electrical rates. This agreement placed his firm in a strong competitive position and led to construction of two new mills by 1926. Reversing the earlier pattern in Anniston and Birmingham, Russell decided that his mills had created more employment for women than for men. So in 1926 he began a cast-iron pipe foundry to furnish jobs for males. During the remaining years of the decade he created an integrated textile network that transformed raw cotton into finely finished cloth products. Using his farm as an experimental facility, he conducted research on ways to upgrade cotton. By adding bleaching and weaving mills, he was able to produce the finest quality finished products. He also established a phone company and the community's first chamber of commerce.

Although the Russell and Comer families left the strongest family legacy on the textile business, the city of Huntsville enjoyed the most spectacular growth. At the end of the nineteenth century, Huntsville was a small town known for its many nurseries; but the city had acquired its first mill in 1881 and two more in 1891 and 1892. The real boom began at the turn of the century with the coming of Merrimack Mill in 1899. This was fol-

Ships were using the state-owned docks at Mobile for a year before they were officially opened in June 1928. The long overdue port modernization was a boon to Alabama agriculture and industry, and put Mobile in the first rank of American seaports. In this photograph taken in May 1927, ships are being unloaded on the right, while warehouses for the cargoes are under construction on the left. Courtesy, University of South Alabama

World War I brought the modern shipbuilding industry to Mobile. In this 1920 photograph, taken at the U.S. Steel-owned Gulf Shipyards in Chickasaw, just north of Mobile, the S.S. Mobile City is being launched. Begun during the war, the conflict had ended before the ship was completed. Gulf Shipyards was one of Mobile's major employers in both world wars. Courtesy, University of South Alabama

Constructed in a swamp north of Mobile's
older docks, the size of the Alabama State
Docks is evident by comparing its angled slips
to the small railroad-owned berths at the bottom of this picture. The state docks, which
could berth eighteen ships at once, boasted its
own railroad warehousing facilities. Courtesy,
University of South Alabama

lowed by Lowe Manufacturing in 1900, Rowe Knitting and Eastern Manufacturing in 1901 and Erwin Mills in 1925. By 1904 seven companies operated eleven cotton mills employing nearly 8,000 hands. A little more than a decade later Huntsville's textile factories consumed 60,000 bales of cotton annually, worth $3.5 million, and shipped 30 million pounds of textiles each year, worth nine to ten million dollars. Its employees tended 240,000 spindles and earned a million dollars a year in wages, making their hometown one of the largest cotton-mill cities in the South.

Like the iron and steel industries, much of the capital funding Huntsville textile growth came from the North. For instance, 52 percent of the stockholders of Dallas Mills in 1894 lived in Huntsville, but they owned only 16.7 percent of the common stock and 1.8 percent of the preferred stock. The 22 percent of stockholders living in New York controlled 43 percent of the total stock. Lowe Mill was organized in 1900 by Arthur H. Lowe of Fitchburg, Massachusetts, who served as president of the New England Manufacturing Association. W.H. Rowe, Jr., of Troy, New York, established Rowe Knitting Company in 1901. New York capitalists also provided most of the funding for Eastern Manufacturing begun the same year.

The history of two of the city's mills reflects the pattern common to all. Dallas Mills began in 1891 funded by a mixture of Nashville, Huntsville, and New York capital. By 1900 the investment in factory and equipment represented more than a

million-and-a-quarter dollars. Some 1,200 employees operated 50,000 spindles. About 1900, the company built a mill village outside the city limits to try to retain a work force in an intensely competitive period of industrial expansion. By 1916 the village contained 120 houses and 74 tenement buildings. Rent amounted to a dollar per room per month. In 1902 laborers worked a twelve-and-a-half hour day from 5:45 a.m. until 6:15 p.m. Profits grew steadily from $91,000 in 1900 to $206,000 in 1910, and $762,000 in 1920.

Merrimack Mill located in Huntsville in 1899, moving from Lowell, Massachusetts. The mill's managers planned to operate 200,000 spindles, three times as many as any other mill in the South. Such a facility would provide jobs directly or indi-

Above: In 1912 Thomas W. Martin became the general counsel of Alabama Power Company, which had been founded six years earlier. He went on to become its president in 1920 and chairman of the board in 1949. Under his direction the company grew from its small beginnings to become the state's largest private producer and distributor of electricity. Courtesy, Alabama Department of Archives and History

Opposite: In 1886 Montgomery built the nation's first practical electric streetcar system. It was known as the "Lightning Route" because of the swiftness of the cars which traveled at speeds up to six miles an hour. In this 1907 photograph streetcars move along Dexter Avenue. Courtesy, Alabama Department of Archives and History

Above: *Benjamin Russell opened a textile mill early in this century in Alexander City after brief careers in the mercantile and banking industries. After successfully negotiating favorable terms for electricity from Alabama Power, he built more mills in Alexander City and eventually expanded into the manufacture of cast iron pipe. Courtesy, Auburn University*

Above, right: *This interior view of an unidentified garment factory shows working conditions which differed little from the sweatshops of New York. The female employees pose with Brother Bryan of Birmingham's Second Presbyterian Church* **(upper left-hand corner).** *Bryan was determined to bring the Gospel to workers who could not easily attend services. Courtesy, Birmingham Public Library*

rectly for 20,000 people and double the population of Huntsville. The company constructed two brick mills, a warehouse, company school, churches, stores, and 280 houses. It opened in 1900 with 750 employees amid much civic hoopla proclaiming Huntsville's coming of age. Actually the mills represented a chronic city problem: heavy reliance on a single industry vulnerable to the vagaries of a changing economy. Some three-quarters of a century later Merrimack was the only Huntsville mill still operating. The city's mills also demonstrated the problems created by manufacturers anxious to find cheap, tractable labor. Factory owners rationalized that women and children operatives were only supplementing the family wage and paid salaries accordingly. Wages averaged well below a

dollar a day for most textile workers. In fact, Alabama's 1890 industrial work force of 31,137 earned an average annual wage of $350. By 1900 average salaries of the state's 52,902 industrial workers had fallen to only $285 a year. Factories and mills successfully recruited labor because even these salaries greatly exceeded the $50-to-$100 per year income of a typical Alabama sharecropper. But as southern industry rapidly expanded competition for labor intensified. Such rivalry developed that mills began to recruit each other's operatives, even offering free transportation from one mill to another. In 1902 cotton-mill executives from Alabama, Mississippi, and Georgia gathered in Montgomery in an unsuccessful attempt to resolve labor problems.

One device in the battle to recruit and retain labor was the mill village, which served dual purposes. It isolated workers from outside influences, where rival mills tried to lure them away or where labor organizers attempted to unionize them. Since the company owned the land on which their houses, churches, and schools operated, workers realized that strikes could cost them more than just jobs. On a more positive side the cheap housing, recreational facilities, and schools were often the best poor white families had ever known. The active social life of the mill village and the close proximity to neighbors appealed especially to women and children. Many of the mills also provided educational opportunities for adult illiterates. Huntsville's Merrimack Mill conducted a night school for employees above the age of sixteen who could not read or write. It met for two hours each Tuesday, Wednesday, and Thursday night. The state paid half the expenses for eleven teachers and the mill furnished the other half. When the school opened in 1921, a survey indicated that 200 residents of the mill village were eligible, although only half that number actually enrolled.

Such efforts won the praise of local ministers, businessmen, newspapers, and civic boosters, who praised the civic-mindedness of mill owners. An editorial in the July 23, 1916 issue of the Huntsville *Mercury Centennial* praised the city mill villages which had done "as much if not more than any other similar communities in any part of the world in uplift work . . ." As a result "any man or woman, boy or girl (of proper age) can find employment at good wages in buildings that are kept in a perfectly sanitary condition, heated and electrically lighted and at a character of work that is interesting and not laborious; where there is plenty of room at the top for those who are energetic, industrious and ambitious."

The praise was not altogether deserved nor the opportunities so numerous. Upward mobility in a mill was slow and unlikely. Rates of illiteracy for children who worked in mills, many of them below the age of fourteen, were three times as high as for nonworking children. The heat and noise of mills damaged health and hearing. Although ministers, women, and even some businessmen pushed a strong child labor reform bill through the 1907 legislature, many mills ignored it and some parents threatened to move if the mills refused to hire their children. In 1912 Dr. W.H. Oates, the state child labor inspector, filed fourteen warrants against Huntsville's Lowe Manufacturing Company for failure to obtain affidavits from parents of minors who were employed in the mill. Oates also found violations at Opelika Cotton Mill and elsewhere.

Race relations were also strained in mill towns. Managers had long since discovered that poor white textile workers would not work beside blacks, so except for menial jobs such as sweeping or lifting unloaded cotton bales from flatcars, blacks were excluded from the mills. Nevertheless, many unskilled poor whites maintained little pride other than in race and felt constantly threatened

by blacks living in the community. They responded enthusiastically to the resurgent Ku Klux Klan in the 1920s and often participated in lynchings. In July 1900, English Clark, a Negro, allegedly raped a poor white operative at Huntsville's Dallas Mills. A mob of 1,000 mill workers walked off their jobs, effectively shutting down the factory, and marched to the jail. They overpowered guards and lynched Clark in front of a mob that had swelled to 6,000. Dallas Manufacturing acknowledged that its employees had conducted the outrage, even agreeing to repair damages to the jail done by the mob.

Labor problems also plagued Alabama's lumber industry. The rapid exploitation of south Ala-

bama's longleaf pine forests continued unabated. Southern pine provided a larger share of the nation's lumber production than any other species every year but one between 1899 and the 1960s, and Alabama was a consistent leader among the southern states. Many of the mills were located in remote counties along the Florida or Mississippi borders. These counties were almost entirely rural with no alternative to farming. The soil was poorly suited to cotton production, resulting in a high incidence of white farm tenancy. At first such regions provided ample sawmill workers. Lockhart, in remote Covington County, contained the state's largest sawmill in 1913. It could produce 100,000 board feet of lumber a day, but Alabama contained twenty additional mills, each with a capacity of 50,000 board feet or more. Lumbering was exhausting and dangerous work, causing many poor whites to remain tenant farmers or to leave the land altogether rather than cut timber. So the mills increasingly turned to convict labor and immigrants. In 1903 Flowers and Flowers Saw Mill at Bolling hired county convicts who worked from sunup to sundown six days a week supervised by one armed guard per twelve prisoners. Dangerous convicts labored with chains shacked to their ankles. When one man disobeyed, the guards usually punished all. At night the men bedded down in stockade barracks. Alabama abolished the convict lease system in the late 1920s, the last southern state to do so.

Another source of labor came from newly arrived immigrants. Companies sent labor recruiters to New York and other seaboard cities to contract newcomers from eastern and southern Europe. Although some welcomed the jobs, others understood little English and were appalled by conditions in the lumber camps, which were often worse than those they had left behind in Europe. Most immigrants quickly returned to the North, though some unscrupulous owners held others in virtual captivity. One of the South's most spectacular federal peonage cases originated in the Jackson Lumber Mill at Lockhart in 1906.

Workers had sufficient reason to complain. Wages averaged less than a dollar a day for unskilled labor. Company villages were more remote than were those of textile mill communities, and commissaries took advantage of the isolation to charge extravagant price markups. Many of the mills paid in scrip which could be redeemed at full face value only in the commissary. As a result, the company store was often a major source of profit.

Before Progressive leaders passed Alabama's Workman Compensation law in January 1920,

Lewis Brockway, posing here in 1903, was a Monrovia farmer who was also a Watkins salesman selling home remedies and seasonings door to door to rural residents. For those some distance from a store, such traveling salesmen were invaluable. Courtesy, Mrs. Godren Darnell, Huntsville

sawmills assumed little responsiblity for the safety of workers. They sometimes assessed employees a certain amount per month for medical services, usually a dollar for single men and a $1.50 for a family. Injuries occurred frequently. One employee of W.T. Smith Lumber Company claimed that hardly a week passed that a man was not killed. Even managers admitted a high accident rate. Records from Tuscaloosa's Kaul Lumber Company beginning in 1913 indicate that the firm

employed between 400 and 500 men. In 1913 its employees suffered 124 accidents, the next year, 150. Inexperienced firemen allowed boilers to overheat and explode. Falling limbs and trees crushed men, and whirling saws ripped off fingers and hands.

Such conditions caused some timber workers to seek improved treatment, but their efforts to organize the widely dispersed loggers never won many victories. Late in the nineteenth century the

Huntsville's Merrimack Manufacturing Company used chartered railway cars to transport its employees and their families to its annual picnic near the site of the old Bell factory on *the Flint River. Such philanthropy was designed in part to discourage unionization. Courtesy, Huntsville/Madison County Public Library*

Above: *Opened in 1892, the Dallas Manufacturing Company was the state's largest cotton mill. With the Merrimack Mill (1899), Lowe Manufacturing (1900), Rowe Knitting and Eastern Manufacturing (1901), and finally Erwin Mills (1915), the Dallas Mill made Huntsville the largest textile mill city in Alabama. By the 1920s Huntsville mills had a quarter million spindles and produced nearly $10 million worth of cloth a year. Courtesy, Birmingham Public Library*

Left: *In an effort to obtain workers more used to the discipline of the machine age, Birmingham firms sent labor recruiters to European countries, including Norway, which was the homeland of the Morrison family. The various immigrant communities brought cultural diversity to Birmingham, which set it apart from the rest of the state. Courtesy, Alabama Department of Archives and History*

James G. McGowin purchased the W.T. Smith Lumber Company in 1905. Turning away from the "clear cutting" practices common in his day, McGowin harvested selectively and practiced reforestation. Courtesy, University of South Alabama

Knights of Labor tried to organize loggers at Brewton. Efforts to unionize the Harold Mill failed when the owner, a German immigrant, made good on his promise to shut down the mill if his 200 employees joined. The manager of Tuscaloosa's Kaul Lumber Company noticed employees holding meetings behind one of the mills. He assigned a Pinkerton detective to attend the meetings and fired a worker who was trying to organize a union. He later allowed skilled machinists to unionize with the warning that he was "still going to damn well run the company."

Changes in technology altered lumbering in the years after 1900. Logging railroads and eight-wheel ox carts dominated transportation. In 1913 south Alabama's longleaf pine belt contained some 424 miles of narrow-gauge track. By 1918 the inexpensive and efficient internal combustion engine gave new life to the portable or "peckerwood" sawmill. Trucks and tractors slowly replaced expensive logging railroads, and small mills once again competed successfully with larger firms.

Although the use of trucks and tractors allowed small producers to compete, large family-owned mills still dominated the industry. The small town of Chapman in Butler County represented for the lumber industry what Huntsville did for textiles. K.L. Davis had built the first sawmill in the entirely rural county in 1883 or 1884 after the L.&N. opened it to transportation. W.T. Smith of Birmingham had purchased the company in 1891. Chapman became a company town whose houses, churches, and schools all belonged to W.T. Smith. The T.R. Miller and McMillan families, who also carved prominent empires out of south Alabama's forests, also resided there.

James G. McGowin arrived in Chapman in 1905. A native of Escambia County, McGowin left his Brewton mercantile business in 1903 to join his two brothers in a Mobile lumber exporting venture. Two years later the three McGowins and their brother-in-law purchased the W.T. Smith Lumber Company, and J.G. McGowin moved to Chapman as secretary-treasurer and general manager. In 1907 they merged with a neighboring mill, establishing a tradition of expansion by acquisition. This strategy required McGowin to adopt a new philosophy of forest management. Instead of cutting timber and then abandoning the land, as previous lumbermen had done, McGowin proposed a concept of sustained yield and careful harvesting. By practicing reforestation, he could plan cutting operations for a number of years in the future. When older timber began to run out in the 1920s, he diversified operations. He built mills to construct crates, barrels, boxes, and veneers, and thereby weathered the depression. His election as president of the company in 1925 strengthened his control, as did the training he afforded his three sons. He put Earl, Julian, and Floyd to work in the mills at the ages of thirteen or fourteen during their summer vacations. He encouraged each to attend college, and Earl won a Rhodes Scholarship to attend Oxford University. When they completed their education he welcomed them back into the family business. Julian took charge of growing and harvesting trees, Floyd of lumber production, and Earl of sales.

They turned the company town of Chapman into what the family called "a benevolent dictatorship." McGowins provided the mayor of the community, no real problem in a town that contained only fifteen or twenty voters. No blacks were allowed and the McGowins established a close, paternalistic relationship to the community's whites. The McGowin and T.R. Miller families were Universalists. Appalled by the emotionalism and anti-intellectualism of a Baptist evangelist who visited the community, they constructed a Universalist Church to enlighten local citizens, though with meager results. They also championed higher education and professional approaches to the state's timber industry. Alabama retained its share of unregulated exploitive industry and individualistic businessmen who gave no thought to the public welfare, but conditions were changing. Between

Alabama's Progressive two-term governor, Bibb Graves, served from 1927-1931 and from 1935-1939. His administrations were characterized by aid to education, road and bridge construction, and a generally activist and progressive pro-business attitude. However, the Depression dashed many of Graves' hopes for substantial economic development. Courtesy, Alabama Department of Archives and History

1900 and 1929 the business community tried to restore order and provide some guidelines for doing business. Under businessmen governors such as B.B. Comer and Thomas Kilby, the state regulated railroads, provided workman's compensation, restricted child labor, and abandoned the convict lease system. Individual businessmen such as George Crawford initiated innovative systems of welfare capitalism, and entrepreneurs such as the McGowins began to realize that the state's resources were finite and had to be conserved for future generations. In many ways the first three decades of the twentieth century ended Alabama's industrial adolescence and ushered in an age of maturity.

Progressive governors such as Thomas Kilby (1918-1922) recognized the need for responsible management of the affairs of business and government. He supported measures to provide workman's compensation, restrict child labor, and end the convict lease system. With business leaders such as James McGowin and George G. Crawford he charted a new and more mature course for business and industry in Alabama. Courtesy, Alabama Department of Archives and History

Wartime crowds were commonplace in Mobile and other cities across Alabama where defense-related industries were located. But this crowd was special as it gathered to celebrate V-E Day in April 1945. Courtesy, University of South Alabama

Chapter 5
A NEW DEAL
A NEW DAY

The passing of years has dimmed memories of the Great Depression. Stories still remembered usually involve personal or family tragedies and triumphs, not institutional crises; but the dreams of profits, prosperous industries, and steady economic growth long cherished by businessmen became casualties as readily as personal goals. Factories and mills, laboriously nurtured for decades through good times and bad, floundered and sank upon a sea of troubles. No region of the state nor type of industry escaped the cataclysm. Only three southern states registered a total decline of white employment during the 1930s, and Alabama had the sharpest decline of the three. Total nonfarm employment fell by 15 percent.

The textile industry collapsed like a house of cards. Huntsville, the state's leader, fell on particularly hard times. Dallas Mill, which had reported a profit of nearly $800,000 in 1920, earned only $6,559 in 1929; in 1930 the company lost $279,039. Lowe Mill was sold at a bankruptcy auction in 1932. By June 1930, 7 percent of Huntsville's population was unemployed. Between 20 and 25 percent of the unemployment resulted from shut down textile mills. The Alabama School of Trades in Gadsden tried desperately to keep its doors open, but industries no longer needed their own employees, much less the newly graduating craftsmen. In order to continue operations the school allowed boys to pay tuition, room, and board by trading a cord of wood or working on the school's farm. The catalogue instructed poor boys from out of town that they need bring only a quilt, a pair of overalls, and sheets. During one depression year legislative appropriations to the school totaled one dollar, that representing only a formality to ensure continued state control. Three different directors

Opposite: Of all America's cities, Birmingham was hardest hit by the Depression. However, by the mid-thirties the city's heavy industry was recovering. As this 1936 Walker Evans photograph suggests, the recovery still left many people untouched. Full employment lay two to four years in the future. Courtesy, Farm Security Administration, Library of Congress

tried to keep the school afloat, each in turn succumbing to disappointment and frustration.

Birmingham suffered worst of all. Although Alabama had become the third largest producer of iron ore and the fourth leading pig iron manufacturer by the 1930s, the state's prominence only made it that much more vulnerable to economic cycles. President Franklin D. Roosevelt called Birmingham the "worst hit town in the country." In June 1932, the city counted 100,000 wage and salary earners. One-quarter of these, 25,000, were jobless; 60,000 more worked only part-time. More than 12,000 unemployed men registered for municipal jobs, and the Red Cross estimated that between 6,000 and 8,000 people lacked adequate food, fuel, and housing. The county almshouse, designed to house 220, held 500.

Just as iron and steel had paced the prosperity of the previous three decades, they led the 1930s decline. T.C.I.'s operation at Docena employed 1,000 men in the late 1920s; by 1933 it retained only seventy-eight. The company tried to lessen the impact of layoffs by deferring rent on houses and utilities and by extending credit at the commissaries. Embittered miners called the credit vouchers "pity slips."

Events at the national level did not favor workers either. U.S. Steel chief executive Judge Gary died, and management less favorable to welfare capitalism assumed leadership. Funds previously used to support welfare programs disappeared with company profits. George G. Crawford resigned as T.C.I. president in 1930 to accept the presidency of Jones and Laughlin Steel Corporation in Pittsburgh. After he left three different chief executives served T.C.I. during the 1930s, each with less autonomy in an increasingly centralized administration. Once the federal government instituted the Federal Emergency Relief Administration, T.C.I. quickly transferred its unemployed workers to relief rolls. By 1939 T.C.I. welfare expenditures amounted to only 14 percent of the 1928 outlay. The head of the company's welfare department wrote former president Crawford in 1932 that the new U.S.S. management viewed its work as "needless expense." However, the company did continue its extensive health services program.

Newer companies struggled just to survive.

Birmingham Slag, building its prosperity by constructing the South's highways, suffered the only operating loss in its history in 1932. Southern Natural Gas Corporation began constructing its first natural gas pipeline in 1929, extending from northeastern Louisiana to Birmingham. The company began gas deliveries on the last day of that propitious year and extended service to Atlanta in 1930, but the stock market crash and Depression plunged the company into immediate trouble, finally forcing it into receivership.

At a personal level the strain was overwhelming. Entrepreneurs who had invested both personal fortunes and enormous amounts of time and talent saw careers crashing down around them. Some, like Crawford, could leave for new opportunities elsewhere, but others had no alternative but to stay in Alabama and see the crisis through. John A. Peterson owned a Montgomery bridge construc-

tion business. Like Birmingham Slag, his firm reacted to cuts in the state and federal highway programs, and by 1931 road building had virtually ceased. Like many businessmen, Peterson had invested some of his profits in the 1920s bull market. When a bear market swept the Wall Street exchange in 1929 he was caught short. But playing stocks was like a poison for which there was no antidote. He felt compelled to continue buying and selling in order to recoup his losses. In his diary he left an account of the folly:

Sept. 8 (1931). Stocks went into further decline after the three day holiday.
Oct. 4. Stock at new lows but have nothing to turn into money except at a great sacrifice.
Oct. 6. Stocks took big rebound and I wonder if the big opportunity is past. I think any rally of any proportions will not be sustained.

July 3 (1932). Have cold feet in investing further in stocks as it looks as if invested money is slipping way.

Despite such realistic appraisals, he kept investing in stocks anyway. When the harsh realities impinged too much he found solace in flying his plane or by attending the annual Auburn-Alabama football game.

Even had management and labor reached a consensus on the nature and extent of the crisis facing them, recovery would have been difficult, but in an atmosphere of layoffs, stretch-outs, mutual animosity and recrimination, industrial relations were as troubled as industrial conditions. No industry escaped entirely, but the textile, iron, steel, coal mining, and rubber industries bore the brunt of the conflict.

Huntsville textile workers led the protest

Above: *In Alabama's cities, towns, and countryside, car sales grew throughout the decades before the Depression. However, by the time this photograph was made in 1931 at the Long-Lewis dealership in Bessemer, sales of durable goods such as cars had fallen off by 90 percent of their 1929 levels. Courtesy, Bessemer Hall of History Museum.*

Opposite: *In 1929 the Southern Natural Gas Corporation began construction of a natural gas pipeline which would go from northeastern Louisiana to Atlanta via Birmingham. The pipeline reached the "Magic City" late in the year and gas deliveries began, but the Depression nearly claimed Southern Natural Gas as one of its victims. The company was in receivership for several years beginning in 1930. In this photograph, made in the summer of 1929, workmen lay pipe outside Fultondale near Birmingham several months before the devastating stock market crash. Courtesy, Southern Natural Gas Company, Birmingham*

against layoffs of some workers and "stretch-outs" which extended the labor of others. Even for those who continued to work, salaries declined more than house rents or prices in the commissary. Membership in the United Textile Workers of America grew from 40,000 in 1933 to 270,000 in August 1934. On July 17, 1934, nearly 4,500 Huntsville mill workers launched a strike which spread across the state and by September throughout the nation. Of the state's 30,000 textile workers, nearly two-thirds joined the walkout, demanding a $12 weekly wage, a thirty-hour week, and union recognition. U.T.W. organizer John Dean and Huntsville native Mollie Dowd coordinated the strike. Though both the organizers and strikers were native southerners, the Huntsville Chamber of Commerce insisted on referring to them as "outsiders." Clashes between strikers and police occurred with increasing frequency, and the city took on the appearance of an armed camp. "Flying squads" of strikers filled worn-out trucks and cars bound for other Alabama mills to persuade fellow "lint heads" to walk off their jobs. By September 7, half the South's 400,000 mill workers had struck and ten people had died in shootings. Four governors, including Alabama's, had mobilized state militias. John Dean had been abducted from his Huntsville hotel room at gunpoint, pistol-whipped, and driven to Fayetteville, Tennessee. He called friends in Huntsville who collected a variety of weapons, packed a dozen cars, and traveled by caravan to Fayetteville to get Dean and return him to Alabama. When rumors circulated that the kidnap had been planned at a party by some of the city's leading citizens, a crowd of several hundred guntoting, torch-carrying mill workers marched through the streets after midnight bound for the home of a man allegedly involved in the plot. Luckily Reuben Chapman, grandson of an Alabama governor, awakened to see the torches lighting Maysville Road and fled out the back door. The 1934 strike marked the decline of Huntsville's textile industry. Further south at Gadsden's Goodyear Rubber Plant, conditions turned just as violent. Sherman H. Dalrymple, president of the United Rubber Workers, tried to organize the facility. Local toughs beat him up and ran him out of town. Bands of thugs roamed through the plant

beating up union members. A subsequent attempt to organize the plant in 1941 resulted in another assault on a union organizer; eighty-six stitches were required to close gashes in his head. Gulf States Steel also defeated efforts by the Steel Workers Organizing Committee to unionize its employees.

Not all organizing drives ended in defeat. The New Deal applied substantial pressure on companies to allow collective bargaining. Section 7(a) of the National Industrial Recovery Act (June 1933) gave employees the right to organize. The National Labor Relations Act (July 1935), often called the Wagner Act for its sponsor, outlawed a number of company strategies for defeating unionism. The Walsh-Healy Act (1936) established minimum labor standards for firms receiving government con-

tracts, and the Fair Labor Standards Act (1938) set minimum wage and maximum hours for companies engaged in interstate commerce.

Union successes came primarily in the coal, iron, and steel industries. When John L. Lewis began an organizing drive in 1933, only 225 of Alabama's 17,500 miners belonged to the United Mine Workers. The series of strikes and confrontations that followed resulted in union victory. In March 1934, thirty-eight companies representing 90 percent of the mines in the state signed an agreement with the U.M.W. The major exceptions were Henry DeBardeleben's coal corporation and Charles F. DeBardeleben's Alabama Fuel and Iron Company. They fired miners who joined the union and broke a strike by planting dynamite under a road leading to their coal mines and mounting machine guns at

Steel mill housing was photographed by famous photographer Walker Evans when he visited Birmingham in March 1936. The typical millhouse had a four-cornered roof with a central chimney, running water to kitchen sinks, but no indoor bathrooms. Courtesy, Library of Congress

mine entrances. A Department of Labor investigator upheld complaints against the DeBardelebens, but his report did not prevent a gun battle between 1,500 striking miners and company guards in October 1934, which left one man dead and ten wounded.

When Lewis organized the Steel Worker's Organizing Committee in June 1936, he dispatched organizers to Birmingham. U.S. Steel quickly capitulated. The company was making profits again after years of losses, Roosevelt had been overwhelmingly reelected, and the company decided if unionism must come it preferred a single industrial union to a collection of craft unions. So the company, including its T.C.I. affiliate, peacefully accepted collective bargaining. Some other Birmingham-area steel mills followed U.S. Steel's lead; but Bethlehem, Youngstown, Inland, Gulf States, and Republic successfully resisted unionism until the early 1940s. By 1940 the United Steel Workers had thirty-three lodges in the South with half of them in the Birmingham district. Of 10,000 southern union members, 5,700 worked in Alabama. By the end of the decade, Alabama had become the most heavily unionized southern state.

Alabama industrial leaders left no doubt how they felt about New Deal labor policies. Scott Roberts, president of the Alabama Cotton Manufacturers Association, blasted New Deal officials for putting striking textile workers on relief during the 1934 strike. Alabama's Associated Industries condemned relief director Harry Hopkins for feeding striking coal miners, and lumber company officials leveled the same charges regarding lumber workers on strike.

The New Deal attracted fire from both directions. Workers complained that industry representatives dominated county relief committees and denied aid to union workers. The New Deal did appoint businessmen and industrialists to important

Birmingham miners are shown taking a break from work in November 1946. Following the bleak years of the Depression, World War II stimulated local industries. The demand for coal, iron, and steel had never been higher and the population of Jefferson County increased by 17 percent as men and women came from across the South to work in wartime industries. Courtesy, Jackie Dobbs, Old Birmingham Photographs

jobs in an attempt to create bipartisan support for its relief efforts. Algernon Blair, a prominent Montgomery real estate developer, served as chairman of the Alabama Relief Administration. Other agency members included Birmingham textile tycoon Donald Comer, son of the former governor and head of Avondale Mills, and Montgomery newspaper editor Grover Hall. Harry Hopkins had appointed Milton H. Fies chairman of the agency in the first days of the new administration, but his appointment brought down a torrent of abuse from union activists. Fies served as vice-president of DeBardeleben Coal Company and had personally discharged miners for joining the U.M.W. Major controversy swirled around the question of whether strikers were eligible for relief, and despite strong opposition from manufacturers and businessmen, the administration decided in favor of labor. By September 1934, nearly 8,200 of the 20,000 striking textile workers were on relief rolls; and of 18,000 coal miners, 13,000 received assistance by October 1935.

The dispute over unionism and relief reflected the variety of business responses to the New Deal in Alabama. Some industrialists painfully acquiesced to unions despite private opposition. Others bitterly held out, resisting any compromise. Still others agreed to serve on New Deal relief agencies. Most accepted, however reluctantly, a new reality regarding the role of the federal government in the nation's economy. Editor Reese T. Amis of the *Huntsville Times* editorialized about the proposed Social Security bill in 1935. Had such a proposal been introduced in 1933, he wrote, it would have been called "dangerous experimentation" or an "un-American form of coddling . . ." By 1935, however, most critics believed the bill did not go far enough:

We have had a revolution in this country, after all, and it has taken place in our minds. Our point of view has shifted. We don't look at things with the same eyes that we used half a dozen years ago.

Yesterday's dangerous radicalism is the height of today's conservatism . . .

Grover Hall, conservative Pulitzer Prize-winning editor of the *Montgomery Advertiser,* wrote a journalist friend in Atlanta of his affection for the old economic system of the 1920s which had been so profitable to their class. That system, Hall added, had been "disastrous to the great majority":

However much we may love the days of Harding and Coolidge, they are gone forever—they will not be recaptured, no matter how much the newspapers of the land may rant and strain. Personally I fared much better under Pickle Coolidge than I have under any subsequent President—but I saw his world and mine die. Under Roosevelt I saw a new world born, even though much that Roosevelt has done annoys me and will not receive my approval . . . But a new day, a new world, a new leadership, a new responsibility are here and you and I would be foolish to ignore the fact.

Newspaper editor Grover Hall received a Pulitzer prize for his articles attacking the Ku Klux Klan in the 1920s. In the thirties he lent support to the New Deal, recognizing its popular appeal despite his personal reservations about it. Courtesy, Alabama Department of Archives and History

Much also remained to be done by manufacturers to mitigate the effects of New Deal regulation and to promote their own interests within the new order. Alabama Power Company chose the path of litigation, challenging the authority of the Tennessee Valley Authority in the courts. Arguing that T.V.A. constituted a government entity in competition with free enterprise, attorneys for the company kept the issue before the bench for half a decade. The company finally reached an informal agreement in 1939 dividing the state into T.V.A. territory in the northern third and Alabama Power's domain in the remainder. Partly as a result of what industrialists viewed as growing federal and state encroachment on their prerogatives, Alabama Power president Thomas W. Martin helped organize the Alabama State Chamber of Commerce in June 1937, with headquarters in the state capital.

During the first three decades of the twentieth century the state government had steadily increased industry regulation. By 1929 Alabama's Public Service Commission governed activities and rate structures of railroads, telephones, telegraph lines, and all other public utilities. Factory and mine inspectors supervised working conditions and enforced restrictions on child and convict labor. The state insurance and banking departments administered regulations on those industries.

Like other southern states after World War I, Alabama had established an agency to publicize the state's advantages and to contact prospective investors. Initially the agency worked with local chambers of commerce to attract new manufacturers.

Birmingham is viewed at night, looking west toward the Alabama Power Company Building. The statue of Electra can barely be seen in the blaze of the light atop the building. Be- yond the Temple Theatre the First Methodist Church steeple is visible. Photo by Charles F. McFarlin. Courtesy, Betsy Bancroft

Since 1914, Alabama Power Company had been building hydroelectric power generating dams. This photograph shows one of the larg-est, the Jordan Dam, on the Coosa River in east central Alabama in 1937. By the end of the thirties, Alabama Power and TVA had

come to terms, with Alabama Power supplying
electricity to most of the state, while TVA limited itself to the Tennessee Valley. Courtesy,
Alabama Department of Archives and History

The Depression lent a sense of urgency to this undertaking. Some Alabama communities provided land and buildings to any industry willing to locate in their town. In 1935 the legislature created the Alabama State Planning Commission to solicit new businesses, but the most lasting effort was imported from Mississippi. Hugh Lawson White, owner of White Lumber Company, began to promote his Balance Agriculture with Industry (BAWI) idea in the early 1930s. As governor of the magnolia state he persuaded the legislature to enact the program in 1936. The idea was relatively simple. A community could sell municipal bonds to construct factories for industries willing to hire a stipulated number of employees or pay a certain payroll. A three-member state industrial commission and a local referendum had to approve the agreement. The bonds were exempt from federal taxes. The community then charged the company a nominal rent which it could show as a tax write-off. The industry paid no property taxes because technically the building remained public property and thus tax-exempt. The BAWI plan spread to Tennessee, Kentucky, and Alabama, though with some modification. Alabama relied more on revenue bonds backed by the industry's rental payments instead of using municipal bonds; but revenue bonds were still tax-exempt and represented a substantial state subsidy for new industry. The rationale for state effort was that industry

created jobs, the most immediate need during the 1930s. The crusade failed not so much because the idea was flawed as because of national conditions. When America's economy began to recover, the BAWI campaign succeeded in attracting many industries, especially low wage, labor-intensive types.

Primarily, Alabama's economic salvation came neither from its own efforts nor from federal largess. Instead, the rains that caused prosperity to sprout came from storm clouds gathering over Europe. As international tensions diverted attention from domestic problems, the state once again profited from its natural advantages. Good climate, abundant water, a large idle labor force, and a

Above: The state's rich deposits of natural minerals included some of America's finest marble. In this 1930s photograph made at Grantt's Quarry, Alabama, in the factory of the Alabama Marble Company, workmen are cutting and polishing the stone which has a variety of uses, especially in fine buildings throughout the state and nation. *Courtesy, Alabama Department of Archives and History*

Opposite: These shotgun houses, photographed in 1937 in Mobile by Arthur Rothstein for the Farm Security Administration, were inhabited by blacks, but many whites also lived in shotguns. With lingering high rates of unemployment and underemployment, few people could afford anything better. *Courtesy, Farm Security Administration, Library of Congress*

huge, underutilized industrial capacity waited for investors; and as America mobilized for war many investors looked south.

The Tennessee Valley Authority furnished Alabama with the additional advantage of cheap power which attracted both civilian and government facilities. Huntsville's Chamber of Commerce had been working industriously all during the 1930s to diversify the city's economy. Finally on July 3, 1941, its long campaign bore fruit. So ju-

bilant were city fathers that they dispatched fire engines clanging bells to dispense an extra edition of the *Huntsville Times.* Headlines announced that a new $40-million war chemical plant was coming to town. By July 7 more than 500 men had applied for site preparation and construction jobs. Within months Huntsville and Redstone Arsenals joined the chemical plant, producing artillery shells and bombs. Together the military facilities on 40,000 acres invigorated the economy to the

Above, left: *The Wilson Dam, begun in 1916, became the cornerstone of TVA after the agency was established in 1933. The dam's power-house is shown in this photograph taken during the 1930s. The cheap electricity provided by TVA was a key element in the economic revival of the Tennessee Valley. Courtesy, Birmingham Public Library*

Above: *In addition to generating hydroelectric power, TVA also improved navigation along the Tennessee River, especially around the treacherous Muscle Shoals. The result was a dramatic upturn in economic activity in north Alabama. When this photo was made at the Wheeler Lock and Dam in 1939, barge traffic had grown to 35 million tons a year from little more than a trickle before TVA. Courtesy, Alabama Department of Archives and History*

tune of some $70 million and ended exclusive reliance on textiles. The arsenals employed more than 11,000 at their peak. By May 1944, Huntsville contained 17,000 manufacturing employees. Even textile employment recovered to more than 5,500, who worked in the remaining three cotton mills. In a pattern familiar around the country, a large percentage of the new employees, both in traditional industries as well as in the arsenals, were female.

The Alabama School of Trades at Gadsden recognized the new realities regarding sex and workplace. During the early 1940s enrollment mushroomed but the composition of the student body changed. The traditional student, a young single male in his late teens, was a prime candidate for military service. So women and older males took his place, attracted to the school both by a sense of patriotism and a desire to aid the war effort as well as a desire to obtain high-paying jobs in Alabama's booming defense plants. As the *Birmingham News* described it, "The Alabama School of Trades is now a school of Maids."

Above, left: *With so many mothers working in defense-related industries, some provision had to be made for the care of their children. Larger corporations and the federal government made various efforts to deal with the problem. These children at Washington Avenue nursery in Mobile were lucky since there were always far more children than such institutions could serve. Courtesy, University of South Alabama*

Top: *The rapid expansion of Mobile's ship-building industry during World War II brought women into fields previously closed to them,*

such as welding. By the war's end women were not only doing such jobs, they were training others to do them, as this ADDSCO picture illustrates. Courtesy, University of South Alabama

Above: *In this 1939 photograph students of Tuskegee Institute are working in the machine and welding department. Unfortunately, too few Alabamians, black or white, had such skills as these men were acquiring as the war-time boom swept over the state. Private industry had to train most of the workers it hired. Courtesy, Tuskegee University*

T.V.A. and the war effort also furnished new opportunities for Birmingham Slag. The company received a lucrative contract in 1939 to prepare a site for a T.V.A. dam and generating plant at Watts

Opposite: Despite the Depression's severity, businesses, even in Birmingham, survived the hard times. Federally funded construction projects kept Birmingham Slag busy building roads and bridges, which required large quantities of redi-mix concrete provided by facilities such as this one photographed by Dorothea Lange in 1936. Courtesy, Farm Security Administration, Library of Congress

Below: When Arthur Rothstein photographed these coal miners in 1937, unemployment in Birmingham was falling as demand for iron and coal rose. Courtesy, Farm Security Administration, National Archives

Bar, Tennessee. A series of T.V.A. contracts followed this first one. The company also furnished aggregates and concrete for the Manhattan Project at Oak Ridge, Tennessee; Redstone Arsenal at Huntsville; the Anniston Ordnance Depot at Bynum; and for several large military installations. Such activity helped Birmingham's economy recover as rapidly as Huntsville's. Steel factories, which had gathered cobwebs for a decade, began running three shifts a day. Only recently designated as one of the cities hardest hit by the Depression, Birmingham became the "great arsenal of the South." Citizens even rejoiced upon learning that the enemy had listed their city as its second bombing priority behind Pittsburgh.

By the fall of 1939 T.C.I. was operating at 100-percent capacity. During the war the company enlarged its Wenonah ore plant, added a blast fur-

Franklin D. Roosevelt's innovative programs such as TVA had a great impact on the lives of Alabamians. His popularity was such that despite the opposition of large vested interests, politicians welcomed the chance to appear with him. Here Roosevelt is accompanied on a 1939 visit to Auburn by (left to right) Governor Frank Dixon, Senator Lister Hill and Congressman George Grant. Courtesy, Auburn University

nace and a plate mill at Fairfield, constructed a shell-forging plant at Ensley, opened a coal mine at Short Creek, and installed a new electrolytic tin-plating process at its Fairfield tin mill. It added 2,500 employees between January and September 1941. The total work force increased by 7,000 between 1938 and 1941, to a total of 30,000. Even with these increases labor shortages plagued the company throughout the war. Several new industries located in the city. Bechtel-McCone Aircraft Modification occupied a plant at the Birmingham airport where it equipped and modified half the B-29 bombers used in the war. O'Neal Steel manufactured steel fabrications for bombs and became one of the largest independent steel companies in the

South.

Elsewhere, Mobile prospered through the acquisition of a large ship-building complex and expansion of dock facilities. The city's population doubled between 1940 and 1944, creating severe housing shortages. The cultural and political landscape changed as thousands of poor whites poured into the city.

Maxwell and Gunter Air Force bases in Montgomery pumped millions of dollars into the capital city's economy and spawned a network of satellite auxiliary training fields such as Deatsville, Elmore, Dannelly, Taylor, and Shorter. By 1943 Maxwell had become the training base for 9,000 cadets per class and graduated a total of 100,000 airmen. Ap-

Top: "Rosie the Riviter" could have lived in Mobile. Women of all ages found work in the shipyards or at Brookley Field as the war turned Mobile's old Southern society upside down. When it was over, most women went back to more traditional jobs or left the labor force altogether, willingly or not, but few forgot the sense of achievement and independence their wartime careers gave them. These women were working at ADDSCO in 1943. Courtesy, University of South Alabama

Middle: In the frenetic days of World War II thousands of workers poured into Mobile's shipyards to build, repair, and overhaul vessels for the war effort. ADDSCO was then the largest employer in the city. Courtesy, University of South Alabama

Bottom: Led by E.A. Roberts, chairman of Waterman Steamship Corporation, Mobilians convinced the state government to expand the state docks after World War II. The expansion stretched south from the original facility almost to the foot of Government Street, adding much needed new warehouse and berthing space. This photograph shows a portion of the construction during the winter of 1949. Courtesy, University of South Alabama

Below: Mobile's population exploded between 1940 and 1943 as thousands of war workers crowded into the city looking for jobs at the shipyards, docks, and Brookley Air Field. In an effort to deal with the housing shortage, Mobilians rented every available room, and the federal government built eleven housing projects and opened the War Housing Center, shown here. Nevertheless, many people spent the war years living in tents and trailers. Courtesy, University of South Alabama

proximately one of every sixteen employed civilians worked at one of the bases and one of every seven families was related directly or indirectly to the Air Force. Contractor Algernon Blair received a $9 million army contract for construction near Maxwell Field.

The Dupont Alabama Ordnance Works, located at Childersburg, was the largest ordnance plant in the South making smokeless powder and explosives. Workers from Georgia, Anniston, and Birmingham found construction jobs building the huge facility. Foreign war also hastened domestic peace. Prosperity seemed to provide an atmosphere conducive to industrial compromise. In Gadsden, Republic Steel (formerly Gulf States) acquiesced to unionism in 1941. Goodyear Rubber Company followed suit in 1943, pressured by the loss of federal defense contracts unless it allowed workers to bargain collectively.

Alabama's heavy industries expanded in wartime. Goodyear Tire and Rubber Company at Gadsden, shown here in 1946, was no exception. Expansion brought unionization, which came to Goodyear in 1943. Courtesy, Alabama Department of Archives and History

Many feared that the end of hostilities would plunge the economy back into the doldrums as happened at the end of World War I. However, pent-up consumer demand, continued high levels of federal spending, and the G.I. Bill, which kept large numbers of veterans temporarily out of the labor force, ensured continued prosperity.

Of course, slumps did occur. Sharp declines in federal spending resulted in reduced payrolls for towns with military installations. The government deactivated Redstone Arsenal in 1945 causing Huntsville officials to scurry after new industry. In Gadsden the Alabama School of Trades underwent yet another transformation as women dropped out and returning veterans, many of them disabled, took their places.

Changing conditions that were one person's problem were another's opportunity. Light industry poured into the Tennessee Valley, attracted by cheap electrical rates. And two brothers in central Alabama began international business careers.

Winston H. "Red" Blount and his brother Houston had grown up in Union Springs. They left the University of Alabama to enter military service, intending to return to operate their father's small sand and gravel business. As with many other

young men, years of military service interrupted their dreams. When they returned, their father was dead and the family business declining. So the brothers traveled to Atlanta to purchase surplus army equipment and moved the family business to Tuskegee. Red Blount bought four new Caterpillar tractors and scrappers for $28,000, not because they were useful in the sand and gravel business, but because they were such a bargain. When he got them home, Houston inquired, "What are we going to do with that stuff?" Red replied, "We're going into the contracting business." With that simple decision they began Blount Brothers Construction Company. At first they used their new machines to build fish ponds and highways. In 1949 they completed their first million-dollar project ahead of schedule by dividing crews into two teams and promising Thanksgiving turkeys to the one finishing first. In the 1950s they moved company headquarters to Montgomery and began specializing in highly technical jobs.

John Murdock Harbert also spotted opportunity in the changing postwar economy. He ended his military career with $6,000 which he had won shooting craps. He invested the money in a concrete mixer and tools, and set out building a financial empire in mining, real-estate development, and construction. Despite facing insolvency three times in his first twenty years of operation, he prospered with the same steady nerves that served him well in wartime dice games.

Birmingham Slag succeeded in the same general business climate as the Blount and Harbert companies. Between the end of the war and a 1956 merger its number of employees swelled to 600, sales increased to $22 million, and net profits ran between $1.5 and $2 million annually. The company continued expanding, constructing ready-mix concrete plants at Fairfield, Birmingham, Alabama City, and Montgomery, and adding asphalt and concrete plants at the Fairfield and Montgomery sites. The firm also constructed concrete brick and block plants at Alabama City near Gadsden and adjacent to its Stockbridge Stone Quarry in Georgia. The company remained under family ownership with Gene and later Charles Ireland serving as president.

Older industries paused to adjust to peacetime conditions, then raced rapidly ahead. T.C.I. consolidated its position as the South's premier steel producer. By 1948 the company managed four major facilities—the Ensley Steel, Fairfield Tin, and Fairfield Wire Works, and the Bessemer Rolling Mills. At these locations, the corporation operated 572 coke ovens, 9 blast furnaces, 21 open-hearth furnaces, and 3 Bessemer converters. Together these facilities could produce a capacity of nearly three million tons of steel ingots and castings. New coal mines fed the gigantic furnaces which lighted Birmingham nights.

The key element in T.C.I's modernization was a new source of iron ore. Ample supplies of Red Mountain ore remained, but the quality had reached such low levels as to be unprofitable. The company discovered that it could import rich Venezuelan ores and blend them with poorer-grade Alabama minerals cheaper than it could mine and upgrade native ores. In 1950 T.C.I. purchased Turner Terminal Company of Mobile to receive some three million tons of Venezuelan ore a year.

Another change occurred in T.C.I.'s attitude toward company welfare programs. During the New Deal, government assumed many of the burdens previously borne by the company. With George Crawford gone and federal programs operating, T.C.I. phased out its Community Service Bureau in 1946. By that time only 10 to 15 percent of its employees still lived in company houses which were sold to employees beginning in 1948. New T.C.I. president Arthur V. Wiebel began closing down the medical and hospital programs in 1951.

Industrywide, Birmingham maintained its margin over other iron and steel producing cities. Jefferson County (Birmingham) led the South in the number of establishments employing more than 100 employees, with forty-three in 1947. Harris County, Texas (Houston) trailed in second place with thirty-four, and Dallas County, Texas, and Hamilton County, Tennessee (Chattanooga), tied for third with twenty-six. Birmingham also led in the number of production workers engaged in metal industries with slightly more than 30,000 to Houston's 18,600.

Alabama's statewide iron and steel employment grew from nearly 39,000 in 1939 to 61,000 in 1947, but Texas outpaced the state during the same period, gaining from 24,000 to 76,400. In 1947 the manufacturing value of the iron and steel industry in Alabama amounted to $208 million or 20 percent of the state's total industrial output. It funneled $132 million in wages into the economy that year. By 1939 the industry had made the port of Mobile the largest Gulf Coast shipper of steel products to domestic and foreign ports, although the city fell to second place behind New Orleans by the late 1940s.

The textile industry lagged behind iron and steel. Although Huntsville remained one of the largest cotton textile centers east of the Mississipi River, the nine mills operating in 1930 had fallen to three by 1945. In a town with only twelve small industries, these three mills were both critical and unstable. In January 1946, Merrimack Mill sold out to M. Lowenstein and Company of New York and changed its name to Huntsville Manufacturing Company. Under that name the company stabilized, and even constructed a third building in 1953. By the 1980s it was the only mill left in town. Dallas Mills followed the pattern of most other companies and sold its village houses to their residents in the mid-1940s, but that move did not substantially improve labor relations. A strike in 1947 crippled the plant. It reopened with only 300 employees, down from 700 when the strike began. In 1949 the mill closed permanently.

Not all mills entered the doldrums. Benjamin Russell had brought his three sons into the textile business, and they had shifted production to athletic wear during the middle of the Depression. This proved to be both an amazingly durable and profitable line and allowed Russell Mills to weather the 1930s in good shape. During the war Russell converted to military uniforms. When hostilities ended, the mills shifted back to athletic wear. So profitable was Russell Mills that the company dou-

The Lowe Cotton Mill, which went bankrupt in 1932, was converted into a shoe factory by the General Shoe Company in the 1940s. Eventually it too succumbed, a victim of cheaper imported shoes. In this picture made in the 1940s, women are sewing uppers together. Courtesy, Huntsville/Madison County Public Library

bled floor space and quadrupled production between 1945 and 1960.

Although the industry did not match the dominance of iron and steel within the region, textile manufacturing did remain a major sector of the state's postwar economy. In 1950 forty companies operated 72 mills in Alabama which employed 54,000 workers.

Another traditional industry, lumbering, also underwent changes. When James McGowin died in 1934 he owned 140,000 acres of largely cutover land. His three sons followed his lead in conservation and reforestation, paying careful attention to replanting, forest fires, and marketing patterns; but they had to contend with numerous problems. For one thing, national paper companies entered Alabama after the war, with Gulf States Paper leading the way. These companies began to buy up available land. In time Union Camp bought the W.T. Smith Lumber Company and closed the company town of Chapman.

The large companies had little experience operating in a southern environment and often struggled with problems. The major difficulty concerned provision of timber. In other regions lumber companies hired their own cutters. Whether because of unreliability of the work force or desire to avoid possible unions, medical liability, and other problems, Gulf Coast firms began to use the wood dealer system. Instead of hiring full-time em-

ployees, companies would contract with prominent people in a community—perhaps a sheriff, judge, attorney, or businessman—to provide a specified number of board feet of lumber annually. The local dealer, in turn, purchased wood from small farmers and independent cutters, who could get into the business with no more capital than it took to buy a secondhand log-hauling truck and a chain saw. Perhaps beginning by cutting timber on their own land, they might expand by harvesting trees belonging to neighbors. Some loggers became prosperous businessmen and substantial landowners themselves; others languished in a condition scarcely better than poverty. Sometimes high-handed local sheriffs and judges used coercion to furnish enough lumber to fill out a contract, but the system worked, and lumber and pulp production contributed a steadily rising percentage of Alabama's manufacturing wealth.

Although shifting patterns of industrial growth sometimes seemed haphazard, in actuality Alabama officials spent more time planning and soliciting than ever before. The State Planning Commission, created in 1935, was replaced in 1943 by the State Planning Board. In 1955 it gave way to the State Planning Board and Industrial Development Board. Some years later the Alabama Program Development Office and the boards were merged to form the Alabama Development Office. Unfortunately the agency was highly political, often furnishing governors a convenient place to employ highly paid campaign aides. Sometimes the political functionaries managed the position well; other times they performed poorly. Usually the key to the office's success was a vigorous governor who helped local community leaders approach potential developers. Governor George C. Wallace became so personally involved in industry hunting that he oftentimes gave potential new industrialists his own phone number to call if they had questions or problems. The legislature enacted an industrial revenue bond act in 1953 as a way of financing manufacturing growth.

Education also contributed to the campaign. In 1947 George C. Wallace, just released from the Army Air Force and a new member of the House of Representatives, sponsored a Regional Trade School Act. Using the Alabama School of Trades

as a model, he proposed to pattern four additional institutions on it and locate them at strategic points across the state.

Alabama officials were sometimes more unified on the desirability of new industry than were businessmen themselves. Persistent rumors circulated through Birmingham's business community that T.C.I. officials used their political clout to prevent automobile manufacturers from locating in the city because they feared competition for skilled workers or higher wage scales. In Montgomery some influential members of the Chamber of Commerce wanted to keep out industries that might introduce strong labor unions into the area. As a consequence pro-industrialists organized the Men of Montgomery in the early 1950s to recruit industry.

Huntsville probably experienced the greatest long-term success courting new plants. Concerned at the cloudy postwar future of Redstone Arsenal, the city established the Huntsville Industrial Expansion Committee in 1944. The committee real-

For veterans of World War II, black or white, the postwar years held great promise. However, blacks' efforts to end segregation would affect the kinds of jobs these veterans might be able to get. Courtesy, Tuskegee University

ized that new jobs must be created and to that end purchased a site near the University of Alabama Research Institute. The move proved fortuitous when the government reactivated Redstone Arsenal in the late 1940s as a rocket and missile research facility. When America's rocket program fizzled, the government decided to rely on former German scientists. Dr. Wernher von Braun had been sent to Fort Bliss, Texas, and resided there until the Korean War, when anxious officials, alarmed at the technological successes of the Soviet Union, transferred him and a number of associates to Huntsville. At the previously deserted Redstone facility they began design and development of a whole series of advanced rocket engines including Redstone, Jupiter, and Saturn which ultimately carried Americans into space and to the moon.

Aerospace firms began to fill the site purchased earlier along the Tennessee River. I.B.M., Lockheed, and Northrop located plants there. Some local firms developed to fill the need for engineers. Brown Engineering Company, founded in 1953 by five local businessmen who borrowed $50,000 for capital, specialized in research, engineering, and manufacturing related to aerospace technology. By 1964 the firm employed 3,000 people, paid a weekly payroll of $422,500, and had established branches in Houston and Cocoa Beach, Florida. The Huntsville Planning Commission, established in 1948, helped the Chamber of Commerce in a vigorous expansion effort.

Perhaps Huntsville recognized earlier than any other Alabama community that future manufacturing growth depended on factors never before prominent. Attracting what would soon be called "high tech" industries required quality education and facilities, a clean environment, cultural amenities, beautification, professionally competent public employees, and efficient local and state governments. Such requirements placed Alabama, and indeed the entire South, at a distinct disadvantage. At the end of World War II research scientists were five times more numerous in the nation as a whole than in the South. Southerners took out patents at a rate less than one-third the national average. Education lagged at all levels. Few regional universities contained distinguished fac-

Mobile's shipyards made an average of one ship a week in addition to repairing and overhauling thousands of others during World

War II. This photograph of the launching of
the SS Touchet was made at ADDSCO on
November 20, 1943.

ulties working at the frontiers of their disciplines.
Even states that tried to fund education ade-
quately suffered from low per capita income that
strangled state budgets. Most southern states, including Alabama, were slow to grasp the new
trends. No amount of courting or financial favors
could convince a technical firm to locate where
there was no pool of highly skilled technicians and
scientists, where employees could not acquire
graduate degrees or enroll their children in decent
schools, or where racial strife imperiled domestic
tranquility.

Despite Alabama's generally dismal record on
such issues, some farsighted leaders perceived the
future clearly. In 1941 Thomas W. Martin, president of Alabama Power, helped organize the
Southern Research Institute in Birmingham. Sur-
viving at first mainly on military and engineering
projects, S.R.I. slowly emerged as a major state resource. By 1952 it employed eighty-eight scientists
and staff and conducted $600,000 worth of re-
search a year. Though a small beginning, at least
a few people of vision were prepared to offer leadership in a new and troubled world.

Mobile did not aggressively seek new industry
after World War II, relying on established
firms, the state docks and Brookley Air Force
Base to provide jobs. Brookley seemed secure
during the Cold War years, but began phasing
out in the 1960s, finally closing in 1967. The
resulting loss of thousands of civilian and military jobs had a catastrophic impact on the
port city. Courtesy, Mobile Press Register

Chapter 6

TWILIGHT TIME
AND NEW BEGINNINGS

JIM'S PLACE
CAFE

CENTRAL S
PAR
OPEN 2

HOT DOG BAR
HAMBURGER 10¢ HOT DOG 10¢
Coca-Cola

MOBILE
CA M CREDIT CO.
ANS
DANGER
WATCH FOR CARS

RCH 1, 1948

Remote from Alabama, events occurred which dramatically altered the state's economic life. The Supreme Court decision in the case of Brown v. Board of Education of Topeka, Kansas, finally resolved the legal question of whether racially segregated schools violated Constitutional guarantees of equality. The unanimous 1954 decision sent tremors through the South. Southerners mobilized for a last stand which would be as tenacious, if less heroic, than gray clad soldiers had mounted in defense of the South ninety years earlier. Businessmen played a major role in the ensuing drama.

The initial crisis occurred in Montgomery. A number of factors converged to cast Alabama's capital city in the national spotlight. A young minister, the Reverend Martin Luther King, Jr., became pastor of Dexter Avenue Baptist Church, located only one block from the capitol. Political division within the city created a leadership vacuum. And the Men of Montgomery organized to try to invigorate the city's economy by attracting industry. The Montgomery bus boycott, which pioneered the strategies of America's civil rights movement and furnished its most important black leaders, crippled the city for 381 days, from December 5, 1955, until December 21, 1956. When blacks selected their own seats on city buses in early 1957 some whites responded with a wave of bombings and violence that jolted the city's leaders.

Montgomery's business community was alarmed by the impact of racial conflict on their attempts to recruit industry. Rumors circulated that the city had lost a Dupont factory and four other plants during the months of turmoil. The Men of Montgomery, consisting of forty businessmen determined to diversify the economy, adopted as a theme "We Mean Business," but the slogan rang hollow in the midst of such conflict. Their campaign to build a new terminal at the airport gave way to the racial confrontation downtown. Privately they tried to mediate between the city's white politicians and black boycott leaders. Their efforts failed but established an important precedent. Believing that a connection existed between a community's image on race relations and its record of economic growth, businessmen became a major force for racial moderation. In the aftermath of a series of January 1957 bombings, Montgomery's newspaper editors, white ministers, and businessmen spoke out against terrorism. The Men of Montgomery went even further, warning quite specifically that the city's economy was stagnant, its image besmirched, and its future imperiled. Although in retrospect their statements seem mild, such public stands demanded a great deal of moral courage in the mid-1950s.

Nearly a decade of conflict followed the Montgomery bus boycott with numerous symbolic clashes and some physical ones. At the University of Alabama, Governor George C. Wallace tried to prevent admission of black students. In Birmingham racial tensions grew steadily in an atmosphere where white civic, religious, and business leaders ignored their responsibilities for the welfare of the community. Threats of violence or social ostracism quieted the few who believed that actions had to

Above: *After Mrs. Rosa Parks' arrest in Montgomery for not giving up her seat for a white passenger on December 1, 1955, blacks in the state capital boycotted public transport for over a year until the U.S. Supreme Court banned segregation on the city's buses. Courtesy, UPI/Bettmen Newsphoto*

Opposite: *With the expansion of the state docks and new downtown construction, Mobile continued to grow in the postwar era. Courtesy, University of South Alabama*

be taken to implement peaceful change. Major industries such as U.S. Steel played no appreciable role in defusing the potentially explosive situation. The crisis steadily worsened following the 1961 freedom rider incident when civil rights workers were beaten with the acquiescence and connivance of local police. Bombings of black churches and homes preceded school desegregation which began in the fall of 1963. Finally the bombing of a black church which killed four young black girls as they put on choir robes and the loss of numerous industrial prospects forced businessmen to act. Biracial groups such as the Young Men's Business Club, the Downtown Action Committee, Community Affairs Committee, and Operation New Birmingham determined to stop the violence, reach a racial accommodation, and start the city moving economically. Sid Smyer visited with President John F. Kennedy, then returned to Birmingham with some frank advice to fellow businessmen: "If we're going to have good business in Birmingham, we better change our way of living. I'm a segregationist from bottom to top, but gentlemen you can see what's happening. I'm not a damn fool . . . We can't win. We are going to have to stop and talk to these folks." And talk they did. The various new organizations brought together leaders of both races to work toward common objectives, including improved economic opportunities.

Paradoxically, at a time when racial violence undermined efforts to attract new industry, Alabama's business and political leaders were conducting an unprecedented campaign to entice manufacturing. Birmingham's Chamber of Commerce established a metropolitan development board and hired a director. The board's task was to diversify the city's industrial base. Governor Wallace tried to help. He had sponsored a bill to provide industrial bonds for new factories while in the legislature. As governor he actively solicited industry.

The state had much to offer both in natural resources and financial enticements. Between 1958 and 1961 Alabama, Louisiana, Mississippi, South Carolina, and Kentucky granted tax exemptions to new industry valued at $143 million. The states offered millions more in revenue bonds to finance factory construction. Alabama purchased a fleet of

mobile classrooms ready to be located on any plant site needed to train workers. Governor Wallace sponsored the most ambitious educational program in the state's history which resulted in one of the nation's most extensive networks of community colleges and trade schools. The state tried to tell its story through national media. A March 1966 advertisement in *Business Week* announced: "Alabama has got what industry looks for. Our Cater and Wallace Acts finance $50 million plants as easily as $50 thousand plants."

Even large national companies began to respond to such inducements. Of 212 firms utilizing Alabama's industrial development bonds, 46 (21.7 percent) were national corporations with stocks listed on one of the major stock exchanges. Between 1952 and 1960 their average investment per job created amounted to $2,448. During the years 1961 to 1968 this figure rose to $20,473, a 740-percent increase. State revenue bonds seemed especially attractive to low wage, labor-intensive industry, but less important to skilled high-tech

Protesting the refusal by white election officials in Dallas County to allow blacks to register to vote. Dr. Martin Luther King, Jr., led the historic Selma-to-Montgomery march in 1965. In this photograph, taken on the second day out of Selma, Rev. Ralph Abernathy catches up on the news while Dr. King leads the marchers. Courtesy, UPI/Bettman Newsphoto

191

firms. The industries which located in Alabama during these years might have done so anyway; but the state subsidy in the form of industrial bonds was probably the deciding factor in many cases.

Alabama's manufacturing growth seems to have been largely unaffected by the Montgomery and Birmingham crises despite the dire predictions of business leaders. More racially moderate states such as Georgia, Florida, Texas, North Carolina, and Tennessee grew faster, but other factors explained their progress.

Some isolated incidents did occur in addition to the general economic stagnation of Montgomery and Birmingham. When Hammermill Paper Company announced its decision in 1965 to locate in racially troubled Selma, clergymen and civil rights leaders threatened to boycott the company. The message was not lost on other national firms contemplating investment in the state.

During these troubled times many of the state's entrepreneurs became reluctant advocates of racial moderation, not so much out of personal conviction as from economic necessity. However reluctant they may have been, they often took the first uneasy steps toward reducing racial tension and ensuring compliance with law. They sometimes acted at considerable risk to themselves and ahead of religious and educational leaders who might have been expected to show more vision. When the racial crises eased most of them gladly returned to more pedestrian and appropriate concerns and left politics to a hopefully more enlightened generation.

Actually industrialists had their hands full trying to cope with rapid changes in American manufacturing. Foreign competition and technological change imperiled Alabama industry at two points. Aging steel and iron plants in Birmingham, Annis-

ton, and Gadsden could no longer compete with new Japanese and German factories built after the Second World War. Imported automobiles not only threatened the domestic steel industry, they also closed down many auto parts factories in the Tennessee Valley. America's commitment to free trade hit hardest at "smokestack" industries. In this sense Alabama's economy was similar to Pennsylvania's and Michigan's rather than to other Sun Belt states. Long the South's industrial leader with the region's heaviest concentration of union members, Alabama suddenly found such prominence more liability than asset. This new insight seemed a terribly unfair irony to business leaders who had labored for 100 years to develop Alabama's heavy industry. Just as they succeeded, America entered the post-industrial age.

The Magic City of Birmingham had clearly lost its magic. Pipe shops that had prospered since the

Opposite, below: The textile industry, Alabama's largest employer after World War II, saw a steady increase in sales of imported fabrics and a steady decline in the number of jobs in Alabama mills. However, when this photograph was made at the Dan River Cotton Mill at Alabaster in 1955, the state still had well over 100 mills operating. One in every five persons employed in Alabama factories worked in mills such as this. Courtesy, Birmingham Public Library

Below: Alcoa Corporation was one of Mobile's largest employers for over thirty years from just before World War II until 1982 when it closed its doors. Imports of bauxite and exports of aluminia, shown here being loaded in 1955, had been a valuable part of the port activities. However, shifting market conditions, international competition, aging facilities and rising labor costs all conspired to bring an end to this part of Mobile's industrial economy. Courtesy, University of South Alabama

Located next to the L & N Railroad yards, with abundant supplies of coal and iron ore close at hand, the Sloss Furnace complex continued to be a productive part of the Birmingham economy for nearly a century. When this picture was made in the 1950s, Sloss belonged to the Alabama Cast Iron Pipe Company (ACIPO). Courtesy, Sloss Furnaces National Historic Landmark

Above: The 1950s saw a severe decline in Alabama coal and iron production as many mines were shut down forever. This is a photograph taken about 1960 of one of Birmingham's oldest, the Sloss-Sheffield Bessie mine, which had opened in 1905, as men leave at the end of their shift. Courtesy, Sloss Furnaces National Historic Landmark

turn of the century began to lose money, then closed altogether. Between 1950 and 1970 the city lost more than 25,000 steel-related jobs and the cornerstone of its historic economic structure. The last underground hematite iron ore mine, Pyne Mine near Bessemer, closed in the 1970s.

The decline of one major industry would have been traumatic, but Alabama had to grapple with problems stemming from the collapse of two. Competition from the Orient eroded the state's major manufacturing employer, the textile industry. In 1962 Alabama contained 125 textile plants employing about 40,000. Apparel manufacturers and other finished product plants employed an additional 21,000. One of every five persons employed in Alabama factories worked in the industry, and one in every eight dollars paid in manufacturing wages came from the mills. They used one-fourth of all electricity consumed by industry in the state, more raw cotton than Alabama farmers grew, and employed more women than any other industry.

Some companies managed to cope. Russell Mills in Alexander City prospered with its line of athletic uniforms. In 1959 the mills' twenty-three million garments sold for $29 million. By the early 1960s the company operated six mills, which occupied two million square feet of floor space, employed 3,700, and paid more than $12 million annually in salaries. Russell Mills had become America's largest manufacturer of athletic uniforms.

The Alexander City Company was an exception to the rule. Elsewhere textile factories went out of business with discouraging regularity. West Boyl-ston Manufacturing in Montgomery closed and Opelika Manufacturing entered receivership. Because the industry was widely dispersed in small towns its decline was especially painful. Often a small community's only source of industrial employment, the closing of a mill affected it much more dramatically than in larger cities which might attract alternate sources of employment.

Economic malaise affected the entire population. At a time when racial violence had tarnished the state's image, and when economic opportunities had struck bottom, many of the state's people migrated elsewhere searching for better lives. Well-educated Alabama students of both races decided not to return home where opportunities seemed so limited and turmoil so constant.

Across the state business leaders worked valiantly to reverse the decline. In Birmingham they helped elect a series of racially moderate mayors—Albert Boutwell, George Seibels, Jr., and David Vann. Seibels persuaded voters to approve the city's largest bond issue of $50 million to reinvigorate the economy. With the proceeds from the

The Alabama State Docks was one of Mobile's largest employers when this picture was made in the late sixties. The stevedores are shown unloading general cargo which has gradually been supplanted by bulk shipments of grain, coal, and forest products in recent years. Increased mechanization has led to a reduction in the number of stevedores the port employs even as its overall tonnage rises. *Courtesy, University of South Alabama*

bonds, he began the Birmingham Green Beautification Program, the Birmingham-Jefferson Civic Center Complex, Morris Avenue restoration, the Red Mountain Expressway, and expansion of the Municipal Airport and Legion Field. Governor Wallace belatedly appropriated money to construct the interstate system through the city, unsnarling one of the worst traffic problems of any large American city. The economy began to diversify as Birmingham became a major center of health care, education, research, utilities, telecommunications, finance, and insurance. Rapid expansion of the University of Alabama in Birmingham made that institution the city's largest employer and mirrored the transformation from an industrial to a service economy. Research grants poured in as the University of Alabama, Birmingham

medical college recruited a distinguished faculty. Outside funding exceeded U.A.B.'s state appropriations by a ratio approaching ten to one.

Older industries tenaciously held onto life. U.S. Steel began a multimillion-dollar modernization which did not result in appreciably higher levels of employment but at least made the Fairfield plants technologically competitive again. Some cast-iron pipe shops such as ACIPCO and McWane survived. McWane even expanded and diversified, purchasing Empire Coke Company (formerly DeBardeleben Coal), SIMSCO foundries, Atlantic States Cast Iron Pipe Company, Union Foundry, and American Foundation Insurance. Although cast-iron pipe and fittings remained McWane's basic product, it did place itself in a more favorable competitive position. Hugh

Above: *After World War II, Wynton "Red" Blount built the family business, Blount Brothers Construction, into a major construction company with projects all over the globe. Blount has also served in a variety of political positions, including United States Postmaster-General, and as the major philanthropic supporter for the Alabama Shakespeare Festival in Montgomery. The Blounts gave the Alabama Shakespeare Festival its $21.5 million theater complex. Courtesy, Auburn University Archives*

Left: *The Turner terminal complex was one of Mobile's largest privately owned docking facilities. Its facilities for handling bulk commodities such as iron and coal, shown here, attracted TCI, which purchased it in 1950 to handle three million tons of Venezuelan iron ore a year. Courtesy, University of South Alabama*

Bigler brought a new technology to an old industry when he established Southern Electric Steel in 1954, an electric furnace operation.

Montgomery's businessmen put aside their bickering over the city's economic future when the Men of Montgomery became the industrial arm of the Chamber of Commerce in the late 1950s. In 1958 Montgomery's metropolitan area provided only 6,675 industrial jobs, far less than the smaller town of Huntsville, but by 1976 the area's 239 manufacturing establishments employed 13,216 and provided a payroll of $110 million a year.

Montgomery's industry varied widely. Union Camp located a paper mill employing 300 across the Alabama River from the capital. Blount Brothers Construction earned an international reputation for its skill in building highly technical

facilities such as Air Force wind tunnels, atomic piles, missile bases, the Atlanta air terminal, and the Cape Canaveral rocket launch complex. Red Blount took time away from his business for public service during the late 1960s, serving both as president of the U.S. Chamber of Commerce and as Postmaster General in the Nixon administration. In the 1970s he resumed direction of Blount Brothers, skillfully managing the acquisition of a number of companies. The business expanded its construction projects to include the New Orleans superdome as well as the $3.4-billion University of Riyad in Saudi Arabia. In the process, the company grew into a one-half-billion-dollar-a-year worldwide giant.

Opelika compensated for the loss of textile jobs by attracting a Uniroyal tire plant and by the

Above: *Thanks in large part to TVA projects, north Alabama enjoyed a wealth of recreational opportunities on the Tennessee River and its manmade lakes. Sail and power boating enthusiasts flocked to the area, its appeal further enhanced by five state parks. These facilities helped attract business and industry to sites throughout the Tennessee Valley after World War II. Courtesy, Huntsville/Madison County Public Library*

Opposite: *Despite the expansion of the Alabama State Docks and more tourist-oriented activities, Mobile's growth in the 1950s was not spectacular. The city retained much of its pre-war look through the decade, with the revolution brought by urban renewal and interstate highway construction yet to come. Courtesy, University of South Alabama*

growth of Ampex Corporation and Diversified Products. Ampex became a national leader in magnetic tape technology and Diversified pioneered a new line of athletic equipment for a nation entering the first stages of a health and physical fitness craze.

One traditional industry that remained strong was lumber. By the 1960s Alabama produced more timber than any other southern state. Despite years of cutting and the virtual exhaustion of the state's longleaf pine forests, Alabama remained one of the most extensively wooded southern states. In 1971 forests covered 21.3 million acres or 65 percent of the state's land, a decrease of only two percent since 1963. As farmers abandoned land that had borne crops for 100 years or more, fields sprouted undergrowth, scrub pine, and sweet gum trees. Experts at Auburn University brought order to irregular forestry procedures by explaining proper management to small wood lot producers as well as to large family-owned companies.

Dean Gjerstad's research with chemical herbicides at Auburn demonstrated that pines grew much faster when farmers sprayed surrounding vegetation which competed for nutrients. Pines relieved from such competition remained healthier and more resistant to the ravages of pine beetles.

Alabama's climate suited the industry perfectly. Research indicated that pine trees growing in the state experienced virtually no dormant period during the year. Heavy annual rainfall, high humidity and temperatures, and a mild winter of only three month's duration combined to produce mature pines in a shorter time than in other regions. As a consequence the most promising future for America's timber industry seemed to be in the Gulf South.

Although the industry remained strong, it did undergo change. Demand for southern pine was pegged to the housing market. General economic problems quickly affected the volatile housing industry, causing lumber sales to slow. As a conse-

quence the forest products industry was highly cyclical.

Most Alabama timberland also remained in small tracts. Wood industries owned 4.1 million acres of timber and the government another million acres, but farmers owned 7.6 million acres and businessmen, doctors, lawyers, and estates another 9.1 million. Dispersed ownership resulted partly from the Alabama legislature's 1967 decision to exempt timber from ad valorem taxes.

Lumber interests successfully argued that treating growing trees as property to be assessed constituted double taxation because lumber was taxed again when it was sold. As a result Alabama, which boasted the lowest property taxes in the nation, exempted timber from ad valorem levies.

Small sawmills which had flourished since the appearance of logging trucks fell upon hard times. In 1971 Alabama had 323 sawmills, only one-half the number active in 1962 and one-tenth those operating in 1946. Yet the remaining mills increased the timber harvest by 70 percent between 1962 and 1971. Loggers cut 30 percent more softwood (mainly pine) in 1972 than in 1963.

Consolidation and greater efficiency characterized the industry. Many small firms could not compete and merged or were bought out. The number of large mills cutting in excess of three million board feet annually increased from 74 in 1962 to 135 in 1971. These large mills paid higher wages and utilized new technology. Chipping head rigs produced more chips and less sawdust than conventional band and circular saws. Production figures reflected the mechanical advances. In 1951 the average Alabama sawmill produced less than one million board feet annually. By 1962 the average had increased to almost two million; by 1971 the average stood at almost 4.5 million. Although the industry did become more sophisticated, producing three times as much wood veneer in 1971 as nine years earlier, it continued to provide mainly basic products. In 1971 the state supplied more pulpwood than any other Gulf state, mainly for the paper mills which had moved in. Alabama remained one of America's top producers of pine poles for power lines.

Natural resources also constituted the basis for another industrial giant. In 1956 Vulcan Materials emerged from a merger of Birmingham Slag and Vulcan Detinning of New Jersey. The northern corporation offered what Birmingham Slag needed: capital to support expansion, widespread business recognition, listing on the New York Stock Exchange, capabilities for research and engineering. Birmingham Slag offered Vulcan access to the nation's interstate highway business, one of the most promising economic ventures of the 1950s.

Charles Ireland devised the conceptual part of the merger and corporate lawyer Bernard "Barney" Monaghan handled negotiations. Effective December 31, 1956, Birmingham Slag became Vulcan Materials. The new company issued stock worth $10 million. During its first year Vulcan earned $3 million on sales of $37 million. In 1959 Ireland advanced to the chairmanship of the board and Monaghan became president. Together they devised a strategy for expanding Vulcan. They acquired Union Chemical and several southern aggregate companies, which established the firm

both in chemicals and the midwestern construction materials market. Sales jumped several hundred percent. Then they bought out the Lambert brothers' rock crushing operations in Tennessee, several Georgia and North Carolina rock quarries, and a number of family-owned concrete businesses. In less than four years Vulcan Materials became the nation's largest aggregates producer, spreading from its original base in the deep South as far north as New Jersey and Wisconsin.

Under the leadership of Houston Blount, who left Blount Brothers' Construction to work for Vulcan, the company broadened its operations to include Saudi Arabia, China, and Latin America. Its products ranged from chemicals, metals, oil, and gas to construction materials. With more than 6,000 employees, Vulcan Materials became a Fortune 500 company and one of the most prosperous industries headquartered in Birmingham.

Southern Natural Resources, Inc., was another old Birmingham company that adopted a broader economic vision. During the twenty years between 1960 and 1980 the company grew rapidly and diversified. Annual revenues increased more than twelvefold to nearly $1.5 billion, and earnings increased to $109.4 million in 1979. Southern Natural Gas Company's pipeline network, begun so modestly in 1929, extended 7,800 miles fifty years later and delivered 600 billion cubic feet of gas a year. The company invested heavily in offshore oil and gas exploration through SONAT Exploration Company. By 1979 it owned eighty-nine oil and gas lease blocks in the Gulf of Mexico and one in the Atlantic. A subsidiary, the Offshore Company, owned and operated one of the world's largest fleets of offshore drilling rigs and ships. SONAT also owned oil and gas leases in some two million acres onshore in the South and Rocky Mountains. It helped map and develop Alabama's own gas resources around Tuscaloosa, in Baldwin County and Mobile Bay, and off Dauphin Island and Gulf Shores.

Like Vulcan Materials SONAT diversified into both related and unrelated industries. In 1969 the company acquired Georgia Natural Gas Company. It also formed a joint venture with Boise Cascade Corporation, gaining control of more than 400,000 acres of prime southern timberlands. In 1969 the companies began construction of what was then the world's largest paper mill complex at De Ridder, Louisiana. Together they controlled some $450 million worth of timberlands, paper, pulp, plywood, and lumber mills. Under the direction of Henry C. Goodrich, the corporation formed Southern Natural Resources in 1973, a holding company suited to its varied businesses.

Industrial cycles proved as painful to SONAT as to U.S. Steel. Oversupply of oil and gas rigs built during the 1970s energy crisis resulted in decreasing demand. Falling petroleum prices hurt most energy companies, especially those heavily involved in exploration. Heavy losses in Iran due to political revolution there also eroded profits, but the company remained a flagship of the state's economy, and its new corporate headquarters in Birmingham's First National-Southern Natural Building helped transform a skyline that had changed little since the 1920s.

The decision of American Telephone and Telegraph to reorganize also contributed to Birmingham's new landscape. During the 1970s A.T.&T. created a new division, South Central Bell, and established its headquarters in the Magic City. The infusion of highly skilled computer operators, engineers, and management-level people broadened the city's economic base and added an impressive building downtown.

Birmingham also prospered from the burgeoning growth of the insurance industry. Of seventy-six Alabama companies licensed to sell insurance, twenty-nine were headquartered in Birmingham. TORCHMARK Corporation led the way as one of America's largest and best managed companies. It began in 1900 when a group of Huntsville textile men organized a fraternal benefit society by issuing certificates. In a flourish of patriotism they christened their new company the Heralds of Liberty. The concern did not prosper and in 1903 a group of Michigan businessmen bought it and transferred it to Detroit. The troubled company remained in the Midwest only one year before a Philadelphia group bought and transferred it again. It remained in Philadelphia from 1904 until 1927 when it returned to Birmingham. After a name change to Liberty National it became a life insurance company in 1929 with assets of about 1.3

Frank Samford built one of the nation's largest insurance companies, Liberty National Life Insurance, and supported a wide range of philanthropic activities. His lifelong devotion to and financial support of Howard College was recognized in 1965 when the school changed its name to Samford University in his honor. Courtesy, Knox Collection, Auburn University Archives

million. The company suffered through hard times during the first half of the Depression, nearly collapsing in 1929 when it could not remove deposits from a Birmingham bank for fear such action would close the bank. In 1931 Liberty National introduced a line of industrial insurance (life and burial insurance paid for in small weekly payments) which proved the company's salvation. The years from 1936 to 1940 brought prosperity, with dividends of 10 percent each year and total assets which increased from $3.51 to $6.44 million. During these years ordinary life insurance grew from $30 to $40 million while industrial insurance nearly doubled in force to $47.8 million. In 1944 Liberty National purchased Brown Service Insurance Company, an important early acquisition.

The chief architect of the company's recovery was Frank P. Samford. A native of Troy, Alabama, and a graduate of Auburn University, Samford descended from one of the state's most prominent families. His grandfather had served a term as governor and his father was a successful Montgomery attorney. Frank Samford and a cousin took over the insolvent Heralds of Liberty in 1921 and nursed it back to health. By 1941 he had transformed Liberty National into a $100 million company. At his death in the 1970s it was the leading insurance company in the Southeast and one of the twenty largest stock life insurance companies in America. His philanthropies extended to many causes but especially to his namesake school, Samford University.

Perhaps the next best-known insurance firm in Birmingham was the Booker T. Washington Company. A.G. Gaston, founder of the firm, was born in 1892 and began his business career at age eleven selling rides on a swing at his Demopolis home in exchange for buttons and pins. He moved to Birmingham with his mother and attended Tuggle School through the tenth grade. During the First World War he served in the army, then returned to Birmingham to work at T.C.I. making railroad cars and mining coal. His entrepreneurial skill had suffered no decline during his military service; he sold box lunches at T.C.I., opened a peanut and popcorn stand, and lent money at an interest rate of twenty-five cents on the dollar collectible every two weeks. He also organized a burial society that ultimately became Booker T. Washington Insurance Company. From such humble beginnings he formed Smith and Gaston Funeral Directors, Booker T. Washington Business College, and the Citizens Federal Savings Bank. His insurance company and bank were the largest black-owned facilities of their kind in Alabama.

Like Samford, Gaston invested both his money and energy in his adopted hometown. In 1963 he provided bail for Martin Luther King, Jr.; terrorists bombed his home in retaliation. He was kidnapped in a racially related incident in 1976. In 1968 he provided $50,000 to begin A.G. Gaston's Boys Club. The club grew to a membership of 2,300, affording recreation and opportunity to black boys from deprived backgrounds. He also established a revolving loan fund for black students attending local universities.

Companies such as Vulcan Materials, SONAT, Liberty National, and Booker T. Washington rep-

resented an important component of Birmingham's economic recovery. All of them had existed for a long time but experienced important growth in the 1960s and 1970s. Rust Engineering fitted the same pattern but was also typical of a new trend in American industry. Many firms became engineering-intensive even if engaged in a traditional industry such as construction. The levels of complexity and sophistication demanded such expertise. Rust Engineering provided conventional Alabama industries state-of-the-art technology. The company specialized in design and construction of highly automated pulp and paper plants, a staple item in Alabama's late twentieth-century economy. The firm also built U.S. Steel's mammoth seamless pipe mill at its Fairfield works.

Actually the company was no Johnny-come-lately to Birmingham. The Rust family had joined the trek from Pittsburgh to Birmingham in the

first years of the century and founded Rust Engineering in 1905. Like Birmingham Slag it had remained a family-owned engineering and construction company until the Rust family sold it in 1967 to Litton Industries, a defense and electronics firm. The company then sank into a sea of corporate mergers characteristic of the times. In the early 1970s Litton sold Rust to Wheelabrator-Frye of Hampton, New Hampshire. The parent company merged in 1983 to form Allied-Signal, the sixteenth largest corporation in America. Rust gained both national exposure and international business as a result of the mergers. Although its headquarters remained in Birmingham where 1,100 of its 1,800 employees worked, the firm established offices in Pittsburgh, Portland, Oregon, and Singapore. In 1985 Allied-Signal reorganized its complex operation with Rust International absorbing some new construction responsibilities within a sub-

group called Kellogg-Rust, Inc. As often happened in such corporate mergers, the future of the company depended on decisions made in corporate boardrooms elsewhere, but Rust seemed destined to play a significant role in Birmingham's engineering future.

Huntsville provided an even more significant insight into the world of high technology and engineering. When the U.S. Army reactivated

The United States Army Guided Missile School began operations in 1952 with one instructor and seven students meeting in this abandoned ammunition loading building which was left over from World War II. From such humble beginnings the modern Redstone Arsenal and Marshall Space Flight Center in Huntsville have developed. Courtesy, Huntsville/Madison County Public Library

Above: *Dr. Wernher von Braun, pictured here in 1955, left Huntsville in 1970 after serving ten years as director of the Marshall Space Flight Center. Thousands of people bid him farewell. Courtesy, Huntsville/Madison County Public Library*

Opposite: *The centerpiece of high-tech Huntsville is the Marshall Space Flight Center. Its crowning achievement was the program which put a man on the moon using rockets developed in Huntsville. These technicians are working on the F-1 engines which powered the Saturn V, America's moon rocket. Courtesy, NASA*

Redstone Arsenal in 1949, Huntsville was a sleepy Tennessee River town of 17,000 inhabitants. The next year the military transferred 130 German scientists, 500 military personnel, 180 General Electric technicians, and 120 Civil Service employees to Huntsville as the vanguard of a work force to come. In February 1956, the U.S. Army established its Ballistic Missile Agency at Redstone,

and in July 1960, the National Aeronautics and Space Administration officially opened the largest of its ten facilities, the George C. Marshall Space Flight Center. The center, directed by Wernher von Braun, assumed responsibility for planning and directing America's non-military space activities with special responsibility for design and development of launch vehicle systems. The testing facility formally dedicated in the fall of 1960 cost $100 million. From Huntsville's Marshall Center America figuratively launched its manned space flight program.

The economic boom that resulted reminded old-timers of Birmingham's frenetic growth in the decades following 1900. The Marshall Center, whose 1964 budget of $1.7 billion provided employment for 9,000, led the way. Dozens of private aerospace firms rushed into the city, flourishing in a symbiotic relationship with NASA. By 1963 thirty-one such companies employed 10,500 engineers, scientists, and technicians. Local people established Brown Engineering and Space Craft, Inc. Space Craft, established in July 1961 with seven employees, designed launch vehicle instrumentation systems and conducted advanced engineering studies concerning space problems. Its first year's sales reached one million dollars, a figure which nearly tripled in 1962. By 1964 Space Craft employed 250 people. National firms such as Boeing, Chrysler, General Electric, Lockheed, Northrop, RCA, and many others opened plants or research facilities in the city.

The economic impact of such vast spending concentrated in a decade and a half transformed Huntsville. Manufacturing employment actually declined from 14,000 to 8,000 between 1957 and 1963 as textile mills closed, but government employment doubled to 20,000 during the same period. NASA employees spent an estimated $100 million in the area during 1962. Huntsville's population increased seven times to 120,000 and the median family income rose 166 percent; the average 1962 income per household of $6,695 led the state.

Such growth brought negative side effects. A compact town with lovely historic buildings suddenly became a sprawling metropolis scattered over thousands of acres and filled with drab apartments and hastily constructed fast-food restau-

rants. Longtime residents raised questions about the price Huntsville paid for progress. The city's mayor told a reporter from *Fortune* magazine that many citizens wondered "why in the hell did it have to happen here—as long as we've got buttermilk and cornbread we're all right? They don't want you to move a bush. But we've got to. We've got to change."

And Huntsville did change. Marshall Space Flight Center acquired one of the largest collections of electronic computers in the world. Increasing numbers of engineers from Auburn University, Georgia Tech, and the University of Alabama settled in the city. The sense of local pride in the space program became almost proprietary. A local writer, sitting with two children of German engi-

neers the day astronaut Alan Shepard blasted into space, shouted at lift-off, "children, that's our Dixie doin' it."

Not all the problems associated with the space industry stemmed from environment and too-rapid growth. In a sense the fifteen years of frantic activity had transformed Huntsville from one kind of single-industry town into another type of single-

When Apollo 11 successfully landed on the moon, all Huntsville celebrated the achievement. As part of that celebration, crowds carried Wernher von Braun, head of the Marshall Space Flight Center, through the city's streets. Von Braun's dream of manned space flight had been fulfilled. Courtesy, Huntsville/Madison County Public Library

industry town. By the mid-1960s Huntsville derived 90 percent of its income from aerospace activities. At first local business leaders assumed this new industry would be immune from the cycles that had plagued textiles. Unfortunately they were wrong.

Completion of the manned lunar missions and new spending priorities necessitated by the war in Southeast Asia ended the city's spectacular growth. Huntsville lost 17,400 NASA-related jobs in the decade after 1965. Before Marshall Center employment stabilized at about 5,200 in 1977, the city suffered substantial economic dislocation. "For Sale" signs sprouted in neighborhoods like fall mushrooms. Boarded-up restaurants dotted new avenues, and business leaders confronted the

President John F. Kennedy and Vice-President Lyndon B. Johnson visited Redstone Arsenal in September 1962. Also pictured are General R.M. Hurst, Deputy Commanding General, Ballistic Missiles, and Dr. Wernher von Braun **(background, left).** Courtesy, U.S. Army Missile Command

specter of the late 1940s all over again. How could they diversify the economy to absorb thousands of highly skilled workers laid off by the government and more thousands of semi-skilled laborers displaced by the decline of textiles?

Vigorous industrial promotion solved the problem. Relying on traditional attractions (cheap TVA power, excellent Tennessee River barge transportation, a plentiful industrial water supply, strategic location midway between Birmingham and Nashville, a large pool of unskilled and semi-skilled labor) and new appeals (cultural amenities, the concentration of high-tech industry), business leaders made their case. They attracted a steady stream of non-aerospace light industry including tire, chemical, machinery, and metal manufacturers. Between 1965 and 1978 Huntsville added 14,000 new non-NASA industrial jobs, for a total manufacturing employment of 86,000. During the two decades following 1965 the city added one billion dollars in industrial investment and 34,000 new jobs. Nearly 12,000 jobs resulted from the location of 87 new firms in the city, the rest from industrial expansions.

Although the city's economy was far more diversified than ever before, the core remained the Marshall and Redstone facilities together with the aerospace firms related to them. While Marshall Center employment fluctuated widely, U.S. Army employment at Redstone remained steady. Department of Defense civilian employment also held constant at about 10,000.

Huntsville's experience highlighted a new era of industrial growth. Critical to most of the new firms was the city's quality of life. A close relationship to the University of Alabama in Huntsville provided local expertise and important cultural and educational opportunities. A clean environment, beautiful landscape, and excellent recreational facilities helped attract high-tech firms.

Taking a cue from Huntsville's experience, the state's universities became more directly involved in industrial growth and problem-solving. Budgets for higher education, especially at critical institutions such as Auburn University, and the three University of Alabama campuses in Tuscaloosa, Birmingham, and Huntsville, increased dramatically.

In 1971 the Alabama legislature passed stringent anti-pollution laws to control irresponsible industry. The new water quality act levied daily fines of up to $10,000, the highest in the Southeast. Although state officials selectively administered the laws governing strip mining, air and water pollution, even a modest effort improved the possibility of attracting more environmentally sensitive industry. Finally Alabama seemed on its way into a new industrial era.

Above, left: *As the port of Mobile has grown over the years the nature of the cargo it handles has changed. More and more of the goods arrive in containers ready to reship via road or rail. Giant cranes, such as this, are used to handle cargo, reducing the number of stevedores employed by the port, but increasing its efficency and competitive position among the Gulf ports. Courtesy, Mobile Press Register*

Top: *Huntsville's growth brought many of the problems of urban sprawl found throughout America. Courtesy, Huntsville/Madison County Public Library*

Above: *On May 25, 1971, President Richard Nixon came to Mobile to inaugurate construction of the Tennessee-Tombigbee Waterway. In this photograph, President Nixon greets Governor George Wallace at the dedication ceremony in Mobile. Courtesy, Mobile Press Register*

Birmingham, Alabama's metropolis, has grown far beyond its beginnings a century ago as a center for Alabama's coal and iron industry. Now the view from Red Mountain is of a modern cityscape with skyscrapers housing home offices for a variety of national and regional companies. Gone too is the smog and coaldust haze which once blanketed the valley when the old open-hearth furnaces flourished. Photo by Michael Thomason

Chapter 7

A RENEWED VISION

FOR THE 21ST CENTURY

labama in the 1980s shared the nation's economic upheaval. A serious depression during the first years of the decade closed factories and sent unemployment spiraling above 16 percent. Foreign imports continued to weaken the steel, textile, and automotive parts industries. New businesses in the service sector anticipated a promising future. Tourism gained rapidly as a chief source of revenue, and Huntsville strengthened its position as a major research and technology center. Survival in an increasingly unstable and complex manufacturing economy demanded adaptation and imagination.

Although foreign imports of steel and textiles cost those industries markets and jobs, many Alabama companies survived because of improved equipment, productivity, and specialty markets. The U.S. Steel facilities in Birmingham modernized, installing the most up-to-date equipment and producing more distinctive products. The city's iron pipe shops also trimmed down to a lean, competitive work force. Marginal operators lost out to the most efficient firms which managed to survive and even prosper in a narrower market.

Consolidation dominated traditional Alabama industries. The number of timber companies continued to decline in the 1980s even as production increased. Improved technology and a favorable climate placed Alabama in an excellent long-term economic position. Economists projected a doubling of southern timber production by the year 2000 in order to satisfy demand, a prospect that ensured steady growth.

Insurance experienced the same phenomenon of mergers, buy outs, and takeovers. In 1979 and 1980 Liberty National's Chief Executive Officer Frank P. Samford, Jr., orchestrated the purchase of Globe Life and Accident Insurance Company (headquartered in Oklahoma City), United Investors of Kansas City, and United American Insurance Company of Dallas, Texas. In a period of less than two years Samford spent $500 million, transforming Liberty National from an insurance company selling one product in one region into TORCHMARK, a widely diversified corporation selling life, health, and accident insurance and financial services in a national market. In the acquisition of Globe, he also gained the services of Ronald K. Richey, a lawyer by training who became president and chief executive officer of TORCHMARK when Samford retired and moved to chairman of the board in 1984. The company's string of consecutive earnings and dividend increases between 1952 and 1985 exceeded any other company's listed on the New York Stock Exchange. Earnings in the early 1980s grew at the rate of 20 to 25 percent a quarter. The new subsidiaries increased profits 55 percent in 1984 and 57 percent during the first half of 1985. In that year assets reached $3.5 billion with almost $45 billion of life insurance in force and estimated revenue of one billion dollars.

Above: In 1979 Frank P. Samford created Torchmark, an insurance holding company, and built it into one of the fifty largest insurance companies in the United States and the largest life insurance company in Alabama. Courtesy, Torchmark Corporation

Opposite: The crew of Spacelab conducted experiments in such areas as solar physics, astronomy, life sciences, and atmospheric physics. Here astronauts determine heart functioning under weightless conditions in the Spacelab simulator at the Marshall Space Flight Center in Huntsville. Courtesy, NASA

Above, left: *William J. Rushton III has piloted Protective Life Insurance Company to a position of respect in the industry. He has also been active as a civic leader in Birmingham where the company has its home office. He has been an officer of the company since 1954 and has served as president and CEO since 1967. Courtesy, Protective Life Insurance Company*

Above, right: *The founder of several large businesses, including the Booker T. Washington Life Insurance Company, Birmingham's first black millionaire, nonagenarian Dr. A.G. Gaston continues to play an active role in his company. His economic success has been accompanied by a life of activism on behalf of full civil rights for all Alabamians. Courtesy, Birmingham Public Library*

Samford and Richey represented a new breed of sophisticated, knowledgeable chief executives who competed successfully in a national market. In 1984 the *Wall Street Transcript* gave its Gold Award as one of America's top executives in the life insurance industry to Frank Samford, Jr. The following year the magazine presented its award to Samford and Richey.

Other insurance companies prospered also. Protective Life Corporation, although not as diverse as TORCHMARK, operated a highly regarded universal life program under the imaginative direction of William J. Rushton III. Rushton also became deeply involved in developing new and more professional leadership in the city of Birmingham.

One of his co-workers in civic endeavors was Louis J. Willie, vice-president of Booker T. Washington Insurance Company. Willie, a native of Fort Worth, Texas, came from a family of limited education and means, but one committed to a better life for its children. Their sacrifices made it possible for him to enter Wiley College, but war interrupted his schooling in 1943. Following two years in the army, he entered business school at the University of Michigan in 1946 on the G.I. Bill. He washed dishes at a fraternity house in exchange for meals. After earning a master's degree in Business Administration in 1947, he taught at Tennessee State University briefly, then worked as an office manager in Nashville. In 1952 A.G. Gaston began searching for a controller for his insurance company. While attending a national Republican convention, a friend from Memphis recommended Willie. Gaston hired him and the eager young businessman rose rapidly through management. By 1985 Willie was a director of Citizens Federal Savings Bank and executive vice-president of Booker T. Washington Insurance Company. He headed day-to-day operations although the remarkable A.G. Gaston, then 93, continued to work at his office for several hours each morning. Willie maintained Gaston's quiet activism in 1984 when he and an attorney became the first black members of the downtown Kiwanis Club.

If insurance seemed the most stable Alabama industry, textiles seemed the most vulnerable, but even that industry emitted mixed signals. Historically textiles had experienced a series of major geographical shifts; the center of production moved from Great Britain to New England in the nineteenth century, and from New England to the South in the first half of the twentieth. In the 1980s many predicted a third shift to Asia.

Some experts remained more optimistic about the industry, if not about jobs. In 1984 American textile production reached an all-time high, though it did so with a labor force some 15 percent smaller than a decade earlier. Although increased mechanization threatened the loss of additional jobs by century's end, it also held the prospect of new materials and markets. The future of the traditional industry based on all-natural fibers looked bleak, but the manufacturing of blends of natural and synthetic fibers held its own in the 1980s due to increased mechanization. And rapidly advancing technology promised a boom in new textiles.

America led the world in new kinds of fibers. Some experts viewed this technology as the second phase of a revolution that began fifty years earlier when scientists developed chemical synthetic polymers. Many of the new textiles combined fibers and plastics. These "geotextiles" or "geomembranes" provided fiber-plastic sheets increasingly employed in road building, drainage, erosion control, waste disposal and stabilizing building foundations. By the mid-1980s the market for such textiles used in construction grew at a phenomenal rate of 25 percent a year.

Other fibrous composites possessing tremendous strength and stiffness despite their light weight replaced metals in aerospace construction. They served as stiffeners for fuselages in transport planes and comprised 70 percent of the airframes of new fighter aircraft. They also replaced coaxial cables in telephone systems and found widespread use in fiber optics.

Non-woven textiles provided new uses as wrapping or sealing materials. Hospital clothing, bedsheets, and disposable diapers all used such substances. This use also integrated two important southern industries, forestry and textiles. Timber companies increasingly explored the possibilities of non-woven textiles as a hedge against overreliance on housing and pulp production.

The success of such efforts depended heavily on factors that had long determined the future of southern manufacturing: high entrepreneurial ability, large-scale capital investment, and linkage between the frontiers of scientific/technological/industrial research and the application of this research to manufacturing.

This linkage of theoretical research and applied industrial technology held the key to Alabama's economic future. Education played a central role,

The Neutral Buoyancy Simulator at the Marshall Space Flight Center in Huntsville approximates the zero gravity of outer space and serves as a training ground for many of the astronauts. In this 1981 photograph the space-suited engineers are experimenting with a mobile work station. Courtesy, NASA

Since its opening in 1970, the Alabama Space and Rocket Center has become a major tourist attraction. Today it features an extensive "rocket park," the Spacedome Theatre, bus tours, and a space camp for junior high students.

Courtesy, Huntsville/Madison County Public Library

especially those units of major universities willing to work closely with industry. The University of Alabama began such a project in 1982 when its professors undertook research into possible cost-efficiency measures at a General Motors plant near Tuscaloosa. Such research, fostered by the cooperation of both GM and the United Auto Workers, cut costs by $1.5 million and saved a plant from closing. The bilateral cooperation worked so well that two additional firms, Stockham Valves and Tuscaloosa Steel, entered similar arrangements. Then in 1985 Alabama Power Company gave the university $300,000, to be matched by $150,000 from the school, to establish a "productivity center." The center provided the services of university experts to help recruit new businesses and make existing companies more productive. The center, housed in the College of Commerce and Business Administration, helped clients capitalize on the latest advances in technology, such as robotics, and in management techniques. Although the University of Alabama in Birmingham was not so directly involved with business, it contributed significantly to improving the quality of urban life.

Auburn University began a similar, more modest program both in business and engineering. Through its cooperative extension program the university had long engaged in academic-industry cooperation in forestry and textile engineering. Auburn completed a $110 million-development drive in the early 1980s, one of the largest ever undertaken by a southern university. Modernization made possible by this funding put it in an excellent position to take advantage of the new scientific and engineering opportunities. Engineering specialists in robotics made the university a major center for developmental research. An interdisciplinary team of mechanical and electrical engineers and physicists won a $12 million contract as the lead school in a five-university consortium to design non-nuclear power systems. These systems would provide energy for space vehicles developed as part of America's Strategic Defense Initiative (S.D.I.) program.

The University of Alabama in Huntsville received a similar grant for laser research associated with S.D.I., the so-called "Star Wars" program. U.A.H.'s Center for High Technology, Manage-

The Ciba-Geigy plant in McIntosh, north of Mobile, today employs 1,100 workers and makes over 75 products. When the plant opened in 1951, there were only 32 employees making just one product: DDT. Ciba-Geigy has been joined by many other firms whose

plants, making primarily agricultural chemicals, are scattered from Mobile to McIntosh. Courtesy, Mobile Press Register

ment and Economic Research also provided the city assistance in attracting aerospace and computer firms. By the end of 1985 Alabama ranked second only to California in contracts granted for S.D.I. research. The army's Ballistic Missile Defense Organization, headquartered in Huntsville, received roughly one-third of the contracts which totaled $355.4 billion. Many private Huntsville firms, some of them homegrown such as Sparta, Inc. and Nichols Research Corporation, received contracts for computer software development for ballistic missile detection, interception, tracking, and destruction. Smaller contracts went to universities led by the project underway at Auburn.

As unusual as it seemed to rank second only to California in S.D.I.'s sophisticated research and development contracts, it seemed even stranger to woo and win international corporations. Taking a cue from the Carolinas which had long attracted European firms, Alabama officials discovered that the state's abundant raw materials could compete in an internationalized world economy. A Michelin Tire plant located at Dothan and hired more than 1,000 employees. Other French companies included Citadel Cement in Demopolis, C. and T. Chemicals near Mobile, and Liquid Air with plants in Decatur, Birmingham, and Montgomery. In the fall of 1985, Harbert Corporation of Birmingham entered into an agreement with France's Sita Corporation to construct solid waste facilities in the United States using Sita's technology. By the end of 1985 French firms employed 2,000 Alabamians.

Ironically, one of Alabama's most promising new industries utilized the skeletons of some of its oldest. Tourism had long been the major source of revenue for Florida, but Alabama's troubled racial past and poverty did not appeal to most travelers. Yet once again the state's amazing variety of natural resources waited for development. Some of its mountains in the northeast matched all but the highest Appalachian peaks, and many considered the stretch of beach from Pensacola to Mobile as good as any in the world.

In Birmingham citizens voted a bond issue to restore Sloss Furnace, a vintage turn-of-the-century iron furnace. Although its newly painted stacks no longer belched forth industrial pollutants, it provided jobs of a different kind, attracting thousands

Alabama Space and Rocket Center features hands-on exhibits and displays of actual rockets and other space-related hardware. It is a successful example of support by private industry, federal, and state government. Although many people find the displays like those in the main exhibit hall fascinating **(above)**, rides like the "Lunar Odyssey," in which space flight is simulated using centrifugal force **(opposite)**, are equally popular, especially with children. Courtesy, Huntsville/Madison County Public Library

Above: *The Riverview Hotel and office complex is a part of a major effort to revitalize downtown Mobile. In this view of construction, made a few months before the hotel's grand opening in June 1983, the nineteenth-century Pincus building is in the foreground. It was then being restored, and today houses offices and a bank. Courtesy, Mobile Press Register*

Opposite: *As part of Mobile's continuing efforts to attract tourists and in celebration of the nation's bicentennial, a portion of the eighteenth-century French Fort Conde was rebuilt. Since its opening in 1976 it has proved to be one of the city's top attractions and the keystone for plans to develop surrounding property. This is a photograph of the grand opening festivities in July 1976. Courtesy, Mobile Press Register*

of visitors a year to hear about, see, and even feel a heavy industrial world fast receding into memory.

When NASA cut back the Marshall Center in the 1960s, the agency helped Huntsville establish the Alabama Space and Rocket Center. It rapidly emerged as the state's premier tourist attraction, drawing nearly 686,000 visitors in 1984. Its economic impact, estimated at $10 million a year, boosted the economy both of Huntsville and Madison County.

The port of Mobile obtained the U.S.S. *Alabama* as the center of an aviation-naval exhibit on the shores of Mobile Bay. The city's historic preservation program began late but salvaged many of the older neighborhoods with lovely nineteenth-century homes. Its hint of Old World architecture and charm, its proximity to the Gulf of Mexico, and its profusion of brilliant early spring azaleas brought tourists in increasing numbers.

At the east end of Mobile Bay one of the least developed stretches of the Gulf Coast underwent a building boom in the early 1980s. Condominium developments with incongruous names such as Gulf Shores Plantation sprouted from the sand dunes. Wolf Bay and Orange Beach welcomed tens of thousands of tourists searching for warm weather, sparkling white beaches, and soft gulf breezes, which sometimes strengthened to menacing hurricanes and periodically reminded developers how fragile the coastal environment was.

As in earlier projects, developers with short-term goals made a bad name for all, and many local residents wished for more tranquil times; but Gulf Shores possessed too much beauty, too many miles of empty beaches, and too many down-home, friendly folks to maintain its pristine innocence. One national television network sent a reporter to film a story on Gulf Shores. He spent much of his time on camera recounting the hospitality and helpfulness of a truckload of local "good old boys" who piled out of their pickup to push his car out of the sand when he wandered off a main road.

Alabama's tourist industry became big business. It pumped tens of millions of dollars into the economy without polluting the state or adding large numbers of new residents demanding public services and necessitating chaotic growth.

Not only did Alabama develop new industrial patterns, it also attracted a new kind of leadership. In Birmingham the involvement of Bill Rushton III and Louis Willie symbolized a racial merging on behalf of the economic future of both races. A city that once symbolized America's racial divisions came to represent in the 1980s the determination of blacks and whites to live together in peace. For example, Birmingham citizens elected Richard Arrington mayor for two terms.

Elected mayor of Birmingham in 1979, Dr. Richard Arrington symbolized the Magic City's economic revitalization and its commitment to racial harmony. Mayor Arrington is seen here dedicating the new Jefferson County Courthouse in October 1986. Courtesy, Office of the Mayor of Birmingham

Born in 1934 to a sharecropper family in Livingston, Alabama, Arrington's family had moved to Birmingham where he attended high school and Miles College. He went on for his master's degree in biology at the University of Detroit, then in 1966 earned a Ph.D. in invertebrate zoology at the University of Oklahoma. He returned to Birmingham to teach at his alma mater, became dean of Miles College in 1966, then in 1971 executive director of an eight-college consortium, the Alabama Center for Higher Education. That same year he was

elected to the city council and in 1979 as mayor. His quiet professional leadership and his determination to involve whites in his administration helped avoid the extreme racial polarization that plagued Chicago, Philadelphia, and other northern cities. Although his political support came mainly from the black community, he won enough white votes to provide the critical winning margin in both mayoralty campaigns.

Birmingham also produced a woman whose meteoric rise broke solid male dominance of the city's

industry. Hall Thompson, a Vanderbilt graduate who built Thompson Tractor into the state's premier heavy equipment company, decided to retire and devote more time to his athletic interests. Having promoted both Samford University and U.A.B. basketball in order to bring big-time collegiate sports to the Magic City, he turned his attention to golf. His dream of a premier professional golfers' association course gave birth to Shoal Creek Country Club, one of the South's finest. When he retired he turned Thompson Tractor over to his daughter, Judith Thompson. A remarkable businesswoman, she skillfully managed the company and also played a major role in bringing horse racing to Birmingham. Her successful efforts to arrange a financial package for the Turf Club taxed her managerial skills but also provided a boost to the city's changing economy. Another woman, June Collier of Montgomery, became chief executive officer of National Industries, which employed 2,400 and sold $103 million in automobile wiring assemblies in 1985.

Alabama's political climate continued to provide mixed signals. Younger politicians offered a less personality-oriented future, but George Wallace continued to dominate the scene in the mid-1980s as he had for nearly a quarter century.

As CEO of National Industries, based in Montgomery, Ms. June Collier (below) directs a multimillion dollar business which employed 2,400 people and sold $103 million in automobile wiring harnesses in 1985. The photo (below, right) is a view of the plant floor. Courtesy, National Industries

In an attempt to influence the legislature more directly, the State Chamber of Commerce and Associated Industries of Alabama merged in 1985 to form the Alabama Business Council. During its first legislative skirmishes it succeeded in repealing a co-employee liability law which business claimed invited litigation between workers and disrupted business; but in a state long dominated by a conservative political climate, the alleged threats of liberal organizations seemed a shadow issue.

Perhaps the larger challenge was not a better organized political effort but a less adversarial relationship between management and labor. America's shrinking share of the world market and declining productivity cost workers their jobs and corporations their profits. As both sides suffered they became more inclined to make concessions. Following the record post-war unemployment levels of the early 1980s, union members primarily sought job stability. Their employers were willing to grant such guarantees in return for greater productivity. The compromise resulted in a period of labor-management peace. Businessmen also moved further away from the chaotic individualism of the nineteenth century. Although some continued to operate as if they bore no responsibility for the public welfare, the environment, or future generations, most adopted a partnership model of corporate enterprise. Civic responsibilities and philanthropies consumed a larger share of their time and resources.

Telephones are assembled in a two-phase process at GTE's Huntsville plant. Skilled workers undertake several operations, rather than repeating the same single task over and over again. In order to prepare workers for such jobs, Huntsville has emphasized quality education both in its public school system and also in the area's colleges and universities. Courtesy, Huntsville/Madison County Public Library

John Murdoch Harbert, III, made *Forbes'* list of America's 400 wealthiest Americans in both 1984 and 1985. His estimated wealth of $600 million came mainly from his construction business, much of it conducted in risky Third World countries. In 1984 and 1985 Harbert gave more than $7 million to Auburn University in order to upgrade and modernize its engineering facilities.

Although Harbert was the only Alabamian to make the 1985 *Forbes* list, other businessmen matched his philanthropy. In 1984 Montgomery

businessman Winton Blount decided to deed 100 acres of land and give $21 million to construct a theater complex to house the Alabama Shakespeare Festival. The festival had begun in 1971 as a professional summer repertory company in Anniston. By the early 1980s it had attracted both critical acclaim and a large and loyal following, but the physical facilities were inadequate and local support limited. Carolyn Blount served on the festival's board of directors and brought the theater's plight to her husband's attention. Blount made the project a family affair. His son Thomas, a Montgomery architect, used inspiration from the Renaissance architect Palladio for the massive and impressive theater. A Montgomery firm made the warm red bricks especially for the building, even naming them the Shakespeare Blend. The result of this cooperative endeavor was a masterpiece of architecture and drama, a blending that promised to improve Alabama's cultural life as much as its ailing economy. Blount's financial contribution, by some estimates, was the second largest of any gift made to the arts in America during 1985.

These new patterns of industry and entrepreneurship occurred within national and even international environments. The integration of Alabama's economy into this broader system gave certain areas a distinct advantage. Huntsville with its diversified industry stood poised to develop its share of high-tech industry. The term high-tech industry, the magical elixir of the 1980s, referred to companies relying on in-depth knowledge and application of advanced technology.

A 1982 congressional economic report identified twenty-four states with important high-tech employment. Alabama was not among the twenty-four. Unfortunately the study accounted only for statewide strength and ignored states which might contain one or more strategic centers of such industry. The report attracted considerable attention from economic planners because during the years from 1955 to 1979 high-tech industries accounted for 75 percent of the job growth in manufacturing.

For years Huntsville had sought to attract such firms, with an amazing record of success. Operating with a hefty budget of a million dollars a year, the city's development board sent a delegation of

Perched atop a Boeing 747, the Space Shuttle Enterprise *arrives in Huntsville. Marshall Space Flight Center developed the external tank, solid rocket boosters, and the main engines, and conducted the tests that enabled sistership* Columbia *to be launched. Courtesy, NASA*

seventy to California in early August 1982. They met with representatives of forty-four high-tech companies.

A study completed in 1985 revealed how successful such efforts had been. Comparing Huntsville to more famous concentrations of high-tech firms in San Jose, California, Raleigh, North Carolina (the Research Triangle), Orlando, Florida, and Austin, Texas, the report concluded that the Alabama town more than held its own. It ranked second to San Jose in the concentration of high-tech

workers to total employment, and Huntsville's scientists-engineers led in average salary. Within Alabama 35 percent of all the state's engineers worked in Huntsville.

The economic spin-off from high-tech employment was significant. NASA planned to spend about 40 percent of the $8 billion allocated for its manned space station at the Marshall Space Center. Much of the $9 billion designated for Star Wars research also found its way to Huntsville. The Marshall Center began to emerge from the shadows of Houston and Cape Kennedy and return to the role it played during the Redstone days. In September 1985, state officials announced that they would locate Alabama's new $22 million supercomputer at Huntsville because of its concentration of high-tech industry. The same year Boeing announced a major expansion of its Hunts-

ville facilities.

Such development had an enormous multiplier effect on the Huntsville economy. Harbert Construction Company and Kovach and Associates began a $60 million office park in November because the city was the fastest growing market for new business in Alabama. Planning began to connect Huntsville to Alabama's interstate system at a cost of some $300 million. Water, sewage, and housing projects got underway anticipating a doubling of the city's population to roughly 320,000 by the year 2000. During 1983 growth in personal income ranked ninth among all U.S. cities, increasing 10.7 percent over the previous year.

Despite such industrial prosperity Huntsville confronted historic problems. The city's economy remained too dependent on the high-tech sector and federal priorities. In Austin, Texas, the government employed 21.2 percent of all engineers. Comparable figures were 10.6 percent in Orlando, 18.9 in Raleigh, 20.1 in Mobile, and 7.2 percent in Birmingham, but in Huntsville government employment accounted for 52.3 percent of these professionals. The median age of Huntsville's

Above: Alabama's interstate highway system is ostensibly complete, though construction projects in Mobile, Birmingham, and Huntsville are still in progress. The volume of traffic has also necessitated upgrading older sections, as is being done in these 1986 Mobile photos. Courtesy, Mobile Press Register

Opposite: The construction of a bridge across the Mobile River delta completed the linking of Alabama's port city, via I-65, with the rest of the state. With the earlier construction (1973) of the I-10 Bayway and the George C. Wallace twin tunnels, the city now has uninterrupted interstate highway connections coast to coast and border to border. Courtesy, Mobile Press Register

engineers, 43.3 years, reflected the stability of government employment but was much older than Raleigh's average of 35. State universities had to produce and Huntsville firms recruit and retain a new generation of highly skilled engineers, mathematicians, and scientists.

Birmingham presented a more traditional and varied prospect for the future. More profoundly af-

President Frederick P. Whiddon and USA Board of Trustees member Ernest Cleverdon, two of the founders of the university, joined to celebrate its twentieth anniversary in 1984. From its beginning as a two-year branch of the University of Alabama, the University of South Alabama has grown to a major independent institution of higher education with graduate programs in a variety of fields, including a college of medicine, in just two decades. Courtesy, Mobile Press Register

fected by the economic convulsions of the previous decade, it loosened traditional ties to iron, steel, and textiles. Education and health care provided more jobs by 1985 than other industries. Utilities and wholesale and retail trade were the next most important employers. The insurance industry followed with some 10,000 jobs and banking came next with 7,000. By 1985 the insurance industry furnished about the same number of jobs as U.S. Steel had in 1979 before its significant job losses, and unlike steel, insurance was pollution-free and nearly depression-proof. Although Birmingham's ratio of engineers to total work force lagged behind Huntsville's, its total number ranked second in the South behind Houston.

Tourism, much of it associated with sports, invig-

orated Birmingham's economy. Hall Thompson's Shoal Creek development attracted a major P.G.A. golf tournament. The All-American Football Bowl game filled the city's hotels as did a number of University of Alabama football games and the annual Auburn-Alabama football game. Both the Sun Belt and Southeastern Conferences scheduled their annual basketball tournaments in the civic center convention complex. This wider economic base did not necessarily absorb displaced steel workers, but it did promise a more prosperous long-term future for the city.

Birmingham's image as a grimy industrial town battered by racial discord was hard to change. Although the image bore little resemblance to 1980s realities, the Metropolitan Development Board received a budget of only $200,000 a year to alter the image. That figure allocated to attracting industry compared poorly to Huntsville's investment of more than a million dollars annually. Chasing smokestack industry cost a great deal more than recruiting high-tech firms. Although the development board brought in many small factories, it failed to attract major new plants.

Put in perspective, Alabama's economy remained in the late twentieth century about where it had been a century earlier. It contained enormous resources but lacked the capital, leadership, and vision to fully develop its potential. Per capita personal income increased 8.6 percent from 1983 to 1984, which ranked thirty-first among all states and below the national average. The state's 1984 per capita income of $9,992 was only 78 percent of the national average and 89 percent of the average for the Southeast. Alabama ranked ninth in per

Opposite: The Medical College of Alabama, opened in Mobile before the Civil War, eventually found its way to Birmingham after World War II. It has prospered in the "Magic City" and its hospitals and medical research facilities are world renowned. Growing up around the medical school, the University of Alabama in Birmingham has become one of the state's major institutions of higher education and a key element in the city's high-tech revival. This is the Hillman Hospital which is the center of UAB's medical education program. Photo by Michael Thomason

SCHOOL OF MEDICINE

Opened as Alabama Medical College in 1859 in Mobile by Josiah C. Nott and other physicians as part of the University of Alabama. Closed by the Civil War in 1861, it reopened in 1868. Reorganized in 1897, it became the Medical Department and in 1907 the School of Medicine of the University of Alabama. The Mobile School was closed and moved to Tuscaloosa in 1920 as a two-year basic medical science program, which was offered through 1944.

Below: Mobile's aging Bates Field received a major renovation with the construction of the multimillion dollar M.C. Farmer terminal facility. Coupled with important improvements in its interstate system and the Tenn-Tom Waterway and major harbor improvement, the new structure exemplifies the style of the progressive leadership in Alabama and its port city. Courtesy, Mobile Press Register

capita income among southeastern states and tenth in per cent increase during that year.

But forecasts by the Federal Bureau of Economic Analysis contained better news. By the end of the century Alabama would gain some 324,000 new jobs with only a 202,000 increase in population. Heavy reliance on food manufacturing, textiles, farming, and apparel industries would decline, but increases in electronics, transportation, motor vehicles, trade and services, machinery, and fabricated metals would provide new opportunities. The increase in personal income, projected at 2.4 percent between 1985 and 2000, would lag slightly behind the national average of

2.6 percent, a fact accounted for mainly by the slow growth in highly skilled jobs.

Factors that would change the prediction and accelerate manufacturing growth depended largely on historic intangibles—education, leadership, and vision. Alabama could take a lesson from Florida, one of the Sun Belt's leaders. The 1970s Florida boom depended on certain basic elements, some of which Alabama contained: the advantages of geography, abundant cheap labor, low taxes, a cooperative state government, publicly financed industrial support, a good educational system, moderately affluent consumers, a relative absence of political demagoguery, overt prejudice, and racial up-

heaval, and a sophisticated, respectable image. Individual Sun Belt cities that flourished—such as Austin, Atlanta, and Houston—relied on the same advantages. Whether Alabama produces the leadership and vision to close the gap between other Sun Belt states in areas where it is lacking will determine how accurate are the economic forecasters.

Some things are certain. The same bountiful resources exist. Citizens possess the same tenacious spirit and the same desire for a better life, and creative and imaginative people still invest their futures in a gamble that new leadership and a renewed vision will finally bring together promise and reality.

Scott and International Paper Companies are located on the north side of Mobile. The city's largest industrial employers, Scott **(shown here in the foreground),** *and International Paper* **(above and to the left),** *produce a wide variety of paper products using the area's abundant timber and water resources. Both companies have been in Mobile for many years and are key components of the local economy. Courtesy, Mobile Press Register*

Despite price fluctuations, Alabama's reserves of oil and natural gas, concentrated in the southwestern portion of the state and offshore from Mobile and Baldwin counties, are an enormous asset. This offshore rig will sink a well 22,800 feet to explore for natural gas. Revenues from royalties, lease payments, and enhanced employment prospects all make this industry one of the state's most promising. Courtesy, Mobile Press Register

An employee of the Harco Drug Company, an Alabama pharmaceutical firm, is seen setting up an assembly line for the company's expanding operation. Photo by Chip Cooper

Above: *The McDuffie Island coal handling facility in Mobile is one of the nation's largest and most modern bulk handling operations. Photo by Michael Thomason*

Left: *One of Birmingham's first iron-making blast furnaces, the Sloss furnace historic site is now open to the public as a park and museum. Photo by Michael Thomason*

Above: *Cool autumn days bring a special beauty to Huntsville's residential neighborhoods. Photo by Chip Cooper*

Left: *An outstanding example of antebellum architecture, the President's Mansion in Tuscaloosa is open for public tours. Photo by Chip Cooper*

Visitors can perform a variety of hands-on experiments relating to NASA space flight programs at the Huntsville Space and Rocket museum. Photo by Michael Thomason

Outside at the Space and Rocket Center in Huntsville are examples of all of America's rockets from the V-2 to Saturn V, whose exhaust nozzles in the foreground dwarf visitors. Courtesy, Michael Thomason

The old iron smelting furnace, now a teaching museum and public park, is an interesting reminder of high-tech Birmingham's iron and coal roots. Courtesy, Michael Thomason

Right: *Electric power transformers, symbolic of the abundant energy that drives Alabama industry, are seen here in striking silhouette. Photo by Chip Cooper*

Below, right: *The University of Alabama system promotes advanced research to attract new industry to the state. Photo by Chip Cooper*

Left: *A barge makes its way down the Warrior River to deliver coal to the port city of Mobile. Photo by Chip Cooper*

Below: *The spectacular scenery of Little River Canyon in DeSoto State Park draws thousands of visitors to the region each year. Photo by Chip Cooper*

Above: *Powdery white-sand beaches meet the blue waters of the Gulf of Mexico on the islands in Mobile Bay. Photo by Matt Bradley*

Right: *Mobile's historic Fort Morgan has been restored and is now open to the public. The fort played a major role in the 1864 Battle of Mobile Bay. Photo by Matt Bradley*

Opposite: *Each spring Alabama is graced with blossoming dogwood trees, prolific throughout the state. Photo by Chip Cooper*

Huntsville's premier high-tech center, home of the Marshall Space Flight Center, was once the center of the state's textile industry. This view of its downtown skyline was taken from the Von Braun Civic Center. Courtesy, Michael Thomason

Top, right: *A dazzling display of white azaleas provides an appropriately elegant foreground for the Battle/Friedman mansion in Tuscaloosa. Photo by Chip Cooper*

Above: *This handsome spiral staircase is a distinctive feature of Oakleigh, Mobile's official nineteenth-century house museum. Photo by Chip Cooper*

*Mobile's shipyards still hum with activity,
turning out U.S. Navy and Coast Guard ships,
workboats, tugs, barges, drilling rigs, and
dredges. Photo by Chip Cooper*

New retail malls featuring upscale merchandise and pleasant surroundings are springing up all over Alabama. Photos by Chip Cooper

This picturesque railroad bridge, one of the longest wooden train trestles in the United States, spans the Warrior River in Tuscaloosa. Photo by Chip Cooper

The setting sun bathes this Greene County scene in pastel hues. Photo by Chip Cooper

Fort Conde and the restored City Hall can be seen in the foreground of this view of old and new Mobile. Photo by Michael Thomason

One of Alabama's most frequently photographed sites, the fountain at Court Square in Montgomery is both a city and state landmark. Photo by Wendell Metzen/Southern Stock Photos

An employee at Phifer Wire Products in Tuscaloosa is seen working at a wire loom. The
company, which makes window screens and
wire mesh, among other products, is an international business. Photo by Chip Cooper

Chapter 8
ALABAMA'S ENTERPRISES

The University of Alabama, with campuses at Birmingham, Huntsville, and Tuscaloosa, is actively promoting education in the burgeoning high-tech industries. Photo by Chip Cooper

The corporate and institutional biographies of the Alabama Enterprises, who helped make this volume possible, are illustrative of some important truths concerning not only Alabama but also American economic development.

In contrast to some of the world's industrialized societies, the United States did not develop its economy through the planning of any single group, individual, or agency. Instead, economic development has been largely left to the free market mechanism and the forces of capitalism. The role of the entrepreneur—alert for unmet needs, new opportunities, new products, and opportunities for expansion—is central to American economic history. The individual histories of the organizations that follow reflect the way in which Alabama businessmen and women and Alabama business and institutional entities have met those needs, seized opportunities, persevered through hard times, and soared during good times.

The biographies also mirror the diversity present in the state. The variants of Alabama in geography, politics, and social and cultural life are matched by the diversity of the history of the regions and their economic development.

The colonial history of the state begins on the Gulf Coast in a Hispanic past that dates to explorations of the 1500s. The French established the first permanent settlement in the early 1700s at the terminus of a watershed encompassing six rivers making their way to the sea through a great bay that became known as Mobile. The Southern port city of the same name would always be primarily water oriented in its economic development. The beginning was river traffic of fur-laden canoes, which progressed in the antebellum period to barges and steamboats bearing Alabama cotton to northern and foreign textile mills. When the Civil War permanently altered the cotton economy, Mobile's water trade diversified to timber, naval stores, coal, and products of the iron and steel industry developing to the north.

A century after the French settlement on the Gulf Coast, the story of Alabama's economic development jumped to the rich bottomland of the Tennessee River valley in the far northern reaches of the territory. Early pioneers such as John Hunt, who gave his name to the settlement of Huntsville, built cabins and staked claims to farmland. Richer "squires" followed the squatters into the region and set up a cotton aristocracy, and a virtual folk migration followed the War of 1812. Many of the early settlers were veterans of Andrew Jackson's militia of Indian fighters; they became the farmers, wagonmakers, carpenters, blacksmiths, and merchants of north Alabama. With marketing and financial structures integrated into the Mississippi River system and New Orleans, north Alabama's economic separation from the rest of the state contributed to economic and political regionalism.

Moving north of the wiregrass and Gulf Coast plain, the Black Belt region of Alabama—a crescent of rich black soil girdling the south-central area of the state—rivaled the Tennessee River valley in cotton growing, but developed later because an Indian population stymied the westward migration of Georgia settlers. Ultimately the city of Montgomery built its economic life around the cotton trade. The waterway linked the fortunes and the economic development of central Alabama with the burgeoning port city of Mobile, 345 miles downriver.

Thrusting between the Black Belt and north Alabama was the last wedge of the Appalachian Mountain range that trailed down the East Coast of the United States. The settlers of the rocky, infertile valleys and hills did not share in the bustling antebellum economic development of the other regions of the state. But the Civil War and the South's desperate need for iron and forges called attention to the real wealth of the region—the mineral resources of iron ore, coal, and limestone. Ironically, the disruption and impoverishment of the Alabama rural economy in the postwar South would furnish another necessity: an available labor force.

Enterprising Alabamians, followed in subsequent decades by outside entrepreneurs, flocked to the mineral region and engaged in real estate speculation, railroad building, and industrial development. Isolated mining camps and small communities grew up beside deposits of iron ore and coal. New urban centers, such as Anniston, Gadsden, Bessemer, and, most important, Birmingham, sprouted in previously sparsely populated valleys. Mines, quarries, blast furnaces, and steel plants spawned hundreds of industrially related businesses, suppliers, and services.

Although cotton was no longer the sole focus of Alabama's economy, technology and the New South movement brought textile mills south to the home region of the raw materials. Thousands of rural Alabamians left farms to enter the mills.

But the story does not, of course, stop with the period of the New South, nor does it remain static. As the nineteenth century progressed, an expanding transportation system transcended some of the regional divisions of the state. Local enterprises often became part of major national corporations as consolidation became the hallmark of American "big business." National and international economic cycles influenced times of boom and bust for Alabama business and industry.

The twentieth century brought the technological promise of automobiles, radios, indoor plumbing, telephones, and electricity, as well as the diversification of business opportunities that such developments promised. The new century also brought the Great Depression. Birmingham, now the largest urban center in the state, earned the dubious distinction of being labeled the worst-hit city in the nation. In 1945—for the first time in Alabama's history—more of the state's citizens worked in industry than on farms. The postwar decades saw such dramatic changes as the development of a high-tech space industry in Huntsville. In Birmingham, the industrial heart of the state, the largest employer was no longer a steel company but a university-medical center complex.

The organizations whose stories are detailed on the following pages have chosen to support this important literary and civic event. They are a mixture of the recently founded juxtaposed against the long established, of the small family enterprise beside the corporate giant, of the locally owned contrasted with the subsidiary of an international corporation, of the service oriented beside the product oriented, of the educational institution beside the business that needs its graduate; but more important, the mosaic is the story of enterprising individuals within a particular time and place.

—Marlene Hunt Rikard

THE BUSINESS COUNCIL OF ALABAMA

The Business Council of Alabama (BCA) serves as a unified voice in promoting free enterprise, healthy economic growth, and a favorable business and industrial climate for its membership as well as for Alabama's entire business community.

The Business Council was established in 1985, when the Alabama Chamber of Commerce and Associated Industries of Alabama consolidated to form a single, major organization to represent the state's businesses and industries.

BCA is comprised of some 60 business classifications, both manufacturing and nonmanufacturing, from a two-employee partnership to a 10,000-employee textile operation. The average member company has fewer than 50 employees.

In a variety of areas the Business Council seeks to achieve goals that would enhance the lives of all Alabamians:

1. To promote the general welfare of the State of Alabama by advancing its educational, civic, social, commercial, and economic interests.

2. To encourage the establishment of new industries as well as to further agricultural, commercial, and recreational pursuits in Alabama.

3. To identify and define governmental, educational, industrial, and other types of problems affecting Alabama business and industry; to encourage cooperative action to address these problems; and to act as a united spokesman for business and industry on matters of national and statewide interest.

4. To maintain the integrity and

Built in 1848, this Greek Revival antebellum home was purchased from the Teague family in 1955 to house The Business Council of Alabama. Listed on the National Register of Historic Places, the house was one of the most pretentious in Montgomery at the time of the Civil War. In 1865 it was occupied by Wilson's Raiders as division headquarters, and martial law was declared from its portico. Some 50 of the council's members financed the purchase of the residence not only as a home for the council but also to preserve it as a showplace in the state capital.

efficiency of the free enterprise system.

5. To cooperate in bringing about equitable and efficient government administration and to encourage interest in governmental affairs.

6. To promote fair and amicable relationships between employer and employee and a closer affinity between agriculture, education, business, and industry.

7. To engage in research and publicize the findings to enhance public understanding of issues affecting business and industry.

The Business Council of Alabama has become the state's preeminent representative of business and industry. Through its efforts progress is being made in areas such as environment, industrial relations, health care cost containment, international trade, and governmental relations. The Alabama business community is unified as never before, and better able to speak with one voice on issues affecting the lives of all of the citizens of the state.

ASSOCIATED GROUP SERVICES, INC.

"People business" always interested Henry Wallace Willoughby. That interest took him from selling books door to door for a publishing concern in order to put himself through college to a career with a major employee benefit company and then to establishing his own business—Associated Group Services. Recently AGS was absorbed by a major national joint venture operation, where Willoughby serves as president of various TPAs.

A math and physics major in college, Willoughby joined Blair, Follin, Allen, & Walker, Inc.—an employee benefit company—after graduation, owing to his sales experience and the counsel of a friend who was a stockholder in BFAW. Later to become Corroon and Black Benefits, Inc., BFAW was a predominant firm in group insurance and specialized in trade association business.

Willoughby worked the western third of his native Kentucky. In 1967 he was sent to Birmingham to start operations for the company in Alabama. He was given a force of six salesmen brought in from other states.

When BFAW merged with another organization in 1970 Willoughby decided the time was right to begin his own venture, Willoughby & Associates, Inc., a consulting insurance agency. In 1982 he founded Associated Group Services to provide third-party administrative services to his clients. The two firms coexisted, with Willoughby acting as president of both.

Drawing upon his experience in working with trade associations, Willoughby contracted with Associated Industries of Alabama (AIA) to manage all of the insurance programs. AIA, the largest employers' organization in the state, included firms that ranged in size from the very large to the quite small. For all members, but of particular benefit to the smaller, insurance programs obtained through the association offered benefits that could not be obtained if acting alone.

Henry Wallace Willoughby, president.

In 1985, alert to the changes occurring in the insurance field, Willoughby considered several offers from hospital companies seeking third-party administrators. In 1986 Associated Group Services was bought by HCA-Hospital Corporation of America. Later that year HCA and The Equitable Life Assurance Society of the United States formed EQUICOR-Equitable-HCA Corporation. The new joint venture operation links the largest hospital company in the world—owning and/or managing 480 hospitals worldwide—and the nation's third-largest insurance firm. Principal offices will be in New York City and Nashville, headquarters of HCA, but the Association Division of EQUICOR will be based in Birmingham.

When he was 17 years old, Willoughby was awarded a trip to the "shocking big-city atmosphere" of Pittsburgh by the book company for which he was working; in his first year the young man from rural Kentucky had become the number two salesman among thousands of college students. His pattern for a future career was set: He always appreciated a challenge and he enjoyed working with people. The merger of Associated Group Services, Inc., into EQUICOR allows him to continue along both paths.

ALABAMA GAS CORPORATION

Although Alabama Gas Corporation was formed in 1948, the roots of the company can be traced to the antebellum period in Montgomery and the New South period in Birmingham. In 1852 the city council of Montgomery granted a franchise to John Jeffrey and Company of Cincinnati, Ohio, to provide manufactured gas for street lighting.

Later John Jeffrey and Company sold its rights, and the Montgomery Gas Light Company was organized. The subsequent history of the organization would be one of mergers, diversification, innovation, and numerous name changes.

With the invention of the incandescent electric lamp, the use of gas for street lighting began to wane. As a result, the firm diversified and in 1898 changed its name to Montgomery Light & Power Company. Alabama Power Company purchased the enterprise in 1923 but sold the gas properties to Alabama Utilities Service Company in 1929. That organization, under the control of Central Public Service Corporation of Chicago, had been formed to acquire the gas properties of Alabama Power.

In the meantime other manufactured gas distribution systems were developed elsewhere in the state: Selma, 1854; Birmingham, 1880; Anniston, 1897; Tuscaloosa, 1901; and Gadsen, 1905. Through a complex series of mergers and acquisitions, the growing Alabama Utilities Service Company began to absorb the smaller manufacturing systems.

In 1936 Alabama Utilities Service Company came under the control of Southern Natural Gas Company and changed its name to Alabama Gas Company. That same year Southern Natural gained control of Alabama Natural Gas Corporation, which had constructed natural gas systems in Auburn, Heflin, Leeds, Opelika, Reform, Tuskegee, and Wetumpka in 1929 and 1930, and which had acquired the distribution system in Huntsville in 1930. Those operations were

In the early days most of the work involved in laying main was done with picks and shovels. Today most of the work is done with heavy machinery.

merged into Alabama Gas Company in 1946.

The creation of Alabama Gas Corporation came two years later with the merger of Alabama Gas Company and Birmingham Gas. The origin of Birmingham Gas was in

Birmingham Gas & Illuminating Company, chartered in 1878—seven years after the city's birth. That enterprise was also destined to have a complicated history of name changes and reorganizations. In 1887 a new firm, Birmingham Gas and Electric Light Company, was formed because of the electric light systems started in 1886. Burdened with debts, the company was sold at public sale two years later, and another new corporation, Birmingham Gas, Electric Light and Power Company, resulted. The name was quickly shortened to Birmingham Gas Company.

In 1890 the sale of gas and electricity became separate enterprises, with Birmingham Gas and Consolidated Electric Light Company each holding an exclusive franchise for the sale of its services in Birmingham. In 1901 the gas company and electric light services were again consolidated under the auspices of the Birmingham Railway Light & Power Company (BRL&P); however, BRL&P suffered in the 1907 panic and was in receivership from 1910 to 1924. Birmingham Electric Company purchased the assets and

An Alabama Gas construction crew from the mid-1950s takes time out for this photo.

in 1929 transferred by deed all of its gas properties to a newly formed Birmingham Gas Company.

That same year Birmingham Gas entered into a 10-year contract with Southern Natural Gas Corporation for delivery of natural gas through its new pipelines from Monroe, Louisiana, to Birmingham and Atlanta. The Birmingham gas companies had previously used manufactured coal gas, manufactured water gas, and, in the 1920s, coke oven gas.

In 1945 Southern Natural purchased almost 85 percent of Birmingham Gas' common stock. Southern Natural then owned both Alabama Gas Company, headquartered in Montgomery, and Birmingham Gas. The merger of these two businesses in 1948 created Alabama Gas Corporation.

Southern Natural owned approximately 98 percent of the common stock of Alabama Gas Corporation until 1953. That year Southern Natural was forced to di-

One of the earliest locations of the Birmingham offices of Alabama Gas (right) and its replacement (below), built in the same location in the early 1960s.

vest itself of all its distribution subsidiaries, and Alabama Gas Corporation became an independent organization.

During World War II material shortages created problems for Alabama Gas; the firm needed additional gas supplies, particularly as postwar demand increased. Purchasing all the area's available supply of coke oven gas by 1946 and finding it insufficient for its needs, Alabama Gas began a program of converting to natural gas, which was

completed in 1954.

The 1960s saw the birth of a new corporate symbol—a little Indian boy with a blue feather in his headband to represent a blue flame. The little Indian, called "Alagasco," made his debut in the 1960 annual report. As the firm's advertising expanded, Alagasco became Alabama Gas to the public and remained the company's symbol for nearly two decades.

Alabama Gas was also making innovations on the technological front, placing the nation's first liquified natural gas plant in service in Pinson Valley in 1965. In 1979 Alagasco Energy Company, a subsidiary created in 1971, entered into a highly successful joint venture for drilling in Fayette and Lamar counties and another joint venture in West Virginia. The energy company's exploration and production of gas and oil has continued in the 1980s.

Faced with the energy crisis of the 1970s, the management of Alabama Gas believed it would be advantageous to form a holding company with utility and nonutility subsidiaries. A holding company would separate the regulated utility's distribution function from its other activities. The firm's leadership wanted to expand its exploration program and develop other energy sources. The stockholders' annual meeting in January 1979 saw the birth of Alagasco, Inc.

Since the name "Alagasco" had been synonymous with Alabama Gas to the public for many years, the name of the holding company caused some confusion. That confusion was one reason for the change of the holding company's name to Energen Corporation in 1985. In addition, the name change represented the holding company's intention to further expand its role in the energy field. As a company spokesman noted, "Energen, a name that cuts across all energy-related businesses and is not geographically limiting, appropriately reflects the future growth and diversification of the company."

THE UNIVERSITY OF ALABAMA AT BIRMINGHAM

The first president of the University of Alabama at Birmingham (UAB), Dr. Joseph F. Volker, has often noted the symbiotic relationship of UAB and the host city. "One cannot flourish unless the other prospers," he observed. Although iron and steel provided the initial impetus for Birmingham's growth, that industry now languishes, its future uncertain; but the high technology and service-oriented economy that has created a healthier, more diversified city is symbolized by the evolution of the urban university.

UAB, currently enrolling 15,000 students, is now the city's largest employer with more than 10,000 faculty and staff and an annual payroll of $224 million. The entire community enjoys the university's cultural, entertainment, and sports programs. The city, state, and region benefit from the superior medical treatment available at the UAB Medical Center and from the training of health care professionals. The Birmingham community also profits from dynamic interaction with UAB research and service centers such as the Office for the Advancement of Developing Industries, the Center for Aging, and the Center for Urban Affairs.

The rapid development of UAB is tied to the growth and change of the city, as well as the meeting of statewide needs. The history of the university also merges the two separate educational developments: the expansion of a Birmingham extension center of the University of Alabama and the establishment of a four-year medical college for the state.

The Extension Center opened in 1936 in a converted clapboard residence at Sixth Avenue North and 22nd Street with 116 students. Returning servicemen benefiting from the G.I. Bill of Rights swelled the enrollment to 400 in 1946. Needing more space, the center spilled over to Phillips High School, and the board of trustees of the University of Alabama began planning for a new facility. In 1954 the Extension Cen-

The University of Alabama at Birmingham's campus features a mix of modern buildings intermingled with older structures put to new use.

ter moved to a new building on 20th Street South, and for the first time came into physical association with the medical center that had been developing on the city's Southside since 1945.

In 1945 no four-year medical school existed in the state of Alabama. After two years of basic sciences at the University of Alabama in Tuscaloosa, students had to leave

The UAB campus is noted not only for its medical and academic achievements but also as a focus of community cultural and entertainment activities.

the state to complete their medical education. Faced with the drain of medical students and practicing physicians, a committee appointed by the Medical Association of the State of Alabama studied the formation of a four-year institution.

Citizens of Mobile, Tuscaloosa, and Birmingham competed for the proposed school. The Citizens' Committee of Birmingham presented the strongest arguments: the city's central location, the proximity to Tuscaloosa, a fund of $160,000 to supplement the legislature's appropriation, and the donation of the Hillman and Jefferson hospitals as the teaching facility for the school. In 1944 Birmingham was chosen as the location for a four-year school of medicine under the board of trustees of the University of Alabama. The county conveyed the hospitals to the university, and the first class of 22 juniors started in October 1945.

That same year the state legislature established the University of Alabama School of Dentistry to be located in Birmingham; the first class enrolled in 1948. Dr. Joseph Volker—former dean of Tufts College School of Dental Medicine in Boston—came as the new dean.

Volker's organizational abilities and vision were important to the future of the young educational complex. In 1962 he became vice-president for health affairs, covering all the medical center units. Dr. S.

Richardson Hill, Jr., was named dean of the School of Medicine and Charles A. McCallum, dean of dentistry. In 1966, when the board of trustees decided to transform the Extension Center, now serving 4,600 students, into the degree-granting College of General Studies, Volker became vice-president for Birmingham affairs. The designation "UAB" came into use to cover the growing complex that now included the College of General Studies, School of Medicine, School of Dentistry, School of Community and Allied Health, and University Hospitals and Clinics. UAB was now one of three campuses of the University of Alabama System. In 1969 UAB was granted autonomy within the system and established its own administrative structure, which reported to the board of trustees. Volker became UAB's first president, serving from 1969 to 1976.

Guided by Volker and Hill, UAB's phenomenal growth continued. Physically, the campus absorbed

The roots of UAB's medical complex lie in the historic Hillman Hospital, which is now part of the institution's medical center.

a large area of the Southside through purchase and urban-renewal projects. Today the campus stretches across 64 city blocks with an eclectic mix of modern, new buildings and older structures modified for the university's needs.

However, the more important growth is reflected in health services, research, and degree programs. UAB first established a national and international reputation in health care, gaining particular recognition in cardiac surgery and later, in organ transplantation programs. Schools of nursing, optometry, and public health were added to the medical center.

The university now has 17 major health care facilities. The faculty and staff conduct an extensive range of research, ranking UAB among the top 40 public universities nationally in the amount of federal research grants and contracts awarded. The Graduate School, established in 1970, offers some 40 master's and 22 doctoral programs; undergraduates may obtain degrees through schools of business, education, engineering, humanities, natural sciences and mathematics, and social and behav-

Since a basketball program was launched in 1977, the UAB Blazers have won two conference titles and have been to the NCAA basketball tournament seven times.

ioral sciences.

In 1976 Volker became chancellor of the University of Alabama System, and Hill assumed leadership of the UAB campus the following year. Although a physician, Hill's interest was in the overall university, and he worked to continue UAB's rapid advancement to an institution of international reputation and caliber. When he announced his sabbatical and retirement in 1986, McCallum, senior vice-president for health affairs and director of the medical center, became acting president. In April 1987 he became UAB president.

From its beginnings the University of Alabama has grown and evolved with the city of Birmingham, but its combination of high-tech research, outstanding medical care, and degree programs extends its influence far beyond the city and the state.

AMSOUTH BANCORPORATION

The story of Alabama's largest bank begins with the dreams of a Swedish sea captain who sailed to America in 1833 to make his fortune. The captain's name was Charles Linn, the bank, AmSouth.

Linn indeed found prosperity as a prominent Montgomery businessman, and was sufficiently enchanted with the fledgling city of Birmingham to construct its first bank. Founded in 1872, The First National Bank of Birmingham was the first bank organized in northern Alabama under the National Bank Act. The institution was initially housed in a wooden structure, but the next year Linn bought a rear lot at First Avenue and 20th Street and built a three-story structure that, because of its unusual height, became known as "Linn's Folly." To celebrate the formal opening on December 31, 1873, the Calico Ball, the most famous social event of early Birmingham history, was held at the bank.

In 1883 the City Bank of Birmingham was incorporated into Linn's bank, the first in a series of mergers, becoming The First National Bank of Birmingham. After a 1902 merger with the Berney National Bank of Birmingham, growth was steady until 1930, when another merger occurred—this time with the American Traders Bank. That year deposits soared to $72 million. Oscar Wells, president of First National, became chairman of the board, and General John C. Persons, president of Traders, became president of the new and larger First National.

In those same eventful years six neighborhood banks became the institutions' first branches, beginning a tradition that now includes 143 AmSouth branches or affiliates across Alabama, more than any other bank in the state.

In World War II General Persons was called into active service as commanding officer of the 31st Infantry Division—the only break in his 37 years of service to the bank. In 1967 he retired as chairman of the board of directors.

Charles Linn, a Swedish immigrant and Montgomery businessman, founded The First National Bank of Birmingham, predecessor of AmSouth Bancorporation.

In 1940 the bank headquarters moved to a newly renovated building at First Avenue and 20th Street. This location remained the heart of its operations until 1971, when the bank moved into its present headquarters, the 30-story First National/Southern Natural Gas Building.

Growth continued through the 1950s under the leadership of John A. Hand and Harvey Terrell. In the early 1970s, with total deposits of $700 million, the bank ac-

quired Engel Mortgage Company. Robert H. Woodrow was named chairman and chief executive officer in 1972; John W. Woods, president since 1969, became vice-chairman of the board and M. Eugene Moor, Jr., president.

A significant step in the bank's development took place in 1972, when it became the lead bank and first affiliate of Alabama Bancorporation. Later that year American National Bank and Trust Company of Mobile and the First National Bank of Decatur affiliated with the new corporation. Woods became chairman of the board, president, and chief executive officer.

The corporation was the first financial institution in Alabama to record one billion dollars in assets, and by the end of the 1970s the $3-billion mark rapidly approached.

One of the people instrumental in that growth was Newton H. DeBardeleben, elected chairman of the board and chief executive officer of The First National Bank in 1976. Dan L. Hendley, who had served as

---

Known as "Linn's Folly" because of its unusual three-story height, The National Bank of Birmingham building was completed in 1873 at the corner of First Avenue and 20th Street in Birmingham.

To celebrate the formal opening of The National Bank of Birmingham, founder Charles Linn held the Calico Ball on the new bank's third floor on December 31, 1873. At the stroke of midnight Linn pulled the curtain and revealed the new year, 1874.

president of First National since 1977, was named chief executive officer following DeBardeleben's death in 1979, and later that year became chairman of the board; William A. Powell, Jr., was named president of the bank and AmSouth Bancorporation.

In 1981 the corporation took a giant step forward in its development, changing its name to AmSouth to express more accurately its scope of activities, which would no longer be limited to Alabama, and to prepare for growth and future business opportunities. That May AmSouth became the first Alabama bank holding company to be listed on the New York Stock Exchange. In November the board of directors agreed to merge all 20 affiliates into one statewide institution, AmSouth Bank N.A., executing the plan in 1983.

Woods became chairman and chief executive officer of the bank, and Hendley became president and chief operating officer. Powell was named vice-chairman of the bank and president of AmSouth Bancorporation.

Today Alabama's largest state-wide banking institution, AmSouth operates more than 143 bank offices in 24 of Alabama's 69 counties, where approximately 70 percent of the state's population and personal income is concentrated.

The largest bank merger in the state's history occurred in August 1985. AmSouth's merger with First Gulf Bancorp, Alabama's fifth-largest banking institution, brought AmSouth's total number of employees to 4,500 and assets to more than five billion dollars. In early 1987 AmSouth was expected to affiliate with the First Tuscaloosa Corporation, which operates nine branches of the First National Bank of Tuscaloosa, thereby raising assets to some $5.7 billion.

AmSouth continues to offer a portfolio of banking services, using a functional superstructure that divides the state into regions and the overall responsibilities for the bank's services into specialized divisions. Service delivery divisions include corporate banking, retail banking, bond, and trust. Bank-related services are also provided through AmSouth Mortgage Company (formerly Engel Mortgage), AmSouth Financial Corporation, and AmSouth of Louisiana, Inc., an affiliate that specializes in business lending.

AmSouth continues to be the largest provider of corporate credit in Alabama, with more than two billion dollars in corporate loans outstanding. Its 86 automated teller machines outnumber those of other banks in the state. The AmSouth Trust Division is Alabama's largest provider of trust services and a leader among those in the Southeast, with a national reputation for successful capital management and currently managing securities and other properties exceeding four billion dollars in value. As one of the top 10 land managers in the country, the Natural Resources Department manages more than 500,000 acres of farm and forest lands and another one-half million mineral acres.

As AmSouth enters the latter 1980s, it remains proud of its 114-year history and its continuing commitment to providing excellent customer service, developing worthwhile new products, and maintaining its premier financial position in the state while actively exploring opportunities for involvement in interstate banking.

It is a legacy and a future of which Charles Linn would be proud.

Headquarters of AmSouth Bancorporation is the First National/Southern Natural Gas Building at Fifth Avenue and 20th Street, Birmingham.

GOLDEN FLAKE SNACK FOODS, INC.

Golden Flake Snack Foods, Inc., originally named Magic City Food Products, was founded in 1923 in the basement of a Hills Grocery store on 15th Avenue in North Birmingham by Frank Mosher and Mose Lischkoff. Mosher and a cook peeled and sliced potatoes and dropped the slices into kettles of furiously boiling oil. The cooled potato chips were then put in grocery bags and "sealed" with staples. The fresh, kettle-cooked potato chips quickly caught on, and two salesmen with one truck were hired to handle the demand.

Mosher and one of his first employees, Helen Friedman, were the key figures in the early growth of the company. In 1924—the year she graduated from high school—Friedman became the bookkeeper

Making peanut butter cracker sandwiches in the late 1930s.

and girl Friday. So essential was she to the operation, she became known in Birmingham as the Golden Flake Girl. In 1928 she and Mosher were married.

Despite the impact of the Great Depression, the chips sold well, and other product lines were added, including peanuts, almonds, and hand-spread peanut butter crackers packed four to a package. However, Mosher and his partner, Lischkoff, quarreled when Mosher bought too many 55-gallon wooden barrels of peanut butter that began to go rancid. Later Friedman and her mother financed a buy-out of Lischkoff. Subsequently, when Mosher and Friedman divorced in 1934, Friedman received the business in the settlement.

Under Friedman's direction, the company instituted "store-door service." Prior to that time orders were largely handled by mail, which meant merchandise was two to three

days old before it reached the point of sale. Freidman sent out a fleet of trucks and salesmen to take the orders, which were filled from the trucks. By 1939 she was operating 12 trucks and had 50 employees. She also had a modern brick plant at 916 Fifth Avenue North, with 8,000 square feet of floor space, housing the latest in equipment.

In 1946, with 16 routes and sales just under one million dollars, the firm was incorporated and sold to the Bashinsky family. Under the direction of Leo Bashinsky as president and Cyrus Case as vice-president, the company entered a remarkable period of growth. Previously 75 percent of the operation's business had been in Birmingham. However, beginning in 1946 new routes were opened, and the company expanded its sales network, picking up some fallen competitors along the way. Since 1946 the corporation's sales have doubled every five

years.

Bashinsky's son, Sloan, bought the firm from his father in 1956. Although he had been one of the charter members of the board of directors and secretary/treasurer, Sloan Bashinsky had worked both route sales and production and knew the business from top to bottom. President Bashinsky and vice-president Halsey Townes changed the corporate name to Golden Flake, Inc., and initiated the construction of a new plant at the company's present Birmingham location, 110 Sixth Street South. Production at the new plant began in 1958. Two additional plants were later added in Nashville, Tennessee, and Ocala, Florida.

Route salesman Clyde Sharpe in the 1950s.

In 1968 Golden Flake became a public corporation and diversified into insurance, real estate, fasteners, and advertising. Later the snack food operation became Golden Flake Snack Foods, Inc., a wholly owned subsidiary of a holding company, Golden Enterprises, Inc. Sloan Bashinskyt is now the chairman and chief executive officer of Golden Enterprises, Inc. The holding company has since divested itself of the real estate and insurance businesses.

John S. Stein is president and chief operating officer of Golden Enterprises and president and chief executive officer of Golden Flake Snack Foods, Inc. Thomas L. Davis and F. Wayne Pate are executive vice-presidents of Golden Flake Snack Foods, Inc.

The company's product line has gone far beyond Frank Mosher's

original kettle-cooked potato chips. Although chips remain one of the major items, Mosher would hardly recognize the large variety of types, flavors, and sizes. Still included, however, is a line of old-fashioned, kettle-fried potato chips. Other products include corn and tortilla chips, nachos, tortilla strips, baked cheese puffs, cheese nuggets, fried cheese curls, cheese popcorn, butter-flavor popcorn, fried pork skins, roasted peanuts, and peanut butter and cheese-filled cracker sandwiches—many lines in a variety of flavors.

Today Golden Flake Snack Foods, Inc., is one of the top five independent snack-food-producing firms in the United States, and has sales of $130 million per year. The company's market covers 12 southeastern states.

ALTEC INDUSTRIES, INC.

In 1952 the unexpected death of his father brought a 19-year-old university student, Lee J. Styslinger, Jr., home to the heavy responsibility of managing the Alabama Truck Equipment Company. With a degree in engineering and a dream, his father, Lee Styslinger, Sr., had moved from Pittsburgh to Birmingham in 1929—an ominous year. Despite the desperate economic conditions the customizing truck body firm Styslinger founded on Vanderbilt Road had grown steadily.

To his employees his ethical standards were as outstanding as his business acumen. One longtime employee noted that "his moral values were of the highest, and he constantly thought first of what was right rather than what was expedient from a business point of view."

Working in the plant during the summers, the young Styslinger not only learned the business; he also absorbed the visionary instinct and the business philosophy of his father. The lessons served the young man well when he became general manager before he reached the age of 20. Carefully studying the market he made a decision in the early 1950s that would launch the company into a period of unprecedented growth and, ultimately, into national and international prominence in its field. Styslinger decided that the com-

Lee Styslinger, Sr. (left), founded Alabama Truck Equipment Company in 1929. His son, Lee Styslinger, Jr. (right), guided the business, renamed Altec Industries, Inc., to national and international prominence in its field.

pany, renamed Altec, Inc., in 1956, should specialize in meeting the needs of electrical, telephone, and related utility industries. In 1963 he established Altec Manufacturing Company.

Expanding rapidly, Altec opened an assembly and service facility in Indianapolis, the Northern Division, and a service center outside of Atlanta. In 1974 Altec, Inc., and Altec Manufacturing Company merged to become Altec Industries, Inc. Two years later the organization opened a plant in St. Joseph, Missouri, the Midwest Division, to manufacture digger/derricks. The company later began producing the aerial devices

used by electrical firms as well as reel lifters. The Southern Division continued to manufacture truck bodies.

To give the Southern Division more space and more autonomy, Altec moved the corporate group to a new headquarters building in the Inverness office complex south of Birmingham. Completed in 1983, the office, nestled comfortably among the trees on the shoreline of a meandering lake, serves as the corporate headquarters for an ever-widening Altec network.

From a small Alabama enterprise Altec has expanded to become a worldwide manufacturing and distribution organization. In 1985 it acquired a Canadian firm, which is an assembly and service facility. In addition to its regional divisions, Altec has 30 distributor organizations in the United States and in other countries.

Lee Styslinger, Jr., refined and enlarged the vision of his father. Since the 1929 founding of a truck body customizing shop, Altec Industries, Inc., has grown into the largest designer, manufacturer, and marketer of aerial devices, digger/derricks, and reel lifters in the world. The corporate management has continued to emphasize a philosophy that embodies a strong sense of business ethics and a team approach among associates.

Altec's new corporate headquarters building in the Inverness area south of Birmingham also serves as the home of a computer-based telecommunications system that connects each operating division to the home office.

INDUSTRIAL PRODUCTS, INC.

From a small rented office above a drugstore in Mountain Brook, a Birmingham suburb, Gerald "Gerry" W. Wiggins and a friend, who shortly went into another line of business, launched Industrial Products, Inc., on September 4, 1958. Today the company serves a six-state area of the Southeast as manufacturers' representative and distributor for leading national manufacturers of corrosion-resistant materials.

A native of Gadsden and a graduate of the University of Alabama, Wiggins established Industrial Products with eight years of experience in the field and a small unsecured loan from a banker friend. Beginning as a commissioned agent for Atlas Mineral & Chemicals, Inc., of Pennsylvania, he entered a highly competitive arena that specialized in finding solutions for corrosion problems in chemical processing, steel mills, food processing, and the pulp and paper industry. After a move to larger quarters in Homewood, Industrial Products also became a distributor for several national manufacturers.

Since no single product will take care of all the corrosion problems existing in industry today, the company's product line is diverse—including plastic-lined piping, Teflon expansion joints, Teflon chemical hoses, fiberglass-reinforced piping and tanks, corrosion-proof masonry products, and protective coatings. In addition to nationally recognized products, more than 25 years of experience enhance the company's effectiveness in achieving solutions to the complicated problems of corrosion.

The move to the present site in Irondale, east of Birmingham, gave Industrial Products two warehousing facilities in addition to the headquarters office. A shop at the Irondale location allows the firm to custom fabricate such items as Teflon-lined pipe to meet specialized needs of the customer. For more efficient servicing of the southeastern market, the company has a

Industrial Products serves a six-state area of the Southeast as a manufacturers' representative and distributor for leading manufacturers of corrosion-resistant materials.

branch in Knoxville, and warehouse and fabricating facilities in Augusta, Georgia, and Gadsden, Alabama.

A lean, efficient, team-oriented operation, Industrial Products has a sales force of six and a total work force of only 12—but serves more than 250 clients. From the outset Wiggins encouraged an egalitarian atmosphere where titles were simply a business necessity, and everyone was willing to do whatever was needed to get the job done—whether operating a pipe machine or sweeping the floor. The top management of Gerry Wiggins, Milton Wiggins, and Bill Porter stresses teamwork, cooperation, and a sharing of information and technical expertise within the company, a formula in which they take great pride and that has built a successful business in the southeastern United States.

AMERICAN CAST IRON PIPE COMPANY

Shortly after the nation entered a new century, a new industry arose in a sparsely settled area to the north of Birmingham. The story of that business, the American Cast Iron Pipe Company (ACIPCO), is not only the story of the industrializing New South and the city that symbolized the New South movement, but also of challenges to the usual ways of doing things.

Out of those challenges came an unusual company—ACIPCO. While the unique corporate structure continues to reflect the heritage and philosophy of its founder, John J. Eagan, the ACIPCO of today ranks as one of the world's largest producers of ductile iron pipe and other tubular products.

The firm has changed drastically since its founding in 1905. The payroll has risen from $151 per week to $1.25 million per week. Atlanta was the market for the first carload of pipe cast 80 years ago; today the corporation's products are in use throughout the world. Recently ACIPCO, with $300 million in sales and more than 3,000 employees, was one of five Alabama companies named to the *Forbes* 400 list of the largest private companies in the United States.

"From a small pipe shop founded in 1905 we have made a tremendous effort in adapting to the demands of the marketplace," says Paul Green, ACIPCO's ninth president. "I would like to think that our founder, John Eagan, would be proud of what we've done, and even prouder of our ambitions for the future."

In 1906, on land purchased from the North Birmingham Land Company and other individuals, ACIPCO's facilities consisted of a small office building, a wooden commissary, a pipe foundry, a powerhouse, a machine shop that also housed the chemical laboratory and a doctor's office, and 24 frame houses for some of the company's workers.

Today ACIPCO's modern facility sprawls over 550 acres. The company's products are marketed from sales offices in leading cities throughout the country, and American International Sales is responsible for the marketing of the products of the various ACIPCO divisions for export from the United States to all foreign markets. The firm also has three wholly owned subsidiaries: American Valve & Hydrant Manufacturing Company in Beaumont, Texas; Specification Rubber Products in Alabaster, Alabama; and Kristin Shipping Company in Birmingham.

ACIPCO products are manufactured through four divisions. The American Ductile Iron Pipe Division produces the ductile iron pipe that transports water for millions of homes, provides fire protection, and safeguards public health through sanitary sewer systems. Throughout its history the company has pioneered in the technology of pipe production and has set high standards for the modern pipe industry. ACIPCO was the first to patent such innovations as cement-lined pipe for water service and various mechanical and restrained joints for pipe and fittings. The firm also pioneered the development of ductile iron, which replaced cast iron as the predominant piping material.

The products of the company's American-Darling Valve Division effectively control the flow of con-

The modern administration building of American Cast Iron Pipe Company today.

veyed liquids. In 1969 ACIPCO purchased the waterworks valve and hydrant product line from Darling Valve & Manufacturing—a respected name in the field since 1896. An ideal complement to the firm's ductile iron pipe and fittings, the acquisition was one more step in a progressive diversification program. The division's valves and hydrants are widely used not only throughout the waterworks industry, but also for petroleum, chemical, marine, and other industrial applications.

ACIPCO Steel Products Divi-

American ductile iron pipe rolls off the line at the firm's central lining/pipe coating building.

The first office building of the American Cast Iron Pipe Company, shown soon after the firm was organized.

American steel pipe is hydrostatically proof tested.

---

sion produces centrifugally cast steel and alloy iron tubes, static castings, and fabricated assemblies. These products serve as hydraulic cylinders, rolls, and in countless diversified applications in steel, chemical, paper, and other industries. The division has supplied such diverse materials as jack-up legs for offshore oil-drilling rigs, the television antennae atop the John Hancock Building in Chicago, and the carrier for the Saturn rocket. Developed and patented by ACIPCO, the Ceram-Spun process makes it possible to cast steel tubes with a variation of thicknesses and diameters.

The company's American Steel Pipe Division has been established as a manufacturer of premium quality pipe for conveying gas and petroleum products to help meet the nation's energy needs.

Progress and an innovative spirit are not new to ACIPCO; they are part of the firm's heritage. ACIPCO is an organization with a strong sense of its history, and that history gave it a unique corporate structure. Although a woman, Charlotte Blair, is credited with the idea of a new southern cast iron pipe plant, it was a young Atlanta businessman, John J. Eagan, that shaped the company's destiny.

Wholly financed by southern businessmen and thus escaping the onus of absentee ownership that plagued many New South industries, ACIPCO was located in Birmingham because of the plentiful raw materials. Eagan, the principal founder, was not only a successful businessman and industrialist but also a prominent Christian layman who firmly believed in translating his religious beliefs into corporate policy—or, as he called it, the "Golden Rule." At ACIPCO he attempted to initiate a system whereby employees not only earned a living wage but also had occupational security and an adequate medical and pension plan before these were industry standards.

Projecting his philosophy and dreams into the future, Eagan created a plan of industrial cooperation in a codicil to his will. He set up a permanent trust of all of the firm's common stock, with the board of management and the board of operatives acting jointly as trustees. According to The Eagan Plan, each employee, from laborer to manager, is entitled to a supplement to his normal pay to be paid from the company's earnings—an incentive that has enabled ACIPCO to become one of the nation's leading foundries.

One of the stated goals of the current management of American Cast Iron Pipe Company is to keep alive the spirit of cooperation inherent in Eagan's philosophy and plan.

ACIPCO Steel Products Division's argon oxygen decarburization (AOD) facility enhances the quality ACIPCO Ceram-Spun® tubing.

Machining of an American-Darling butterfly valve on a numerical control mill in the No. 1 machine shop.

"The employees of Eagan's company," notes the current president, "are beneficiaries not only of the founder's will but also of an ideal of industrial achievement based on 'everyone working together toward the same end.'"

279

UNITED STATES PIPE AND FOUNDRY COMPANY

The industrial family tree of United States Pipe and Foundry Company is the story of two businesses: Sloss-Sheffield Steel and Iron Company, founded in Birmingham as Sloss Furnace Company in 1871, and U.S. Pipe, formed in 1899 by the consolidation of several small pressure pipe companies. With the merger of Sloss-Sheffield into U.S. Pipe in 1952, the company became a fully integrated producer of cast iron pressure pipe.

The story of Sloss began in 1876, when James Withers Sloss, an Irish farmer's son from north Alabama, rode into the raw, new town named Birmingham. Already a successful businessman and railroad executive, Sloss joined other entrepreneurs seeking to develop the mineral wealth of Jones Valley. Sloss placed his first blast furnaces in operation in 1882 on the eastern edge of the new town.

In 1887 he sold his interests, and a new enterprise, Sloss Iron and Steel Company, was organized by a group of financiers. Growing rapidly, Sloss Iron built two new furnaces in North Birmingham and purchased coal and ore properties to ensure a steady supply of raw materials. In

The Concrete Batch Plant was located at the Sloss City Furnace of Sloss-Sheffield Steel and Iron Company in Birmingham.

Molten iron flowing from the Sloss furnaces adjacent to First Avenue North was a familiar sight to Birmingham residents.

the 1890s the firm expanded further with the purchase of the properties of the Sheffield Iron Company, which included additional blast furnaces and iron ore and coal properties. In 1899 the expanded operation became Sloss-Sheffield Steel and Iron Company, the second-largest company in the Birmingham district.

In the early twentieth century the original Birmingham furnaces were dismantled and replaced by those presently standing on the site. Technological improvements and a process of acquisitions continued.

U.S. Pipe was incorporated in the same year as Sloss-Sheffield Steel and Iron Company, and both were incorporated in New Jersey. Consolidation was a hallmark of American business at that time, and U.S. Pipe came into being through the consolidation of numerous small companies located in Alabama, Kentucky, New Jersey, New York, Ohio, Pennsylvania, Tennessee, and Wisconsin.

In 1911 U.S. Pipe purchased the Dimmick Pipe Company, giving the firm another Alabama plant. Dimmick, organized in 1900, had a plant in North Birmingham producing cast iron pipe. In 1951 U.S. Pipe opened a plant for the production of cast iron products for the water industry near Oakland, California. An-

other Alabama property, the T.C. King Foundry Company in Anniston, was added in 1961.

As the largest consumer of merchant pig iron in the country, U.S. Pipe was the primary customer of Sloss-Sheffield. In 1942 U.S. Pipe purchased holdings amounting to about 55 percent of the common stock of Sloss-Sheffield from Allied Chemical and Dye Corporation. The merger of Sloss and U.S. Pipe took place in 1952. For a short time the management of the enlarged corporation was in the U.S. Pipe headquarters office in Burlington, New Jersey, but soon the general office of the company was moved to Birmingham.

U.S. Pipe has continuously updated plants and technology in a process that has led to the concentration of operations in fewer and larger plants. In the 1920s the company purchased the rights to a revolutionary new process of producing pipe. The original plants manufactured pipe by the "pit cast" method in which molten iron was poured into vertical molds lined with sand. The new method, developed by Dimitri Sensaud deLavaud, introduced molten iron into a rapidly rotating mold.

The chimneys of the complex of Sloss-Sheffield City Furnaces loom in the background behind furnace employees and vice-president Daniel E. Watkins (right) after retirement, city manager of Mountain Brook.

The centrifugal force of the rotating mold distributed the molten iron uniformly around the inner surface of the mold. Not only was the process more efficient and less costly, the result was a higher quality product.

Ductile iron has replaced cast iron in the production of pressure pipe. Ductile iron retained all the long-life attributes of cast iron but had the advantage of far greater strength and resistance to damage.

In 1969 U.S. Pipe was purchased by the Jim Walter Corporation of Tampa, Florida. For more efficient operations U.S. Pipe was ultimately divided into several divisions.

In 1971 the Sloss furnaces standing beside Birmingham's First Avenue North viaduct were closed. Since the furnaces were adjacent to the downtown area, generations of Birmingham residents and visitors to the city had enjoyed the spectacular sight of the glowing molten iron flowing from the furnaces when they were tapped. The Sloss furnaces symbolized an important part of the city's heritage.

The Jim Walter Corporation deeded the Sloss furnaces property to the Alabama State Fair Authority with the hope that the site could be preserved and developed as a mu-

seum of industrial history. Believing the project to be unfeasible, the Alabama State Fair Authority proposed that the furnaces be dismantled.

A public outcry resulted. A group of citizens, organized as the Sloss Furnace Association, succeeded in having the furnaces deeded to the City of Birmingham. City voters passed a special bond referendum to raise funds for preservation and development of the historic property. The support of the Jim Walter Corporation, the Sloss Furnace Association, the city, and such institutions as the National Trust for Historic Preser-

Pipe production continues at the Bessemer plant of U.S. Pipe. The plant was one of the original facilities in the formation of the company in 1899.

The Sloss furnace complex of U.S. Pipe and Foundry symbolized the early iron and steel industry upon which the City of Birmingham was founded. Today the past stands preserved in the Sloss Furnace National Historic Landmark.

vation resulted in the opening of the Sloss Furnace National Historic Landmark—a museum and community center as well as historic symbol of Birmingham's past.

Just to the east of the Sloss furnace monument to Birmingham's past stands the headquarters building of United States Pipe and Foundry Company, representative of a technological future. Today U.S. Pipe is one of the largest producers of ductile iron pressure pipe in the world.

AMEREX CORPORATION

E.K. "Ned" Paine, president, owner, and chief executive officer of Amerex Corporation, was the 1986 Birmingham Area Chamber of Commerce Small Business Person of the Year. He received the same honor for the State of Alabama and for the region encompassing 10 eastern states.

The growth of Amerex stands behind Paine's awards. Paine began the company in Trussville in 1970 with a $375,000 loan from the Small Business Administration, 10 acres of land, a 28,000-square-foot building, and 27 employees. In the first year production ran at 2,000 to 3,000 fire extinguishers per month.

Today Amerex Corporation, a manufacturer of portable fire extinguishers, has expanded to 100 acres, 200,000 square feet, and 458 employees. Production ran at 200,000 per month or 2.4 million per year. Today the firm is one of the largest manufacturers of industrial/commercial fire extinguishers in the world and is one of the largest fire extinguisher suppliers to the U.S. government.

Paine brought years of experience to the founding of Amerex. Leaving a position as national sales manager for General Fire Extin-

guisher Corporation in Illinois, he and John W. Howard purchased the Badger Fire Extinguisher Company of West Virginia in 1964. When Badger was bought by ATO, a Cleveland-based conglomerate, Paine was made group vice-president over seven ATO-owned companies.

But he longed to be in business for himself again, and he began a search for "just the right place." Among his considerations were "lots of sunshine," an available work force, and good community support. Paine made contact with Birmingham's newly formed Metropolitan Development Board and found what he was looking for in Trussville.

Ned Paine brought more than just his own experience with him. Howard, formerly chief designer and engineer at General and then Badger, and 10 co-workers joined him in Alabama. Paine's wife, Goldie, became office manager for Amerex.

Paine also brought with him a dedication to quality and to safety standards. Active in the National Fire Protection Association, he was instrumental in drawing up the National Fire Research and Safety Act of 1967 and was present for the signing of the bill at the White House by President Lyndon B. Johnson. When the Occupational Safety and Health Administration (OSHA) be-

After almost two decades of rapid growth, Amerex now employs over 450 workers. Ned and Goldie Paine are shown here in the Trussville office.

gan to strictly enforce its fire safety regulations in 1971, Paine's determination to produce only a high-quality product paid off—the Amerex products met OSHA's criteria. In addition, the firm went to three shifts a day the same year it opened.

By the early 1980s Amerex had secured about 30 percent of the commercial/industrial domestic market. Goldie Paine believed Amerex should venture into the international market, and today she runs Amerex Fire International as a separate corporation. Export sales have grown to $3.5 million, with 7 percent of total sales now generated by Amerex International.

Ned and Goldie Paine are "people-oriented" in their business philosophy. They attribute much of their business success to a loyal network of suppliers and clients across the country. In the international branch, Goldie places an emphasis on learning the customs of a particular country.

But the people orientation is most obvious at the Trussville plant. Amerex Corporation, in effect, has trained its own management team from the work force recruited in the Trussville area. A Management Council includes many of the firm's longtime employees. The Paines encourage a familial atmosphere and are now hiring children of some of their first employees.

In 1970 E.K. "Ned" Paine founded Amerex Corporation in Trussville. Currently the company is one of the largest manufacturers of portable fire extinguishers in the world.

CENTRAL BANK OF THE SOUTH

Central Bank of the South, Alabama's third-largest bank, was organized in 1964. The original paid-in capital totaled one million dollars. On March 31, 1987, 23 years later, the youngest of the four major banks in Alabama reached $222 million in capital and $3.5 billion in assets.

According to the bank's chairman and chief executive officer, Harry B. Brock, Jr., the phenomenal growth of Central is the result of a deep-rooted sales culture that has been embraced by the board of directors on down through the organization. Incentive payments to reward performance have been a part of the management system at Central ever since the bank was formed and includes the directors as well as the employees.

Central's emphasis on sales pushed its market penetrations among commercial banks up from zero in 1964 to make it a leading force in 1986. Even though Central spearheaded statewide banking and achieved the distinction in 1981 of being the first statewide bank in the state of Alabama, its entry into new markets has been accomplished with de novo offices or mergers with small banks in major markets.

This strategy was more a necessity than choice. When Central started the ball rolling toward statewide banking in 1968, it caused a storm of protest from almost every other banker in Alabama. This protest included a lawsuit filed by the state's largest banks and a lobbying effort by the Alabama Bankers Association to pass a bill in the Alabama Legislature to outlaw statewide branching as well as the formation of bank holding companies. Even though Central prevailed at the end of what was a bitter fight, the battle left Central without many friends

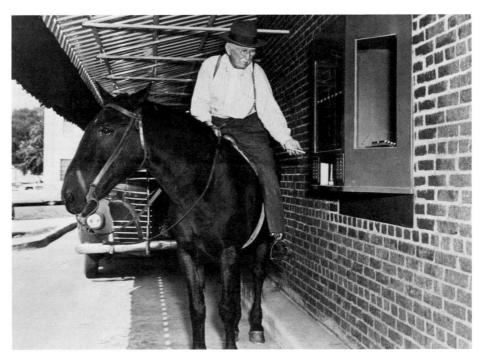

with whom to merge.

In 1987 Central had 78 offices in 41 communities in Alabama with more than 2,700 employees.

Central Bancshares of the South, parent company of Central Bank of the South, took the lead in interstate banking by being the first bank holding company in Alabama to acquire an out-of-state bank. This was accomplished through its purchase of a bank in the Houston,

One of the earliest drive-in windows was installed in Decatur by State National Bank, which would join the Central team in 1968.

Texas, market in February 1987. According to the *Houston Post*, the purchase also represented the first acquisition of a Texas bank by an out-of-state bank holding company. Central's strategies for growth continue its tradition of being an innovative leader among its peers.

An early photo of Central Bank's founders and directors. Seated are Harry B. Brock, Jr. (left), and Schuyler A. Baker. Standing (left to right) are Frank L. Hardy, John R. Israel, Jr., R. Hugh Daniel, Wendell H. Taylor, and Stewart H. Welch, Jr.

SPRING AIR MATTRESS COMPANY DIVISION OF ALABAMA BEDDING MANUFACTURING COMPANY, INC.

Alabama Bedding Manufacturing Company, Inc., has been manufacturing mattresses and boxsprings in the same Birmingham location since 1924. George P. Dupree, Beauregard Miller, and Frank Ridout left another mattress factory to form their own corporation, and set up shop at 200 Third Avenue North. Naming their business Alabama Bedding Corporation, they used Alabama Brand as their product trade name.

Within the first decade of operation, Dupree became the sole owner. In 1937 he sold one-third interest to Goode Price, Jr., who had an option to buy up to 50 percent. After World War II and five years of Army service, Price exercised his option in 1945.

Mrs. Jack Mitchell, who was with the company for 57 years until her death in 1985, had a 9.5-percent interest in Alabama Bedding. George Dupree eventually gave his interest to his son Carl. Price bought out Carl Dupree's interest in 1966.

In 1955 the owners created an affiliated business, Foam Rubber Distributors of Alabama, Inc., to supply foam rubber products to Alabama Bedding and to fabricate products for the foam seating and cushion industry. To accommodate the new business and provide storage space for the raw materials for the mattress company, they purchased a 25,000-square-foot building behind the mattress factory.

Price made a major decision concerning the future of the Alabama-based firm in 1967, when Alabama Bedding joined the Spring Air Company as a licensee to manufacture Spring Air products and use Spring Air as its trade name. It was a successful union. Spring Air has proven to be one of the fastest growing mattress manufacturers in the United States. In the past decade and a half Spring Air's U.S. sales increased 550 percent. Now an international organization, Spring Air has more than

5,000 dealers.

Price expanded his operation in 1977 with the purchase of Spring Air Mattress Company of Georgia, currently serving the state of Georgia from a base in Atlanta.

Price's son, Goode Price III, grew up working during the summer at Alabama Bedding and joined the firm on a full-time basis in 1978. Four years later he became president and chief executive officer and continues to serve in those capacities for Alabama Bedding and its affiliates. Because of the successful growth as a Spring Air licensee, the new president decided to add an additional 28,000 square feet of manufacturing space in 1984 along with new office and showroom space.

Spring Air Mattress Company, Division of Alabama Bedding Manufacturing Company, Inc., operates as a manufacturer and wholesale distributor that delivers its products in its own trucks. Goode Price III attributes the firm's success to having a broad dealer base and to the implementation of innovative ideas that have established the company as a leader in the bedding industry.

Beauregard Miller (left), one of the founders of Alabama Bedding Manufacturing Company, Inc., with an unidentified friend in front of the original facility. This was the predecessor of today's Spring Air Mattress Company.

J.F. DAY COMPANY, INC.

J.F. Day Company—the largest distributor in the Southeast for Pella windows, doors, skylights, and sunrooms—celebrated its 50th anniversary in 1986. The current president, J.F. Day III, represents the third generation of the family that founded the Birmingham-based firm in 1936.

Originally from Edgefield, South Carolina, J.F. Day, Sr., became familiar with Birmingham while working for a meat-packing company. After marrying a local young lady, he decided to settle permanently in the area. In the 1920s he went into business building portable garages for the growing population of automobiles in the city.

When J.F. Day, Jr., finished school in 1936, the father-and-son team opened J.F. Day Company—which specialized in venetian blinds, insect screens, and weather stripping for residential and commercial structures. The industry was in its infancy, and the father-and-son duo saw the possibilities for growth. Originally, the enterprise handled primarily the blinds manufactured by Rolscreen Company of Pella, Iowa. In 1939 J.F. Day Company began manufacturing its own blinds, but in the 1960s the firm renewed its relationship with Rolscreen and ultimately became a distributor for the full line of Pella products.

Although national manufacturers were dubious, the Day family believed that the southern states presented a market for insulated windows. In the 1960s the organization began promoting the idea; found a strong, viable market; and built a good foundation even before the energy-conscious 1970s. As sales increased, the company made a commitment to carry a full inventory of Rolscreen's Pella products so that immediate delivery was possible.

Although venetian blinds are still a part of Day's line of products, energy-efficient windows, sunrooms, bay windows, and patio doors are among the "specialties of the house." The primary markets for the firm include new construction by individuals and contractors, remodeling projects of older homes and structures, and replacement of original installations with more energy-efficient products in modern homes.

The third generation of the Day family, J.F. "Frank" Day III, began working in the operation while in high school, became full time in 1970, and was named president in 1976. In the 1970s the corporation was assigned Pella distributorships in Memphis, Tennessee, and Jackson, Mississippi, and now has warehouses, showrooms, and administrative and sales staffs in those areas as well as in Birmingham. Other cities with J.F. Day's Pella Window Stores include Shreveport and Monroe, Louisiana; Tupelo, Mississippi; Jackson, Tennessee; and Huntsville, Florence, Tuscaloosa, Montgomery, Auburn, and Dothan, Alabama.

J.F. Day Company, Inc., celebrated its 50th anniversary in 1986. Its Alabama stores are located in Huntsville, Florence, Tuscaloosa, Montgomery, Auburn, Dothan, and this one in Birmingham at 2820 Sixth Avenue South.

PROTECTIVE LIFE INSURANCE COMPANY

In 1907, when William Dorsey Jelks, former governor of Alabama, founded a new insurance company, the name he chose—Protective— had a reassuring sound in a year of turmoil. It was the year of the San Francisco Earthquake, the great fire in Baltimore, and a financial panic on Wall Street. Country banks in the South limited withdrawals, and many people in Birmingham used clearinghouse certificates in lieu of currency. The takeover of Birmingham's largest iron and steel producer by United States Steel Corporation possibly saved the southern industrial giant from economic catastrophe.

But Jelks had a vision that was not deterred by short-range problems. He was a child of the Old South, born in 1855 in Macon County, whose father died in the service of the Confederate Army. Growing up in the New South, Jelks graduated in 1876 from Mercer University, moved to Eufaula, and purchased the *Eufaula Times,* building it into the largest paper in the state. His knowledge of the political issues of the day and grasp of state problems led to his election as governor. Serving from 1901 to 1907, he became known as "Alabama's business governor."

Protective Life's headquarters building from 1928 to 1976 was dubbed a "Cathedral of Business" by a noted local columnist because of its elegantly appointed interior and the unusual copper roof.

His two terms as chief executive further enlarged his knowledge of the state and region, its problems and potential. He was aware not only of the wealth the South was capable of generating but also of the flow of

that wealth out of the South. He particularly noted the insurance premiums going out of the state.

In 1907 he moved to Birmingham and organized the Protective Life Insurance Company, serving as the firm's first president. Jelks' emphasis on regional development, a conservative business philosophy, and an ethical, value-oriented company structure set a pattern built upon and enlarged by subsequent leaders of Protective Life.

Beginning with all desks and all files in one room, Protective sold its first policy in September 1907 and had $183,500 worth of insurance in force at the end of the first year. In spite of the national financial distress of 1907, Protective survived and thrived. In 1915 the company moved to a two-story building at 2112 First Avenue North, and one year later paid its first dividend to its stockholders.

On its 10th birthday Protective saw so many of its employees going into military service that the company secretary reported the staff "shot to pieces." However, financially the firm could point with pride to assets that had more than doubled, legal reserves that had mounted over threefold, and $7,149,499 of insurance in force.

The year 1918 brought severe tests to all insurance companies. Protective suffered because of the influenza epidemic and the bitter death toll among citizens and soldiers. The company paid its full dividend to participating policyholders, but, for the first and only time in its history, had to pass on the dividend to stockholders.

In 1927, on Protective's 20th anniversary, the company merged with another Birmingham firm, Alabama National Insurance. Since Protective was approximately 50 percent larger, the organization retained the Protective Life name. A major contribution of Alabama National to the

Even in its early years Protective Life supported physical fitness for its employees.

merger was its management team. Jelks became chairman of the board and Samuel Clabaugh of Alabama National was appointed president, becoming chief executive officer when Jelks retired three years later. The Rushton family, so important to later developments, also became associated with Protective Life through the merger.

The following year Protective erected a new 14-story building on First Avenue and 21st Street at a cost of $900,000. Clabaugh, a Tuscaloosa editor and banker before entering the insurance business, guided the company through the worst of the Depression. The firm weathered the troubled times, showing an increase in life insurance in force every year except 1931 and 1932. During Clabaugh's tenure, Protective's insurance in force doubled, and assets increased by 67 percent.

In 1937 William J. Rushton, then president of Birmingham Ice and Cold Storage Company, was persuaded to leave the family business and become Protective's chief executive officer. A native of Birmingham and graduate of Washington and Lee University, Rushton had served on the boards of both Alabama National and Protective Life. In years to come the Rushton name would become synonymous with Protective Life in Birmingham circles.

In the fall of 1940 Rushton, a major in the Army reserves, was called to active duty. He rose to the rank of colonel and had the responsibility for the manufacture and procurement of all Army ordnance material in five southern states. When he returned to civilian rank, he was thereafter known as Colonel Rushton.

Under Rushton's leadership the growth of Protective continued to exceed the average growth of all life insurance companies in the nation. Following the Jelks tradition, Rushton believed strongly in furthering southern economic development. A 1940s annual report noted: "When you buy life insurance

In the 1930s Protective Life hoped to teach the value of money and the wisdom of investing through juvenile thrift clubs.

from Protective Life, your money serves you twice. First, you buy protection at competitive rates. . . . Second, your premium money stays at home."

At the end of Rushton's first 20 years Protective's life insurance in force, assets, and net worth had grown to eight times the 1937 figures. In 1963 Protective made a change in marketing strategy, deciding to concentrate on the upper-income market. The company also decided to expand geographically and become a nationwide organization. In 1968 the firm also made a commitment to the college senior market. Rushton leadership continued in 1969, when William J. Rushton III, son of the Colonel, became chief executive officer.

In 1976 Protective moved to a new home office situated dramatically on a 28-acre wooded site in suburban Mountain Brook.

Today William J. Rushton III, chairman and chief executive officer, and Drayton Nabers, Jr., president and chief operating officer, echo a theme consistent with the history of Protective Life Insurance Company: "Our philosophy rests on two overriding values, quality and growth, which by tradition and choice transcend all others. We are dedicated to creating value for our customers, reward and fulfillment for our people, and profit for our owners."

Twenty-eight acres of wooded mountainside provide a dramatic setting for the new headquarters of Protective Life Insurance Company.

DURR-FILLAUER MEDICAL, INC.

Financial analysts hail Durr-Fillauer Medical, Inc., as one of the most successful corporations in Alabama and the Southeast. Based in Montgomery, it is best known as a wholesale distributor of pharmaceuticals and a supplier of medical and surgical goods.

From a historical perspective the three founders would not now recognize what they started in 1896 as a small wholesale drug operation. They sold mostly petroleum jelly, sulphur, and Coca-Cola syrup. Today Durr-Fillauer's wholesale drug division is the largest such organization headquartered in the Southeast. From its five wholesale drug distribution centers in Montgomery, Mobile, Tampa, Shreveport, and Meridian, the company disperses 25,000 products to thousands of customers in the Sunbelt states.

Durr-Fillauer has a long history of serving the physician and non-hospital segment of the health care industry, so it has not been badly damaged by cutbacks in the acute care hospital area. Physicians' offices, outpatient clinics, emergency centers, and home health care programs account for the fastest-growing segment in health care delivery, and Durr-Fillauer's cost-efficient operation, combined with a state-of-the-art computer system and a fleet of company-owned vehicles, serves this area well.

Lean times in the health care industry have threatened company earnings, but the chief executive officer, William A. Williamson, Jr., believes that creative diversification will keep Durr-Fillauer financially healthy in a changing market. Its small but profitable orthopedic division manufactures and distributes orthotic and prosthetic devices to more than 2,200 wholesale customers. Two retail facilities custom fabricate artificial limbs and braces.

Veterinary supplies have been added to its distribution line, and the firm entered the home entertainment field in 1985 with the purchase of Source Video Distribution Co.,

The main floor and front offices of Durr Drug Company in 1917. The predecessor of today's Durr-Fillauer Medical, Inc., it was then located at 209 Commerce Street.

Inc., and initiation of distribution of prerecorded video cassettes and accessories to retail outlets in 48 states.

Durr-Fillauer Medical, Inc., has undergone many changes since 1896, but the key to its success has been a commitment to asset management, a disciplined management approach designed to target higher profit market segments, and value-added marketing. The value-added concept—matching products with a customer's needs—is not just a catchy phrase in Durr-Fillauer's book. It gives this company an edge in a highly competitive market.

A 1917 photo of the warehouse and chemicals laboratory.

BRADFORD & CO., INC.—FOOD BROKERS

Growing up in Sweetwater, Alabama, Tom Bradford was only seven years old when his father died in 1916. His mother took in boarders, gave piano lessons, and worked in the bank. She saved enough money for Tom to attend Birmingham-Southern College in Birmingham.

Today a 250-acre park in Birmingham bears Bradford's name, testimony to his longtime civic service. Man of the Year in 1965, president of the chamber of commerce in 1971, Distinguished Alumnus of Birmingham-Southern College in 1973, and induction into the Alabama Academy of Honor in 1981 give further recognition of his achievements. When Bradford headed the United Way campaign in 1967, he retired from active, day-to-day direction of Bradford & Co.; and his son, Tom Jr., became president of one of the largest food brokerage concerns in the South.

However, his path from college to the business world was not direct. A talented singer, Bradford left Birmingham-Southern before graduating and made his way to New York where he sang in the chorus of the Broadway musical *Hit the Deck* with Kate Smith. After traveling with the road show, he decided to complete his education at Birmingham-Southern and then Harvard Business School.

In Depression-wracked Birmingham in 1932, Bradford took a job pumping gas for B.F. Goodrich. He also persuaded the company to sponsor him on a radio show six nights a week as MC and vocalist. Throughout his business career, his singing talent has made him a popular performer at parties and meetings. At age 78, he still entertains crowds with his theme song, "I'm a Ding Dong Daddy from Dumas."

In 1934 his radio career ended when he was transferred to Atlanta. After traveling the Southeast for six years with B.F. Goodrich and *This Week* magazine, he moved back to Birmingham to become a junior partner in Ormand Brothers Broker-

age Co., a food brokerage firm with four employees covering the northern half of Alabama.

Ormand and Bradford continued as partners through Bradford's service in the Navy during World War II, changing the name to Ormand-Bradford Brokerage Co. Ormand passed away in 1947, and in 1958 the firm became Bradford & Co., Inc. That same year Tom Bradford, Jr., joined the company after graduating from Washington and Lee University.

During Tom Jr.'s career, the food brokerage business underwent a dramatic transformation. The primary function had been to sell merchandise to wholesalers and chain warehouses with no particular effort to help merchandise the products at the retail level. However, today merchandising has become the most important facet of the business.

In 1972, realizing that changing conditions necessitated a statewide operation for company growth, the Bradfords purchased Mrs. Strat-

ton's Salads, Inc., which had a distribution system covering retail grocery stores throughout Alabama and the Florida Panhandle; and Bradford's younger son, John, took over as president. This acquisition gave Bradford & Co. the opportunity to open a very successful branch office in Montgomery.

Added to the family business in 1978, Sunbelt Sweeteners, Inc., makes liquid sugar and also distributes high-fructose corn sweeteners in tank trucks to the industrial trade in Alabama, Tennessee, and Georgia.

With resident salesmen in Georgia, Florida, Mississippi, and Tennessee, Bradford & Co. now covers a six-state area. Today three companies stand witness to the business acumen of the "Ding Dong Daddy from Dumas."

Three generations in the food business—Tom Bradford (seated) with grandson Jim and two sons, Tom Jr. (left) and John.

THE GEO. F. WHEELOCK COMPANY

The growth of The Geo. F. Wheelock Company mirrors the development of Birmingham itself. Among the northern entrepreneurs attracted to the new city in the post-Civil War period was Charles Wheelock—native of New York, former major in the Union Army, and talented architect. Arriving in 1882 Wheelock designed and built many of Birmingham's churches, residences, and offices, but experienced difficulty in obtaining the fancy sheet-metal work needed for the ornate Victorian designs of the time. Taking advantage of the entrepreneurial opportunity, the architect's son, George F. Wheelock, came to Birmingham in 1887 and the following year founded the Wheelock Company—which specialized in sheet-metal work, galvanized cornices, skylight window caps, and roofing contract work.

Flourishing at its South 21st Street location, The Geo. F. Wheelock Company was well established when the founder died in 1904. His young widow, Addie, became president. Unsure of customer reaction to a female executive, she remained behind the scenes but ran the business firmly while grooming her son to assume control.

For continuity, Frederick Carlisle, 16 years old when his father died, legally changed his name to George Frederick. After learning all aspects of the sheet-metal trade, he became president in 1916, two years after the company moved to larger quarters on Fifth Avenue South. At that time the firm ventured into wholesale distribution by establishing the Phoenix Supply Company.

After a move in 1928 to Second Avenue South, Fred Wheelock restructured the company from retail to wholesale, eliminated the roofing contract business, and merged the Phoenix Company with the parent firm. Although the changes marked the corporation's future path, the next decade was one of struggle as Birmingham plunged into the Great Depression.

World War II brought a new set

of problems. The demand for war material created a scarcity of domestic products for the company to sell. Wheelock survived with a temporary partnership with E.M. Quintana to manufacture metal ammunition boxes, shell casings, and bomb crates under contract with the Department of War. Remaining in the forefront of technological advances after the war, the firm began selling air-conditioning equipment and added

Prior to the company's conversion to a wholesale distributorship, Wheelock trucks delivered the firm's sheet metal and heating products to construction sites around the rapidly growing young city.

---

new insulation products such as duct wrap and duct liner.

After a 60-year tenure Fred Wheelock died in 1965; his son, George F. Wheelock, Jr., became president. George Jr., who joined the firm in 1949 after his wartime service, guided the organization until 1982 when his son, George F. Wheelock III, succeeded him. The latter also followed the family tradition of learning the business by beginning in the warehouse.

By diversifying its product line and modifying the corporate structure, The Geo. F. Wheelock Company has continued its successful growth, changing with the times and meeting market needs in the Magic City.

The office building of The Geo. F. Wheelock Company, on South 21st Street in Birmingham, featured the company's window cap and galvanized cornice work. In this 1896 photograph the founder of the business and his son are second and third from the left.

ERNST & WHINNEY

The first of the national accounting firms to open an office in Birmingham, Ernst & Whinney initiated its Alabama practice October 1, 1929. Few would have predicted the imminent crash of the stock market later that month. Birmingham and E&W survived the ensuing Great Depression together. E&W is now the largest public accounting firm in Alabama, and a 1986 survey rated Birmingham's business conditions among the best in the nation.

E&W's offices were originally located in the old First National Bank building (now called the John Hand Building) on 20th Street at First Avenue North. In 1971 E&W moved four blocks north to more spacious quarters in the newly completed First National/Southern Natural Building.

Started as Ernst & Ernst in 1903, the firm was founded by A.C. Ernst in Cleveland. In 1979 the company's name was changed as the result of a long-standing relationship with Whinney, Murray & Company, an affiliate based in England. E&W, an international partnership with more than 350 offices, serves a diverse clientele in over 75 countries.

Four managing partners have directed client services from the Birmingham office: Henry J. Pratt, John L. Badeau, Donald C. Brabston, and Pat J. Bell, who has been managing partner since 1979. Many of E&W's early clients in Alabama—companies and organizations that have helped shape life in the Magic City and in other Alabama towns and cities—remain valued clients today.

In 1955 E&W established a Mobile office to accommodate more effectively the growing needs of the business community in south Alabama and northwest Florida. Originally managed by W.T. Mars, this office has been under the supervi-

Birmingham office partners of Ernst & Whinney are (left to right) Larry E. Newman; G. Marc Neas; Charles E. Simon; R. Travis Kirkpatrick; Pat J. Bell, managing partner; Richard L. Dandurand; T. Richard Horn, Jr.; Bill Stephenson; and Leroy W. Woody.

sion of Charles R. Chamblee as managing partner since 1976.

Pat Bell and eight additional partners in Birmingham, along with a staff of more than 120 audit, tax, and management consulting profes-

Ernest & Whinney opened an office in Mobile in 1955. Stephen W. Mixon (left) is a tax partner, and Charles R. Chamblee (right) is managing partner.

sionals, work closely with the Mobile office. "We are sufficiently experienced and diversified to assist with a broad scope of professional services," says Bell, "and we have the flexibility to provide new specialties as the need arises." He adds, "Our clients range from multinational corporations to small, family-owned businesses. We have a very strong presence in banking and health care. Regardless of size and company identity, our aim is to anticipate client needs and to provide productive solutions."

From its early days E&W has also demonstrated a strong commitment to the community. Founder A.C. Ernst exhorted his associates, "Never overlook opportunities. . .to make life more pleasant for those around us." Indeed, Ernst gave much advice that remains remarkably apt; he counseled that "the essential qualities for success are character, ability, and industry" and that "the reputation of our firm for impartial service is the most valuable asset we have."

The current managing partner, Pat Bell, notes, "At Ernst & Whinney, commitment still has a dual meaning—community needs and client service."

MAYER ELECTRIC SUPPLY COMPANY

In Birmingham, a city in the grip of the Great Depression, the dream of Ben S. Weil appeared to be at an end. In 1930 Weil had founded The Electric Supply Company; in July 1932 the bankruptcy court sold his business. He had found it impossible to collect his accounts receivable.

Max Mayer purchased the operation, renamed it Mayer Electric Supply Company, and gave Weil 50 percent of the stock to continue running the business; the dream was revived. In 1934 Weil and his wife purchased the balance of the stock but elected to retain the new name.

Locating on the 21st Street viaduct near an older, established hardware and electrical supply firm, Weil began to build his business with the spillover of customers from the other establishment. If he did not have what the customer wanted, he had it the next time. Espousing a philosophy of "hands-on" management, he kept his office near the front counter. With only three employees in the 2,000-square-foot facility, Weil remained personally involved in all aspects of the business—from opening the mail to manning the counter.

In 1949 Mayer Electric, now 15 employees strong, moved to larger quarters at 3200 Third Avenue South. Weil's son, Leonard, had

In 1949 Mayer Electric Supply Company moved to larger quarters at 3200 Third Avenue South in Birmingham, allowing the firm to set up a large lighting showroom.

joined the firm the previous year and assumed responsibility for setting up a lighting showroom. Since contractors generally had their own display rooms, the company had previously used only a limited display. Gradually, the contractors came to depend on the Mayer showroom and sent their customers there to make selections.

Weil's son-in-law, Charles Collat, joined the firm in 1953. After serving two years in the armed forces in Japan, he returned to Birmingham and worked in all aspects of the business—including the warehouse, inside and outside sales, and finance. Becoming operating manager, Collat initiated Mayer's data-processing operation, which was to make possible the company's rapid growth in the coming decades.

Leonard Weil became president in the mid-1960s, but his father broke ground for a new facility at 35th Street and Fifth Avenue South before his death in 1970. Mayer Electric Supply moved into the new quarters on Labor Day that same

Employees celebrated a grand opening at the electric supply company's new quarters in 1949.

Leonard Weil (left) joined his father, Ben S. Weil (right), in the management of Mayer Electric Supply Company in 1948.

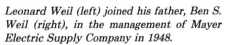

year. With almost 70,000 square feet, the building covered a full city block, and the showroom tripled in size. The organization was expanding in the geographic scope of its operations as well, opening a Montgomery branch in 1973, an Atlanta office in 1975, and moving into Decatur in 1978.

When Leonard Weil retired in 1979, Charles Collat and his family acquired the stock of the company and became sole owners with Collat as president. Under his leadership, expansion continued as Mayer opened branches in Muscle Shoals, Huntsville, Gadsden, Tuscaloosa, Anniston, and Madison, Alabama; Tampa, Florida; as well as an additional five operations in Georgia. In 1983 a new and larger residential lighting showroom fully occupied the completely remodeled site of the 1949 location, thus providing space for further expansion at the company's corporate headquarters.

Although Ben Weil's hands-on management technique was no longer Mayer's mode of operation, the careful attention to the needs of the customer that had marked his era continued, but in a manner appropriate to the changing times. Working from a good stock position, Collat introduced the concept of strategic planning in 1979. The March 1983 issue of *Electrical Distributor,* the official publication of The National Association of Electrical Distributors, showcased Mayer's strategic planning procedures.

In 1983, despite adverse economic conditions in Birmingham and throughout the state, a poll of electrical supply manufacturers and their representatives throughout the United States conducted by *Electrical Wholesaling* magazine (a division of McGraw-Hill) selected Mayer Electric as the top overall distributor performer in the nation. The managing editor of the magazine noted that Mayer Electric had "taken the stuff of management theory and applied it to their daily business."

The management team as-

On Labor Day in 1970 Mayer Electric Supply Company occupied its present modern quarters at 35th Street and Fifth Avenue South.

sembled by Collat includes Jim Summerlin, Alabama Division vice-president; Vic Kester, Georgia Division vice-president; and Jay Ziff, vice-president of finance. The team approach is illustrated by a favorite story told by one of the corporate officers. During a management meeting Collat received the nickname, "The Lead Duck."

"We were talking about the case

Charles A. Collat, president, became chairman of the National Association of Electrical Distributors in 1986.

of how at times when the lead duck is flying in one direction, he looks back and finds that the flock has veered off in another direction," recalled a Mayer executive. The president, however, saw more than the obvious humor. Collat pointed out that "a good leader is one who understands that if he looks around and sees the flock heading off, he better reassess the situation and respond accordingly."

Under Collat's leadership Mayer Electric has also responded to the needs of the community at large. In 1986 the company endowed The Ben S. Weil Chair in Industrial Distribution at the University of Alabama at Birmingham. The private endowment, matched by funds from the Alabama Endowment Trust Fund for Eminent Scholars established by the Alabama Legislature, created a one-million-dollar endowment. The degree program will combine business and basic engineering courses to prepare students for careers in either distribution or manufacturing, and will be one of fewer than a dozen such offerings in the nation.

From the bankruptcy courts of the 1930s, Mayer Electric Supply Company emerged to become one of the leading electrical supply firms in the nation. In 1986 the innovative leadership of Charles Collat was given recognition by his selection as chairman of the National Association of Electrical Distributors.

BARBER DAIRIES, INC.

George H. Barber was one of the new breed of dairymen who advocated pasteurization of milk and distribution from centrally located plants. Moving from Wauwatosa, Wisconsin, he and his family arrived in Birmingham in 1921 with a truckload of milk-processing equipment.

Birmingham and Jefferson County were in the midst of a transition in the milk-producing industry, and the Barber family would play a leading role. At the instigation of the health officer of the Birmingham-Jefferson County Health Department, Birmingham instituted a stringent and modern milk ordinance in 1920, which provoked much opposition from small, family-owned dairies and customers suspicious of pasteurization. Health officials and the producers of pasteurized milk had an educational and public relations task before them.

In 1922 only eight municipalities in Alabama had milk ordinances, and few pasteurizing plants were in operation. Men like George Barber were very aware that pasteurization was the way of the future to ensure sanitary milk supplies. Barber was one of the instigators behind the Alabama State Board of Health's approval of the Alabama Standard Milk Grading Ordinance in 1923.

In this atmosphere of change and confrontation George Barber and his brother Warren founded Barber Brothers Dairy at 715 South 10th Street. George had an extensive background in the dairy business in Wisconsin. Barber Brothers Dairy obtained its milk supply from some of the 300 family-owned farms near Birmingham. As the business grew and local supplies proved inadequate, George imported dairy herds from Wisconsin and Minnesota and arranged financing for farmers in the Black Belt.

In 1929, having built one of the largest dairies in the county, George and Warren sold their operation to Foremost Dairies, Inc. The brothers and George's son, George W. Barber, were Foremost employees until 1934.

George W. Barber, Jr., owner and chairman of the board; W.P. Langston, executive vice-president; and Albert E. Geiss, president (left to right), checking a machine that forms, fills, and seals approximately 120 half-pint cartons of milk per minute.

In the Depression years opposition increased from raw milk producers and from local dairy farmers as Barber, now with Foremost, began to bring in milk supplies from ever-widening areas. In 1931 the company's new stainless, seamless tankers—first in the area—were twice the target of bombs. On a third occasion the plant itself was bombed.

On February 9, 1934, George and his son bought the Hansen Pure Milk Company. The firm pasteurized milk and produced buttermilk, butter, cottage cheese, and other dairy by-products. The Pure Milk Company also had its own ice plant with a capacity of about 10,000 pounds per day—an important factor in the days of nonrefrigerated delivery trucks. The "Barber banner" was introduced to all the products that fall, and soon Barber ads began appearing in the local papers.

Barber purchased White Dairy in 1935. In business in Birmingham since 1912, White Dairy contributed significantly to the growth of the Barber operation. White Dairy became primarily the home-delivery enterprise, and Barber Pure Milk supplied supermarkets, food services, and institutions.

In the mid-1930s the second generation of the Barber family became involved in state action concerning the dairy industry. Milk supplies were erratic, and price wars plagued processors. George W. Barber was appointed as a member of the committee that drew up the bill establishing the Alabama Milk Control Board. As with the earlier milk ordinance, the Milk Control Board was also the subject of long-running controversy.

In 1938 George H. Barber passed away, and George W. assumed leadership of the company as the nation approached the war years and a new set of problems. Milk supplies were not readily available, employees were called into the armed services, and gas, tires, sugar, and other commodities were rationed. Trucks had to be kept running because new equipment was not available.

To alleviate the shortage of milk supplies, Barber brought in seven carloads of dairy cattle from Minnesota and distributed them to farms supplying Barber. The Barber/White Dairy operation began a tremendous expansion in the postwar years, growing from nine to 24 routes by 1950.

The final chapter of the long-running competition between pasteurized and raw milk came in 1948, when the county passed a law that all fresh milk sold in Jefferson County must be pasteurized.

The postwar years also saw the introduction of the wax-coated paper carton into the Birmingham market and the expansion of Barber into a number of new markets. The purchase of Carr-Myers Dairy of Tupelo, Mississippi; the Ruffin Graham Dairy in Mobile; and the Teague Farms Dairy in Montgomery all occurred in the 1950s. In 1962 the company acquired Turners Dairies in Anniston, and two years later Barber opened two retail routes to service the Huntsville area.

The year 1964 was an active one. The third generation, George W. Barber, Jr., began his formal career with the company. The firm introduced Barber's All-Natural French Ice Cream to its product line and began production of 100-percent pure Florida Orange Juice. The corporation also began planning a new plant for Barber Pure Milk Company and Barber Ice Cream Company. Located on a 27-acre site in Homewood, the first phase of the plant became operational in 1970.

That same year George W.

The milk-processing plant and administrative offices can be seen on the left, and the ice cream manufacturing plant is on the right. Built in the mid-1970s and located on 27 acres just south of Birmingham, Barber's facilities are continuously modernized to maintain state-of-the-art capabilities.

Barber, Sr., died, and George W. Barber, Jr., became chief executive. In 1973 he was elevated to chairman of the board, and Albert E. Geiss became president.

Currently Barber Dairies, Inc., operates milk-processing plants in Birmingham, Anniston, Montgomery, Mobile, and Tupelo. Distribution facilities are located in Nashville, Tennessee; Panama City and Pensacola, Florida; and Dothan, Alabama. The company employs 800 people and has an annual payroll in excess of $15 million.

Barber Dairies, Inc., uses in excess of 290 million pounds of milk annually, and Barber Ice Cream Company produces in excess of six million gallons of ice cream and novelties per year. The firm continues its leadership in the industry and annually receives quality award recognition from the Association of Manufacturers.

DRUMMOND COMPANY, INC.

In a nation increasingly aware of its energy problems, coal is recognized as the most abundant, most secure, and least expensive of our resources. In Alabama, a state whose economic development has been closely tied to its natural resources, the largest producer of coal is Drummond Company, Inc. Drummond coal is used—in Alabama and around the world—for the generation of electricity, the production of steel, and in a variety of other uses. The largest producer of foundry and industrial coke in the United States is also part of the Drummond organization.

The company has 3,400 employees, most of them operating personnel located at seven surface mines and three underground mines in Walker, Jefferson, Tuscaloosa, and Cullman counties, and at the coke plant in Tarrant. Headquarters is at Jasper, with some executive and staff offices in Birmingham.

The mammoth and modern equipment used today is far removed from the picks and shovels that were the tools of Heman Drummond, founder of the firm, at his first mine in 1935. An innovative and energetic man, he had worked for another mining venture for several years before deciding to go out on his own.

Garry N. Drummond (seated) is chief executive officer of Drummond Company, Inc., and E.A. "Larry" Drummond is president.

At his small underground mine in a Walker County hillside, the coal was cut, loaded on small cars, hauled out of the mine, and dumped—all by hand. Mules were brought in to haul the cars soon after the mine opened, and an electric drill and cutting machine were added in 1937.

When one mine was exhausted another would be opened, and Drummond acquired additional land as his revenues permitted. The company's first surface mine was opened in 1943, using a 3/4-cubic-yard-capacity power shovel to scratch coal from the edges of an outcropping. The hard times of those years are attested to by a loan note executed in 1943 by "Mr. Heman," as he liked to be known. To secure his three-month bank loan of $300, he mortgaged three mules—described in the note by color, age, and weight, and one by name: "Tobe."

Through the 1940s and early 1950s the firm moved on to new mines, purchased some larger equipment, and grew slowly. Heman Drummond died in 1956, but his two older sons, Segal and Don, continued to work and held the business together. They were joined later by the three younger sons, Garry, Larry, and John, as each completed his schooling. The 1960s were a period of growth for Drummond, which was leasing new reserves, developing mines, and acquiring equipment. Sales had risen to eight million dollars by the late 1960s.

The giant step that moved Drummond into the major leagues of coal mining was taken in 1969. Garry Drummond, who then had been with the company eight years since receiving his civil engineering degree, negotiated a contract with a Japanese steel corporation for the delivery of $100 million worth of coal over the next 10 years. The firm's first export sale, it opened the way for what became a major part of the business.

The company expanded rapidly in the 1970s to complete the original Japanese contract and to compete for additional business worldwide as well as in the United States. The organization's surface mines had primarily used power shovels to remove overburden up to that time. Now, larger equipment was needed, and the mines began to use draglines. The first of Drummond's giant electric draglines had a bucket capacity of 40 cubic yards. This was followed by others with even larger buckets, on up to today's machines with 115-cubic-yard capacity, moving 170

Heman Drummond, shown with one of the coal cars pulled by mules at his first mine in 1935.

tons of material in a single load. One of these behemoths is named "Ol' Tobe II," commemorating its little four-legged predecessor in a Drummond mine 40 years earlier.

As production and sales grew, so did the company's dedication to the protection of the environment and restoration of mined lands. Reclamation of land to a productive state is a combination of science, art, and engineering, and Drummond has won recognition from several conservation groups for its innovative and effective approaches.

A major step in the growth of Drummond Company, Inc., has been the merger of Alabama By-Products Corporation, which was incorporated in 1920, with antecedent enterprises dating back to 1894. The ABC coke plant at Tarrant is the largest single producer of foundry coke in the United States, shipping its product throughout the country and to several foreign destinations. The firm also operated numerous coal mines throughout its history.

Drummond Company acquired majority control of ABC's voting stock in 1977, and eight years later completed acquisition of all ABC stock through a tender offer. At the end of 1985 ABC was merged with Drummond, and its coke plant, three underground mines, and one surface mine became part of the latter organization. The coke plant continues to operate as the ABC Coke Divi-

"Ol' Tobe II," one of Drummond's large draglines, has a boom longer than a football field and a bucket that will hold 115 cubic yards of material.

sion of Drummond, maintaining its equity in the nationally recognized ABC name.

Also in 1985 Drummond began its first venture into real estate development with Oakbridge, a $500-million residential, commercial, professional office, and business park

Hay is produced on land that was recently a Drummond surface mine. A crucial part of the surface mining process is reclamation—restoring the land to productivity.

community. The 1,450-acre site is located in Lakeland, Florida.

Garry Neil Drummond has been chief executive officer of Drummond Company, Inc., since 1973; the other four brothers have also been involved continuously in its management. E.A. "Larry" Drummond is president of the company, Segal E. Drummond is executive vice-president and assistant to the chief executive officer, Donald D. Drummond is president of the Drummond Coal Division, and John H. Drummond is vice-president/asset management.

Other senior officers are executive vice-presidents Charles W. Adair, administration; Donald M. Baxter, operations; and Joseph E. Nicholls, finance; senior vice-presidents Hubert D. Hagen, land management; and R. Weaver Self, project management; president G.A. Pribbenow, Jr., of Drummond Coal Sales, Inc.; president Walter F. Johnsey of Perry Supply Company; and vice-president and general counsel W.B. Long.

Contemporaries of Heman Drummond describe him as a man of imagination and hard work. Continuing and applying that legacy in today's complex energy market, Drummond Company, Inc., has grown to become the largest privately held firm in Alabama and a prominent leader in America's coal industry.

SOUTH CENTRAL BELL

Alexander Graham Bell invented the telephone in 1876, and just three years later Alabama's first telephone exchange was operating in Mobile.

Albert Danner introduced the new invention to Alabama in 1879, using telephones to link the office and shipping shed of his coal and lumberyard. He demonstrated the phone to his friend C.G. Meriwether, and together they created the first telephone exchange in Alabama.

The Mobile exchange opened November 15, 1879, with Governor Rufus W. Cobb on hand for the celebration. Meriwether managed the office on the third floor of the Western Union Building. When Southern Bell Telephone Company incorporated in 1882, Mobile's exchange became one of the 11 original exchanges.

During 1879 the phone was used for the first time in Birmingham by F.H. Britton, train dispatcher for the South and North Railroad. He installed one in his office and another at the railroad's Decatur office, connecting them via Western Union's cables. At a prearranged time one Sunday afternoon all telegraph communications were cut off. A clear and distinct conversation could then be

Telephone operators were closely supervised at Birmingham's main switchboard in 1890.

heard between the two offices.

The next year Alabama's second exchange was established in Selma, followed by one in Montgomery. Not until May 1882 was an exchange founded in Birmingham.

Before such an exchange was feasible, 25 subscribers had to be enlisted. A Southern Bell representative initially approached James A. Van Hoose (a Birmingham grocer who later became mayor), who agreed to head the list. Three days later the discouraged representative came back with only 17 subscribers.

Van Hoose offered to find the remaining eight subscribers. He approached eight different people, asking each to be the 25th subscriber if he could find seven others. They all agreed, and a Birmingham exchange was created with 17 original and eight "25th" subscribers.

One of the first long-distance lines in Alabama connected Mobile and Montgomery, crossing the Mobile and Tensaw rivers over a drawbridge. Every time the bridge was raised, the line had to be disconnected. One of the first really *long* long-distance lines reached from Huntsville to New York. It opened July 7, 1895, with a conversation between Huntsville Mayor W.T. Hutchens and D.I. Carson, general superintendent of the Southern Bell Telephone Company, who was in New York.

By the turn of the century the telephone had grown into big business in Alabama. Exchanges had reached cities in all regions of the state. Changes took place rapidly. Females replaced males as operators because men had a tendency to be rowdy and rude to the customers, while women were much more dependable and patient. Alabama's phone system grew so large that an Alabama division of Southern Bell had to be created in 1923. Birmingham became division headquarters

This early telephone construction crew is ready to tackle whatever comes along. Some of the men are wearing climbing spikes on their legs.

with W.E. Bare as manager.

The growth of dial service, introduced in 1936, was stunted by the Great Depression. At the Depression's outset Alabama had 106,000 phones; at its depth, only 78,000. Other catastrophes during the 1930s included a fire on March 10, 1934, which started in downtown Birmingham at Loveman's Department Store and spread to the exchange's central office. Some 8,300 phones were knocked out of service—a loss of $500,000. Within 10 days the combined efforts of Southern Bell, Western Union, Long Lines, and AT&T had completely restored telephone service.

The "boom" caused by World War II brought the phone business out of the Depression and a speedy renewal of dial service growth in Alabama. In Montgomery, John Cason pulled the switch that transferred service to the dial. He had done the same thing 30 years earlier during the conversion to manual operations.

Alabama's one-millionth telephone was installed on June 30, 1966, in the office of Samford University's president, Dr. Leslie S. Wright. By September Southern Bell had become the largest operating company in the Bell System.

On July 1, 1968, Southern Bell split into two operating companies. The eastern area—Georgia, Florida, North Carolina, and South Carolina—continued as Southern Bell. The western area—Louisiana, Mississippi, Alabama, Tennessee, and Kentucky—became South Central Bell. At its founding South Central Bell was the largest new corporation ever formed and the sixth largest of the 22 operating companies in the Bell System. Headquartered in Birmingham, the company had 40,000 employees and 5.5 million phones. Cecil Bauer was the first president.

Another important milestone in 1968 was the conversion of the last manual exchange in Alabama—York—to dial.

On August 17, 1969, tragedy

This ancestor of the upright desk set was made in 1897 and represents a refinement of earlier, similar models.

struck southern telephone networks. Hurricane Camille devastated Alabama's Gulf Coast region, silencing more than 186,000 phones, isolating 18 exchanges from the network, and knocking out 1,668 long-distance lines. But forces from around the Bell System showed the spirit of service by completely restoring telephone service in less than a month.

A new South Central Bell headquarters building in Birmingham was occupied in 1972; at the time the 30-story structure was the largest in Alabama. Ten years later South Central Bell's Alabama state headquarters organization moved into its unique office building off U.S. 280 South. A remarkable example of the blending of nature and man-made structures, the building hovers over a small lake.

As South Central Bell began life as a separate entity, rapid changes started taking place in the telecommunications business. In 1964 Decatur had become the first southern city to receive Touch-Tone service. The "911" Universal Emergency Service was also in its early stages. The 1970s and 1980s saw the introduction or modernization of Directory Assistance, Direct Distance Dialing, coin-operated pay phones, and electronic central offices.

Fundamental changes taking place in the telephone industry led to divestiture of the Bell System through an agreement between AT&T and the Department of Justice. On January 1, 1984, AT&T's 22 operating companies were split into 22 individually run corporations under seven regional holding companies. The largest of the seven in terms of assets, BellSouth Corporation, manages South Central Bell, Southern Bell, and a number of other subsidiaries. BellSouth is headquartered in Atlanta.

The rapidly growing southeast United States offers virtually unlimited opportunities in telecommunications, and South Central Bell is on the leading edge of new technology with fiber optics, computerized call switching, and digital and light-wave communications.

South Central Bell's corporate foundation rests on a series of five values: "Customer First, Respect for the Individual, Pursuit of Excellence, Positive Response to Change, and Community Mindedness." These values mirror a proud heritage of service for South Central Bell in the past and an exciting future of service for the nation's Sunbelt.

In 1969 Hurricane Camille silenced 186,000 telephones along the Alabama Gulf Coast area, including this pay telephone booth.

SHOOK & FLETCHER

Founded in 1949 to meet the demand for insulation specialists, Shook & Fletcher Insulation Co., is an outgrowth of a business founded in Birmingham in 1901.

On May 14, 1901, Paschal G. Shook and John F. Fletcher, Jr., who had resigned executive positions with one of Birmingham's leading iron and steel companies, announced that they would open a brokerage office in Birmingham to "conduct a general commission business, covering the purchase and sale of pig iron, bar iron, steel, coke, coal, fire brick, and all manufactured products." The mill and mine supply firm prospered and grew, becoming the representative for a large number of manufacturers in the iron and steel, mining, and electric utilities industry.

James Warner Shook, the brother of Paschal Shook, bought Fletcher's interest in 1913. Warner Shook's background was in brown iron ore mining, and Shook & Fletcher branched into mining, becoming the largest independent iron ore producer in the Southeast. Within Alabama the company operated mines in Blount, Franklin, Bibb, Tuscaloosa, Shelby, St. Clair, and Jefferson counties, as well as one mine in Georgia and two in southeast Missouri. The mines operated successfully until they were phased out in the early 1970s.

The corporation further diversified its operations in the late 1920s with the addition of a mechanical contracting division for the installation of heating and cooling equipment. Eventually, Shook & Fletcher received the franchise of the Carrier Corporation of Syracuse, New York.

Needing insulation for use in its installation, Shook & Fletcher obtained the Johns Manville franchise in 1949. Manville, however, believed the franchise should be operated separately from the mechanical contracting division; therefore, Shook & Fletcher Insulation Co. was founded in 1949.

The mechanical contracting di-

Shook & Fletcher displayed mill and mining equipment at a 1926 trade show in Ohio.

vision operated as part of Shook & Fletcher until it was sold in 1972 to the firm of Banks, Ellett and Ramsey. It operates today as Shook & Fletcher Mechanical Contractors.

Two generations of the Shook family contributed to the growth of Shook & Fletcher, serving directly in the management of the company. Paschal and Warner Shook were followed by A.M. Shook III, Paschal G. Shook, Jr., and Chas L. Gaines, Jr., a son-in-law of the family. In 1967 the Shooks sold Shook & Fletcher Insulation Co. to a group of men who had become the working management of the firm. This group included James P. Ennis, an engineer who was an expert on thermal insulation, and Wayne W. Killion, who is today president and chief executive officer of the company.

Killion came to Alabama in 1934 as a nine-year-old child of an Iowa farming family seeking to escape the drought of the Midwest. Coming for the "winter only," Killion's grandfather decided Foley, Alabama, was a great place, and the family stayed. When the nation entered World War II, the young Killion joined the Navy and was sent to Birmingham's

Howard College and Tulane University for further training. When the war ended, he returned to Howard to finish his education and graduated with a degree in business administration with a major in accounting.

After working in public accounting he moved into private accounting

---

Shook & Fletcher is a leading marine insulation contractor providing insulation for piping, ductwork, and mechanical systems on ships for the U.S. Navy and for private companies.

and at age 23 joined Shook & Fletcher in August 1949 on the same day the Manville franchise was obtained. Killion's responsibilities included both Shook & Fletcher Supply and Shook & Fletcher Insulation until 1964, when he was made controller of the insulation company. Eventually, he served as vice-president of finance, vice-president, and then president. When Killion and the others bought out the business in 1967, Ennis became president and Killion became vice-president. Ennis died in 1972, and 14 years later Killion became sole owner. In 1982 he bought Shook & Fletcher Supply Co.

Today Shook & Fletcher Insulation Co. has nine division offices strategically located in five states. A materials warehouse is maintained at each location, ensuring one-day delivery to most customers. Each warehouse has a full inventory of insulation products and finishing materials so no backordering is necessary.

As one of the leading independent distributors and contractors in the country, Shook & Fletcher maintains an extensive inventory of insu-

Steam lines insulated by Shook & Fletcher at a nuclear power plant have been covered with an insulation of calcium silicate pipe covering and aluminum jacketing.

lation products drawn from all the major manufacturers. Products inventoried include many forms of fiberglass, calcium silicate, ceramic fibers, mineral wool, polyurethane, polystyrene, foam plastic, glass cloth, metal and PVC jacketing, fittings, and various accessories.

The firm also offers contracting services in commercial, industrial, and marine installation. Industrial insulation involves complex systems operating under extreme temperatures in a variety of conditions. Shook & Fletcher has insulated systems for extreme hot and cold processes, underground, above ground, on towers, on hortenspheres, and under other conditions.

The company is also a leading marine insulation contractor, insulating piping, ductwork, and mechanical systems on ships for the U.S. Navy and for private businesses. Shook & Fletcher is one of the few firms in the country that fabricates hull board, used widely as an insulation material and finish on the interior of a ship's hull.

Today Shook & Fletcher's facilities are located in Birmingham, Mobile, and Decatur, Alabama; Evansville, Indiana; Knoxville and Chattanooga, Tennessee; Savannah and Atlanta, Georgia; and Pascagoula, Mississippi.

Surrounded by scaffolding, these petroleum cracking towers are being covered by an insulation of calcium silicate, one of the wide varieties of insulating products installed by Shook & Fletcher.

MAYNARD, COOPER, FRIERSON & GALE

"Our history is what happened last week," says one of the founding lawyers of Maynard, Cooper, Frierson & Gale. The Birmingham firm is, indeed, quite young—founded in February 1984. The average age of its lawyers is only 33.

However, youthfulness in history and in personnel has been no handicap. The firm serves as principal external counsel for the largest bank and bank holding company in Alabama, one of the largest ductile pipe manufacturers in the world, an Alabama-based life insurance organization with more than $22 billion of insurance in force, the 10th-largest coal producer in the United States, and one of the largest pulp and paper corporations in the southeastern United States.

Maynard, Cooper, Frierson & Gale began with a commitment to a stated philosophy concerning the legal profession and the role of the lawyer within the community. Eleven attorneys who were partners in a larger Birmingham firm shared common principles that they believed could be the foundation of a new and dynamic law firm. Fifteen younger attorneys joined them. As

they began, they took time to set down the founding principles that had drawn the group together—and which would be used as the standard for the future. Embodied in those principles is a dedication first and foremost to professional excellence in the service of their clients; but, at the same time, there is a commitment to the personal happiness and professional development of the firm's lawyers. Recognizing that they are "quasi-public servants," the attorneys are mindful of broader civic and social responsibilities.

That commitment to public service in their chosen profession and in the community at large is manifested in a wide variety of outside activities. One member of the firm has served as chairman of the Litigation Section of the American Bar Association and as a member of the board

---

The founding partners of Maynard, Cooper, Frierson & Gale include (seated, left to right) John D. Johns, Meade Frierson III, Cathy S. Wright, George G. Lynn, H. Thomas Wells, Jr., and (standing, left to right) Douglas T. Arendall, George F. Maynard, Kirby Sevier, N. Lee Cooper, J. Hobson Presley, Jr., and Fournier J. Gale III.

of directors of the American Bar Endowment; another serves on the board of directors of the American Judicature Society; and two members are active in the American Law Institute. Community service includes involvement with the Alabama Symphony, the United Way, Big Brothers and Big Sisters, the YMCA and YWCA, the Business Council of Alabama, and church activities in a number of different denominations.

The full-service law firm—encompassing virtually all aspects of legal practice—now has 37 lawyers, approximately half of whom are partners. Symbolic of its commitment to the city, the group now occupies six floors of the renovated Watts Building, a 1927 Art Deco structure in the center of downtown Birmingham.

The lawyers of Maynard, Cooper, Frierson & Gale reflect a diversity of legal specialties, community interests, and personalities, but they share a commitment to a personal and professional philosophy. It is that commitment that serves as the cornerstone for a flourishing new law firm in the heart of the city.

BUFFALO ROCK COMPANY

Headquartered in Birmingham, the Buffalo Rock Company is the nation's largest privately owned Pepsi Cola bottler. It operates 14 franchises with 17 distribution points in Alabama, Florida, and Georgia.

The story of Buffalo Rock and the Lee family began in the late 1800s with the founding of the wholesale Alabama Grocery Company by Sidney W. Lee. The firm moved into the soft drink business when Lee and a chemist cousin developed Buffalo Rock Ginger Ale. The popularity of the new drink soon eclipsed all other products and became the sole business of the renamed Buffalo Rock Company. For 30 years the main products were Buffalo Rock Ginger Ale, Mission Orange, Mission Grape, and B-1. In 1951 the firm purchased the Birmingham Pepsi Cola franchise and soon added Dr Pepper and Seven Up.

Originally located on First Avenue North, the company moved to 10th Avenue and 26th Street North in 1919. A huge sign erected on the roof of the 26th Street plant fascinated Birmingham residents. Lit by hundreds of bulbs, the sign showed a Buffalo Rock bottle with its contents pouring into a glass.

Buffalo Rock has remained a family business. Sidney Lee passed it on to his son James C. Lee, Sr. When James Sr. died in 1951, his son James C. Lee, Jr., who had begun working when he was 19—hand

A delivery man with a load of Buffalo Rock Ginger Ale in the early 1930s.

loading drink cases, as well as delivering and selling—assumed leadership. He developed a reputation for his keen business sense and commitment to community service.

When it outgrew its 26th Street location, Buffalo Rock moved, in 1966, to a 15-acre site on Oxmoor Road, south of Red Mountain. Acquisitions and expansions have made continuing demands for increased warehouse and production facilities as well as office space. Today, following a multimillion-dollar expansion, the firm occupies 350,000 square feet in three buildings on 27 acres in Birmingham and Homewood.

An early Buffalo Rock sign, circa 1930.

wood.

Billed as The Year of the Super Rock, 1985 saw a flurry of franchise acquisitions that marked the greatest period of growth in the history of Buffalo Rock. The firm acquired the Pepsi Cola franchises of Albany and Columbus, Georgia, and Dothan, Alabama, and the Seven Up franchises in Pensacola and Fort Walton Beach, Florida, and Mobile, Alabama. These were added to Pepsi franchises in Birmingham, Gadsden, Huntsville, and Tuscumbia, Alabama; Newnan and LaGrange, Georgia; and to the 1981 purchases of the Mobile franchise and the acquisition of worldwide rights to Grapico. In 1986 the corporation continued its expansion with the acquisition of the Panama City, Florida, and Tuscaloosa Pepsi franchises.

Known throughout the beverage industry as a leader and innovator, Buffalo Rock developed the highly successful three-liter package, which is now a common sight in stores across the country.

The fourth generation of the Lee family is now involved in operating the business. In addition to James C. Lee, Jr., who is chairman and chief executive officer, James C. Lee III is president. Currently serving as senior vice-president of corporate affairs, Peyton Lee, the daughter of James Jr., is the first woman of the family to seek a career with Buffalo Rock Company.

BRUNO'S, INC.

Picture a room 20 by 40 feet. That would make a pretty big living room. Or maybe a living and dining room together. But suppose it were a whole grocery store that was trying to supply meat and vegetables and canned goods to an entire neighborhood—plus support a family of 10! Now you have a picture of the very first Bruno's store on the north side of Birmingham. It was 1932 in the depths of the Great Depression. Joe Bruno's father, Vincent, had been laid off from the steel mills since 1929. He might never get another job and, in fact, he didn't. So Joe's mother, Theresa, took $600, all the money she had scrimped and saved over the years, and gave it to Joe to start a grocery store. Talk about a gamble! Joe and his 17-year-old brother Sam

bought their stock on credit and paid the bills as the customers paid theirs. Sales that first week were $75!

Meanwhile, mother Theresa kept the vegetable garden going and still made most of the eight children's clothing out of remnants and flour sacks. The store was obviously a family affair. Husband and wife worked together and the children came in after school to help.

Somehow it all worked. As one brother after another grew to maturity, each branched off and started a store of his own. In 1959 they incorporated and actually rented their own warehouse. This was progress!

The visible prices date this to the early days of Bruno's.

Each of the brothers developed his own field of expertise. Joe was in charge of administration and finance and also meat buying. Lee was the produce man. Sam was a general "Mr. Fixit." Angelo was in charge of merchandising. At this time Bruno's started a revolutionary advertising idea—a two-page newspaper ad, sometimes in color, full of bargains to attract both new and old customers. It was not to be the last revolutionary idea from this small company.

One ironic note: When Bruno's began, and for years thereafter, 80-90 percent of all grocery business in Birmingham was in two chains— A&P and Hill's. How things change. Hill's sold out to Winn-Dixie, and in 1980 Bruno's bought the last seven

The Bruno family, who established Bruno's, Inc. in 1932. Some members are still active in the business today.

A&Ps in Birmingham.

By 1970 the firm had 29 stores in operation from Birmingham to Huntsville to Tuscaloosa. And two years earlier the first Big B Discount Drugs had opened its doors in Birmingham. The business was moving right along. But a trip Joe Bruno took to Europe was to give a new direction and a new impetus to the company. Joe saw the first hypermarchés, high-volume, low-margin discount stores, and became convinced that the future of supermarketing lay in this direction.

To help raise capital for this new venture, the brothers decided to go public and had their first stock offering. This was in 1971. The underwriters set the price at $14.75 a share. What an investment that would have been: At 1987 prices that one share of stock would now be 32 shares worth $640!

In 1972 the first Food World opened its doors. Today, of the more than 100 stores in the chain, 65 are Food Worlds. Food World started a trend that is going on to this day—discount every item every day, no loss-leaders, no stamps, no games, no gimmicks. Customers grew to appreciate and trust Food World and sales grew accordingly. New stores soon joined in: Consumer Foods for areas too small for a Food World; Food-Max, giant, deluxe warehouse stores; and the new Bruno's Food & Pharmacy, the "Best of Everything" stores designed for upscale areas. The company has the right store for any clientele and has the ability to operate several formats within the same area.

In 1986 Bruno's moved past the billion-dollar mark in sales, probably the only Alabama company of its size that derived the bulk of its income primarily from within the state.

Bruno's has come a long way from that little 800-square-foot store, but some things haven't changed. By 1987 the firm had grown to over 10,000 employees but the feeling of "family" still endures. Three of the five original brothers are still active in the company. Angelo Bruno's son, Ronald, is now president and chief operating officer. "We're all in this together," is the motivating influence for the business—together with the basic idea of "let's give the customer the best value we can."

Bruno's has grown by keeping costs down and passing the savings on to its customers. Year after year, the stores have been upgraded and new departments—seafood, cheese, floral sections—have been added. The promise to the customer is that no matter which store you enter, it will offer the best values and the widest variety that money can buy. That's a pretty good promise.

BLOUNT, INC.

Now entering its fifth decade, Blount, Inc., is a giant among American corporations. Blount people have distinguished themselves as entrepreneurs—first in the Southeast, then across the United States, and around the globe.

From its international headquarters in Montgomery, Alabama, the company employs more than 10,000 people. Today Blount is a billion-dollar, worldwide construction and manufacturing company. It is demonstrating how to make steel profitably in the United States, how to adapt Japanese manufacturing and management techniques to American industry, and how to utilize Swiss technology to reduce the reliance on landfill in disposing of garbage while producing energy. It is hard to believe that it all began in 1946 as a small, sand and gravel business in nearby Union Springs.

The man behind this company is equally remarkable. Winton M. "Red" Blount has demonstrated his foresight and ingenuity right from the start. Red and his brother, Houston, left the University of Alabama to serve in World War II. While they were gone their father died. The sand and gravel business he owned had deteriorated and the brothers, after returning to Alabama, decided to rebuild the company. They bought Army surplus equipment and based their operation in Tuskegee. The Army surplus

people offered Red four D-7 Caterpillar tractors and scrapers for $28,000, a very low price even in 1946. Although the tractors were useless in the sand and gravel business, he bought them anyway. When he told his brother what he had done Houston asked, "What are we going to do with that stuff?"

"We're going into the contracting business," Red replied. That decision marked the start of Blount Brothers Construction Co., the original Blount, Inc., business.

The first contracts were for fish

The year 1979 marked Blount's acquisition of Washington Steel, the industry's low-cost producer of flat-rolled stainless steel.

ponds, and soon the enterprise was subcontracting for the state highway department. In 1949 it won a million-dollar bid to complete the superstructure for a viaduct in Birmingham. In the next few years the company's reputation for quality grew, and the Blounts moved the headquarters to Montgomery. In 1952 the brothers received a contract to build an Air Force wind tunnel and began developing a high level of technical expertise. Shortly afterwards, Blount constructed the first atomic reactor ever built on a fixed-price basis.

Houston Blount left the company to help found the Vulcan Materials enterprise in Birmingham, but remains on the Blount, Inc., board. Red Blount's firm continued to pros-

Blount acquired Omark Industries, which invented the modern cutting chain, in 1985.

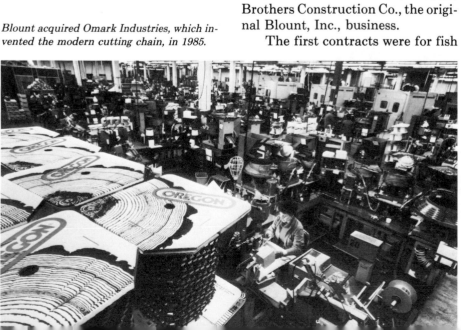

In 1985 Blount completed an academic campus in Riyadh, Saudia Arabia, the largest fixed-price construction project ever awarded.

per and in 1958 built the nation's first intercontinental missile base. This project was followed by other missile and space industry jobs, including Complex 39A at Cape Canaveral from which all flights to the moon were launched.

Contracting almost exclusively with the government, a decision by the directors to enter the private sector proved difficult but timely. In 1968, when Red Blount resigned to serve as U.S. Postmaster General, he prohibited the operation from bidding on federal contracts. This restriction meant a tremendous financial loss, but laid the base for Blount's long-term growth. The firm went public, and a carefully planned series of acquisitions was begun.

In 1979 Washington Steel Corporation was acquired. It has since become one of the lowest-cost producers of stainless steel in the United States and is a trend-setter in this fast-growing segment of the market. Washington Steel has never had an unprofitable year or layoff in an industry that has experienced significant difficulty. Under Blount's ownership it has become a leader in technical and managerial innovations. Blount again made history in 1985 by acquiring Omark Industries, the most advanced user of just-in-time manufacturing systems in America. Omark is the world's leader in saw-chain cutting technology.

Blount, Inc., has become one of the nation's largest diversified service companies, continuing to change but not abandoning a rich heritage. Past achievements fuel future growth as the organization focuses on its core businesses of tomorrow: construction and engineering, resource recovery, specialty steel, saw chain, hydraulic materials handling equipment, and sporting apparatus.

Perhaps those four tractors Red Blount bought in 1946 have turned out to be one of the best buys in the history of American industry.

Blount completed Launch Pad Complex 39A, from which all lunar launches were made, in 1969.

307

A.G. GASTON ENTERPRISES

The business philosophy of Dr. A.G. Gaston is simple: Find a need and fill it; if you are filling a need, the public will support you. The interrelated network of businesses founded by Gaston met needs he observed in the Birmingham black community.

Born in rural Marengo County in 1892, Gaston moved to Birmingham and found work in the steel mills. Not content to work for someone else, Gaston organized a burial insurance society in 1923. Incorporated in 1931 as the Booker T. Washington Burial Society, the company later expanded its services and became the Booker T. Washington Insurance Company. With his father-in-law, Gaston also founded Smith and Gaston Funeral Directors, Inc.

As his enterprises grew, Gaston discovered a shortage of skilled black clerical employees. With his wife, Minnie Gardner Gaston, he founded the Booker T. Washington Business College in 1939. Still flourishing today, the college was for many years the only school in which blacks might obtain training as secretaries, accountants, and bookkeepers.

The business network related to the original insurance company expanded in the 1940s, when Gaston purchased the New Grace Hill Cemetery and later the Zion Memorial Gardens and Mausoleum. Gaston's entrepreneurship continued in the 1950s with the formation of Vulcan Realty and Investment Corporation. The Citizens Federal Savings and Loan Association, chartered in 1956, was the first of the Gaston-inspired enterprises established as a public corporation rather than a family-controlled business. The motivation, however, was the same; if other financial institutions would not make sufficient capital available to build homes, churches, and businesses in the black community, Gaston would organize his own.

The establishment of the A.G. Gaston Motel in 1954 met an immediate need for blacks traveling in the segregated South, but the motel

Dr. A.G. Gaston, one of the most widely respected entrepreneurs in Birmingham, has spent six decades building a business network.

played an unanticipated role in the civil rights struggles of the 1960s in Birmingham. The motel became the headquarters and haven for Martin Luther King, Jr., and other civil rights leaders who succeeded in creating a more open Birmingham society.

Although Birmingham became a more integrated community in the

1960s, Gaston believed there was still a need for providing services for senior citizens that could be met through the A.G. Gaston Home for Senior Citizens—opened in 1963. After a period of consolidation, he ventured into a new arena in 1976; two radio stations, purchased from bankruptcy court, are now successful competitors in the Birmingham market. Gaston's entrepreneurial energy continued in 1986 with the founding of Gaston Construction Company.

Now 94 years old, Dr. A.G. Gaston continues to work six days a week. Although he never attended college, his business talents have earned him honorary degrees from such schools as the University of Alabama, Tuskegee Institute, and Pepperdine University. Widely respected in the state and nation, he has spent his life meeting needs and making life better for the black community in Birmingham.

At the center of Dr. A.G. Gaston's business enterprises in Birmingham is the Booker T. Washington Insurance Company, which is headquartered in the same building as the Citizens Federal Savings Bank.

STERNE, AGEE & LEACH, INC.

Sterne, Agee & Leach, Inc., is the largest and oldest investment banking firm with headquarters in Alabama. The only member firm of the New York Stock Exchange headquartered in Alabama, the organization acts as underwriter, distributor, dealer, and broker in municipal bonds, corporate bonds, common and preferred stocks, and is a market maker in many regional stocks.

Originated as Ward, Sterne & Company, the firm began in Birmingham on August 1, 1919, when George B. Ward—twice mayor of the city—and Mervyn H. Sterne entered into partnership. Each man had previously operated a securities firm in Birmingham, dating from 1901 and 1916, respectively. Rucker Agee joined the organization in 1919; Edmund C. Leach, who opened the Montgomery office, joined in 1921. Becoming known as Ward, Sterne, Agee & Leach until the death of George Ward in 1940, the firm then became Sterne, Agee & Leach.

In 1955 Henry S. Lynn, who had first joined the firm in 1930, acquired a seat on the New York Stock Exchange and is the only resident of Alabama to have been a member of that organization. Alonzo H. Lee, who had joined the company in 1926, became an associate member of the American Stock Exchange in 1955. Changed from a partnership to a corporation in 1964, the firm became Sterne, Agee & Leach, Inc. Ten years later it acquired the business of Shropshire, Frazer & Company, an investment banking firm operated for many years in Mobile by H. Ogden Shropshire and Frank B. Frazer. A Selma office, opened in 1984 by Thomas R. Boyd, was followed in 1985 by an office in Crestline, a Birmingham suburb, managed by Reynolds D. Whatley. In 1987 a Huntsville branch was opened with Mark Custer as manager.

Since its founding the company has been especially active in public finance. In the 1920s, faced with archaic municipal bond laws and no Alabama attorneys specializing in the field, the firm helped draft the first modern municipal bond code for the state. During that decade the company assisted the government of Jefferson County through a difficult bond situation. After an election authorizing road bonds, the county let contracts for road construction, but the bond market collapsed. With bond interest legally limited to 5 percent, the bond issue could not be sold; local headlines announced that the county was bankrupt. Ward, Sterne & Company arranged with the county to issue warrants bearing interest at 8 percent to the road contractors, took options from the contractors on the warrants, and proceeded to market them.

In 1923 the firm purchased the first highway bonds issued by the State of Alabama—the first internal improvements bond issue by the state since the days of Reconstruction—and in 1928, as co-underwriter with Lehman Brothers, purchased the first revenue bonds issued by a state agency. During the 1930s the firm took the lead in revising the Alabama School Warrant Act, under which local boards of education have financed capital improvements for the past 50 years.

Sterne, Agee & Leach actively assisted in the development and passage of legislation that established the Alabama Housing Finance Authority in 1980. The authority has issued more than one billion dollars in single-family and multifamily mortgage revenue bonds.

Recognizing for several years a need among the state's investors for an Alabama Tax-Exempt Bond Trust, in 1984 Sterne, Agee & Leach offered the first registered public offering of a tax-exempt bond trust with interest exempt from both Alabama and federal income taxes. It was well received, and five series of the trust are now held by Alabama investors.

Through the years Sterne, Agee & Leach has served as investment banker and financial adviser to the State of Alabama and its counties, cities, and other bodies to bring their debt securities to market. It has also served as investment banker to a number of institutions of higher learning in the state.

The firm specializes in research coverage of Alabama companies. In addition to the traditional offerings of stocks and municipal and corporate bonds, the company also provides options, limited partnerships, money market and mutual funds, industrial development and pollution-control revenue bonds, as well as other investments. In recent years the firm has expanded its investment banking activities, not only in the municipal bond area but also in corporate finance as an underwriter and distributor of securities for both existing and new enterprises.

Present executive officers of the corporation are William K. McHenry, Jr., chairman of the board; Will Hill Tankersley, chairman of the executive committee; Henry S. Lynn, vice-chairman of the board; Henry S. Lynn, Jr., president, treasurer, and chief executive officer; and W. Warren Belser, Jr., executive vice-president and secretary. With offices in Birmingham, Montgomery, Mobile, Huntsville, Crestline, and Selma, Sterne, Agee & Leach, Inc., continues a tradition of offering quality investment services to clients.

O'NEAL STEEL, INC.

Kirkman O'Neal, grandson of Alabama Governor Edward A. O'Neal and son of Alabama Governor Emmet O'Neal, might have followed his father into the practice of law; but instead he chose to attend the Naval Academy at Annapolis. The discovery of an old eye injury, however, prevented him from pursuing a naval career after graduation in 1913.

He served for a time as his father's private secretary in the governor's office and then as his law clerk in Birmingham. But just as he began deliberating on more permanent job offers, world events intervened to pull him back to the Navy. A German submarine sank the *Lusitania;* as the nation entered World War I, O'Neal sent in an application to the Naval Department and was commissioned as an ensign.

After his discharge from the Navy following the Armistice, he was back to job hunting again. A brief stint with U.S. Steel at the Chickasaw shipyard and Ingalls Iron Works Company introduced him to steel fabrication. Not content to work for someone else, soon he was searching for a way to go into business for himself.

In 1921 O'Neal borrowed $2,000 and invested in a small steel-

The original fabrication facilities of Southern Steel Works, predecessor to O'Neal Steel, Inc., were on Birmingham's west side.

fabricating firm in West End. At the time Southern Steel Works had no orders on the books. O'Neal Steel, Inc., was to grow from this small firm. The beginning was not easy. The first day brought many revelations. O'Neal had been assured that there were no outstanding debts, but soon discovered that there was an overdue note at the bank, the rent was two months past due, and the tool company was threatening to

The current Birmingham service center has more than one-half million square feet of metals storage and processing capability under roof.

take back the air compressor. "I had no idea so many things could happen to one person in a single day, and all bad!" recalls O'Neal.

But he began working to make things happen: getting the tool company to leave the compressor for another month, working out an agreement with the bank to obtain the money necessary to get the steel needed for a job, straightening out a contract for bridge construction for a coal company, and making business contacts that would enable him to compete with much larger firms that had equally large inventories. In the 1920s O'Neal bought out the other partner in Southern Steel. O'Neal Steel was on its way.

By the time of the Great Depression the company had built up an annual sales of $350,000. As with all Birmingham companies, however, O'Neal Steel struggled to stay afloat in the Depression. O'Neal recalls that during one month total sales were less than $700.

As the nation's entry into World War II approached, business conditions began to improve. O'Neal moved into a large new plant on the east side of Birmingham and went into round-the-clock production. During the war O'Neal plant resources were converted to the munitions effort, manufacturing bomb casings, gun platforms, and superstructures for aircraft carriers. In mid-1945 O'Neal was making twice as many bombs as any other plant in the nation. For its efforts in meeting wartime needs, O'Neal Steel re-

ceived Army and Navy "E" awards with two citations for excellence. At the conclusion of the war O'Neal moved back into structural fabrication.

Even before the war O'Neal had begun a warehouse service. Becoming one of the largest fabricators in the area, O'Neal not only maintained its own inventory but also was able to sell to other fabricators. From that, the concept of service centers or "supermarkets for steel" grew. In the early 1950s the company established a branch location in Jackson, Mississippi, that was exclusively a service center. That was the beginning of a widespread network. Today O'Neal operates 18 service centers with two of the major operations located in Birmingham and Mobile.

Through the 1950s and 1960s the company added a number of specialty metal products and began a significant switch from fabrication to service center. The shift in emphasis followed trends in the manufacturing community. More and more manufacturers began going to a "just-in-time" or zero-inventory method of operation. Distributors, therefore, began to play a larger role in the metals industry, acting as middlemen between the producers and consumers of raw steel products.

O'Neal Steel is recognized as being a leader in the service center industry. The company was one of the first to utilize mechanized vertical storage and computerized inventory control. A sophisticated in-house data-processing system allows sales, purchasing, and credit personnel to have instant access to information. As a result of being on the leading edge, O'Neal Steel has grown more rapidly than the industry in general.

Also contributing to the firm's growth is its service of "first-stage processing." The old warehouse business did virtually no processing; today in the service center industry approximately 50 percent of material shipped to a manufacturer has had some form of first-stage processing performed. O'Neal has been a

Flame cutting of parts from steel plate is but one of many processing functions performed in the modern Mobile service center facility.

leader in adding equipment and processing services.

The second and third generation of the O'Neal family is now active in the business. Kirkman O'Neal retired as president in 1959 and became chairman of the board. He was succeeded by his son, Emmet O'Neal II. When Emmet II became

Facilitated by an advanced computer network, inside sales/customer service representatives are virtual banks of up-to-date information regarding inventory availability, order status, and pricing.

chairman of the board, Kirkman O'Neal became chairman of the finance committee. Emmet O'Neal III now serves the company as vice-chairman.

In looking back to the little shed in West End, Kirkman O'Neal proudly recalls that "no outside money except the original $2,000 has ever been put into the business. Our expansion has been through funds generated within the company." From that disastrous first day in the offices of Southern Steel Works, the O'Neals have built O'Neal Steel, Inc., into the largest privately owned metal service center in the nation and a leader in the metals service center industry.

THE DAUGHTERS OF CHARITY

Sufficient medical facilities were sorely lacking in the State of Alabama in the late 1800s, as they were in a great many areas in the Southeast at the time. As the population grew and industry expanded, the need for such facilities became more and more apparent. It is a handful of very special individuals that the state has to thank for being the primary instruments in remedying the deficiency. They belonged to the Daughters of Charity, an international organization that was founded in 1633 and that has a centuries-old tradition of involvement in the healing ministry.

A group of the Sisters, located at the Provincial House of the Daughters of Charity at Emmitsburg, Maryland, was visited by the Reverend Patrick O'Reilly, pastor of St. Paul's Church in Birmingham. It was he who convinced several of the Sisters to come to Birmingham to establish and staff a hospital. Birmingham's citizens were in favor of the effort and were responsible for donations that would finance a portion of the construction costs.

On June 8, 1898, a meeting was held at St. Paul's Church where citizens of Birmingham formed a committee and agreed that the name of the organization would be the Sisters of Charity Hospital Association. A 10-acre site for the hospital was then selected in Fountain Heights. In the

Sister Chrysostom Moynahan, the first nurse to be registered by the State of Alabama, founded the school of nursing at St. Vincent's.

meantime the residence of Mr. H.F. DeBardeleben had been leased to serve as a temporary hospital until a new, permanent building could be completed. The DeBardeleben residence also became the home of the Sisters, who arrived from St. Louis, Mobile, and Knoxville to begin operating the temporary facility.

The doors of the hospital were officially opened on December 20, 1898, equipped to accommodate 30 patients. Shortly thereafter, on March 11, 1899, ground-breaking ceremonies were held at the site of what would become a permanent facility. Eighteen months later the Sisters began moving into the first completed wing of the hospital, and the next day the first five patients arrived. Formal dedication of the new hospital was held on Thanksgiving Day in 1900; Mayor W. Mell Drennan called it the new "palatial home of widest human charity."

The hospital contained 100 beds and, according to reports in local papers, offered its patients the best of everything in the South—from electric lights to operating rooms. A room and the care that went along with it cost patients a total of $12 per week. At the end of its first year in operation, the hospital had cared for more than 1,200 patients, 500 of whom were charity patients, paying nothing for the medical attention they received. In 1901 the Hillman Hospital and Clinic was built to take over the care of the charity patients, establishing St. Vincent's status as a private hospital.

Father O'Reilly, largely responsible for the establishment of St. Vincent's, was thrown from his horse while serving as chaplain in the National Guard of Alabama in 1904 and died a few days later. He was buried on the grounds of St. Vincent's where a monument was later erected in his honor as testimony to his great contributions to the hospital's beginnings.

Early in 1900 the first school of nursing to open in north Alabama did so at St. Vincent's, founded by Sister Chrysostom, the first nurse to be registered in the State of Alabama. Her certificate of registration bears the prestigious #1. After nearly a century of operation, however, the nursing school, because of many issues facing diploma nursing programs, will close after graduating the

Birmingham's first ambulance is parked in front of St. Vincent's in the early 1900s.

final class in 1987.

A new, seven-story structure was completed and dedicated in 1972 at a cost of $12 million, followed in 1975 by a $4-million Professional Building that houses suites for physicians and a parking deck with 325 spaces. Since 1975 more additions and expansions have been completed, virtually doubling the hospital's size. Today, with its 338 acute care beds, St. Vincent's is considered to be a specialty referral hospital.

During the formative years of St. Vincent's, another hospital was being established in Alabama's capital city, again by the Daughters of Charity. In 1901, $10,000 was raised in the city of Montgomery with which the Sisters began construction. Again a home in the area housed the Sisters and also served as a temporary facility. On April 3, 1902, ground-breaking ceremonies were held for St. Margaret's Hospital, and one month later the first cornerstone was laid. By June 1902 the hospital was open for business. That same month Dr. Luther L. Hill performed the hospital's first surgery.

In 1919 the first of many additions was made to the hospital and, along with physical expansion, technological advances were made at a rapid pace. A tumor and cancer clinic was established in 1927, and in 1940 a school of nursing was opened to the public.

With the addition of an east wing in 1956, Montgomery experienced several firsts. St. Margaret's became the first hospital in the state to house a recovery room, an intercommunication system between patients' rooms and nurses' stations, and a cafeteria for visitors and family members. More wings were added, a new school of nursing was built in 1967, and a six-story professional office building and parking deck were completed in 1978.

Montgomery's first hospital was completely renovated in 1981 at an investment of $17 million, refacing and modernizing the structure to offer some of the most modern and spacious medical facilities in the state.

The Daughters of Charity had brought their ministry to south Alabama prior to the other two ventures. Providence Hospital, administered by the Sisters, was established in Mobile in 1854 with the capacity to care for 60 patients. Since that time the hospital has gone on to establish a tradition of change, growth, and development for the betterment of the community.

Providence Hospital was the site of numerous firsts in Mobile, including kidney dialysis, a school of nursing, health and wellness services, pastoral services, and family-centered maternity care. The institution has been constant in its philosophies about the dignity of each person, the sanctity of life, and service to the poor.

St. Vincent's today.

Ground was broken for St. Margaret's in April 1902 in Montgomery.

The institution has advanced today to state-of-the-art equipment and service and offers the latest in technology and design. These advances that will culminate with the opening in 1987 of a new 245-acre health care complex, encompassing a 349-bed hospital, an ambulatory services center, a rehabilitation hospital, a psychiatric and substance abuse hospital, an extended care facility, and a wellness and sports center. A retirement community is being planned and commercial development within the complex will include a hotel, shopping areas, and restaurants.

The presence of Providence will be felt in Mobile more keenly than ever with the completion of this new facility, continuing on in the tradition of healing through modern innovation and technology.

These hospitals and the care they offered the residents of Alabama represented monumental efforts by the Daughters of Charity; but hospitals were not the only organizations the Sisters were responsible for founding. At the time that St. Vincent's hospital was being established, the same Father O'Reilly was also charting the course for the first orphanage in north Alabama. He obtained permission from the local bishop to purchase a parcel of land to use for the orphanage. More Sisters from the Provincial House of the Daughters of Charity in Maryland arrived to assist in operating the institution.

On the acquired property was a large, redbrick building in a beautiful, tranquil setting of trees atop a hill. This building had originally been built sometime in 1890 and, on July 13, 1903, welcomed Manley Webb as the first orphan to enroll at the home. Formal blessing and dedication services for the building were held six days later. Many children soon followed, children bereft of one or both parents or whose parents were unable to care for them. They were welcomed and cared for by the Sisters.

Following Father O'Reilly's tragic death, the Reverend James E. Coyle became the pastor of St. Paul's Church and the champion of the orphanage for some 17 years before his own death. In 1925 the first swimming pool was constructed on the grounds, and in July 1938 the orphanage was presented with its first bus.

In 1948 the name of the institution was changed from East Lake Atheneum Orphanage Home to St. Thomas Home-on-the-Hill. Five years later, on its 50th anniversary, there were 57 children living at the home which, at that time, began to care for emotionally disturbed children. In the mid-1950s the institution began to emphasize its temporary nature, encouraging the placement of children in boarding houses or in adoptive homes.

St. Margaret's was completely renovated in 1981 and is now one of the most modern medical facilities in the state.

Ground was blessed and broken on August 30, 1954, for a new St. Thomas Home that was completed in 1956. In August 1958 the home welcomed its first "Housefather," who not only assisted in teaching school, but also joined in on sports and helped the boys solve their "man-to-man" problems.

Sadly, due to the decrease in the number of children being housed over the years, the increase of annual expenses, and the costly maintenance of buildings and unused space, it was decided that the home would be phased out in June 1971. The facility became the St. Thomas Day Care Center and, later, the St. Tho-

The first Providence Hospital, in Mobile, was located at St. Anthony and Broad streets.

mas Catholic Life Center.

Another early contribution of the Daughters of Charity to the State of Alabama was St. Mary's Home in Mobile, which was begun in 1838 at the encouragement of the first bishop of Mobile. He requested the Sisters' presence to form a Society of Catholic women who would work to alleviate the extreme poverty and suffering that existed. The organization would also work to give aid to the many destitute and orphaned children in Mobile.

The asylum for children opened its doors on December 26, 1838, and survived not only the Civil War and an explosion in 1866 that completely destroyed the building, but also the citywide epidemic of yellow fever in 1897, two major hurricanes, the Great Depression, and both world wars. Originally an orphanage for Catholic girls, St. Mary's, in 1950, began to focus on residential pro-

grams for neglected girls of all religious persuasions, and in 1967 began caring for boys as well.

St. Mary's is the oldest residential program for children in the state and today operates as a school for both girls and boys. Based on the belief that the family is the natural unit of society, when that unit is disturbed every effort is made to correct the family union or substitute a family for the children involved. In 1987 St. Mary's will celebrate its 150th anniversary.

The Allen Memorial Home, another Daughters of Charity institution established in Mobile, was begun in 1911 by Sisters who were housed temporarily at Providence Hospital. Allen Memorial was begun as a home for abandoned babies and orphans, and included a program for unwed mothers. Its first child was received on Christmas Day in 1911. Today, with 940 beds, the facilities offer 24-hour nursing care for sick and primarily elderly individuals. Short-term nursing is also available to those who will be able to eventually return home. The Allen Memorial Home currently employs a staff of 92 who work to meet the physical as well as spiritual needs of its patients.

St. James Major School, located near Mobile in the once all-black parish of St. James, was established in 1913. It was staffed originally by lay-teachers, but was taken over by the Holy Ghost Sisters in 1924, and finally by the Daughters of Charity in 1964. The school was built on the grounds of the St. James Church with education and service to the poor as its primary interest. Still in

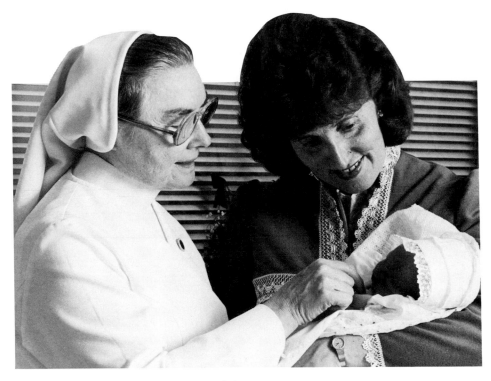

The Daughters of Charity, an order founded in 1633 with a centuries-old tradition of involvement in the healing ministry, has provided care for the residents of Alabama since the founding of Providence Hospital in 1854.

its original location in what is now the city of Prichard, the school is supported largely by contributions from individuals and organizations in the area. Visits are still made regularly by the Sisters to the families of the schoolchildren and to the needy in the city.

The two newest establishments in the state operated by the Daughters of Charity are Cathedral Place in Mobile and Seton Haven in Montgomery. Cathedral Place began as a dream of Bishop John L. May of Mobile to provide a home for the elderly. That dream was realized in 1975, when two Daughters of Charity

The 349-bed Providence Hospital features state-of-the-art equipment and the latest in technology and design.

were assigned to the 190-unit complex that experiences a 100-percent occupancy rate at all times. The Sisters work hard to meet the social and spiritual needs of the elderly residents by driving them to doctors appointments, grocery stores, bingo games, and shopping centers. Other periodic outings are planned in and out of town that keep the residents active and healthy.

Seton Haven was opened in October 1979 as a housing facility for the handicapped and elderly who wish to live independently but not isolated. The Daughters of Charity provides most of the staff for the facility that is owned and operated by the Catholic Housing Authority of Montgomery. The 100 units of the complex are located on five acres near St. Bede's Church.

From glancing at the histories of these organizations of healing, education, and care with which the Daughters of Charity have been closely aligned for well over a century, the importance of their role in Alabama's spirit of brotherhood, or "sisterhood," toward their own—whether orphaned or elderly, sick or well, poor or wealthy—is evident. Their ministry and the philosophies they have brought to the State of Alabama will forever be remembered as an integral part of its past and looked to in the future for inspiration.

LONG-LEWIS, INC.

Inspired by Alabama iron boom towns such as Birmingham, the new town of Bessemer—named for Sir Henry Bessemer, the British inventor of the Bessemer process of steelmaking—was incorporated in 1887 in the western area of Jefferson County. That same year William J. Long, a native of Xenia, Ohio, decided that the new town offered promising opportunities for a man skilled in the metalworking trade.

Born of immigrant parents from Ireland and Holland, Long had become an apprentice tinsmith at the age of 12 and a journeyman at 15. In addition to employment as a tinsmith, he also sold farm implements for an Ohio hardware establishment and worked with the Pennsylvania Railroad. In 1885, at the age of 26, he left Ohio to work on a canal project in Panama. After a short time at the Isthmus, Long returned to the Birmingham district through which he had passed on his way southward. Securing a contract to put a metal roof and cornice work on a school, as well as other tinsmithing assignments, he decided to open a business in the new town of Bessemer.

The entrepreneur built a shop of red corrugated metal at First Alley and Second Avenue and opened the Bessemer Cornice Works. His shop produced the highly ornate cornice

Long-Lewis replaced its buggy line with a Ford dealership, currently the oldest existing in Alabama.

The Long-Lewis Ford dealership was housed in the same building as the hardware store until 1965.

and decorative metalwork used for a number of structures built in boomtown Bessemer: the McDonald Block, the I. Rosen Store, the Kartus Korner Building, and the First National Bank. Purchasing additional property on Second Avenue North, Long erected a corrugated-iron structure and began stocking a mercantile line of tinware, stoves, ranges, padlocks, screens, and nails—the beginning of the hardware phase of the enterprise. Additional expansion allowed him to add a line of buggies, wagons, and harnesses.

The rapidly expanding business suffered a major disaster in 1899, when fire destroyed the buildings and the stock; insurance covered only a small part of the value. John C. Perry, Long's stepson, took charge of the temporary store opened after the fire. By January 1901 Long and Perry had built a new brick structure on the original site with a sales area for hardware, stoves, and ranges on the first floor and stock storage on the second. They soon added a two-story addition for the buggy and harness line.

The expanding services of the Bessemer Cornice Works formed the foundation for the Long-Lewis Hardware Company, incorporated on June 29, 1906, with William J. Long as president and Isaac Arthur Lewis as first vice-president. Lewis withdrew in 1908 to form another establishment in Bessemer. A contracting service, growing out of plumbing

business done by Long as early as 1890, ultimately became the general contracting firm of Sullivan, Long & Hagerty but was not formally severed from the parent company until 1939. By then the firm had earned a solid reputation all over the South in municipal improvement work such as waterworks and sewage construction, and road building and paving work. Both the son and stepson of William Long worked with the contracting firm.

As the nation entered the automobile age, Long-Lewis ultimately replaced its buggy line with the horseless carriage. The first automobile handled by the company was a two-cylinder International made by International Harvester; however, in 1911 Long purchased a Ford from a Bessemer merchant who had won the car but was afraid to drive it.

In 1915 Long-Lewis became an official Ford dealership—currently the oldest existing in Alabama. Since the automobile showroom was in the same building as the hardware store, salesmen did not know if a customer entering the front door wanted an ax or an automobile. In the early years trusted customers could buy cars on "open account" just as they bought hardware items. The sales receipt for a new car read "Long-Lewis Hardware Company" at the top.

William Long died in 1920, a successful businessman and faithful community servant to his adopted city. The following year, at the annual meeting of the Long-Lewis directorate, John T. Hagerty became president. He was succeeded by Long's stepson, John Perry, in 1924.

Charles A. Long, son of the founder, began work at the firm during his first year of high school. He resumed work with the company after earning a degree in mechanical engineering from the University of Alabama in 1914, but service overseas in World War I interrupted his association with Long-Lewis. Elected a director of the organization in 1922, he subsequently served as secretary, second vice-president, and

Long-Lewis Hardware served the Bessemer community from this location until the company began operating exclusively out of its Birmingham store in 1980.

first vice-president, then followed Perry as president in 1938.

In 1929 Long-Lewis opened a wholesale and retail outlet in Birmingham at Fifth Avenue and Ninth Street North that became a very successful venture. Although the Bessemer store remained more retail oriented, the Birmingham operation became exclusively wholesale in 1946. As a distributor organization, Long-Lewis had salesmen blanket-

The hardware store carried a mercantile line that ranged from stoves to tinware, and from hammers and nails to buggies and harnesses.

ing the state, calling on hardware dealers and contractors. When the Bessemer store was closed in 1980, Long-Lewis Hardware began operating exclusively out of the Birmingham location.

The automobile dealership remained in the same facility as the Bessemer hardware store until 1965, when it moved to the current location on the "Bessemer Superhighway" near the Brighton turnoff. In 1986 Long-Lewis Ford led the car dealerships of Alabama, with sales of $60.8 million.

Today the company begun by the tinsmith from Ohio is known officially as Long-Lewis, Inc. Charles A. Long, Jr., grandson of the founder, serves as chairman of both the hardware and automobile dealership divisions. On December 29, 1986, Vaughn Burrell, who managed the Ford division for 22 years, purchased the company from the Long family.

FONTAINE GROUP, INC.

The Fontaine Group is a diversified group of companies, with corporate headquarters in Birmingham, providing essential products and services to the heavy-duty trucking industry. The group employs 900 people at 21 locations with a combined plant and office capacity exceeding 774,000 square feet. Annual sales are in excess of $100 million. The Fontaine Group is an outgrowth of the Fontaine Truck Equipment Company.

Entreprenurial drive led John P.K. Fontaine to form the Fontaine Truck Equipment Company in 1940 to produce various specialized trailers for the U.S. government. Shortly after World War II began, a critical shortage of fifth wheels, cast-steel devices that coupled tractors to trailers, developed. In 1942 Fontaine invented the "fabricated" fifth wheel,

by welding together steel plate and support structures, as an alternative to the cast-steel fifth wheel.

Following the war Fontaine Truck Equipment evolved from a government contractor to a producer of platform and heavy-duty specialty trailers as well as fifth wheels for commercial use. In 1947 Fontaine developed the "No-Slack®" locking mechanism for the fabricated fifth wheel, designed to automatically adjust the "slack" connection that results when the fifth wheel locking mechanism and the trailer kingpin continuously rub together. Although this development gave Fontaine a superior product in the marketplace, he still found it difficult to break down heavy-duty truck distributors' loyalty to the cast fifth wheel.

Fontaine fought the distributors' prejudice by marketing his

products directly to truck dealers and factory branches. He stood behind the quality of his product by offering a no-questions-asked warranty. And he was able to offer his products at a value price because he bypassed the middleman, the distributor.

In order to further support his warranty program, and to provide wider distribution with more complete service to his customers, Fontaine conceived of a nationwide network of branches that would sell and install fifth wheels and other truck equipment the company man-

Fontaine Truck Equipment Company both sells and installs a wide variety of truck equipment and parts.

The legacy of innovation has been passed from John P.K. Fontaine (right) to new company president, Kelly Dier.

Fontaine produces fifth wheels in scores of type, size, and mount variations for all makes of heavy-duty trucks.

Fontaine Truck Modification Company offers its customers detailed truck modifications and equipment installations.

ufactured. The first full-service branch opened in Los Angeles in 1961, and by 1975 twelve branches were operating in major cities across the country.

Responding to the needs of a growing customer base, Fontaine added its product line dump bodies, lime and fertilizer spreaders, and bulk feed transport equipment. As production of this diverse product line strained the limits of the company's manufacturing and warehouse facility, Fontaine built its first fully integrated fifth wheel manufacturing plant in Rocky Mount, North Carolina, in 1963. Two years later platform and lowbed trailer production was moved to a plant in

Fontaine Body and Hoist is one of few dump body manufacturers in the United States to build its own complete hydraulics systems.

Fontaine Trailer Company, located in Haleyville, Alabama, produces a complete line of platform trailers and many special applications.

Haleyville, Alabama, and integrated manufacture of dump bodies and hydraulics began in a facility in Collins, Mississippi.

A series of record sales years gave Fontaine the confidence to open a second, fully integrated, 50,000-square-foot fifth wheel plant in 1974, located in Burnes Flat, Oklahoma. And, in 1979, a 122,000-square-foot plant was purchased in Birmingham. This facility initially manufactured spreaders, standard lowbed trailers, and heavy-duty specialty trailers, but today is solely dedicated to the manufacture of fifth wheels.

In 1982 the company was reorganized along divisional lines in order to provide a dedicated management team for each product line. Aggressive sales programs were implemented with the addition of product zone managers to service existing accounts, set up distributors, and solicit new business.

In January 1983 Fontaine Truck Equipment Company was purchased by The Marmon Group of Companies headquartered in Chicago. The firm was transformed from a centralized, divisional structure to a decentralized group of "stand alone" business units. The Fontaine Group today consists of five independent companies that work together to supply the diverse needs of heavy-duty truck equipment customers. These include Fontaine Fifth Wheel Company, Fontaine Truck Equipment Company, Fontaine Modifications/Components Company, and the Fontaine Body & Hoist Company.

Fontaine Fifth Wheel Company employs 252 people at two locations: the Birmingham plant (130,000 square feet), which also houses the corporate offices; and the plant in Rocky Mount, North Carolina (123,000 square feet). Fontaine Fifth Wheel produces fifth wheel coupling devises for heavy-duty tractors.

Fontaine Trailer Company employs 160 people at its 170,000-square-foot facility in Haleyville, Al-

abama. It produces a complete line of platform trailers in flat, drop, and lowbed configurations as well as custom designed trailers with hauling capacities up to 300 tons.

Fontaine Truck Equipment Company, headquartered in Birmingham, is the nation's largest full-line truck equipment distributor. The firm both sells and installs fifth wheels, dump bodies, ice control and agricultural spreaders, trailers, service bodies, van bodies, platform and stake bodies, cranes, lift gates, tool boxes, bedliners, tractor accessories, and parts and service for these products. Fontaine Truck Equipment employs 214 people in 12 locations: Atlanta, Birmingham, Charlotte, Dallas, Ft. Lauderdale, Indianapolis, Kansas City, Los Angeles, Louisville, New Orleans, Nashville, and Philadelphia.

Fontaine Modification/Components Company is headquartered in Louisville, Kentucky. The MOD center offers detailed truck equipment installations and modifications for truck dealers and fleet groups. It employs 100 people at three locations, including Louisville, Kentucky; Pontiac, Michigan; and Springfield, Ohio. The Marmon-Herrington division of the Fontaine Modification/Components Company, also located in Louisville, produces custom-engineered, all-wheel-drive kits, including OEM axles and transfer cases, to convert 4x2 and 6x4 vehicles to 4x4 and 6x6 trucks.

Fontaine Body and Hoist produces dump bodies, dump body hoists, and agricultural spreaders and ice control spreaders. Located in Collins, Mississippi, the company employs 155 people.

Sound management, product innovation, and a strong commitment to customer satisfaction are philosophies that have piloted Fontaine to a leadership position in today's truck transportation industry. Aggressive marketing programs are positioning the Fontaine Group for a leadership role in the industry tomorrow and beyond.

KOVACH & ASSOCIATES

Frank Kovach was a successful contractor and manufacturer's representative of conveying equipment when he tried, in 1971, to rent office space at Mountain Brook Office Park on Highway 280 in Birmingham. To his surprise, none was available.

As a result, Kovach decided to build his first office building, and Kovach & Associates was born. From a one-man company it has grown to 50 professionals and 25 buildings with more than one million square feet of office space.

With a seemingly unerring instinct for sites, Kovach has concentrated on suburban office park development. Century Park South, his first major complex, was built on an 18-acre site in Vestavia Hills adjacent to Interstate 65. An award-winning complex of eight buildings, it was entirely conceived, constructed, and leased by Kovach.

Before Century Park South was complete, Kovach had begun a similar project, Chase Park South, on U.S. Highway 31 at the entrance to the planned community of Riverchase. Five rustic cedar-and-stone buildings nestled into 16 acres of wooded land. As Kovach completed the project, he was ready to begin work on Cahaba Park South, located on 22 acres purchased in the Highway 280 corridor near Inverness.

In 1983 Kovach & Associates sold the Century and Chase Park projects, encompassing approximately 350,000 square feet in 13 buildings, to Metropolitan Life Insurance Company for more than $20 million. The sale provided Kovach with the necessary capital for impressive growth and expansion into new markets.

The following year Kovach acquired a site in Deerfield Beach, Florida, and constructed a six-story polished granite 125,000-square-foot building. On behalf of Metropolitan Life, he also acquired additional land and 105,000 square feet in four completed buildings located in the Hillsboro Executive Center in Deer-

Frank Kovach, Jr., president.

field Beach. Kovach & Associates, Florida Division, is now headquartered in the growing complex, with plans to expand it to 500,000 square feet.

Joining with Harbert Corporation in 1984, Kovach began the development of Chase Corporate Centre on a 14-acre site in Riverchase and constructed a Class A 225,000-square-foot building. This cooperative venture led to a third field office for Kovach & Associates in Huntsville, called Perimeter Park

Kovach Centre, headquarters for Kovach & Associates, at 2700 Highway 280 South in Birmingham.

South. The Kovach/Harbert group has completed a 105,000-square-foot office building on a 40-acre site near Huntsville's Research Park, with more than 600,000 square feet planned.

The last four projects completed by Kovach differ from the earlier developments in two ways: They are larger, averaging more than 100,000 square feet, and are Class A high-quality, midrise structures, four floors or higher, in contrast to the earlier two- and three-story buildings. "This new era of polished granite and heavily landscaped buildings featuring artist-designed custom carpets, custom original artwork, and high-speed mahogany elevators is exciting," explains Kovach, "and they are what the corporate client wants."

Diversification and growth continues. An apartment division, established in 1985, joint ventured a 220-unit project, River Place, on the Cahaba River, is constructing a 400-unit complex, Cahaba Forest Apartments, and has plans for a 200-unit group in Vestavia. Kovach & Associates expects to add a fourth field office in 1987 and one a year thereafter. Frank Kovach's philosophy for growth includes highly capable associates with ownership and profit sharing in the projects with which they are involved, and sound business partners such as Metropolitan Life and Harbert International, which can assist with funding for future projects.

CAR & TRUCK RENTAL

Sallie Creel began her car rental business in a service station on Birmingham's Airport Highway in 1972. Inside the office she had two desks and two phones. Under one desk a mongrel dog—dubbed "Union"—took up residence and delivered nine puppies. With gas selling for 37 cents a gallon and premiums still in vogue, Creel put up a billboard: "Free pup with a fillup!" Customers competed to take home the pups, named "Union 76," "77," "78," etc.!

Such innovation has been a key to the business success that earned Creel the title of Small Business Person of the Year from the Birmingham Area Chamber of Commerce in 1984. The Creel franchise increased eightfold, from $150,000 to $1.2 million, between 1972 and 1983. Starting with two people and 20 cars, the firm now has 25 employees and a fleet of more than 400 vehicles in its Rent-A-Car franchise. In 1986 Creel opened a new facility in the booming community of Hoover, targeting the business of a new luxury hotel and the Riverchase Galleria.

Southern coeds of the 1950s were not expected to achieve such success in the business world, and, indeed, Sallie Cole had no particular career goals when she graduated from Ramsay High School and enrolled at the University of Alabama. Only a few hours short of a degree, she left school and soon was married. Ten years and three children later, she found herself divorced and the primary support for her children.

After working for a time in real estate, she accepted a job with a car rental agency and gained valuable knowledge of all aspects of the business. In the meantime she had married John Creel and added his two children to her busy life. Showing her an advertisement for agency franchises in an in-flight magazine, her husband challenged her: "If you are going to work 80 hours a week, why not open your own business?" In spite of her initial doubts, Sallie Creel secured financing from General Motors Acceptance Corporation for 20 cars.

She had to come up with innovative solutions to problems from the outset. When the 20 cars she had ordered for the opening were not delivered in time, she called up everybody in her family and rented their cars to fulfill the reservations she had booked.

In the first years Creel was personally involved in all aspects of the business. She made sales calls, waited on customers, kept the books, washed cars, filled gas tanks, and

Sallie Creel has guided her Rent-A-Car company to success in a highly competitive market.

found homes for puppies while calling attention to her new business. "We have to try harder," notes Creel. "Most of our business is from local companies and repeat customers—not travelers."

Evidence of Creel's creativity and hard work is obvious in her sales figures, her awards, and her positions in Birmingham business and civic organizations. As her business has grown, so has her involvement in community affairs. "I have come to the point," remarks Creel, "where I can do some community work now. . . . If you're interested in what goes on around you with other people's welfare, it is very rewarding both personally and business wise."

JEMISON INVESTMENT CO., INC.

John S. Jemison, Jr., is characterized in Birmingham business circles as a "deal maker"—in the best sense of the term. He is a man who is admired by his associates for getting to the essence of the question or the problem quickly. His reputation for openness in his business dealings has led to trust and confidence in Jemison and in Jemison Investment Co., Inc.

Born in Birmingham in 1908, Jemison is a member of a family that has long been active in the business and civic life of the city and the state. Educated in the public schools of Birmingham, he graduated in 1931 from the University of North Carolina, Chapel Hill, with a degree in business administration.

After graduation he accepted a position with the Bank of Manhattan Company (now Chase Manhattan Bank) and did work in advanced accounting, securities analysis, and economics at the New York University Graduate School of Business Administration. From 1940 to 1947 Jemison was associated with Goldman, Sachs & Co., New York, one of the nation's largest underwriters of industrial securities. During that time he also served with the U.S. Navy, discharged with the rank of commander.

Jemison returned to Birmingham in 1947 and until 1955 was resident partner at Marx & Co., investment bankers, of Birmingham and New York City. When Otto Marx, Jr., was invited to become president of Paribas Corporation in New York, Marx and Jemison dissolved their partnership.

In 1949 Jemison had organized Jemison Investment Co., Inc., as a small side investment firm, but Jemison Investment was not activated until the partnership was dissolved. Since 1955 the company, 100-percent owned by Jemison and his four children, has been Jemison's main business.

From 1955 to 1983 Jemison was president and treasurer of the company; since 1983 he has been chairman and treasurer. James D. Davis currently serves as president. Jemison describes the company as a "small conglomerate." Jemison Investment has a number of subsidiaries and divisions and two controlled affiliate companies. Jemison is chairman of the board of each of the firms, and Davis is on the board of each. However, all businesses operate autonomously, and day-to-day operations are handled by management of the companies.

Jemison Investment's largest subsidiary is Stringfellow Lumber Company, Inc., headquartered in Birmingham. Founded in 1913 by E.D. Stringfellow in Reform, Alabama, the firm moved to Tuscaloosa

---

SIRCO, known originally as Southern States Iron Roofing Company, opened a new office building in 1951. The office is still in use today.

before coming to Birmingham in 1937. Lumber brokerage was the ongoing function of the company, but at various times the firm was involved with operating sawmills and with warehouse distribution and manufacturing.

Jemison Investment purchased Stringfellow Lumber in 1971 from the estate of the founder. Expansion after the acquisition resulted in a larger and more diversified company. Selling only to dealers, not contractors, Stringfellow operates in Birmingham as a broker in West Coast, Canadian, and Southern pine.

The firm operates wholesale lumber distribution yards in Atlanta, Georgia, and in Birmingham and Hodges, Alabama. A lumber remanufacturing plant at Hodges provides lumber to mobile home industries in the Southeast. In Nashville, Tennessee, Old Hickory Lumber Company sells lumber and other building materials to contractors.

Another Jemison Investment subsidiary, Triangle Distributors, Inc., is located in Tupelo, Mississippi. An outgrowth of a wholesale grocery company founded in Mississippi in 1907, the firm began selling staple hardware and building materials products during the years following World War II. In 1955, as the hard goods increased as a percentage of the company's volume, the managers—three Whiteside brothers—decided to move exclusively into the building materials field.

In 1975 Jemison Investment purchased Triangle. The windows, door frames, and other related building materials are distributed throughout north Mississippi, north Alabama, and into Tennessee. A distribution outlet in Jackson, Tennessee, has increased Triangle's overall warehousing facilities to more than a quarter-million square feet.

Another Birmingham-based subsidiary is SIRCO Systems, Inc. Founded in 1914 by Harry Fullenwater as Southern States Iron Roofing Company, the firm made roofing materials. In 1930 Southern States

began to produce light- and heavy-gauge drums. Reynolds Metals Company purchased controlling interest in 1950. Jemison Investment acquired the outstanding capital stock of SIRCO in 1979. As the only non-aluminum subsidiary of Reynolds, SIRCO had not received the attention or capital it needed. Jemison spent a substantial amount on improving the operations, both in quality of product and in costs. SIRCO is the largest manufacturer of nested steel drums in the United States and has two branch locations, in Memphis and Mobile.

Acquired by Jemison Investment in 1985, Thomas Foundries, Inc., is one of the nation's leading manufacturers of dredge pumps, slurry pumps, high-alloy manganese

SIRCO's current nested drum design enables the company to ship up to 2,500, 55-gallon knocked-down drums to a truckload instead of the usual 250.

steel crusher parts, and custom castings in a wide variety of abrasion-resistant iron and steel alloys. Edward L. Thomas, a native of Valdosta, Georgia, organized the Thomas Grate Bar Company in Birmingham in 1911; after his son, E.A. Thomas, became president in 1937, the name was changed to Thomas Foundries. He installed modern

Located on Birmingham's north side, the 75-year-old Thomas Foundries, Inc., has a new headquarters building.

electric melting furnaces, enabling the company to produce high-quality alloy iron and steel castings and broaden its product line.

The two controlled affiliate businesses of Jemison Investment are L. Farber Company of Worcester, Massachusetts, and Gould & Scammon, Inc., of Auburn, Maine. Farber, more than 70 years old, is the largest manufacturer of leather welting for the shoe industry in the nation. Gould & Scammon manufactures synthetic component parts for the shoe industry, primarily counters that give shape and form to the shoe heels.

The latest acquisition of Jemison Investment is B.A.S.S., Inc., of Montgomery, Alabama, a 19-year-old publishing and bass tournament organization. B.A.S.S., Inc., is the publisher of *Bassmaster Magazine*, *Southern Outdoors Magazine*, *Saltwater Magazine*, and other periodicals and books, with total circulation of over one million. B.A.S.S., Inc., also produces "The Bassmasters," a television fishing series.

Basic to the success of Jemison Investment Co., Inc., is a belief in maintaining autonomy at each company: Each organization operates with its own management and liberal incentives for future growth.

ALABAMA TELCO CREDIT UNION

With a capital of $70, seven charter members—C.A. O'Brien, C.H. Stowers, O.S. Sanders, H.C. Caldwell, Ruth Gulledge, J.T. Norman, and M.B. Phillips—organized Telco Credit Union of Alabama on December 1, 1934. The new institution was promptly approved by the superintendent of insurance on December 5.

Founded to serve the employees of Southern Bell, the new credit union was launched in the depths of the Great Depression in Birmingham, a municipality labeled by the President of the United States as the "worst hit town in the country." In Jefferson County 123,000 people had lost their jobs, mines and mills were closed, and furnaces were out of blast. An old Birmingham adage rang true again: "Hard times come here first and stay longest."

But the new credit union was begun on faith and a commitment to service. Acting as temporary chairman, C.A. O'Brien presided over the first annual meeting held on January 3, 1935, in the Assembly Hall of the Telephone Building at 1715 Sixth Avenue North. O'Brien explained the nature of credit unions to those present and stressed the purpose of Telco as an organization to assist the employees in maintaining good credit and offering them a systematic plan of saving. In addition, Telco would be a source from which they could secure money without paying the exorbitant rates of interest charged by some other lending agencies.

The board of directors elected at the meeting included Stowers, Gulledge, Sanders, and O'Brien from the charter members, and J.E. Richardson, J.L. Powell, and J.C. Willox. The board met five days later, elected O'Brien as president, and set the rate of interest on loans to employees at one percent per month upon unpaid balances and the rate of interest on deposits at 2 percent per annum. With no paid employees the Telco office was to be open on alternate Fridays and the first and 15th of each month from 11 a.m. to

Gene Mauldin, president.

1 p.m. By the beginning of the following month the new credit union reported 104 members and total receipts of $308.25.

President O'Brien was followed by C.H. Stowers, F.M. McCauley, B.F. Lunsford, M.J. Plott, R.C. Meacham, and J.K. Davis, serving terms from 1935 to 1969. T.W. Barker served from 1970 to 1983

Rose Ann Wilson, senior vice-president.

during a record period of growth and development for Telco. In 1983 the title of president was changed to chairman, and Mary Outlaw assumed the position. All officers, directors, and committee members serve without pay on their own time.

Slow but steady progress characterized the growth of Telco until the outbreak of World War II. War and military orders brought rapid expansion to Birmingham. Many factories went on three shifts a day, and women moved into the work force in

increasing numbers.

With Birmingham booming, Telco savings deposits began to grow dramatically, from $150,000 in 1940 to almost $400,000 in just five years. The pattern of growth became even more dramatic in the postwar years. Membership accelerated from slightly less than 2,000 at the end of the war to more than 5,000, 10 years later. By 1955 the assets were $2.35 million. The credit union now had a full-time manager and five employees.

Four years later Telco had grown to almost 7,000 members and exceeded $4.5 million in assets. In 1983 the organization experienced its finest year to date with a 31-percent growth in total assets. On its 50th anniversary Telco celebrated having better than 15,500 members and assets in excess of $46 million.

W.R. Glenn, manager of Telco from 1940 until 1978, oversaw many of the dramatic changes, including the construction of offices completed in 1971. Gene Mauldin became manager in 1978, leading Telco into the era of computerization. A branch office in Mobile opened in March 1982, and a new Birmingham-area office at Riverchase opened in November of the following year. Expansion also occurred in services offered, including IRAs, CDs, real estate mort-

The board of directors of Alabama Telco Credit Union (front row, from left): R.C. Meacham, R.E. Day, J.C. Dickerson, and Mary Outlaw. In the second row (from left): D.E. Kines, Dundas Fowler, A.M. Robertson, Earl Cash, and Lowell Bryant. In the third row (from left): Jim Messer, Keith Milling, L.D. Weems, Tom Waddell, and Eugene Grady. Not present, E.N. Struthers, Jr.

gages, and sharedrafts.

Alabama Telco Credit Union recently opened its new headquarters building at 1849 Data Drive. Conveniently located in Riverchase, the 30,000-square-foot building can accommodate twice the number of

ATCU employees as the Southside office.

For the members this means greater convenience and better service. With four drive-through windows, safe deposit boxes, a night deposit, and an automatic teller machine, all of the members' financial needs can be handled at one location. Alabama Telco now has 12 offices statewide to serve its more than 30,000 members.

As 1987 began Telco had assets topping $100 million and more than 30,000 members. Present board members include Eugene Grady, E.N. Struthers, Jr., R.C. Meacham, L.D. Weems, Mary Outlaw, Earl L. Cash, R.E. Day, D.E. Kines, Keith Milling, William T. Waddell, Jim Messer, A.M. Robertson, Jr., J.C. Dickerson, Jr., Lowell G. Bryant, and Dundas Fowler.

As Alabama Telco Credit Union proceeds into its second half-century of service, it is reaching out to an ever-expanding membership that now includes other communications businesses. Recent steps by the government to deregulate the financial community, coupled with the AT&T divestiture, have propelled ATCU into a business environment full of new opportunities.

D. Claiborne Floyd, vice-president/operations.

ALABAMA POWER COMPANY

More than 80 years ago Captain William Lay built a dam and water-powered generator on Big Wills Creek near Gadsden. But, with the same limited vision they had of airplanes and automobiles of the early 1900s, few people saw the potential in the electricity his generator produced.

However, Captain Lay and other men such as James Mitchell and Thomas Martin did see that potential. Overcoming skepticism and financial difficulties with persistence and determination, they built a foundation for a young but rapidly growing Alabama Power Company —a company that is now the state's primary provider of electric power.

Today Alabama Power serves more than one million customers located throughout the state, from the Tennessee River valley south to Dauphin Island in the Gulf of Mexico. In producing electricity for customers in its 44,500-square-mile service area, Alabama Power uses a mix of 14 hydroelectric generating plants, seven coal-fired plants, and one nuclear power plant.

Under the leadership of current company president Joseph M. Farley, Alabama Power has initiated many important developments in the 1970s and 1980s: new technologies that turn sunlight into electricity, productivity advancements that have dramatically improved the company's ability to provide its product more economically, and an economic development effort that has brought thousands of jobs and other benefits to Alabama.

Since the 1920s Alabama Power has considered the state's economic development to be among its most important roles. In 1921, keenly aware of the need for more industry to supplement farming in the state, company officials formed a New Industries Division. Believed to be the first of its kind in the nation, the division began to promote Alabama as an attractive site for new industry through trade journals, at business meetings throughout the Northeast,

Hydroelectric generation of electricity continues to play an important role in meeting the energy needs of Alabama Power customers.

and at trade shows in Boston, Philadelphia, and New York. Through the New Industries Division, business leaders miles away from Alabama began to learn of the state's resources, its people, and a power delivery system only beginning to harness the vast energy available from the rivers of the state.

Between 1925 and 1940 Alabama Power helped bring 275 new industries and businesses to the state. Following World War II paper, chemical, and rubber manufacturers

Alabama Power Company's Joseph M. Farley Nuclear Electric Generating Plant, located near Dothan, consistently ranks among the nation's best performing nuclear facilities.

moved to Alabama, followed in the 1970s by electronics and machinery firms. Between 1946 and 1980 approximately 6,800 new or expanded business operations came to Alabama through the combined efforts of Alabama Power, the state's Alabama Development Office, local chambers of commerce, and other groups.

Today Alabama Power continues that partnership to bring industry to the state with the operation of The Alabama Resource Center. Located near Birmingham, the facility will use state-of-the-art technology to provide facts on available sites throughout the state to individuals interested in locating or expanding a business or industry in Alabama.

Alabama Power Company continues to be one of the best electric utilities in the United States, fulfilling a vision born more than three-quarters of a century ago at a place called Big Wills Creek.

DANIEL INDUSTRIAL METALS, INC.

Experiencing economic blows brought on by depression years, undergoing several name changes and shifts in primary production, and mourning the sudden loss of the fourth-generation heir and recent company vice-president has not deterred Daniel Industrial Metals, Inc., from growing into and remaining a recognized leader in the fabrication of steel and iron—Birmingham's primary products and industrial symbols. Nor has this growth prevented a continued emphasis on the family from which the business sprang.

W. Homer Daniel was an inventive machinist, inspired by the great advancements in technology marking the early years of the twentieth century. It was these inventive capabilities and the patenting of a cutoff valve for municipal water systems that initiated the founding of Daniel Manufacturing Company in 1913, primarily to produce the device. Five years later the firm took its first major turn when Daniel patented a new machine used in the preparation of ice cream cones. Daniel Manufacturing Company was reorganized as The Daniel Machine Company to manufacture the new invention.

For a time Daniel branched into auto repair and maintenance as well as the oil business, ventures that took him out of Birmingham temporarily. But he returned, and the culmination of his ventures led, in 1929, to specialization in metal fabrication, filling both residential and industrial needs for fire escapes, porch and stair railings, heavy mesh, fences, screens, trellises, window guards, and toolroom enclosures.

The fluctuations of a troubled economy peaked with the Great Depression in the 1930s, forcing the retirement of W. Homer Daniel. But the Daniel family would reemerge in the iron and steel industry. In 1940 Daniel's son, W. Harry Daniel, founded his own operation, Daniel Iron Works. James Daniel soon became involved and, at the age of 12, worked alongside his father on Sat-

James E. Daniel, chief executive officer.

W. Homer Daniel at the wheel of his service car.

urdays and during school vacations, finally joined the company on a full-time basis after serving in the U.S. Marine Corps. In 1947 Daniel Iron Works became Daniel Ornamental Iron Company, which it remained until 1985, when James Daniel once again changed the name, this time to Daniel Industrial Metals, Inc.

James Daniel, current president, represents the third generation involved in the family enterprise and sees himself as possibly the last Daniel to be at the helm of the company. The fourth generation, James' son, J. Dashwood Daniel, was operating as vice-president of the firm when he was killed in 1983. However, the business will continue on in the tradition of the past.

The company, soon celebrating its 75th anniversary, prides itself on being progressive and flexible to ever-changing market needs. While growing old in years and holding fast to its family roots and familiar atmosphere, Daniel Industrial Metals is moving with the times, planning for the future, and becoming more technologically advanced. Extensive computerization and AISC Quality Certification in Categories I, II, and III are only a couple of the recent advancements aimed at streamlining the company's production services. A new plant will open soon in Trussville, Alabama, where the firm, along with its offices in Birmingham, will continue to produce a diverse line of commercial and industrial metal products.

At the offices of Daniel Industrial Metals, Inc., at 620 Goldwire Way Southwest, only a few blocks from where Homer Daniel began the business in 1913, the more than 55 employees that are a part of the Daniel "family" plan many more years of contribution to the economic and civic activity of Birmingham.

RUST INTERNATIONAL CORPORATION

In 1985 Rust International Corporation celebrated its 80th anniversary. The story of Rust is the story of three generations of the Rust family; of two cities, Pittsburgh and Birmingham; and for the modern period, a story of corporate mergers.

The founding Rust brothers—Ellsworth Marshall "E.M.," Stirling Murry "S.M.," and Edmund Jennings Lee "E.J. Lee"—were the three youngest sons of Colonel Armistead Thomson Mason Rust, a Virginian and West Point graduate who served in the Confederate Army.

Born and educated in Virginia, the brothers began engineering careers in Pennsylvania. Three older brothers had formed the Rust Boiler Company in Pittsburgh to manufacture and sell an improved and patented type of vertical steam boiler that they had developed. The younger brothers headed south, setting up a sales office in Birmingham in 1902 for the Rust Boiler Company and an office in New Orleans.

Business was brisk, particularly with Birmingham steel plants and the southern sawmill industry. When customers began asking for help with boiler erection and brickwork construction, the younger brothers formed The Rust Engineering Company as a partnership operation from Birmingham and New Orleans in 1905. They soon gained a reputation for being technically expert in their field.

In 1908 the Rust Boiler Company was sold to Babcock & Wilcox; the brothers continued doing work for the new firm and expanded the scope of their own operation. In 1913 the company opened a new office in Pittsburgh run by S.M. Rust, and the following year E.M. Rust opened a Washington, D.C., office. By 1915 Rust also had a number of contracts for general construction work, and subsequently opened offices in New York, Cleveland, Washington, Chicago, and Tulsa.

At the instigation of E.M., the firm also entered the chimney construction business, going on to become one of the major chimney builders in the country. Rust diversified further in 1925 with entry into the industrial furnace field. As a natural corollary, the company moved into the brick-manufacturing field. In 1918 the brothers acquired Birmingham Clay Products Company, and three years later formed the Bolivar Clay Products Company of Bolivar, Ohio, to manufacture high-quality radial chimney brick.

The brothers divided their business into three corporations in 1920 with offices located in Pittsburgh, Washington, D.C., and Birmingham. Each brother held equal stock in the three companies, serving as president of one company and vice-president of the other two.

During the Depression the Birmingham office changed its name to Rust Construction Company and concentrated on smaller jobs, allowing the Pittsburgh office to also accept contracts in Alabama. In 1936 Rust built its first complete pulp and paper mill, launching the firm into future contracts in the pulp and paper field.

That decade also saw the second generation of Rusts begin to enter the business. When E.J. Lee died in 1939, his elder son, G.M., succeeded him as vice-president, director, and general manager of southern operations. Work in the name of Rust Construction Company was discontinued, and in 1940 it was absorbed into the Pittsburgh corporation. S.M. Jr. took over operations management of the Pittsburgh office in 1939 and became president five years later.

Rust formed several additional companies in the 1930s to broaden

Virginia-born brothers, E.M. Rust (left), S.M. Rust (center), and E.J. Lee Rust (right), founded the Rust Engineering Company in Birmingham in 1905.

services and territory. Included were the Rust Gunite Company, Potomac Clay Products, Inc., Loudoun-Rust Company, Woodbridge Clay Products Co., the Allegheny Industrial Electrical Company, and the Rust Engineering Company (Canada) Ltd.

Rust handled major construction work for the government during World War II, including the Atomic Energy Commission plant at Oak Ridge, Tennessee, where Rust had as many as 3,500 employees.

Expansion continued in the 1940s. The Rust Process Design Company was formed in 1948 to handle the firm's expanding work in the process chemical industries. In 1954 the firm merged into Rust Engineering. New subsidiaries, such as The Rust Company, Rust Building, and Industrial Insulation, were also later merged into Rust Engineering.

In the 1950s Rust participated in several large projects in joint ventures with other firms. With two other companies, Rust supplied architect-engineer services for the Air Force Titan facilities program. In the 1960s Rust created an international affiliate, Coppee-Rust, in Brussels, Belgium, by joining with an established European engineering firm. During this period the third generation of Rusts began to join the company operations.

Rust International Corporation headquarters now occupies this complex in Meadow Brook Corporate Park, south of Birmingham.

A dramatic change for the company came in 1967. The Rust family and stockholders sold the corporation and its subsidiaries to Litton Industries, Inc. In 1971 Litton management transferred the engineering headquarters from Pittsburgh to Birmingham.

The following year another ownership change occurred, when Wheelabrator-Frye, Inc., acquired Rust from Litton Industries. Wheelabrator-Frye, a firm known for its leadership in environmental systems, had international offices in 12 countries. In 1981 additional acquisitions by Wheelabrator led to reorganization affecting Rust. Rust's Northeast Regional Operations were merged with the Swindell organization of Pittsburgh, creating Swindell-Rust. Kellogg Rust, Inc., was created to coordinate and direct worldwide operation of Rust and the M.W. Kellogg Company. Rust International Corporation was formed in 1982 as a consolidation of all operating divisions performing engineering services formerly associated with The Rust Engineering Company. The Rust Engineering Company became an operating unit of Kellogg Rust Constructors, Inc.

Following the merger of Wheelabrator-Frye and The Signal Companies, Kellogg Rust, Inc., became one of the Signal Companies in 1983. The year 1985 brought more organizational change when The Signal Companies merged with Al-

From 1945 to 1956 the firm was headquartered in the Exchange Building in downtown Birmingham.

lied Corporation.

In a major reorganization, Allied-Signal spun off over 30 business units into a new company, The Henley Group, Inc. Rust is a unit of Wheelabrator Technologies Inc., a major operating company of The Henley Group.

Today Rust is one of the largest full-service engineering/construction firms in the United States and is consistently listed near the top of *Engineering News Records'* Top 400 Contractors. In addition to its Birmingham headquarters, Rust maintains offices in Pittsburgh, Pennsylvania, and in Portland, Oregon.

In its long history Rust has successfully performed more than 19,000 contracts in a wide range of industries and locations. Rust clients are in the pulp and paper and metals industries, food and beverage, energy, electronics, chemicals, automotive, government, and many more.

UNIVERSITY OF MONTEVALLO

"The 90-year history of the University of Montevallo and its present status are intertwined," notes president Jim Vickrey. "That sense of continuity between the past and the present provides the basis of our prospects and plans for the future."

Located at the geographic center of the state in the Shelby County town of Montevallo, the university is the only one whose *current* mission is incorporated into the laws of Alabama. The recently rearticulated mission and related 24 goals are the culmination not only of careful study of the present and future of the university, but also of a thorough understanding of Montevallo's heritage and its evolution from its founding as state girls' school in 1896 to its status today as Alabama's only *public* liberal arts college.

The statewide mission of the university, "unique in higher education in Alabama," says the state statute, "is to provide to students from throughout the state an affordable, geographically accessible, 'small college' public higher educational expe-

This afternoon scene typifies the architectural appropriateness of "the look of Montevallo," which includes red brick walks and driveways, and large, sprawling shade trees.

rience of high quality with a strong emphasis on undergraduate liberal studies and with professional programs supported by a broad base of arts and sciences, designed for their intellectual and personal growth in the pursuit of meaningful employment and responsible, informed citizenship."

Montevallo evolved to university status in 1969, not from a state teachers college as did many of Alabama's institutions of higher education, but from a fledgling state college for women in the 1920s—one with an emphasis on a liberal education central to UM's purpose and strategy. Vickrey, who began his tenure as president in 1977, stresses that the UM mission directly addresses "the greatest need of the state." If the state is to advance economically and culturally, he says, the percentage of the adult Alabamians with four-year college degrees must be closer to the national average than it now is.

With a history of response to state needs, Montevallo today is educating, "one at a time," a carefully

controlled number (2,500-2,600) of women and, since 1956, men. UM faculty and staff are doing so on one of the South's most attractive campuses via a nationally known core curriculum and via nationally accredited programs in the arts, business, education, and other areas. (In fact, 77 percent of UM's *accreditable* undergraduate programs are nationally accredited.) Is it any wonder then that a recent Capstone Poll revealed that—despite UM's deliberately small size—about one in 5 adult Alabamians reported that one or more members of their families had attended college at Montevallo? Perhaps that is so, in part, because Montevallo's emphasis on liberal education has never precluded professional preparation. Indeed, UM graduates in such disciplines as business, communication science and disorders, home economics, music, and theater are considered to be some of the best prepared professionals coming out of Alabama higher education.

At UM talented teachers for more than 90 years have been educating students not merely for their first jobs but, more importantly, for their last jobs as well. "That," says Vickrey (the university's second-longest-serving president), "is our heritage and so also the hallmark of our mission-directed activities now and in the years ahead."

WILLIAM M. MERCER-MEIDINGER-HANSEN, INCORPORATED

William M. Mercer-Meidinger-Hansen, Incorporated, with offices in principal cities in the United States and around the world, is the world's largest consulting firm dealing with compensation, employee benefits, and human resource management. A Marsh & McLennan company, Mercer-Meidinger-Hansen helps its clients to design, implement, finance, administer, and communicate to its employees their compensation, retirement, group life, health, and disability programs.

Although Mercer-Meidinger-Hansen consultants have the research, resources, systems, and techniques of a worldwide organization behind them, the firm believes that the most important element of its business is the relationship between the consultant and the client. An emphasis is placed on a critical thought process in which the consultant and client work closely together to diagnose the client's situation—determining exactly where the client's business is now and where it wishes to be. Based on that, what are the company's objectives for its benefit programs? Being fee-based and having no specific package to promote, the consultant is free to use creativity and initiative to recommend the best way for the client "to get from here to there."

The Birmingham office of Mercer-Meidinger-Hansen reflects the importance of the consultant/client relationship in its history and its growth. It was opened in 1967 by Robert L. Seiler as part of Meidinger & Associates' efforts to bring its consultants closer to its clients.

After the turbulence of the early 1950s, some businesses were reluctant to enter the Birmingham area. Meidinger, however, already served clients in the area from its home office in Louisville, Kentucky, and believed that a commitment to change in the Birmingham community made the city a good location for a firm offering actuarial services to pension plans—the firm's major emphasis at the time. A relatively small operation at first, Meidinger concentrated on expanding into medium-size cities around the state.

The growth of Meidinger to one of the top 10 consulting firms in the nation before its merger into William M. Mercer-Meidinger-Hansen, Incorporated, affirms the wisdom of the business philosophy of the company; the growth of the Birmingham office reflects the foresight of the commitment to a presence in the southern city. Starting with a two-person office in the Brown-Marx Building, Mercer-Meidinger-Hansen has grown to a staff of 19 employees. Seeking larger quarters, the firm was located in Office Park for a decade before moving to One Perimeter Park South on Highway 280 south of the city.

Serving primarily Alabama, the growth of the Birmingham office and diversification of its services reflects the economic growth and change in the state and regional marketplace and the success of Mercer-Meidinger-Hansen consultants in meeting those changing, expanding needs.

A large part of the company's success is also attributable to changes in the local market. It believes that a willingness in Birmingham to deal as openly as possible with problems has accounted for significant transformation into an increasingly progressive and forward-looking city, better equipped to serve its more diversified and cosmopolitan community.

To meet the expanding needs of a changing clientele, William M. Mercer-Meidinger-Hansen, Incorporated, of Birmingham now offers a wide range of consulting services to businesses, industries, and institutions in the state in the areas of employee benefits, compensation, and human resource management. Its growth in size and service has been dramatic, but the philosophy of Mercer-Meidinger-Hansen has remained consistent: to be "client-driven" and idea-oriented.

AMERICA'S FIRST CREDIT UNION

"We are people helping people"; that was the philosophy from which America's First Credit Union was born in 1936, and which guides its existence today. In August 1936, 19 employees of United States Steel Corporation's Ensley Works in Birmingham—trying to recover from the Great Depression—pooled their resources to organize the original Iron and Steel Workers Credit Union, Alabama's 19th credit union.

Adopting the national credit union motto, "Not for profit, not for charity, but service," these volunteers believed their cooperative spirit would economically benefit their co-workers and community far differently than the neighborhood loan dealer who too often was the only source of credit.

Housed at the general superintendent's office of United States Steel and open only three days a week, the credit union used a cigar box to hold its cash. Only two transactions were offered: savings and cosigned loans. The credit union's first loan was for five dollars.

Eligible members included only employees of U.S. Steel's Ensley Works; the Fairfield division of Tennessee Coal, Iron & Railroad Company (a U.S. Steel subsidiary); and the TCI Employees (now Lloyd Noland) Hospital. The benefit of belonging to a credit union, sharing financial resources with one's co-workers, quickly caught on; by year-end the credit union had 822 members, 357 borrowers, and assets of $17,982.

During the 1940s the credit union opened its first official office outside the U.S. Steel plant in Ensley and had a paid staff instead of volunteers. In 1952 John R. Stephenson joined the credit union as president. During his tenure it has grown to become Alabama's largest state-chartered credit union—with assets of more than $230 million, ranking 60th in size among America's 18,500 credit unions.

The credit union's 98,000 members are served by seven volunteer directors elected by the membership; the board hires a professional staff. Unlike other financial institutions the board serves to promote the unique financial cooperative atmosphere of credit unions. America's First is owned by its members rather than a group of stockholders. Each member who has at least one share ($25) and is over 16 is eligible to vote at the annual meeting.

During the late 1950s financial services other than savings and lending were introduced. Temporary disability insurance became the first in a successive line of supplemental life, home-owners, and automobile insurance policies to become available. The loan portfolio expanded during the 1960s to include pre-approved lines of credit, real estate, and student loans. Today America's First makes almost any type of consumer loan, including MasterCard and Visa.

Membership expansion also took place in the 1960s, when the field of membership was changed to include other steel-related companies and the employees' immediate family members. This action proved to be extremely beneficial in view of the volatile demands on Alabama's steel industry during the 1970s. The credit union dropped "workers" from the name and became Iron and Steel Credit Union in 1976.

The 1970s were one of the credit union's most progressive decades. In order to better serve the expanded membership, the organization began branching into different areas of Alabama outside Birmingham and Jefferson County. New services rapidly appeared to meet increased and changing financial needs. A Telephone Loan Department was created, certificates of deposits and Individual Retirement Accounts were added to the savings program, and interest-earning checking accounts were introduced.

With the advent of computerized technology, all operational procedures were automated, bringing on-line service delivery to members throughout Alabama and the United States. Member transactions immediately post and update the respective accounts. The 1980s will be remembered as an "era of electronics," with the institution of Flash Cash and Flash Talk programs. Flash Cash is a shared network of 24-hour automatic teller machines that allow members to make cash withdrawals, transfers, and payments from participating machines all over Alabama and Florida. Flash Talk is a unique information response system that gives members personal account convenience confidentially from any touchtone telephone in the United States 24 hours a day.

One of the most dramatic developments for credit union advancement occurred in 1983, when the Alabama legislature amended the credit union laws governing membership. The Iron and Steel Credit Union charter was changed to include nonsteel-related companies and associations in Alabama not being served by a credit union. This move, and subsequent requests from hundreds of nonsteel-related groups to be served, prompted another name change to America's First Credit Union. Although America's First is perceived as a fringe benefit for an employee or association member, the services extend to the family and community.

While the loan services provide for transportation, housing, and leisure-time activities, America's First helps its members build a secure financial foundation through a variety of savings programs and financial counseling. The two basic services—savings and loans with competitive rates—were the founda-

Constructed in 1980, the administrative headquarters of America's First Credit Union was hailed as "the most colorful addition to Birmingham's skyline." Designed after the Pompidou Museum in Paris, the bright yellow-colored metal and reflective glass structure has played a leading role in the revitalization of downtown Birmingham's business district.

tion on which the credit union started in 1936, and remain its primary functions 51 years later.

The same cooperative spirit that inspired the 19 volunteers is still evident today in the variety of services offered to meet a growing membership. While buildings, products, and service delivery methods have changed, America's First Credit Union has never strayed from its basic philosophy of people helping people:

"We are committed to helping our members improve their lifestyle, fulfill their personal dreams, and provide a future for their children. We are also committed to helping the community by supporting civic programs such as the chamber of commerce, United Way, and Red Cross, as well as many other charitable and educational programs. We are people helping people."

HARBERT CORPORATION

"From heavy construction to mining—and beyond" might well be the title of Harbert Corporation's story for a major portion of its existence. John M. Harbert III, as founder and president and now chairman of the board, has guided his company's every move since its incorporation in Birmingham in January 1949.

Prior to the firm's incorporation, the young Auburn University engineering graduate built small bridges and roads with a labor crew recruited from cotton fields. Then he took into the business his brother, Bill L. Harbert, and two other young engineers, Edwin M. Dixon and Theodore F. Randolph. During its earliest years Harbert Construction Corporation had 25 to 30 employees, a one-room office, and a small yard of World War II surplus equipment.

Fewer than 10 years later, with its first multimillion-dollar contract to construct a 1,000-mile natural gas pipeline in Florida, the corporation had almost 7,000 employees and 3,500 pieces of equipment. This contract marked the beginning of Florida Gas, a company in which Harbert served as a director for a number of years.

The diversification that had characterized Harbert's rapid growth was due in part to postwar needs in the United States: bridges, water systems, highways, dams, and inexpensive energy. It was also due to the foresight of Harbert and his small group of top executives. Work in Florida had convinced them not only of the need there for natural gas as inexpensive energy; it led to the corporation's first venture into acquisition and development of land. Harbert formed a successful partnership to build a residential area and shopping mall in Sarasota.

Another acquisition of land took place when Harbert assessed the South's increasingly heavy use of natural gas and projected its inevitable depletion. The land was in Shelby County, Alabama, and its value was in coal. When union problems and a National Labor Relations Board decision against Harbert put a damper on the coal operation, the mines were shut down. However, that land eventually became a magnificent site for homes, country club, golf course, shopping, and business facilities. With visionary environmental planning the Riverchase community was built in a pastoral

Harbert Corporation's first headquarters.

setting with urban conveniences.

Just as John Harbert's affinity for the land is discernible in Riverchase and in the nearby natural setting of the corporate headquarters, so his belief in coal as the nation's most plentiful source of energy was substantiated by acquisition of leases and coal reserves in Kentucky in the early 1970s. Harbert engineers and equipment experts readily adapted their knowledge to surface mining, coal car loading, and land reclamation.

Some executives and project managers spent most of their time at the mining operations; others were involved in major projects in the United States, as well as in Central and South America. The Harbert logo also became familiar to residents of the Mid-East, from Abu Dhabi to a vast expanse of the Negev Desert, where Harbert personnel spent two years constructing a large installation.

With the 1981 sale of Harbert's coal mines, along with Three Rivers Rock Company, its fleet of tow boats, and the Savannah Coal Port property, to Standard Oil of Indiana, Harbert Corporation became one of the largest Amoco stockholders and had greater need than ever for broad diversification.

From mining the corporation moved boldly into oil exploration with the acquisition of Plumb Oil of Houston. Having participated in supplying both natural gas and coal as energy sources, Harbert management transferred its expertise to oil, while continuing to look to the future with experimental ventures into agri-fuels. And having "bridged, gas-piped, cabled, water-systemed, and dammed" its share of many states and more than several nations, Harbert management elected to further its diversification into real estate in a joint venture with Brice Construction Company for the South Trust Tower in downtown Birmingham, Alabama's tallest building.

In Hoover, at the intersection of interstate highways 459 and 65,

Harbert Corporation headquarters today.

which Harbert had helped to build, came another opportunity for a real estate investment. This was a joint venture with Jim Wilson and Associates for one of the South's showplaces: the Riverchase Galleria, an attraction that daily draws thousands of visitors and shoppers from a radius of several hundred miles.

Another intersection that provided an opportunity for a joint venture in 1986 for Harbert and AmSouth Bank is at the corner of Sixth Avenue and 19th Street in Birmingham. Said to be one of the finest pieces of commercial property in Alabama, AmSouth/Harbert Plaza is designed to house a skyscraper office building, restaurants, specialty shops, and an atrium connecting it to the adjacent skyscraper, also owned by AmSouth/Harbert.

These projects reflect the corporation's faith in the future of Alabama and John Harbert's personal civic pride in Birmingham. He led the fund drive for a downtown civic club building for use by the Rotary, Kiwanis, and Quarterback clubs, as well as other organizations. It was named in his honor, as was the John M. Harbert III Engineering Center at Auburn University. He has donated funds to many educational institutions and in 1986 gave a building to Birmingham-Southern College to be named for his wife, a Birmingham-Southern alumna.

In addition to philanthropy, Harbert has served the state and the City of Birmingham in innumerable capacities—from the Alabama Commission on Higher Education to the Boy Scout Council, from the Birmingham Art Museum Board to fund-raising board member of the Eye Foundation and the YWCA.

Harbert employees are encouraged, as well as inspired by the founder's example, to be good citizens. A number of summer jobs are offered to college students, and a summer program for high school students annually relieves highways around Birmingham of several tons of litter.

Chairman of the board John Harbert subscribes to the motto, "The harder I work, the luckier I get," having experienced both. His fledgling Harbert Construction Corporation of 1949 is now an international conglomerate, of which Bill Harbert is president. Its subsidiaries include Harbert International, Argus Protective Services, Five Flags Pipeline Company, Harbert Energy (Plumb Oil Company of Houston and The Wil-Mac Oil Corporation of Dallas), Harbert Land Corporation, Harbert Machinery, Inc., Harbert Properties Corporation, Mid-South Machinery Co., Inc., Mincon Supply, Inc., Robbins Manufacturing, Inc., Southland Power Constructors, Inc., and Harbert International Establishment, based in London. Other foreign offices are in Quito, Ecuador; Bogota, Colombia; Santiago, Chile; and Cairo, Egypt.

The recently completed Safaga Grain Silo Complex—a grain unloading, storage, and distribution facility on the Nile River, is an example of Harbert's worldwide construction capability.

GENERAL MACHINERY COMPANY, INC.

The story of General Machinery Company, Inc., supplier of electrical and mechanical equipment to industry, is part of the fabric of the industrial history of its home city of Birmingham. As the young industrial center entered the twentieth century, the city at last seemed ready to fulfill the promises inherent in the nickname—"the Pittsburgh of the South."

Crocker-Wheeler Company, a national manufacturer of electrical equipment headquartered in New Jersey, decided the time was right to enter the Birmingham market. The firm sent B.A. Schroder from New Orleans to the Magic City to open an office to serve the rapidly electrifying industries of Birmingham. Schroder watched developments in the city with interest, and within a few years he concluded that Bir-

In the 1930s the Birmingham warehouse of General Machinery was located at 1600 Second Avenue South. During this era the company primarily sold and serviced Goodman mining products and Cutler Hammer motor controls.

mingham now offered excellent opportunities for a businessman who could meet the needs of expanding industry. In 1908 he left his former employer and founded General Machinery Company.

From the company's first headquarters in the Brown-Marx Building in downtown Birmingham, Schroder carefully studied the Birmingham market through the years and made adjustments in his product line as necessary. Dealing originally in electrical mining machinery, Schroder broadened the firm's scope during a slump in the coal mining industry and began handling pumps.

After Schroder's death in 1954, his son-in-law Ed Wilkinson operated the company until his death in 1972. Francis Crockard, Jr., whose grandfather had provided leadership to several leading Birmingham iron and steel companies in the early twentieth century, became president and majority stockholder of General Machinery. Later that year Michael Balliet and Jerry Hope also became stockholders.

Today General Machinery Company features three groups of product lines integrated by a shop unit. The electrical department is a distributor for Cutler-Hammer and Westinghouse products. This facet of the firm also deals with Gould programmable controls, motion controls that are used extensively in

robotics, and variable frequency and DC drives. Electrical equipment with programmable controls is the fastest-growing segment of the company's market.

The second facet of the corporation is the pump group, which does work with the handling of coal slurry as well as paper mill and process chemicals. General Machinery is a distributor for Goulds pumps and Gorman Rupp equipment.

The company's air group, which specializes in air systems, is a distributor for Joy compressors, Dresser-Roots blowers, and Zurn dryers.

Integrating the products of the other three groups is the shop, which not only does repair work but also fabricates packages for the other groups. The shop is also the warranty station for Yale hoists and can load test units up to 10 tons.

With a total of 45 employees including 11 outside salesmen, General Machinery Company, Inc., also has a facility in Mobile and a sales office in Decatur. The ability of the company to deliver a total package of products has kept it in the forefront of supplying machinery to heavy industry.

The Birmingham headquarters of General Machinery Company, Inc., is a 42,000-square-foot building, which houses an inventory worth in excess of one million dollars.

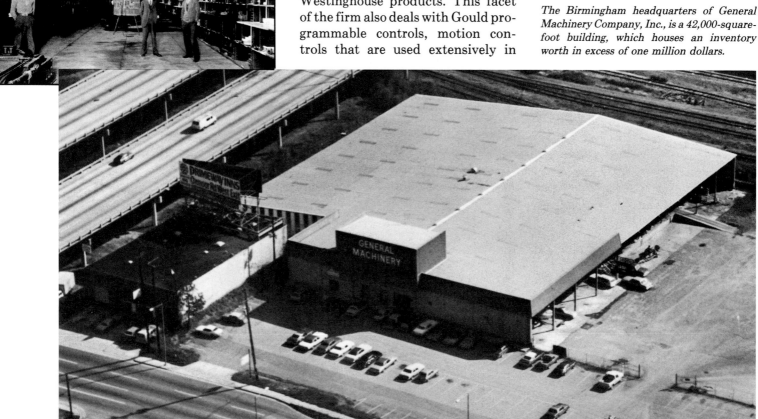

UNION BANK & TRUST CO.

Union Bank & Trust Co. opened its doors on Court Square in the late spring of 1901 with less than $25,000 in assets and more than a little determination. The fledgling enterprise weathered its first years well, under the guidance of some of Montgomery's most prominent and aspiring merchants, but even they did not realize just how quickly the new bank would grow.

Within a very short time Union Bank & Trust Co. was well on its way to local financial prominence. By 1922 the bank had outgrown its building. It then moved to larger quarters in the nearby Vandiver Building, but this new location had to be abandoned for still larger quarters just eight years later, when it relocated to 60 Commerce Street, where Union Bank stands proudly today. The Union Bank Building, completed in 1970, is the tallest in Montgomery.

During its 86-year history Union Bank has had only six presidents. The first was Michael Cody, who served until 1932. He was followed by Walton Harris Hill, 1932-1938; Grover Keyton, 1938-1954; John H. Neill, Jr., 1954-1976; John Maples, Jr., 1976-1978; and Henry A. Leslie, 1078 to present.

Today Union Bank has assets of $448 million, maintains 10 offices in Montgomery, and has more than 100 member banks from the Southeast participating in its Correspondent Banking Program.

While the trend in recent years has been to merge with large statewide holding companies, Union Bank remains actively independent under the leadership of board chairman W. Robbins Taylor and president and chief executive officer Henry A. Leslie. The distinguished "hometown" board members are Richard W. Buchanan, Jr., H.P. Haas, Robert F. Henry, Jr., R.S. Hill, Jr., T. Bowen Hill III, Jim T. Inscoe,

Mark W. Johnston, Robert E. Kelly, Henry A. Leslie, Algie Hill Neill, Samuel L. Schloss, C.B. Shewmake, W. Robbins Taylor, William G. Thames, Harry J. Till, and John M. Trotman.

In the banking industry, the basis of success is the ability to serve the community well with highly qualified personnel, and the bank is certainly proud of the superb caliber of its staff. The directors and staff look forward to continuing to serve the best interests of Union Bank & Trust Co.'s customers and stockholders.

The Union Bank Building has towered over downtown Montgomery since its completion in 1970.

VICTORYLAND GREYHOUND RACING PARK

The dog racing track with the largest pari-mutuel handle in the country emerged from a soybean field in one of the poorest counties in the rural South. To the residents of Macon County, Alabama, VictoryLand Greyhound Racing Park has brought an aura of revitalization and a sense of accomplishment to the people who call this land home.

Nestled on the outskirts of rural Tuskegee, Alabama, VictoryLand is operated by Milton McGregor and Parimutuel Management Company. It is governed by a local racing commission, the members of which are residents of Macon County.

Before VictoryLand's electric rabbit, Richie, began luring greyhounds around the oval track, Macon County's schools were nearly bankrupt and on the verge of closing. The county had one of the state's highest unemployment rates, and its county seat, Tuskegee, was suffering the financial pains of declining federal grants and revenue-sharing dollars. City and county officials have

Milton E. McGregor, president and treasurer.

Willie R. Whitehead, vice-president.

VictoryLand, home of greyhound racing in Tuskegee, Alabama.

welcomed the new life being pumped into the area, generating millions of dollars for the financially strapped school system and channeling hundreds of thousands in funds to local charities.

More than 850 jobs have been created since VictoryLand opened in September 1984, with 75 percent of those positions filled by Macon County residents. The track is the county's third-largest employer, surpassed only by the Veterans Administration complex and Tuskegee University. Several cottage industries have been generated by this

A. Preston Hornsby

Robert M. Burton

Robert C. Carter

enterprise, such as a baby-sitting service, convenience stores, a motel, and service stations, and governing officials believe that additional, larger industries will come into the

Fred D. Gray, attorney.

area because of its success.

VictoryLand's popularity stems from its value as a complete entertainment package. Along with the excitement of fast-paced racing action and the availability of a wide variety of parimutuel wagers, the track offers glass-enclosed, climate-controlled trackside seating. In the fashionable Clubhouse, patrons can enjoy full food and beverage service and tiered table seating. The second-level Lounge provides live monitor viewing of the races, and the Concourse gives patrons a close-up view of the action with row seating and the availability of snack foods and beverages. The Victory Room, with its elegant amenities, is offered for reserved groups and private functions.

Up to 4,000 people a day discover the thrill of the chase in VictoryLand's attractive atmosphere. Open 50 weeks per year, racing is held nightly except Sunday, and there are four weekly matinees. Patrons can wager on win, place, show, quiniela, big Q, exacta, quiniela double, straight trifecta, and a one-

dollar trifecta and superfecta. The twin trifecta is a popular pool wager with a jackpot that builds nightly. Winnings that climb to hundreds of thousands of dollars add excitement to the colorful racing action.

In 1985 the establishment of the Macon County Greyhound Parks, Inc./VictoryLand Scholarships at Auburn University were announced. Students from Macon County are given first priority to benefit from this endowment, which will increase to more than $100,000.

Three Charity Days are held each year, with the money received given to benevolent organizations that have made application for support. The racing commission distributes these funds for such widespread uses as recreation, indigent care, mental health, hospitals, libraries, and numerous additional agencies.

To the citizens of Macon County, VictoryLand Greyhound Racing Park is welcome relief to a failing economy. To the patrons of the track, it is a fun-filled world of entertainment.

LLOYD NOLAND HOSPITAL & HEALTH CENTERS

"Many times I have been asked, or have put the question to myself: 'Why do we go into the study and practice of medicine?' . . . To my mind, then, the answer is because the individual has a craving for adventure into unknown realms, a not uncommon type of curiosity. And, after all, can any great geographic discovery or exploration compare with the marvelous explorations and discoveries listed in the history of medicine?"

These words were penned in 1938 by national public health and industrial medicine leader Dr. Lloyd Noland.

Virginia-born, Noland had a love for adventure that was evident in 1904, when he volunteered to join what became the world's most heralded public health team. Noland served with medical forces in Panama led by Dr. William Crawford Gorgas, who fought yellow fever and malaria to pave the way for the building of the Panama Canal.

In 1913 adventure-loving Noland returned to the United States to take on a mission in Jefferson County, Alabama. Noland came to save a steel company whose workers were plagued by diseases such as malaria and typhoid. Using knowledge acquired in Panama, Noland created the nation's first major experiment

The 319-bed Employees' Hospital of the Tennessee Coal, Iron and Railroad Company, known as TCI Hospital, cast this stately appearance in 1919 when it opened in Fairfield, Alabama, as a nationally recognized industrial hospital.

in industrial medicine. He set up the TCI Health Department to serve employees (and their families) in the Tennessee Coal, Iron and Railroad Company (TCI). A United States Steel Corporation subsidiary, TCI was the largest iron and steel company in the Birmingham area termed the "Pittsburgh of the South."

At the time many companies in the United States were beginning to provide employee health programs; however, the TCI health program had a bigness and a diversity that made it unique.

In 1919 the TCI Health Department opened a showcase hospital in Fairfield, Alabama—the 319-bed Employees' Hospital of the Tennessee Coal, Iron and Railroad Company—or TCI Hospital. The $1.25-million facility soon was attracting

medical visitors from around the world.

Patterned after the Gorgas health system in Panama, the TCI Health Department featured a sanitation system with services such as food supply inspection and spraying for disease-causing mosquitoes. In addition, outpatient clinics called dispensaries were located in plants and near mines where employees worked and in company-owned villages where they lived.

In April 1950, five months after Noland's death, the name of TCI Hospital was changed to Lloyd Noland Hospital. The following year the United States Steel Corporation donated the hospital to the community. The Lloyd Noland Foundation, Inc., was created to operate the hospital, converted from an industrial facility to a community, not-for-profit institution.

In the mid 1980s the Fairfield-based community health care system that began as the TCI Health Department became known as Lloyd Noland Hospital & Health Centers.

Today Lloyd Noland provides a comprehensive array of medical ser-

Children of TCI employees are shown as they lined up for immunization at one of the clinics pioneered by Dr. Lloyd Noland as part of the TCI Health Department in the 1920s.

vices, including internal medicine, surgery, obstetrics/gynecology, pediatrics, psychiatry, and all specialties, as well as modern technology such as nuclear magnetic resonance, computerized axial tomography, cardiac catheterization, and dialysis. Lloyd Noland is the only private medical center in Alabama accredited both by the Joint Commission on Accreditation of Hospitals and the Accreditation Association for Ambulatory Health Care, Inc.

Continuing a tradition of quality patient care and quality postgraduate medical education, Lloyd Noland is staffed by one of the largest physician group practices in the South and offers physician residency training in several medical specialties.

More than seven decades since Dr. Lloyd Noland embarked upon his health care adventure in Jefferson County, Alabama, Lloyd Noland Hospital & Health Centers still reflects that spirit of adventure so characteristic of Noland himself.

In the early twentieth century Noland pioneered in such areas as preventive medicine, care for the elderly, multispecialty physician group practice, outpatient care, prepaid health care, and health maintenance organizations. In fact, Dr. Lloyd Noland established one of the nation's early prototypes of what later would be known as a health maintenance organization, or HMO. Likewise, the Lloyd Noland Hospital & Health Centers of the 1980s is pioneering with modern-day prototypes.

A chain of progressive outpatient centers, the Family Care centers, was launched in 1984. Initial locations were in Pleasant Grove, Hueytown, and Hoover, and future sites are projected.

More than 5,000 senior citizens aged 65 and over enrolled in Lloyd Noland's new ElderCare program within two years of the program's 1984 beginning. ElderCare members need only their Medicare cards and approved supplemental insurance;

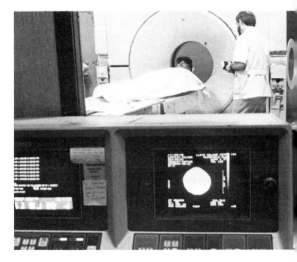

Preparations are made for a patient to undergo computerized axial tomography (CAT) scanning, one of the progressive diagnostic tools in use at the Lloyd Noland facilities in the 1980s.

and ElderCare covers Medicare-approved services with no extra charges, handles paperwork in filing claims, makes available comprehensive health care services under one hospital-clinic roof with an added option of Family Care centers, and offers bonuses such as exercise programs, preventive care, and social activities.

New chapters are being written in the ongoing story of Lloyd Noland's pioneering work in health maintenance organizations. In 1977 Lloyd Noland Hospital became the first hospital in Alabama to participate in the modern-day HMO—a cooperative venture with Blue Cross and Blue Shield of Alabama. Then, in 1986, Lloyd Noland Hospital & Health Centers presented its new HMO program known as Health Advantage.

And, just as Dr. Noland in the early 1900s was planning the showcase TCI Hospital, Lloyd Noland Hospital & Health Centers leaders in the 1980s are planning a new hospital. In 1985 state officials approved

Lloyd Noland Hospital & Health Centers to build a 157-bed hospital, Cahaba Medical Center, on a 200-acre campus in south Jefferson County.

Guided by a spirit of adventure and innovation, Lloyd Noland Hospital & Health Centers continues to dedicate itself to the patients who have entrusted their health care to the institution and to the physicians, staff, and volunteers who have honored that trust.

Lloyd Noland Hospital, shown in 1984 on its 42-acre wooded hilltop site, is a private hospital with a community role much broader than that of the TCI (industrial) Hospital, where it had its beginnings.

TEE JAYS MANUFACTURING COMPANY, INC.

In 1976, just one year after graduation from the University of North Alabama with a degree in accounting, Terry Wylie founded Tee Jays Manufacturing Company in Florence, a verticle mill in the knit goods industry. In partnership with his father, Paul Wylie, 23-year-old Terry envisioned building a quality business that would be competitive in the national garment industry.

That vision quickly became reality for the two partners. Little more than a decade later Tee Jays Manufacturing Company produces more than 22 million garments annually, including T-shirts, sweat shirts, and other knitted items.

Tee Jays has been able to compete with the largest manufacturing facilities in the nation in certain product lines. Today the firm continues to make inroads competitively against some very large domestic companies. Tee Jays has succeeded by achieving a number of corporate goals, among them providing its customers with top-quality merchandise at competitive prices and in a timely manner—considered paramount in the Tee Jays corporate philosophy. These goals have been achieved, too, because of the firm's deep concern for its employees and its endeavor to be a good corporate citizen of Florence.

In 1986 the company's production of 22 million garments was shipped worldwide to a quickly recognized roster of national and international customers, including K mart; JCPenney; Sears, Roebuck and Co.; Zayre Corp.; McCrory Stores; Richway Stores; the Southland Corp., operator of 7-Eleven Stores; and the Shopko Corp.

Tee Jays' garments can also be found on the shelves of some of the premier amusement parks in the country, including Disney World in Orlando, Florida, and Disneyland in Anaheim, California. In addition, the firm has contracted with suppliers of garments to such entertainers as Michael Jackson and Kenny Rogers, whose fans purchase the merchandise at the performers' concerts. The market for Tee Jays' products is diversified, including both large and small retail accounts, wholesalers, theme parks, the resort market, and special and licensed products.

Tee Jays purchases only the highest quality grade yarns. Its cloth is dyed, cut, and sewn in the company's Florence plant by its 817 employees, who produce knit goods and sweat shirts for infants, toddlers, boys, girls, men, and women.

The firm has expanded rapidly in recent years, adding two new facilities with approximately 13,000 square feet of floor space in 1986, as well as expanding one facility by 31,500 square feet in early 1986. This carefully planned growth brings the size of the company's Florence facilities to 165,000 square feet in six buildings in the Florence-Lauderdale Industrial Park. The expansion has resulted in a 100-percent increase in Tee Jays' knitting and dyeing capacity, thus allowing the firm to eliminate the need for outside contractors. This is a particularly important factor for the Florence community because it has resulted in new, local jobs and provided a boost to the northwest Alabama economy. The expansions also have meant an increase in sales of approximately 40 percent.

Tee Jays' full line of goods is available to the public at mill outlet prices at its new retail mill outlet store on Helton Drive in Florence.

Terry Wylie, president of Tee Jays Manufacturing Company, Inc., and Paul Wylie, chairman, have combined their experience and marketing acumen in the textile industry to become owners of one of Alabama's most successful, high-quality manufacturing concerns.

WSFA-TV

On December 25, 1954, WSFA-TV began broadcasting with Charles Dickens' "A Christmas Carol." Originally an enterprise conceived by three Montgomery businessmen, the station is now owned by Cosmos Broadcasting Corporation.

Since its inception TV-12's program service has been anchored by three daily newscasts. Through outstanding news and public service programming, the station has cultivated the respect of both viewers and the television industry. Its superlative tradition in area news service began its first year with news director Frank McGee, of network fame, who cultivated a unique staff and initiated the use of modern electronic news-gathering equipment.

WSFA-TV gained national prominence when Montgomery and the central Alabama region became the testing ground for the initial

This 2,000-foot transmitter tower located in Grady has been serving WSFA since 1977.

WSFA's news and weather team (from left): Lynn Sampson, Rich Thomas, and Bob Howell.

efforts of the civil rights movement. The Montgomery NBC affiliate kept central and south Alabama viewers informed throughout the racial turmoil of the 1950s and 1960s, with the national networks using WSFA-TV's facilities to transmit the news of the human rights effort to the nation and the world.

Channel 12 has always been a pioneer in broadcasting with a long list of area "firsts." It was the first station in Alabama to utilize electronic news-gathering, the first to put cameras on the floor of the Alabama legislature, the first to use computerized vote-totaling in an election cov-

erage program, and the first station in the state to produce a regularly scheduled hour-long newscast. It is the only station in Alabama airing regular editorial comments as part of its news presentation.

In 1955 WSFA-TV signed a contract with Auburn University to telecast playbacks of all Auburn football games. Today the "Auburn Football Review" is networked to many other television stations in the Southeast. In-depth coverage of all Alabama sporting events is another reason for Channel 12's award-winning status.

A vanguard in the field of television, WSFA-TV has been referred to as one of the "jewels in the NBC crown." Certainly it has been a beacon of progress in this area of the New South.

JACKSON HOSPITAL & CLINIC, INC.

The history of Jackson Hospital is integral to the history of medicine in Montgomery. The origins of the "Jackson Hospital Block" go back to 1894, when Watkins Infirmary received its first patients in this location. Dr. T.B. Hubbard, a dedicated physician and educator, assumed ownership of the property and operated a hospital on the site. Later Dr. Clark Hilton Rice opened the first pediatric hospital in south Alabama in one of the buildings.

In 1946, recognizing the need for expanded medical care in the Montgomery area to keep abreast of radical changes in the practice of medicine after World War II, Dr. Franklin Jackson purchased the south half of the Forest Avenue block ending at Pine Street. On September 16, 1946, Jackson Hospital opened with 37 patient beds and five attending physicians.

The entire hospital, comprised of three buildings connected by wooden archways, contained one large operating room and another small suite used for emergencies and minor surgical procedures. With no air conditioning, the only method of cooling was the use of window fans. A common procedure on a muggy summer day was to send to the kitchen for blocks of ice to place in front of the fans.

In 1950 all personal ownership of the hospital was terminated, and it emerged as a nonprofit institution. This same year the first modern construction process began. The physical plant grew rapidly during the decade of the 1950s, including the advent of an obstetrical unit, a medical records library with credentialed personnel, and many innovations such as carpeting in the patients' rooms, the use of attractive homelike furniture, and a lessening of the dreary hospital image. The Joint Commission on Accreditation of Hospitals (JCAH) first accredited the institution in 1955. Since that time Jackson Hospital has passed subsequent accreditation surveys, and in 1972 achieved the position of

being the first institution in the country to receive a 100-percent rating by a JCAH survey team.

To provide better patient care, an adjacent clinic building was constructed in 1971, offering office space to the physicians serving the hospital. For convenience, a branch bank and a pharmacy were located in the building, and a large parking deck was added with links to the clinic building and the hospital.

Today Jackson Hospital & Clinic covers a 10-city-block area, ranking it among the largest hospitals in the state with its 409-bed capacity. It has more than 200 active and courtesy staff members representing all specialties, and is an efficient, cost-effective institution able to respond to the community and economy with programs and services that reflect the climate of the late twentieth century.

While personal attention is the hallmark of Jackson Hospital, the hospital also takes great pride in the technological advances it brings to the community, among them magnetic resonance imaging and dual photon densitometry. To enhance efforts to provide a modern facility with state-of-the-art equipment and to enlarge the scope of treatment, the Jackson Hospital Foundation was formed in 1976. The foundation encourages community participation, ensuring the citizenry an opportunity to become involved in the health care provided in their area.

The Frank McGough Oncology Unit is the focal point for a program at Jackson Hospital to meet the specialized needs of cancer patients and their families. The personal care

required in the treatment of this disease is administered by a staff whose primary concern and training are geared toward cancer patients and their family members, and includes support groups and other activities that can be implemented and coordinated effectively through this special unit. This unit is complemented by a comprehensive radiation therapy department that affords the Montgomery community the very best in cancer treatment.

A leading influence in the area's medical community, this hospital center offers the latest in medical management implemented by a caring staff of dedicated individuals. The area responds by making it Montgomery's hospital of choice.

Opposite page: On September 16, 1946, Jackson Hospital opened at Forest Avenue and Pine Street with 37 patient beds and five attending physicians.

Right: Today Jackson Hospital covers a 10-city-block area, ranking it among the largest hospitals in the state.

ALABAMA FEDERAL SAVINGS AND LOAN ASSOCIATION

The merger of four independent savings and loan associations in April 1982 resulted in the formation of Alabama Federal Savings and Loan Association. These four associations, Home Federal Savings and Loan Association of the South in Birmingham, Heritage Federal Savings and Loan Association in Tuscaloosa, Home Savings and Loan Association in Mobile, and Security Federal Savings and Loan Association in Huntsville, realized the advantage of uniting as a strong statewide organization. Each association had a long and distinguished record of service in its home community.

Home Federal of the South, founded in Birmingham in 1923, reorganized in 1929 and elected J.B. Hill, president of Hill Grocery Company, as association president. Joining Hill in reorganizing the association was Donald Comer, president of Avondale Mills; J.M.G. Parker, of Moore Handley; William S. Pritchard, attorney; and Colonel Wealkly, head of the Boys' Industrial School.

Heritage Federal Savings and Loan Association, founded in 1925 as the Tuscaloosa Building and Loan Association, converted from a state charter to a federal charter in 1936. J.H. Duckworth, Charles Morris, and S.J. Pearson formed the association and guided it through the early years of growth.

Home Savings and Loan Association in Mobile, granted a state charter in October 1921, was formed largely due to the efforts of C.C. Lowder and several concerned Mobile businessmen. Directors of the association, in addition to Lowder, included Stewart Brooks, E.G. Draper, Julius Goldstein, F.E. Overall, H.H. Wifel, Jr., and A.L. Staples. Staples served as a state legislator and was largely responsible for placing on the statute books of the State of Alabama the laws governing the savings and loan associations of Alabama.

Security Federal Savings and Loan Association in Huntsville,

Northern region main office, Huntsville.

founded in April 1958, was the youngest of the four merging organizations. The founding board members were William M. McKissack, M.D., Robert N. Yarbrough, James R. Cleary, Joseph E. Cooper, George H. Gesman, George A. Martin, R.P. Van Valkenburg, Sr., James E. Taylor, and Joseph W. Haskings.

Alabama Federal maintained its headquarters in Tuscaloosa until 1985, when the association moved to 110 Office Park Drive in Birmingham. Several months prior to that move, in April 1984, Jack H. Shannon became chairman of the board and chief executive officer of Alabama Federal. Shannon brought with him an aggressive new management team and a strategy designed to maintain and enhance profits. Alabama Federal's board of directors includes many prominent Alabamians with strong ties to the four merged associations. Currently guiding Alabama Federal, in addition to Shannon, are David H. Marbury III, Harold F. Miller, Jr., Claude H.

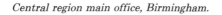

Central region main office, Birmingham.

Southern region main office, Mobile.

The corporate office of Alabama Federal is located in Birmingham.

Moore, Jr., Tom P. Ollinger, James E. Park, Jr., William S. Pritchard, Jr., James O. Screven, Jr., John E. Waller, and Dr. H.K. Wu.

In November 1985 Alabama Federal converted from a mutual association to a stock association with the issuance of 1.41 million shares of common stock. Alabama Federal common stock is traded on the NASDAQ national over-the-counter market with the symbol ALFD.

Primarily in the business of attracting time and demand deposits and originating loans secured by residential and commercial property, Alabama Federal ranks second in asset size among the savings and loan associations based in Alabama and conducts business from 36 offices throughout the state.

In 1986, the first full year Alabama Federal operated as a stock association, it experienced exceptional growth. The year brought expansion into the Montgomery market, the state capital and an important major metropolitan area. Record mortgage loan volume and better control of the cost of funds in 1986 helped the association achieve record profits.

Alabama Federal has plans for continued, controlled expansion and the introduction of new products and services to maintain its leadership as a full-service financial institution. Modernization of its existing offices and systems, including establishing full in-house, data-processing capability, began in 1985. A complete electronic network linking all branches throughout the state now exists.

Present management is confident that Alabama Federal Savings and Loan Association will continue to be a prominent participant in Alabama's future growth—from Huntsville and the Quad Cities to Mobile and the Gulf Coast—contributing to the betterment of life in each area just as the founders of the four merged associations did in Birmingham, Huntsville, Mobile, and Tuscaloosa decades ago.

Western region main office, Tuscaloosa.

ALABAMA-TENNESSEE NATURAL GAS COMPANY
A SUBSIDIARY OF ALATENN RESOURCES, INC.

In the early 1930s the Muscle Shoals area was experiencing rapid growth, and from this growth arose a need for the city and surrounding areas to link to a natural gas supply instead of continuing to rely on manufactured gas.

Amidst war and after struggling through a myriad of bureaucratic channels, Tennessee Gas and Transmission Company received authorization from the Federal Power Commission in 1943 to build a natural gas pipeline from Louisiana through the Muscle Shoals area to Tennessee. The original route of the line, however, was changed, causing it to run miles outside the Muscle Shoals area. It was that change that led to the formation of three new pipeline companies, one of which was Alabama-Tennessee Natural Gas Company, founded by W.S. Eastep in 1944. The resulting planned facilities would finally bring the desired natural gas to the Muscle Shoals area, but not before many more difficulties were overcome.

There was intense competition for the gas supply that was available in the Southeast, and many problems mounted in preparing for the final hearings before the Federal Power Commission. Lacking much of the technical information needed,

B.F. Grizzle, guiding engineer of the project, appeared at the hearing with only $52 in the company's treasury; but, after six days and 716 pages of testimony, availability of gas for the Alabama-Tennessee project was assured. On June 3, 1948, Alabama-Tennessee was granted its certificate of public convenience and necessity.

It was necessary to secure long-term financial commitments before the pipeline could be built. The rising price of steel and the shortage of cash were only two of the stumbling blocks encountered by the company. Five thousand of its 150,000 shares of stock were sold at one dollar per share, and a bank loan for $50,000 was obtained that would allow construction to begin on facilities required to serve the first two scheduled customers, Reynolds Metals Company and Tennessee Valley Authority. More stock had to be sold and another loan for $225,000 obtained. Other delays resulted from the shortage of pipe, but the project was finally begun.

The line began at a connection near Selmer, Tennessee, and ran just south of the Tennessee River all the way to Muscle Shoals. The route ran through woods, rolling countryside, and swampland, even encountering a few whiskey stills along its journey

to completion. Slowly the pipe was welded, coated, and laid.

On February 1, 1950, Eastep's dream of bringing natural gas to the area was realized as the valve was opened and natural gas began to flow through Alabama-Tennessee lines. The company then began to build the facilities that would eventually make natural gas available to more than 500,000 potential customers.

In the summer of 1949 Morton D. Prouty joined Alabama-Tennessee and was elected president and chief executive officer in 1978. Under Prouty's guidance the company has paid dividends to the stockholders since its first quarterly dividend on December 10, 1951. Prouty was also instrumental in restructuring the company into a holding company, AlaTenn Resources, Inc.

Today, under the leadership of Jerry A. Howard, president and chief executive officer, Prouty's successor, the company has continued to grow through two major acquisitions outside the Tennessee Valley. Management intends to continue the company's growth through diversification in response to an increasingly competitive environment, a directive of which Alabama-Tennessee Natural Gas Company's founders would surely approve.

GENERAL MOTORS CORPORATION SAGINAW DIVISION

On 400 acres of rolling farm and woodlands near the marshy backwaters of the Tennessee River at Athens, General Motors Saginaw Steering Gear Division decided, in 1973, to commit millions of dollars for a major automotive plant. General Motors was attracted to the pastoral site off Interstate 65, midway between Birmingham and Nashville, and Atlanta and Memphis, because within 500 miles lies 50 percent of the nation's population and 55 percent of its manufacturing activities.

Construction began in April 1974 on Plant 21—a cavernous 708,000-square-foot building that was to serve as the centerpiece of Saginaw's eventual manufacturing complex. By December 1975 Plant 21 produced its first power-steering pump. The facility also included a powerhouse, waste-treatment plant, primary switchyard, and storm retention ponds.

Just four years after Saginaw announced construction of its first Athens plant, the company unveiled plans for a second facility. Construction of Plant 22 began in July 1977. Production of energy-absorbing steering columns and new, 11-cubic-inch air pumps began in the sprawling, 091,000-square-foot facility the following year.

Yet by mid-1980 Saginaw was again expanding—and rapidly filling its original 400-acre site. This time, seeing the increasing demand for front-wheel-drive axles, Saginaw made the decision to construct a third plant at its Alabama site. The foundation was poured for Plant 23 in 1980, and production began in the 646,000-square-foot building within a year.

With only slight employment fluctuations, General Motors' Saginaw Division at Athens has enjoyed steady growth in the past decade—particularly in the past five years. Today the division employs approximately 3,500 hourly and 360 salaried workers at its Athens plant.

Plant 21, with approximately 2,000 employees, currently produces rack-and-pinion-steering gears and transverse compact pumps. With 600 employees, Plant 22 continues to produce intermediate shafts and 11-cubic-inch air pumps. In 1981 tie rod machining and assembly operations were installed, and three years later toe links were added. In 1985 the consolidation of manufacturing by General Motors resulted in increased manufacturing of products at Plant 22. At Plant 23, with the largest heat-treating facility in the southeastern United States, front-wheel-drive axle assemblies are manufactured for General Motors' intermediate-size automobiles.

In 1986 the Saginaw Division produced 87,400 finished assemblies per day, or 3.4 million pounds each day—the equivalent of more than 85 fully loaded semitrucks per week. Approximately 30 million assemblies rolled out of the three Saginaw plants in 1986.

With an estimated payroll of $154 million in 1986, the community-minded firm spent $26 million with local and state suppliers that year, contributing to a healthy area and state economy. Continued prosperous growth seems almost a certainty for the Saginaw Division, which could be a major on-site supplier of Saginaw components to General Motors' new Saturn facility at Spring Hill, Tennessee, just 80 miles to the north.

General Motors Corporation's Saginaw Division complex is located adjacent to Calhoun Community College and Pryor Field near Decatur.

THE BOEING COMPANY

The Boeing Company, founded in July 1916 in Seattle, Washington, has produced more commercial jetliners than any other company, and in the past two decades also has become a leader in the missile, rocket, helicopter, and space fields.

William Edward Boeing, the son of a wealthy Seattle timberman, took up flying at the age of 34 simply as a way of amusing himself. After riding several times in a seaplane in 1914, however, he became convinced that he could build a better aircraft. Along with G. Conrad Westervelt, a Navy officer assigned to engineering work at a Seattle shipyard, Boeing began construction on a pair of new seaplanes called the B&W seaplane.

In the early 1920s U.S. aviation was involved primarily in the carrying of mail, and it was Boeing seaplanes that were used in the first international airmail route. One year later The Boeing Company obtained its first major order for 111 observation airplanes, followed the next year by a postwar contract for 200 of the craft, the largest postwar contract awarded any airplane manufacturer. For the next several years production was devoted mainly to military planes and a few mail planes.

When the U.S. government stopped flying the mail in 1926, Boeing successfully bid on the contract for carrying transcontinental airmail and established Boeing Air Transport, Inc., to build the planes necessary to fulfill the commitment. This signaled the beginning of regular commercial passenger service over long distances, and served as the vehicle for the first regular pas-

The Boeing Company recently completed its move into $50-million company-owned facilities at the Huntsville-Madison County Jetplex Industrial Park. The three-building, 450,000-square-foot complex is headquarters for the company's Boeing Huntsville operations. The move to the 110-acre site consolidated Huntsville operations in one location for the first time. Boeing will observe its 25th year of continuous operation in the State of Alabama during 1987.

From 1961 to 1973 Boeing built and tested the first stage of the giant Saturn V boosters that helped rocket men to the moon. It also integrated, stacked, fueled, and launched 13 such successful rockets, and provided technical integration and evaluation of the entire Apollo program. At its peak, almost 10,000 Boeing employees were involved in the program.

senger and mail night flights in 1930.

By 1928 the Boeing factory had 800 employees and was one of the largest aircraft plants in the country. To meet what Boeing felt his future activities would require, Boeing Airplane & Transport Corp. stock went on the market on November 1, 1928, and sold briskly. Soon after the Boeing stock sale, Boeing founded United Aircraft & Transport Corp., which included Boeing Airplane Co., Pratt & Whitney, Chance Vought, Sikorsky, Hamilton Propeller Co., Pacific Air Transport, and Boeing Air Transport. In 1931 Boeing Air Transport, National Air Transport, Pacific Air Transport, and Varney Air Lines were combined as United Air Lines. Following a lengthy government hearing and the passage of a law prohibiting air mail contractors from association with aviation manufacturing companies, United Aircraft & Transport Corp. was forced to split up. On September 26, 1934, the corporation split into three new companies: United Air Lines, United Aircraft Corp., and Boeing

Airplane Company.

In the late 1930s Boeing aircraft designs began to appear throughout the country, even in the aircraft produced by competing firms who were quick to recognize the superiority of Boeing designs. The B-17 Flying Fortress; the company's first postwar commercial airlines, the Stratocruiser, and the B-52, which still forms the principal striking force of our military, were productions that kept the company at the head of aircraft design during the 1950s.

In 1952 Boeing announced its new development, a high-risk investment in a $16-million prototype jet

Eddie Hubbard (left) and William Boeing prepare for the first international mail flight in a Boeing B&W seaplane on March 3, 1919.

transport, marking the company's departure from the military bombers. The Model 707 or the Dash Eighty, as it was called, was completed in May 1954 and made its first flight on July 15, the 38th anniversary of Boeing's founding. William E. Boeing, founder of the company, was no longer directly associated with the corporation at that time but saw the fruits of his labor as he watched his wife christen the Dash Eighty when it rolled off the assembly lines. He died in 1956, at the age of 74, before seeing it placed in the Smithsonian Institution in 1972.

In January 1970 the world's largest commercial airplane, the Boeing 747, entered airline service after having undergone the most extensive test program ever undertaken in commercial aviation history. And in the mid-1970s Boeing developed the 767 to meet new fuel-efficiency criteria after completion of years of research and development work.

Just six months before the 747 entered commercial airline service, in July 1969, Neil Armstrong walked on the moon. Subsequent astronauts explored the moon's surface in a buggy—the Lunar Rover—built by Boeing. The Boeing-built S-1C first stage of the Apollo/Saturn V moon rocket played a key role in this new

flight territory of space. In February 1962 Boeing's Huntsville operations were established to support initial development of the Saturn V Stage 1 booster. Huntsville was becoming one of the major sites of the country's space program, and Boeing was there to answer the related needs.

A new chapter in the company's Huntsville history began in 1984, when ground-breaking ceremonies were held to celebrate plans for Boeing's new facilities. The Boeing Technology Complex that resulted represents nearly 450,000 square feet of company-owned facilities at an investment exceeding $50 million. A business base this sizable confirms the company's corporate commitment to Alabama and its faith in the future of high-technology business in north Alabama as well as the importance of the country's military activities and space-related endeavors.

According to officials, the technical expertise, extensive small business network, healthy business climate, and supportive environment in Alabama have created a premier working atmosphere for The Boeing Company, which now has a solid base in diverse programs such as the preliminary design of space station modules, a nationwide telecommunications and computational services network for NASA, support of Army Missile Command's simulation complex, and a host of laborato-

ries that support Huntsville research and development activities. Huntsville is headquarters for the company's military simulation and training systems efforts, and manages the State of Alabama's supercomputer network.

Boeing in Huntsville takes great pride in being a major contributor to the city's economy as well as its people. The firm is instrumental in supplying scholarships that enable students to attend U.S. Space Camp, provides Junior Achievement business consultants to local schools, and loaned executives to United Way. Boeing offers its own employees courses in CPR and a wellness program that promotes an overall healthier life-style. The employees, in turn, offer to Huntsville their time and energy. They act as volunteers at monthly visits to local hospital pediatric wards and, over the years, have established a Good Neighbor Fund that raises, through voluntary contributions from employees, thousands of dollars each year to be dispersed among organizations in the north Alabama area. These organizations help care for children, elderly, and handicapped individuals in need of assistance, and are instrumental in creating wheelchair loan programs and funds that allow diabetic children to attend a summer camp especially designed for them.

The company continues to follow the aims of William E. Boeing who said,

" . . . I've tried to make the men around me feel, as I do, that we are embarked as pioneers upon a new science and industry in which our problems are so new and unusual that it behooves no one to dismiss any novel idea with the statement that 'It can't be done.' . . ."

And in the words of thenpresident of Boeing, William M. Allen, in 1966,

"The years ahead promise to be at least as challenging and revolutionary as those through which we have come. In all likelihood they will be more so. . . ."

GENERAL SERVICES INCORPORATED

L. Paul Banks is a man who inspires confidence, an important quality considering his business—security protection and armored car courier services. The confidence stems perhaps from his qualifications. Banks held top executive positions for more than 15 years in various financing, marketing, public accounting, and business development firms in Birmingham before becoming a leader in a business of his own. Or perhaps the confidence stems from the knowledge that here is a man who has been a key instrument in shaping black history in the South, a man who is accustomed to standing tall in the face of adversity in order to uphold his convictions.

In the early 1960s, a time of extreme racial tension in the nation, Banks was operating a bonding company out of Birmingham, one that made its place in history by assisting a man named Martin Luther King, Jr. The famed civil rights leader planned a demonstration in which over 4,000 people would participate. Experience had proven to King that he needed a reliable bond company in the cities in which he held marches to assist the demonstrators that were inevitably arrested.

Few of the white-owned businesses in the city would agree to help him, and those that did offered assistance only at unheard-of prices. It was Banks' company that agreed to arrange bonding for those that participated in the march. Even though it resulted in his firm being disqualified at times from making further bonds in the city, Banks' company cooperated in making the necessary arrangements for more than 2,500 demonstrators in May 1963, including Martin Luther King, Jr., himself.

In 1978 Banks established General Services Incorporated, a diversified company that provides services in several specialized areas. In 1980 he added a full-service security and armored car division that has since become the first black-owned armored vehicle service in America to receive statewide operating au-

L. Paul Banks, founder and president of General Services Incorporated, which provides security protection and armored car courier services throughout the state of Alabama.

thority.

Banks became interested in the armored vehicle service business after receiving a telephone call from a Birmingham utility company inquiring about the availability of security service from its offices to a nearby bank at specified times. A subsequent survey revealed that a need did exist in Birmingham for specialized, same-day deposit service, and Banks quickly responded to that need. His firm provides armored car services in Alabama.

Today General Services Incorporated, the parent company of Banks Security, continues to operate a uniformed guard service along with its armored vehicle service, recently installing state-of-the-art security equipment to safeguard clients' property. Banks Security also provides seven-day-per-week replenishment service for automated teller machines and a special coin wrapping service.

Currently operating as one of the three largest black-owned businesses in Birmingham, the company employs 125 people and increases that number to 200 during peak

business periods. In 1984 the Alabama Public Service Commission unanimously approved the firm's petition to operate statewide, enabling the company to bid on much larger contracts than in the past and ensuring its continued growth. The awarding of a permit for the firm to operate statewide was challenged in the circuit court of Jefferson County, Alabama, by some companies who were already providing armored car services throughout the state of Alabama.

In 1985 a court issued an order reversing the Alabama Public Service Commission's approval of Banks' application. Upon appeal by Banks to the Alabama Supreme Court, which had reversed an administrative judge's ruling, he finally gained full authority to operate an armored car service statewide.

Growth, however, does not deter Banks from continuing to be a vital contributor to Birmingham civic activities and the betterment of the area. The kind of contribution he offers, Banks believes, only serves to form a closer bond between the city and its businesses. And his beliefs are something L. Paul Banks will go to great lengths to uphold today, just as in the days of Martin Luther King, Jr.

SONAT INC.

Nearly 60 years ago a group of visionary businessmen came up with a plan to challenge the Mississippi River and deliver energy in the form of natural gas to two of the South's largest cities, Birmingham and Atlanta.

At the time natural gas was a by-product of the oil boom. Gas was being flared at oil fields in north Louisiana, when Southern Natural Gas began building a natural gas pipeline system from the oil fields to serve customers in Mississippi, Alabama, and Georgia. With the successful crossing of the Mississippi, the pipeline was completed to Birmingham in December 1929 and to Atlanta the following June.

Today Sonat Inc., parent company of Southern Natural Gas, is a worldwide corporation, headquartered in Birmingham and owned by thousands of shareholders. The natural gas pipeline continues to be the core business of Sonat, and pipelines of the firm and its largest pipeline subsidiary, Southern Natural Gas, are located in eight states and serve the Southeast, bringing natural gas from sources in the Gulf of Mexico and onshore to homes, businesses, and industries across the Southeast through more than 13,000 miles of pipeline.

The early years were difficult ones, however. The young company was dealt some hard blows by the Depression. But Southern Natural Gas Company, the predecessor of Sonat Inc., emerged and began paying dividends in 1936.

Despite the cyclical nature of the energy industry, Sonat expanded, reaching into the areas of domestic exploration and production of oil and natural gas, and services to the energy industry worldwide. Through Sonat Exploration Company, headquartered in Houston, the firm explores for and produces oil and natural gas in the Gulf of Mexico and onshore in the rich oil and gas areas of the United States.

Sonat's oil services subsidiaries offer contract services to major oil companies worldwide. A major oil

services subsidiary and innovative industry leader, Sonat Offshore Drilling, headquartered in Houston, operates one of the world's largest fleets of offshore drilling rigs. The company's drillship, *Discoverer Seven Seas,* has repeatedly set world records for deep-water drilling of oil and gas wells. Other of its units are

The Henry Goodrich, *one of the world's largest semisubmersible drilling rigs is owned by Sonat Offshore Drilling. The advanced offshore drilling rig is substantially enclosed and winterized for efficient year-round operation off northern Norway or in comparable Arctic conditions.*

Muscle and mule power marked the early days of interstate pipeline construction. In this 1929 photograph workers install one of the first Southern Natural Gas pipelines in the Birmingham area.

designed to provide additional high-technology drilling services, including shirt-sleeve working environments in icy North Sea waters. Another of its oil services subsidiaries, Teleco Oilfield Services, headquartered in Meriden, Connecticut, provides measurement-while-drilling services to the industry, utilizing space-age technology developed through aggressive research and development programs.

Today the company that challenged the Mississippi River to bring energy to two of the South's largest cities is still meeting the needs of energy users and the energy industry through its pipeline, oil services, and exploration and production subsidiaries.

Despite nearly 60 years of growing to a $3-billion company, Sonat Inc. has had but five chief executives. Ronald L. Kuehn, Jr., succeeded Henry C. Goodrich in 1985. Goodrich, who was named chairman in 1980, followed John S. Shaw, Jr. Shaw succeeded C. Pratt Rather in 1967, and Rather, in 1965, succeeded Christopher T. Chenery, the company's first chief executive.

BIRMINGHAM REALTY COMPANY

It is not often that a realty company is responsible for the founding of a city, particularly a company that later grows to be among the largest, most opportunistic in the Southeast. However, Birmingham Realty Company, originally Elyton Land Company, is among the few such businesses that can lay claim to such a distinction.

In the late 1860s the South and North Alabama Railroad was under construction between Montgomery and Decatur and would, at some point, be forced to cross the Alabama and Chattanooga Railroad. Several right-of-way engineers involved in the project began to speculate about just where that crossing would be and discovered that the intersection would occur at a point in north Alabama where huge deposits of coal and iron ore lay near the small town of Elyton. This location was sure to attract a great many prospective settlers, and the engineers, anxious to capitalize on their knowledge, decided to form a company for the purpose of building a town there. The title to 4,150 acres was transferred to Josiah Morris of Montgomery shortly thereafter, and on December 20, 1870, the corporation was formed. On January 26, 1871, a meeting of the investors was held in Montgomery where it was decided that the city would be called Birmingham and would be built by Elyton Land Company near Elyton.

Offices were opened in Birmingham and engineers were engaged to begin the surveys necessary to lay out the streets and avenues. In June 1871 the first lot in the city was sold at the corner of First Avenue and 19th Street for $100. Stockholders in the company then agreed to contribute funds to build a hotel nearby, with plans for a waterworks to follow. More lots were sold, and houses began to appear at a rapid pace. The town, it seemed, was off and growing.

The 1873 report to stockholders by Elyton Land Company was a glowing one, reporting an immense amount of growth in a short two-year

Birmingham Realty Company, established in 1870, occupied its own building in 1904.

span. The venture's founders as well as the new settlers in the area all felt certain that the boom of the north Alabama city would continue uninterrupted. However, that was not to be the case.

An epidemic of cholera struck

Heritage Place, part of the historical renovation of downtown Birmingham.

the city in 1873, and population began to decrease as rapidly as it had increased. Gradually, however, Birmingham began to recover and then to enter a boom period in the 1880s. The Elyton Land Company borrowed heavily to finance new streets, utilities, and streetcar lines. Prosperity seemed unlimited. But a severe national recession ended all this in the mid-1890s. The company's bondholders foreclosed forming the Birmingham Realty Company with the remaining assets. William G. Woodward of New York became the firm's largest shareholder. Henry R. Carse of New York was named president in 1904, a position he held for nearly 40 years.

With the growth of the iron works in 1900, the city of Birmingham began once again to flourish, and the new Birmingham Realty Company did the same, developing Norwood, Highland Avenue, and later Forest Park. What proved to be one of the firm's most lucrative investments was founded in 1904. It was the Dolcito Quarry Company, now operating the largest and most modern quarry in the area. Located in the Pinson Valley, the quarry was originally opened by Tennessee Coal

and Iron Company. Dolcito Quarry Company proved to offer its owners access to limestone of a chemical composition that made it suitable for use in the steel industry and as an outstanding aggregate for concrete and highways. The Dolcito Quarry Company continues to be one of Birmingham Realty Company's most valuable assets.

In the 1930s Sidney W. Smyer, Sr., began serving as a Birmingham Realty's board member and as its general counsel. He became president in 1954 upon the retirement of I.C. Beatty. The Smyers were a pioneering family in the Birmingham area and had long been independently involved in real estate development in the city prior to association with the firm. He served until the 1960s, when Sidney W. Smyer, Jr., then vice-president, took the office held by his father.

Major ownership of the company remained with the Woodward family until they and the other major shareholders sold out in 1977. Since World War II, however, Birmingham Realty has been involved exclusively in commercial real estate development and, under the Smyers' leadership, has been instrumental in the development of some of Birmingham's most prominent areas. In the 1950s and 1960s development was concentrated on Southside, where some of the area's first warehouses, shopping centers, and office parks were built.

More recently the firm has been heavily involved in the expansion of Birmingham suburbs, developing office parks and shopping centers. Two of the most notable of these recent projects are Perimeter Park South and Riverhills in North Shelby County. These two developments, along with the Valleydale Business Center project, assisted the firm in increasing its real estate investments almost threefold.

Currently Birmingham Realty is heavily involved in city projects, serving in various capacities on boards and councils in the area that

One (top) and Two (above) Perimeter Park South are two of the most recent buildings in this suburban office park.

are key organizations in Birmingham development. The underwriting of the firm comes from continued close ties with both the Birmingham Chamber of Commerce and The Business Council of Alabama, both strong, business-oriented agencies.

Russell M. Cunningham III was named president in 1982 with Sidney W. Smyer, Jr., chairman.

Still located in historic offices on First Avenue North downtown, Birmingham Realty Company offers

anyone entering its establishment a view of the original documents of its predecessor and the original plats of the city as its first streets were laid and its first businesses built more than a century ago. Looking at these documents displayed on the walls of the offices and glancing around at the magnificent structure housing them, it is difficult not to wander back in time to the place where it all began and marvel at the vast accomplishments of a few far-sighted men and the enterprise that they established. Those few men's dreams and that firm's expertise resulted in a city they decided to call Birmingham.

CHRYSLER CORPORATION

Workers tacked up the first Chrysler Corporation signs in Huntsville, Alabama, in early autumn 1952. They were on a collection of nondescript buildings dotting the former grazelands near the Tennessee River, the Chrysler logo symbolized the firm's commitment to American technological development.

Chrysler assembled in those Redstone Arsenal buildings 26 engineers to provide support engineering services to Dr. Wernher von Braun's then-infant rocket research team. Their first assignment was development of the Redstone and Jupiter missile systems. The parent plant—then called the Chrysler Missile Plant in Detroit, Michigan—was already actively engaged in the production of these missile systems, as well as in support of the Jupiter C, Juno II, and Mercury-Redstone systems that placed the United States' first satellites and first astronauts in space. Chrysler became the first major industrial firm involved in the development and production of large, surface-to-surface missiles, re-entry vehicles, and space boosters.

By 1959—just as President Eisenhower created the National Aeronautics and Space Administration—Chrysler's Huntsville operation saw its boundaries expand and relocated to the Huntsville Industrial Center, a renovated cotton mill on the city's east side where a group of the nation's prime space contractors began to assemble.

In these developmental years of American space exploration, the growth of Chrysler's commitment to the space program witnessed a parallel growth of its professional specialties. Chrysler became an acknowledged leader in the area of electronic controls, developing both systems and components for America's space ventures.

Its work paid off. In 1961 Chrysler was awarded the prime contract for the Saturn S-1 and S-1B launch vehicles. These Chrysler-engineered components hurled manned and unmanned Apollo spacecraft into earth orbit—laying the groundwork for this nation's manned lunar expeditions.

With the expansion of its significant role in the space program, Chrysler Huntsville's growth continued. In 1965, having outgrown its old cotton mill quarters, the firm occupied a new, 65,000-square-foot facility in Huntsville's Cummings Research Park.

The 1970s brought a rapid phasing down of the space program. Government space contracts dried up, and many of the nation's major space contractors closed their Huntsville doors. But in this upheaval, Chrysler saw opportunity: Chrysler's Huntsville division offered tremendous capability as a technical problem solver. Some of the nation's best and brightest engineering and scientific minds had been tested and proven in finding technical solutions to the problems of space voyage. And what better solution to Chrysler's Huntsville dilemma than to redirect those scientific skills from putting man on the moon to developing better electronic control systems for the automotive industry? It was an unexpected—but natural—transition for Chrysler.

The automotive industry was beginning to use advanced electronics in cars and trucks. The transition from space to auto electronics would demand a synthesis of science, engineering, manufacturing, and marketing. Prototypes were conceived and engineered by Chrysler's technical staff, moved into mass production by a newly developed manufacturing team, and introduced to an emerging market.

It was a new arena. But the challenge to reorganize, restructure, and identify new markets was met. Chrysler Aerospace evolved into Chrysler Electronic Components and Systems, and emerged into one of the fastest-growing high-tech, electronic engineering and manufacturing operations in the South.

As it flourished in its new role,

Chrysler Electronics City, Huntsville.

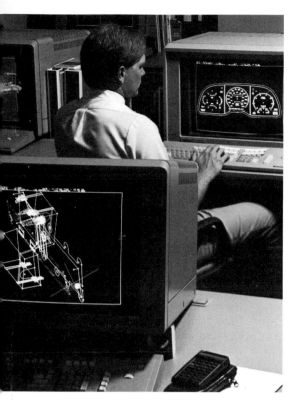

Chrysler Huntsville has moved into the age of robotics and computer-aided design. Much of the mechanical, structural, and electrical design is done through the aid of computers. Here an engineer works on the design of an automobile dashboard.

Chrysler Huntsville's 29-acre facility in Cummings Research Park proved too confining. Entry into the automotive electronics industry had meant mass production. More manufacturing space was needed. In 1972 Chrysler's 65,000-square-foot facility was enlarged to 100,000 square feet to accommodate the manufacturing of Chrysler Huntsville's first products: blocking oscillators for emission control systems, headlamp delays, and car radios. Just two years later the plant was more than doubled in size to house the manufacturing of electronic ignition controls for Chrysler Corporation passenger cars. And in 1977 the Huntsville division again expanded, adding a second 200,000-square-foot manufacturing facility adjacent to the

original plant.

But the company's growth should not be measured solely in square feet. Chrysler implemented state-of-the-art manufacturing methods, refining and updating regularly. In 1984 a $3.6-million robot-equipped assembly line was added to assist the manufacturing and quality assurance of automobile spark control computers. It was just the first step in a $15-million expansion program. But automation doesn't necessarily mean displacement of people. The figures prove that in 1960 Chrysler Electronics employed 910. By 1987 employment jumped to over 3,000 with an annual payroll of $118 million. And Chrysler Huntsville's transition and progression from hand assembly of electromechanical and electronic products to today's highly robotic operation provided the competitive talents necessary to maintain automotive electronic product manufacturing in the United States.

While Chrysler Huntsville's roots were in electronics development for the government, the completion of government contracts in the late 1960s and early 1970s led to extensive organizational restructuring within Chrysler, and a new emphasis on developing products for non-military markets. By the late 1970s the company had tackled this market, securing prominent public contracts, as well as substantive military contracts.

In September 1982, under a major reorganization, the Chrysler Military-Public Electronic Systems (MPES) organization was segregated from Chrysler's Automotive Electronics Division and established as a separate entity. MPES's product lines include automatic test equipment for the U.S. Army M1-A1 Abrams Tank and the M2/M3 Bradley Fighting Vehicles, Supervisory Control and Data Acquisition (SCADA) systems used by utility companies and power plants, and a computerized rail traffic control system for Amtrak. MPES is also in-

volved in designing, building, and servicing Chrysler assembly plant test equipment.

Chrysler also relocated its Introl Products Operation from Ann Arbor, Michigan, to Huntsville. This consolidation and transfer of operations resulted in the relocation of approximately 300 employees to Huntsville and the addition of 10 new products to the Huntsville line up.

It was early 1984 that the new Chrysler Corporation began to lay the groundwork for an expansion that would become one of the most significant developments in Huntsville's storied economic growth. And by summer of 1986, with a vision to the future, Chrysler came armed with plans to purchase 325 acres at the Huntsville-Madison County Airport.

The result: Chrysler Electronics City—a prize sought by cities across the United States, but won by Huntsville through sheer teamwork and cooperation by city, county, state, and federal officials, as well as Chrysler management and the United Auto Workers Union. Chrysler Electronics City is a 700,000-square-foot electronics manufacturing facility featuring state-of-the-art automated material handling, in-line processing, computer-integrated manufacturing, and a new research and development engineering facility. Located within this complex at the Huntsville jetport will also be materials suppliers.

In its three decades in Huntsville, Chrysler Corporation has grown into two divisions—Military-Public Electronic Systems with 600 employees, and Chrysler Electronic Components and Systems with 3,000 employees. And with its growth and seasoned experience came a graceful transition from aerospace technology to the development of sophisticated instrumentation and electronic components and systems for the U.S. military, industrial business sector, and the automotive industry.

CHAMPION INTERNATIONAL CORPORATION

Champion International Corporation, headquartered in Stamford, Connecticut, is one of the country's leading forest products companies. Champion is comprised of four product line business units: printing and writing papers; publication papers; newsprint, pulp, and kraft; and forest products.

In the 1960s the new corporation identified several key growth markets for fine papers. The demand for these papers was ever-increasing as the result of advanced information processing and print communication technologies. In answer to the demand Champion decided it would build a major new pulp and paper mill that would utilize the most modern technology available as well as the most experienced, qualified people. Most importantly, this new mill would be built with the future in mind. It would have to be equipped to accommodate the continual growth that would be necessary in order to keep pace with the markets for its products.

A site was needed for the new mill—one that would provide access to the 50 million gallons of water per day required by the mill processes, a plentiful supply of forestlands, and a variety of energy sources such as coal, gas, and oil. A good transportation network would also be essential. A city that provided just such assets was Courtland in north Alabama, bordered on the north by the Tennessee River. There in that small city, on the banks of the river, a pulp

Champion's 1,850-acre Courtland, Alabama, complex is a showcase of modern pulp and fine paper technology.

The new No. 34 paper machine is the keystone of the latest expansion. Started up in record time on July 19, 1983, it is designed to produce some 400 tons per day of uncoated paper production at Courtland.

and paper giant would soon rise.

Ground was broken at the site in 1968, and by 1971 the first pulp mill, a pulp dryer, and a paper machine started up. Another paper machine was added in 1975. In 1979 the pulp capacity was doubled with the start-up of a second pulp mill followed by a third paper machine in 1980. The last addition was in 1983 with the start-up of a fourth paper machine. This paper mill giant operates today on 1,850 acres surrounded, in a 75-mile radius, by almost a half-million owned or leased acres of timberland that provide the trees essential to the entire papermaking process.

The timber is cut and shipped primarily by rail to the mill site where it is stripped. The bark is then burned to provide energy for the mill and the logs are chipped into small pieces that are cooked in a chemical solution that releases the cellulose fiber from the wood of the tree. The separated fiber is then washed, screened, and bleached. The pulp mixture that results from the 18-hour process is mixed with additives and large amounts of water that allows it to flow over the paper machines where the water is drained away and a continuous sheet of paper is formed and dried. These sheets are then converted into rolls or sheets of various sizes ready for distribution to consumers all over the country.

The modern processes of the Courtland mills produce approximately 1,700 tons of paper per day, a considerable improvement over the methods of 2,000 years ago when people made one sheet at a time by straining a water and pulp wood mixture through a screen, which left behind a mat of fiber that was used as paper.

State-of-the-art technology is continually being added to the mills to improve its processes as well as perform the equally important tasks of controlling air and water pollution and managing solid waste disposal. But still considered its most important resource are the people of the Courtland mill, now numbering approximately 1,500. An additional 100 people are directly employed in the Alabama Timberlands operation.

The Champion industry remains closely tied to the future, since paper is the link between advancing communication technologies and the individuals who utilize the flood of information that is produced by our society, but most importantly, because paper is the communications medium that is still the most compatible with people.

BROMBERG'S

Founded in 1836 in Mobile, Bromberg's is the oldest business in Alabama. It has been under continuous family ownership and management for six generations.

The story begins in 1832, when Frederick Bromberg, who was a native of East Prussia, sailed from Hamburg, Germany, bound for Boston.

Once in his new home, he spent many hours listening to the tales that weathered seamen told about the antebellum South. Determined to be a part of this gracious southern life-style, he arrived in Mobile in 1836. There he and his family opened a mercantile business that sold musical instruments, sheet music, and fancy goods that plantation owners sought to make their lives more elegant. Thus began a 150-year company tradition of supplying the finer things of life to discriminating southerners.

Only three years after its opening, Bromberg's original store was destroyed by the great Mobile fire of 1839. That same year the South suffered a yellow fever epidemic, and Frederick's wife contracted the disease. In spite of adversity, the young company flourished through long hours and hard work.

Frederick W. Bromberg was

An early street scene in Birmingham with F.W. Bromberg Jewelers in the background (right) in 1910.

joined by his son, Charles, who entered the firm full time in 1865, after military service for the Confederacy. Charles, in turn, was joined by his brother-in-law E.O. Zadek, and their management continued until the Mobile store was closed in 1915.

In 1900 F.W. Bromberg, son of Charles, founded F.W. Bromberg Jewelers in the booming new city of Birmingham. After World War I F.W.'s four sons, William, Robert, Charles, and Frank, joined him in the business. They were almost immediately faced with the challenge of the Great Depression, followed closely by the turmoil of World War II. However, steady growth continued in spite of hard times. They were joined in the 1950s by their sons and sons-in-law, whose children became active in the firm in the 1970s and 1980s.

In 1946 the company erected its

current headquarters location on 20th Street in downtown Birmingham, and in 1959 began a period of expansion, with the opening of its first suburban store in Mountain Brook. Soon followed additional locations in Hoover, Montgomery, Huntsville, and Tuscaloosa, and the acquisition of five Underwood Jewelers stores in Jacksonville, Florida.

Bromberg's continues to be noted for offering only the finest quality in jewelry, silver, and ceramics. The firm holds the further distinction of being one of only five companies in the nation to be operated by the same family for six generations.

Today 11 members of the family's fourth, fifth, and sixth generations form Bromberg's management team. They stand as living testimony that a family business that works well together can be successful.

(Left to right) Frank H. Bromberg, Jr., Eugene A. Bromberg, Paul M. Byrne, and Frank H. Bromberg, Sr., in front of Bromberg's corporate headquarters in Birmingham.

359

JACKSONVILLE STATE UNIVERSITY

Jacksonville State University is Alabama's fourth-largest university and the only major institution of higher education in northeast Alabama.

Under the leadership of first-year president Dr. Harold J. McGee, Jacksonville State is committed to assist in the economic development of the region, especially with outreach programs designed to assist small businesses as well as more substantial business and industrial clients.

The College of Commerce and Business Administration, the largest of JSU's eight colleges, works hand in hand with the JSU-based Center for Economic Development, Small Business Development Center, and Management Development Center. Those facets of the university provide best-fit analyses, economic impact surveys, consultation, and

The predecessors of Jacksonville State University date back to Jacksonville Male Academy in 1836. Today it is the major institution of higher education in northeast Alabama with 42 majors within eight colleges.

training assistance to business, industry, and government agencies throughout the region.

The university's mission is to become the most outstanding undergraduate teaching institution in Alabama.

In 1983 the university unveiled a unique program designed to serve the needs of skilled workers in such mid-tech areas as computer-aided drafting and industrial management. The Bachelor of Technology degree enables graduates of technical, junior, and community colleges to continue their education through the baccalaureate level. The program also serves individuals in the work force whose competencies were developed from other sources. The program consists of a combination of business (management), industrial, and engineering courses.

Another new program at Jacksonville State University is the Department of Communications. An existing campus building was extensively renovated to house the department and its state-of-the-art equipment. Unlike many communication programs, the one at JSU focuses on the broadcast industry and trains students in every aspect of the profession. Majors receive part of their training at WJSU-TV in Anniston, a commercial CBS affiliate, as well as at an on-campus closed-

The Department of Communications trains students for the broadcast industry with the latest state-of-the-art equipment, an on-campus closed-circuit television station, and an FM radio station.

circuit TV station and a 3,000-watt FM campus radio station.

Striving to make a college degree possible for everyone in its recruiting area, JSU has kept tuition and fees affordable. At the same time the university is known for the high-caliber academic program it offers approximately 7,000 students annually, most of whom are first-generation college students.

Jacksonville State University offers 42 majors within eight colleges. The eight colleges of JSU are: College of Commerce and Business Administration, College of Education, College of Criminal Justice, College of Nursing, College of Science and Mathematics, College of Communications and Fine Arts, College of Humanities and Social Science, and College of Graduate Studies and Continuing Education.

Jacksonville State University originates from Jacksonville Male Academy, established in the city in 1836. It evolved into the State Normal School at the turn of the century and was elevated to Jacksonville State Teachers College in 1929, Jacksonville State College in 1957, and to a full university in 1966.

HOLIDAY INN OF SHEFFIELD

Nestled in a wooded area in the heart of the Quad Cities, the Holiday Inn of Sheffield is the Shoals' premier conference and convention facility. Just two miles from the Muscle Shoals Airport and one mile from Wilson Dam and the Tennessee Valley Authority Reservation, the 206-room facility is the Shoals area's only Holiday Inn.

The northwest Alabama countryside glistens with lakes, state parks, and recreational facilities, while such historic landmarks as the Natchez Trace, Indian Mound and Museum, Helen Keller's birthplace, and the museum and birthplace of the Father of Rhythm and Blues—W.C. Handy—are all nearby. At the Holiday Inn of Sheffield, don't be surprised to spot a familiar music star, for Muscle Shoals is billed as the "Hit Recording Capital of the World."

Three floors of cheerful suites and rooms await the traveler or conference attendee at the Holiday Inn of Sheffield. Tastefully decorated suites include living, dining, and bar areas. The Inn's Board Room suites include connecting guest quarters. All rooms are just steps away from the inviting garden and pool area, where guests can soak up the warm Alabama sun. An indoor jacuzzi, just off the lobby, allows for all-weather recreation and relaxation.

Entertainment is aplenty at the Holiday Inn of Sheffield. The hotel's lounge is the setting for the most fashionable dancing in town, made even more cordial by its backgammon tables and a large-screen television to enjoy the game with friends. The Marketplace provides an airy, greenhouse setting for breakfast, lunch, and dinner.

As a favorite and comfortable conference and convention facility, the Holiday Inn of Sheffield can accommodate a wide variety of functions. Its meeting space for up to 450 people is unsurpassed in the area. Whatever special event is on the calendar, it's a special event at the Holiday Inn of Sheffield, whether for meetings, banquets, conferences, or wedding receptions. From the Shoals Ballroom to smaller areas, such as the Cedar, Cypress, Willow, or Magnolia rooms, the Inn offers detailed planning and catering for a successful gathering.

The Holiday Inn of Sheffield, opened in the spring of 1982, is backed by a superb parent organization—Servico Management Corp., of West Palm Beach, Florida, owners and operators of fine lodging, meeting, and dining facilities nationwide, as well as in foreign locations.

The Holiday Inn of Sheffield offers a refreshing respite for the traveler or convention visitor in the midst of historic northwest Alabama.

HUNTSVILLE HILTON AND TOWERS

Huntsville's Von Braun Civic Center was rising from the deep red clay, its foundation poured, its steel frame thrusting into the sky. But just across the reflecting lake of Big Spring Park, a seemingly prime tract of land lay vacant, strewn with debris. The weathered shacks that once dotted this landscape had disappeared—victims of urban renewal. But the renewal had not yet come.

The City of Huntsville had advertised the property as a "motel site"—its location directly across from the new, multimillion-dollar arena, convention center, arts complex, and museum ideal to support a first-class lodging facility. But so far, no takers.

In stepped the Huntsville Real Estate Investment Trust, a group of local investors headed by retired Lieutenant General Charles W. Eifler. Armed with the charter of helping Huntsville to grow and prosper, Eifler had scouted the area for investment opportunities for the trust. It was just such an opportunity that he foresaw in that debris-strewn property across from the new civic center.

Under the red topsoil the motel site hid a limestone cave—its solid floor more than 45 feet below the surface. That very soft underpinning had frightened away other developers. But in the site Eifler and his partners saw three prime attributes for business, he recalls fondly:

In January 1984 HJH Associates began a million-dollar alteration of the hotel. Shown is the lobby area.

"Location, location, location."

State Geologist Dr. Walter Jones was brought in to inspect the site. His recommendation: Build the hotel on piles. It was the only way. After weeks of evaluation in late 1973, the completion of a feasibility study, and the assembling of a financial package, construction of the Huntsville Hilton began in May 1974.

Less than a year later—on April 5, 1975—the Huntsville Hilton opened its doors. Its instant success could be attributed to its location: adjacent to the Von Braun Civic Center, a short walking distance to City of Huntsville and Madison County offices, just steps from the city's financial and legal center, and just as close to the city's historic districts as well as its growing medical district.

The Huntsville Hilton and Towers' spacious Lofton's restaurant.

Atop 252 piles driven 40 to 50 feet into a limestone cavern floor, the Huntsville Hilton boasted 205 rooms at its opening, ample meeting areas, a ballroom, two restaurants, and an intimate lounge. Its restaurants, in fact, brought a new sophistication to the city—the Peppertree, with seating for 147, and the elegant Pressed Duck, a specialty restaurant for just 67 diners.

So popular was the hotel that in 1979 its original owners, whose name had changed to Huntsville Industrial Associates, began construction of an additional 90 hotel rooms on the south side of the site. However, this addition took on another dimension. As an enlightened package to attract the small hotel convention,

another ballroom was added to the hotel complex, as well as a second lounge. When construction was completed in a year, the hotel featured facilities for booking two conventions with neither ever having to interfere with the other because of their separate locations within the hotel complex.

In late 1983 Huntsville Industrial Associates decided to liquidate its business holdings, including dispensing of the hotel property. But because of the investors' keen interest in the future of Huntsville, they were reluctant to sell their key hotel property in the heart of the city to

just anyone. The buyer had to be special, with a special interest in the city. That buyer was HJH Associates of Alabama, then operators of successful hotels in Raleigh, North Carolina, and Orlando, Florida.

Shortly after the sale was completed in January 1984, HJH Associates began a million-dollar alteration of the hotel, gutting its center for extensive remodeling of its lobby, lounges, and restaurant. Today the quiet dignity of the design is apparent to each hotel guest, as the lobby opens to reveal a quiet lobby lounge, the spacious Lofton's restaurant, and the rejuvenated and successful nightspot, Bowties. The Huntsville Hilton and Towers is a success story at the city's heart.

FLORENCE TIMESDAILY

The newspaper has been a part of daily life for such a long period of time that it seems to be given very little thought by anyone who is not directly involved in its production. Not, that is, until it fails to appear with its customary regularity. But a great deal of work is involved in the process that makes the newspaper one of the most reliable items in daily life.

In Florence, the daily paper began 118 years ago and nowhere can be found in the history of that long existence a recollection of a single day of publication being missed. What is now the *Florence Times-Daily* was begun in 1869, and existed at that time as two separate publications: *The Florence Times* and *The Tri-Cities Daily.* The *Tri-Cities Daily* was originally located on Montgomery Avenue in Sheffield and was published there until some time during the 1930s, when both papers began to be published in Florence at the Florence Times Building on Mobile Street.

No change was made in that tradition until 1969, when the two publications were combined to form one afternoon edition of the *Florence Times-Tri-Cities Daily.* It was not until 1982 that another major change occurred. At that time the paper was purchased by *The New York Times,* who made it a part of The New York Times Regional Newspaper Group (NYTRENG), a group of 33 daily and weekly newspapers found in the Southeast. The following year the paper was once again redesigned, its name formally changed to *Times-Daily,* and publication switched to morning rather than afternoon.

Still housed in offices on West Tennessee Street that were acquired in 1957, the *TimesDaily* utilizes 32,000 square feet in producing its daily edition. The 32,000 copies of the paper that are printed each day require approximately 2,500 tons of newsprint each year. The larger Sunday edition requires, on the average, 42 rolls of newsprint each week that weigh approximately 900 pounds each. If these rolls were unwound and connected, they would stretch from Florence to Little Rock, Arkansas, and would measure a total of 294 miles. And at $425 per ton of newsprint, the cost of paper for the Sunday edition alone is more than $7,000 each week.

Since the paper was started in 1869, not a day can be recalled when publication was missed. Today the Florence TimesDaily *serves 32,000 customers in the surrounding area.*

The Florence TimesDaily, *located on West Tennessee Street, is owned by The New York Times Regional Newspaper Group.*

News is gathered locally and supplemented with national items obtained over phone lines from The Associated Press and *The New York Times* wire services, which use electrical impulses to generate letters, figures, and words. These images, in turn, appear on computers at the offices in Florence. Additions and deletions are made by editors, who, when satisfied, electronically transfer the stories to a typesetting machine that converts the impulses into flashes of light. These flashes of light are then photographed onto light-sensitive paper, developed much like a roll of film, and arranged on pages. These pages are also photographed and used to make an aluminum printing plate only .009 inches thick that is mounted on the press that prints the paper.

Once printed and folded, the papers are distributed in a variety of ways to more than 40 carriers who then deliver to the 32,000 subscribers in the area. It is this complicated process, beginning with tons of newsprint, ending in the hands of carriers, and exemplified by the *Florence TimesDaily* that makes the daily newspaper the reliable item that it is—a process that, in order to be successfully completed day after day, requires skill, efficiency, and the dedication of many employees.

CHAMBER OF COMMERCE OF THE SHOALS

The Florence Chamber of Commerce has been an influencing force in the Shoals area since the city of Florence was founded in 1818. A century later, as the city celebrated its 100th anniversary, the chamber, with W.H. Mitchell as president, issued its first written annual report. That same year, also for the first time, the chamber designed a specific plan of activities that would allow Florence to function as efficiently and economically as possible.

It was decided that a well-financed chamber was the only type that would be instrumental in moving the town forward, thus, the membership instructed the directors to accumulate a fund of not less than $15,000 to be used in the year 1918. First, the chamber needed publicity for the city, but, even with its new budget, could not afford a national advertising campaign. Instead it brought in renowned southern newspaper writer, David Holt, to work as a correspondent. Holt was responsible for getting publicity matter into outside papers under the heading of "news," and did a masterful job of advertising the virtues and attractions of the city until he was called away to war.

Facing problems of providing adequate transportation between Florence and the nearby nitrate plant employing great numbers of its townspeople and of completing a highway across the top of Wilson Dam, the chamber had its work cut out for it in the first decades of the twentieth century, but successfully met both challenges. Housing was another area in which growth was essential. To ensure this growth, the chamber formed the city's first

Wilson Dam, completed in 1925 by the U.S. Corps of Engineers, forms a 16-mile lake over what was once a reach of shoals and rapids, hampering and sometimes preventing navigation.

Housing Bureau, maintained to list and present available housing facilities to the public. The end of the war brought other improvements to Florence, most of which were the result of chamber efforts. As time went by the focus of the organization shifted from inner-city improvements to the Tennessee River. Great concentration was put into the improvement of the river as well as power development.

In that first annual report of 1918 the chamber outlined as its primary purpose promoting the commercial, industrial, and civic welfare

Before TVA's Wilson Dam was completed by the U.S. Corps of Engineers in 1924, the Tennessee River in northwest Alabama often looked like this. It was called Muscle Shoals, not because of the mussel that were abundant in the river, but because of the muscle power required to move even a canoe through the rocky shallows. Wilson Dam was the first major step in controlling the Tennessee River and providing more dependable navigation past Muscle Shoals, Alabama. Photo circa 1914

of the City of Florence and the chamber of commerce has, in the nearly 70 years since, continued to uphold those ideals held by its founders over a century ago. Today, with more than 40,000 residents, the city houses a vital industrial complex, a major university, and is the home of what is now the world's largest and highest single lift in a waterway at the Wilson Dam.

The membership of the Florence/Lauderdale Area Chamber and the membership of the Greater Shoals Area Chamber of Commerce recently voted to unite the two bodies, effective January 1, 1987, forming the Chamber of Commerce of the Shoals to act as one organization that will promote the exposure and desirable growth of the area.

Key activities in the Shoals area include the Helen Keller Festival held each year during June in the city of Tuscumbia, the birthplace of Helen Keller, and the W.C. Handy Jazz Festival held each year during August honoring the "Father of the Blues," born in a Florence log cabin in 1873, who became one of America's most important contributors to early jazz. Beginning in 1986 and continuing through 1991, the NCAA Division II Football Championship game is held in Florence, a game attracting more than 10,000 spectators each year. These and other important activities in which the Chamber of Commerce of the Shoals plays a key role bring valuable dollars into the Shoals area economy and, as has always been its tradition, promotes the area to all who will come and enjoy its pleasures.

WAPI AM/FM RADIO

Today radio holds a respected position among available communications mediums. But it was not so long ago that radio seemed a curious thing thought sure to be made obsolete by the onslaught of television, an oddity that raised many questions about its viability in the future. Those questions regarding its viability, however, were soon put to rest.

In the medium's early years Alabama had as its initial taste of radio, WAPI AM/FM, the first station in the state and, in fact, one of the oldest AM stations in the country. The station began in Birmingham in 1922 as WSY and a few years later, in 1925, was donated to Alabama Polytechnic Institute (now Auburn University), where its call letters were changed to WAPI. There the station established a community service format, broadcasting programs of local interest on everything from agriculture and industry to home economics

WAPI AM/FM was the first station in the state and one of the oldest AM stations in the country. One of its former homes was in the Protective Life Building.

and education. This format continued even after the station was moved from Auburn's campus back to Birmingham in 1928, where it remained the flagship station of the university for many years. Two years later came the introduction of commercials, which began to demonstrate to advertisers that radio held a power all its own.

The city government, which had acquired joint ownership of the station upon its return to Birmingham, could no longer afford its investment after the Great Depression hit. The state then allocated equal shares of ownership to Auburn, the University of Alabama, and the Alabama College for Women (now the University of Montevallo). Actual management, however, was carried out by local businessmen until 1961, when the Newhouse Broadcasting Corporation purchased the rights to the station.

WAPI proved to be a leader in radio technique by utilizing innovative presentations and unique approaches. Broadcasts such as a speech by the Speaker of the U.S. House of Representatives, William Bankhead, as introduced by his daughter Tallulah Bankhead on the stage of the Alabama Theatre, and Glenn Miller conducting his Army band while stationed at Maxwell Field during World War II are early examples of WAPI's groundbreaking style. And had anyone questioned the station's commitment to its craft, they were proved wrong when the station relocated its towers at one point without so much as a pause in broadcasting.

WAPI-FM began permanent broadcasts as a separate facility in 1947, increasing its power to 100,000 watts in 1964 and introducing stereo broadcasting five years later. While establishing a solid reputation in the industry, the station relocated several times from its original headquarters to such historic sites as the downtown Protective Life Building and Radio Park on Red Mountain before settling into its current facil-

ity on Highland Avenue South, where it operates under the ownership of Mobilian Bernard Dittman.

As WAPI AM/FM nears its seventh decade of broadcasting, it is still on top of innovative trends in radio. WAPI-AM, after nearly 30 years of struggle, was finally granted a power increase to 50,000 watts and is closely watching trends in the AM stereo of the future, while enjoying its reputation as the only area station to cater to the over-35 audience. WAPI-AM continues to be the Birmingham voice of Auburn University, broadcasting all football and basketball games. WAPI-FM is enjoying top ratings as a contemporary hit rock station that is making constant strides in quality of sound and presentation and, like most stations across the country, is relying heavily on its morning show personalities to manifest the station's attitudes and its commitment to Birmingham. And, as in its beginning, it is that commitment that keeps WAPI AM/FM at the forefront of Birmingham's growth.

WAPI AM/FM operates from these modern studios on Highland Avenue South in Birmingham.

WBMG-TV

On October 17, 1965, WBMG began operation with the distinction of being the first UHF television station in Birmingham and the surrounding area. Soon after its birth, founder Jack DuBois relinquished management to Hugh Smith, whose pragmatic approach and expertise in the field kept the station's head above water at a time when UHF television was far from stable.

After several years of operation as the Birmingham UHF station, WBMG underwent some major changes. While at its original offices on Red Mountain in 1969, WBMG-TV became a CBS affiliate. A move to new headquarters on Golden Crest Drive in 1970 was followed three years later by new ownership. The station was purchased at that time by Park Communications, a publicly traded corporation that owns and operates more than 30 daily newspapers, over 20 weekly newspapers, 7 television stations, 10 AM stations, and 9 FM stations across the country. Park Communications was the first broadcast group in the nation to own the legal maximum of seven in each of those categories as set forth by FCC regu-

The WBMG-TV offices on Golden Crest Drive, Birmingham.

lations—the purchase of WBMG pushing it along to that distinction.

Even in its new association with such a powerful and distinctive conglomerate, WBMG did not lose sight of its purposes and priorities on a local level. The station held on to the philosophies of its inauspicious beginning and strove to serve the best interests of Birmingham. It acted as a strong booster of the community's pride in itself as a growing major industrial site as well as the academic pride generated by the University of Alabama at Birmingham (UAB). WBMG became closely associated with the UAB Blazers, carrying the basketball games as well as the

WBMG-TV's Action News anchor team (left to right): Chip Tarkenton, sports; Steve Ross, co-anchor; Marianne Matthews, co-anchor; and Paul Ossmann, weather.

coaches' shows long before the Blazers achieved any type of national acclaim in the sports world. The games and associated shows are still aired today as an integral part of Birmingham viewing.

In its attempts to bring the best technological improvements possible to Birmingham television, the station extended its tower height to the legal maximum, greatly expanding signal distribution and penetration. A new transmitter, at a cost of approximately six million dollars, has recently doubled the station's power. However, aside from the betterment of its technology, WBMG continues to list serving Birmingham as its top priority by providing programming that is relevant to audience interests and needs and that has a positive impact on viewers.

Still at its offices on Golden Crest Drive, WBMG-TV plans to continue a close interaction with the city of Birmingham and, as television leans toward trends in localization, plans to remain solidly involved in activities that will bring improvement to the city.

CAPITOL BROADCASTING CORPORATION

WKSJ RADIO
"Hello Americans, stand by for news!" WKSJ-FM is the only station in Mobile, Alabama, to feature the nation's most listened-to radio personality, Paul Harvey.

A vital component of the communications scene in the Port City, 95 KSJ has been serving the area with imagination and professionalism since its inception in July 1971. Named for then general manager Kenneth S. Johnson, the station is a Capitol Broadcasting Corporation property. This parent organization includes 10 radio stations in eight markets—including Mobile and Birmingham, Alabama; Charleston, West Virginia; Louisville, Kentucky; Charlotte and Raleigh, North Carolina; Nashville, Tennessee; and Austin, Texas.

This ABC affiliate adopted a contemporary country music theme in 1976, attaining the number one

Dr. Bill Williams, meteorologist and climatologist, keeps 95 KSJ listeners abreast of local weather conditions.

ranking in Mobile in 1980. On several occasions it has been rated as the number one country music station in the nation, and has achieved top-ranked status in broadcasting surveys regardless of format. To express appreciation for its tremendous audience support, 95 KSJ sponsors an annual concert featuring nationally known entertainers in the field of country music. Twice yearly, in-depth surveys are conducted to keep the station attuned to the listening appetites of the public.

Commitment to community involvement has been a formula for the success of WKSJ. The station's public affairs outreach acts as liaison between community efforts and the media, and shares its talents for generating publicity toward helping area neighborhoods. To promote civic pride, WKSJ launched the "I Love You Mobile" campaign. Block parties were held in all of the area's major communities and the station sponsored TV commercials and utilized billboards and KSJ-FM air time to promote and publicize Mobile's assets. When the city budget could no longer support the Fourth of July fireworks display, WKSJ originated "Skyshow," a spectacular event for the enjoyment of all. The station has been the primary sponsor of the city's annual Christmas parade since 1985. "Safe Trick or Treat" is held each Octo-

The crowd at the 95 KSJ Family Reunion. The show featured Eddie Rabbitt, the Nitty Gritty Dirt Band, Marie Osmond, T. Graham Brown, and Mel McDaniel.

ber 31 in the area's largest shopping mall under the auspices of WKSJ, the mall merchants joining with the station to assure a protected environment for the children.

Mobile is the birthplace of Mardi Gras. During the two weeks of misrule in the Port City, the KSJ Mystery Reveler walks the streets dispensing gifts. Besides the mystery Reveler, KSJ is involved in many other aspects of Mobile's biggest party.

Commitment to excellence in programming is evident in the area of sports. WKSJ is the official radio station for the Azalea Trail Run, providing live coverage for Alabama's largest participatory athletic event. The station broadcasts all of the University of Alabama football and basketball games, applying the talents of an award-winning team of sports announcers.

A contributor to the information system of the region, WKSJ provides a format for opinion making and community betterment through public service announcements and programs. It supports, promotes, and encourages nonprofit organizations which help create a viable and attractive urban area.

WKSJ-FM is not only an information disseminator, but also an influential innovator in the realm of news broadcasting. It is especially proud of its weather service, which offers the most professional weather reporting in the Gulf Coast region. Accurate prediction of the area's quixotic storms is difficult, and to provide Mobilians with authoritative weather broadcasting KSJ

The 95 KSJ staff with the winner of a new Chevrolet in 1986.

recruited Dr. Bill Williams, meteorologist and climatologist on the staff of the University of South Alabama. Utilizing the latest techniques and an array of data resources which include satellites, radar, weather facsimile, and teletype circuits, "Dr. Bill" provides current climate information, forecasts, and warnings to business and industry as well as the general population. Areas such as the Alabama State Docks on the Mobile waterfront are warned in advance of unusual weather systems that would require special precautions. Correct interpretation of approaching storms is indispensable to the Alabama Gulf Coast shipping and fishing industries, and KSJ furnishes these companies with weather information that will affect their business operation.

Providing information, serving community interests, furnishing a broad spectrum of entertainment—WKSJ-FM is deeply involved in the daily life of Mobilians. In less than 20 years it has become a major community force, touching many people and affecting the cultural, economic, and social aspects of life in this Gulf Coast area.

WMJJ-FM

From the day WMJJ-FM went on the air in December 1982, it has been Birmingham's innovative broadcasting entity. No other station has equaled the excitement, in-

WMJJ-FM is located at 530 Beacon Parkway West.

tensity, and creative leadership of "Magic 96 FM."

Public consideration is the main theme connecting the station's daily offerings. Responding to listeners' wishes, Magic 96 has instituted "Freedom of Choice" weekends. These are offered on special dates from 5 p.m. Friday to midnight Sunday when musical requests are solicited from the public and the station responds—just like the good old days when the radio audience had something to say about what they heard. By popular demand there is a live weekly broadcast from a local nightclub featuring music of the 1960s and 1970s for those who care to reminisce.

Capitol Broadcasting Corporation, owners of WMJJ-FM, continues its policy of strong community involvement in the Birmingham area with this station. A complete line of children's clothing has been designed by the station and marketed by a local department store under the name of "Magic Kid's Clothes" with proceeds benefiting Children's Hospital of Birmingham. Realizing that this specialty institution cannot survive without public support, Magic 96 FM assists Children's Hospital in its efforts to treat area youngsters from all socioeconomic areas who suffer from cancer, muscular diseases, cardiovascular maladies, and those victimized by accidents, with the sale of this collection of children's and toddlers' activewear.

A New Year's Eve Countdown celebration was begun by the station. Held in the historic Five Points South section of Birmingham, it is one of the most successful outdoor events in the city. WMJJ commissioned a special recording of an original song entitled "Dancin' in the Streets" to add to the festivities.

From charitable fund raising to dancing in the streets—Magic 96 FM is a factor in Birmingham's growth. The station is proving that success—for WMJJ-FM and the city—comes with active participation.

PATRONS

The following individuals, companies, and organizations have made a valuable commitment to the quality of this publication. Windsor Publications and The Business Council of Alabama gratefully acknowledge their participation in *Mine, Mill, and Microchip: A Chronicle of Alabama Enterprise.*

Alabama Federal Savings and Loan
    Association*
Alabama Gas Corporation*
Alabama Power Company*
Alabama Telco Credit Union*
Alabama-Tennessee Natural Gas
    Company
        A Subsidiary of AlaTenn
        Resources, Inc.*
Altec Industries, Inc.*
Amerex Corporation*
American Cast Iron Pipe Company*
America's First Credit Union*
AmSouth Bancorporation*
Associated Group Services, Inc.*
Barber Dairies, Inc.*
Birmingham Realty Company*
Blount, Inc.*
The Boeing Company*
Bradford & Co., Inc.—Food Brokers*
Bromberg's*
Bruno's, Inc.*
Buffalo Rock Company*
Capitol Broadcasting Corporation*
Car & Truck Rental*
Central Bank of the South*
Chamber of Commerce of the Shoals*
Champion International Corporation*
Chrysler Corporation*
Daniel Industrial Metals, Inc.*
The Daughters of Charity*
J.F. Day Company, Inc.*
Drummond Company, Inc.*
Durr-Fillauer Medical, Inc.*
Ernst & Whinney*
Florence TimesDaily*
Fontaine Group, Inc.*
Fulton Haley Metal Products, Inc.
A.G. Gaston Enterprises*
General Machinery Company, Inc.*
General Motors Corporation
        Saginaw Division*
General Services Incorporated*
Golden Flake Snack Foods, Inc.*
Harbert Corporation*
Holiday Inn of Sheffield*
Huntsville Hilton and Towers*
Industrial Products, Inc.*

Jackson Hospital & Clinic, Inc.*
Jacksonville State University*
Jemison Investment Co., Inc.*
Kovach & Associates*
Long-Lewis, Inc.*
MacMillan Bloedel Inc.
Mayer Electric Supply Company*
Maynard, Cooper, Frierson & Gale*
William M. Mercer-Meidinger-Hansen,
        Incorporated*
Lloyd Noland Hospital & Health
        Centers*
O'Neal Steel, Inc.*
E.K. Paine
Protective Life Insurance Company*
Rust International Corporation*
Shook & Fletcher*
Sonat Inc.*
South Central Bell*
Spring Air Mattress Company
        Division of Alabama Bedding
        Manufacturing Company, Inc.*
Sterne, Agee & Leach, Inc.*
Steward Machine Co., Inc.
Tee Jays Manufacturing Company,
        Inc.*
Union Bank & Trust Co.*
United States Pipe and Foundry
        Company*
The University of Alabama at
        Birmingham*
University of Montevallo*
Victoryland Greyhound Racing Park*
WAPI AM/FM Radio*
WBMG-TV*
The Geo. F. Wheelock Company*
WSFA-TV*

*Alabama's Enterprises of *Mine, Mill, and Microchip: A Chronicle of Alabama Enterprise.* The histories of these companies and organizations appear in Chapter VIII, beginning on page 266.

BIBLIOGRAPHY

Alabama Department of Industrial Relations. *The Iron and Steel Industry in Alabama.* Montgomery: Alabama Department of Industrial Relations, 1950.

Amos, Harriet E. "Social Life in an Antebellum Cotton Port: Mobile, Alabama, 1820-1860." Ph.D. dissertation, Emory University, 1976.

Armes, Ethel. *The Story of Coal and Iron in Alabama.* Birmingham: Chamber of Commerce, 1910.

Atkins, Leah Rawls. *The Valley and the Hills: An Illustrated History of Birmingham and Jefferson County.* Woodland Hills, California: Windsor Publications, 1981.

Bailey, Hugh C. "Ethel Armes and *The Story of Coal and Iron in Alabama.*" *The Alabama Review,* XXII (July, 1969), 188-199.

Berney, Saffold. *Handbook of Alabama: A Complete Index to the State; With a Geological Map.* Mobile, Alabama: Mobile Register Printing, 1878, 1892.

Bertelson, Daniel F. *Alabama Forest Industries.* U.S. Department of Agriculture, Forest Service Resource Bulletin SO-36, 1972.

Biography of a Business: Tennessee Coal and Iron Division, United States Steel Corporation. n.p.: Tennessee Coal and Iron Division, 1960.

Boyd, Minnie C. *Alabama In the Fifties: A Social Study.* New York, New York: Columbia University Press, 1931.

Buford, James A., Jr. "Some Aspects of Competition in the Southern Pine Industry of Alabama, 1967-1972." Ph.D. dissertation, University of Georgia, 1974.

Carmer, Carl. *Stars Fell on Alabama.* New York: Farrar and Rinehart, 1934.

Chapman, H. H. *The Iron and Steel Industries of the South.* Tuscaloosa: University of Alabama Press, 1953.

Cobb, James C. *Industrialization and Southern Society, 1877-1984.* Lexington, Kentucky: The University Press of Kentucky, 1984.

Cobb, James C. *The Selling of the South: The Southern Crusade for Industrial Development, 1936-1980.* Baton Rouge, Louisiana: Louisiana State University Press, 1982.

Comer, Donald. *Braxton Bragg Comer (1848-1927): An Alabamian Whose Avondale Mills Opened New Paths for Southern Progress.* New York, New York: The Newcomen Society of England, American Branch, 1947.

Directory of Alabama Manufacturers and Manufactures. Birmingham-Montgomery, Alabama: Alabama Industrial Development Board, 1938.

Doster, James F. "Railroad Domination in Alabama, 1885-1905." *The Alabama Review,* VII (July, 1954), 186-197.

Doster, James F. *Railroads in Alabama Politics, 1875-1914.* University, Alabama: University of Alabama Press, 1957.

Duffee, Mary Gordon. *Sketches of Alabama: Being an Account of the Journey from Tuscaloosa to Blount Springs Through Jefferson County on the Old Stage Roads.* Ed. by Virginia Pounds Brown and Jane Porter Nabers. University, Alabama: University of Alabama Press, 1970.

Eisterhold, John A. "Mobile: Lumber Center of the Gulf Coast." *The Alabama Review,* XXIV (April, 1973), 83-104.

Erskine Ramsay: A Biographical Memoir. New York: The American Historical Company, 1953.

Flick, Warren A. "The Wood Dealer System in Mississippi: An Essay on Regional Economics and Culture." *Journal of Forest History,* 29 (July, 1985), 131-138.

Flynt, Wayne. *Montgomery: An Illustrated History.* Woodland Hills, California: Windsor Publications, 1980.

Fuller, Justin. "Alabama Business Leaders: 1865-1900 (Part II)." *The Alabama Review,* XVII (January, 1964), 63-75.

Fuller, Justin. "Boom Towns and Blast Furnaces: Town Promotion in Alabama, 1885-1893." *The Alabama Review,* XXIX (January, 1976), 37-48.

Fuller, Justin. "From Iron to Steel: Alabama's Industrial Evolution." *The Alabama Review,* XVII (April, 1964), 137-148.

Fuller, Justin. "Henry F. DeBardeleben, Industrialist of the New South." *The Alabama Review,* XXXIX (January, 1986), 3-18.

Fuller, Justin. "History of the Tennessee Coal, Iron, and Railroad Company, 1852-1907." Ph.D. dissertation, North Carolina: University of North Carolina at Chapel Hill, 1966.

Fundaburk, Emma Lila. "Business Corporations in Alabama in the Nineteenth Century." vols. 1-111. Ph.D. dissertation, Ohio State University, 1963.

Gates, Grace Hooten. "Anniston: Transition from Company Town to Public Town." *The Alabama Review,* XXXVII (January, 1984), 34-44.

Gates, Grace Hooten. *The Model City of the New South: Anniston, Alabama, 1872-1900.* Huntsville, Alabama: Strode Publishers, Inc., 1978.

Going, Allen J. *Bourbon Democracy in Alabama, 1874-1890.* University, Alabama: University of Alabama Press, 1951.

Griffin, Richard W. "Poor White Laborers in Southern Cotton Factories, 1789-1865." *The South Carolina Historical Magazine,* LXI (1960), 26-40.

Hassinger, Bernice S. *Henderson Steel: Birmingham's First Steel.* Birmingham, Alabama: Bernice S. Hassinger, 1978.

Howard, Gene L. *Death at Cross Plains. An Alabama Reconstruction Tragedy.* University, Alabama: University of Alabama Press, 1984.

Huntsville City Planning Commission. *Huntsville: Its Population, Housing and Economy, April 1979.* Huntsville, Alabama: Huntsville's Department of City Planning, 1979.

"James Greeley McGowin—South Alabama Lumberman." Oral Histories with N. Floyd, Earl S., and Nicholas S. McGowin, conducted by Elwood R. Maunder. Santa Cruz, California: Forest History Society, 1977.

Jarrells, Donald R. "History of the Alabama School of Trades." Unpublished research paper, Gadsden: Gadsden State Junior College, 1971.

John J. Eagan: His Business Practice and Philosophy. Third Edition. Birmingham, Alabama: American Cast Iron Pipe Company, 1943.

Jordan, Weymouth T. "The Industrial Gospel." *AnteBellum Alabama Town and Country.* Tallahassee: Florida State University Studies, 1957.

Knowlton, Evelyn H. *Pepperell's Progress: History of a Cotton Textile Company, 1844-1945.* Cambridge, Massachusetts: Harvard University Press, 1948.

Kranzberg, Melvin. "Rebirth for Textiles," *The Atlanta Journal and Constitution,* November 24, 1985.

Martin, Thomas W. *Forty Years of Alabama Power Company, 1911-1951.* New York, New York: The Newcomen Society of North America, 1952.

Martin, Thomas W. *The Story of Electricity in Alabama Since the Turn of the Century: 1900-1952.* Birmingham, Alabama: Thomas W. Martin, 1953.

Massey, Richard W., Jr. "A History of the Lumber Industry in Alabama and West Florida, 1880-1914." Ph.D. dissertation, Vanderbilt University, 1960.

Massey, Richard W., Jr. "Logging Railroads in Alabama, 1880-1914." *The Alabama Review,* XIV (January, 1961), 41-50.

McKenzie, Robert H. "A History of the Shelby Iron Company, 1865-1881." Ph.D. dissertation, University of Alabama, 1971.

McKenzie, Robert H. "Horace Ware: Alabama Iron Pioneer." *The Alabama Review,* XXVI (July, 1973), 157-172.

McKenzie, Robert H. "Reconstruction of the Alabama Iron Industry, 1865-1880." *The Alabama Review,* XXV (July, 1972), 178-191.

McLaurin, Melton A., and Michael Thomason. *Mobile: The Life and Times of a Great Southern City: An Illustrated History.* Woodland Hills, California: Windsor Publications, 1981.

Mickle, Will. "Huntsville, Alabama: Cotton Textile Center of the New South." *Cotton History Review,* vol. 2, 1961, 92-102.

Miller, Randall M. "The Cotton Mill Movement in Antebellum Alabama." Ph.D. dissertation, Ohio State University, 1971.

Moore, A. B. "Railroad Building in Alabama During the Reconstruction Period." *The Journal of Southern History,* I (November, 1935), 421-441.

Morgan, David T. "Philip Phillips and Internal Improvements in Mid-Nineteenth-Century Alabama." *The Alabama Review,* XXXIV (April, 1981), 83-93.

Morring, Thomas F. "The Impact of Space Age Spending on the Economy of Huntsville, Alabama." M.S. thesis, Massachusetts Institute of Technology, 1964.

Nelms, Jack N. "Early Days With the Alabama River Steamboats." *The Alabama Review,* XXXVII (January, 1984), 13-23.

Nesbitt, C. H. *Annual Reports of Coal Mines State of Alabama, 1914.* Birmingham: State of Alabama, 1914.

1929-1979 Fifty Years: Southern Natural Resources, Annual Report, 1979. Southern Natural Resources, Inc. 1979.

Olmstead, Frederick L. *A Journey in the Back Country.* New York, New York: Mason Brothers, 1860.

O'Neil, Paul. "The Anachronistic Town of Huntsville." *The Space Industry: America's Newest Giant.* Englewood Cliffs, New Jersey: Prentice-Hall, Inc., 1962.

Owens, Harry P. "Sail and Steam Vessels Serving the Appalachicola-Chattahoochee Valley." *The Alabama Review,* XXI (July, 1968), 195-210.

Phillips, William B. *Iron Making in Alabama.* Third Edition. University, Alabama: Geological Survey of Alabama, 1912.

Rikard, Marlene Hunt. "An Experiment in Welfare Capitalism: The Health Care Services of the Tennessee Coal, Iron and Railroad Company." Ph.D. dissertation, University of Alabama, 1983.

Riley, B. F. *Alabama as it is; or the Immigrant's and Capitalist's Guide Book to Alabama.* Atlanta, Georgia: Constitution Publishing Company, 1888.

Rogers, William W. *The One-Gallused Rebellion: Agrarianism in Alabama, 1865-1896.* Baton Rouge, Louisiana: Louisiana State University Press, 1970.

Russell, Robert A. "Gold Mining in Alabama Before 1860." *The Alabama Review,* X (January, 1957), 5-14.

Russell, Thomas D. *Russell of Alabama.* New York, New York: The Newcomen Society in North America, 1960.

Ryan, Patricia. *Northern Dollars for Huntsville Spindles.* Huntsville, Alabama: Huntsville Planning Department, Special Report No. 4, 1983.

Samford, Frank P. *The First Seventy-One Years of the Liberty National Life Insurance Company.* Birmingham, Alabama: n. p., 1972.

Satterfield, Carolyn Green. "J. R. McWane: Pipe and Progress." *The Alabama Review,* XXXV (January, 1982), 30-37.

Schweikart, Larry. "Alabama's Antebellum Banks: New Interpretations, New Evidence." *The Alabama Review,* XXXVIII (July, 1985), 202-221.

Smith, Algernon L. *Continental Gin Company and its Fifty-Two Years of Service.* Ed. by James F. Sulzby, Jr. Birmingham, Alabama: Continental Gin Company, 1952.

Stephens, Elise Hopkins. *Historic Huntsville: A City of New Beginnings.* Woodland Hills, California: Windsor Publications, 1984.

Stockham, Richard J. "Alabama Iron for the Confederacy: The Selma Works." *The Alabama Review,* XXI (July, 1968), 163-172.

Straw, Richard A. "Soldiers and Miners in a Strike Zone: Birmingham, 1908." *The Alabama Review,* XXXVIII (October, 1985), 289-309.

Textile Leaders of the South. Ed. by Marjorie W. Young. Anderson, South Carolina: James R. Young, 1963.

Thorn, Cecelia Jean. "The Bell Factory: Early Pride of Huntsville." *The Alabama Review,* XXXII (January, 1979), 28-37.

Thornton, J. Mills, III. *Politics and Power in a Slave Society: Alabama, 1800-1860.* Baton Rouge: Louisiana State University Press, 1978.

Vandiver, Frank E. "Josiah Gorgas and the Brierfield Iron Works." *Alabama Review,* III (January, 1950), 5-21.

Vandiver, Frank E. "The Shelby Iron Company in the Civil War." *The Alabama Review,* I (January, April, July, 1948), 12-26, 111-127, 203-217.

Vulcan's History. Vulcan Materials Company. n.d.

Ward, Robert D., and William W. Rogers. *Labor Revolt in Alabama: The Great Strike of 1894.* University, Alabama: University of Alabama Press, 1965.

White, Marjorie Longenecker. *The Birmingham District: An Industrial History and Guide.* Birmingham, Alabama: Birmingham Historical Society, 1981.

Wiener, Jonathan M. *Social Origins of the New South: Alabama, 1860-1885.* Baton Rouge, Louisiana: Louisiana State University Press, 1978.

Wilhelm, Dwight M. *A History of the Cotton Textile Industry of Alabama, 1809-1950.* Montgomery, Alabama: n.p., 1950.

Woodward, Joseph H., II. "Alabama Iron Manufacturing, 1860-1865." *The Alabama Review,* VII (July, 1854), 199-207.

INDEX

GENERAL INDEX
Italicized numbers indicate illustrations

Kansas, 189
Building stone, 13, 16
Business Week, 190
Butler County, 152

C

C. and T. Chemicals, 223
Cabaniss, Charles, 24
Cadle, Cornelius, 101
Cahaba coalfields, 16
Cahaba Coal Mining Company, 82, *90-91*
Cahaba Iron Works, 51, 75-76
Cahaba River, 16
Cahawba, 22
Calhoun County, 73, 85
Campbell's Foundry, 52
Cane Creek furnace, 33
Cape Canaveral, 199
Carmer, Carl, 134, 136
Carver, George Washington, 136
Central City Foundry, 52
Central City Iron Works, 52
Central Iron and Coal Company, *120-121*
Chapman, 152, 153
Chapman, Reuben, 160
Chattahoochee River, 16, 77
Chattanooga Railroad, 77
Cherokee County, 51
Ciba-Geigy, *222-223*
Citadel Cement, 223
City National Bank, 94
Civil Rights Movement, 189, 190
Civil War, 49, 56
Claiborne, 22
Clarke County, 52
Clay, H. Lawson, 46
Clay deposits, 13, 16
Clayton, Henry D., 76
Cleverdon, Ernest, *236*
Coal (bituminous) deposits, 16, 28; district of, 30; mining of, 28, 30, 31, 41, *164-165, 177*; production of, 30, 46, 56
Coal Mining Institute of America, 89
Coke production, 34
Collier, Henry W., 26, 39, 42, *58*
Collier, June, 230, *230*
Comer, B.B., 94, 104, 105, 128, 129, 130, 153, *168*
Comer, Donald, 94, 165
Commercial Club of Birmingham, 104
Commerical Review of the South, 24, 39, 45
Community Affairs Committee, 190
Conecuh River, 98
Continental Gin Company, 93
Convict labor, 106, 149
Coosa River, 16, 20, 24
Copper, 16
Cotton, 16; investment of, 41; production of, 25, *34-35,* 39; shipment of, *10-11, 41, 42-43*
Cotton mills, 24, 25, 27, 45, 48, *63, 93, 93,* 140; labor, 27
Crawford, George Gordon, 118, 119, *119;* welfare program of, 123
Croxton, John T., 65
Cumberland Plateau, 13

D

Dallas Iron Works, 52
Dallas Mills, *123,* 144, 145, 148, *151;* during Depression, 157
Dalrymple, Sherman H., 160

Dan River Cotton Mills, *192-193*
Davis, K.L., 152
Dean, John, 160
DeBardeleben, Henry, F. *59,* 76, 79, 80, 81, 82, 161
DeBardeleben Coal and Iron Company, 82
DeBardeleben's Alabama Fuel and Iron Company, Charles F., 161
Decatur, 84
Decatur and Tuscumbia Railroad, 24
Demopolis, 16
Depression, Great, 157, 170
Devil's Backbone Gold District, 28
Diversified Products, 200
Dog River Factory, 27
Dolomite, 16
Dolomite flux, 31
Dowd, Mollie, 160
Downtown Action Committee, 190
Dupont Alabama Ordnance Works, 180
Dutch Bend Gold Mine, 28
Dwight Cotton Mill, *63*

E

Eagan, John J., 126, 127
East Tennessee, Virginia, and Georgia Railroad, 78
Echols, William H., *94*
Education, *134-135,* 219, 236
Edwards, Giles, 75
Elyton Land Company, 77
Empire Coke Company, 198
Ensley, Enoch, 100
Ensley Industrial Town plan, *100-101*
Ensley Steel Works (Mill), *122,* 181; mill village, *61*
Ensley's Pratt Coal and Iron Company, Enoch, D., 101, 120
Erwin Mills, 144
Etowah County, 84
Eufaula, The, 21
Exporting, 18

F

Fairfield Tin, 181
Fairfield Wire Works, 181
Fair Labor Standard Act, 161
Farmer's Alliance and Populist Party, 109, 111
Farragut, David, 56
Federal Bureau of Economic Analysis, 238
Fies, Milton H., 165
Fink, Albert, 78
Fireclay, 13
First National-Southern Natural building, 203
Fish Pond Factory, 27
Fitzpatrick, Phillip, 13
Florence, 84
Flowers and Flowers Lumber Company, 106
Flowers and Flowers Saw Mill, 149
Fort Conde, *226-227*
Fort Sumter, 50

G

Gadsden, 137
Gaines, The, 56
Gary, Elbert, 118 122
Gaston, A.G., 204, 218, *218*
Gaston's Boys Club, A.G., 204
General Electric, 207

General Motors, 221
General Shoe Company, 182
Georgia Pacific Railroad, 87
Georgia Railroad Commission, 104
Georgia's Natural Gas Company, 202
Georgia Tech, 208
Gilmer, Frank, 51, 77
Gjerstad, Dean, 201
Gold, 69; camps, 28; district, 28; mining of, 16, 28
Goldthwaite, Henry, 22
Goldville, 28
Goodyear Tire and Rubber Company, 137, *180;* rubber plant of, 160, 180
Gorgas, Amelia Gayle, 50
Gorgas, Josiah, 50, *50,* 72
Grady, Henry, 69, 87
Graphite, 16
Gravel, 13, 16
Graves, Bibb, 137
Gregory Hill Gold Mine, 28
Gristmills, 17, 49, *76-77*
GTE, *232*
Gulf Coast, 227
Gulf Shipyards, *142-143*
Gulf Shores Plantation, 227
Gulf States Paper, 182
Gulf States Steel, 137, 160
Gunter Air Force Base, 178

H

Hall, Grover, 165, 166, *166*
Hammermill Paper Company, 192; boycott of, 192
Hanby, David, 30, 65
Harbert Corporation, 223, 234
Hargert, John Murdoch, III, 232
Hargreanes, Harry, 101
Harriet, The, 22
Hartford, USS, *52-53*
Hassinger, W.H., 89
Health care industries, 236
Hematite (red iron ore), 16, 30
Henderson, James, 89
Henderson Steel and Manufacturing Company, 89, 92, *92-93*
Heralds of Liberty. *See* Liberty National
Highland Rim, 13
Hilliard, Henry, *48*
Hillman, T.T., 131
Hog Mountain Gold Mine, 28
Hopkins, Harry, 163, 165
House Committee on Internal Improvements, 42-43
Huntsville, *83,* 140, 205, 207, 208, 209, 223, 234
Huntsville and Redstone Arsenals, 172
Huntsville Chamber of Commerce, 160, 172
Huntsville Fire Department, *71*
Huntsville Grocery Company, *85*
Huntsville Industrial Expansion Committee, 183
Huntsville Manufacturing Company, 182, *196*
Huntsville Memorial Parkway, *213*
Huntsville *Mercury Centennial,* 148
Huntsville Planning Commission, 184
Hunstville Times, 165, 172
Hurst, R.M., *210-211*

I

Immigrants, 16, 23, 27, 105, 116, 149, *151*